STEREOTYPES AND THE CONSTRUCTION OF THE SOCIAL WORLD

Stereotypes and the Construction of the Social World explores the complexity of stereotypes, guiding the reader through issues of definition and theoretical explanations from psychology and other disciplines. The book examines why people use stereotypes, which have often been represented as inaccurate, rigid and discriminatory. If that is what they are, then why would people employ such 'faulty' or 'biased' views of others?

While this book presents a detailed and comprehensive analysis of the psychological research into the individual use of stereotypes, it also presents this research within its ideological and historical context, revealing the important sociocultural factors in what we mean by 'stereotypes'. From the politics of representation and intergroup power relations, alongside individual social cognitive issues, the book provides a comprehensive and cross-disciplinary account of stereotypes and stereotyping.

Featuring a wealth of real-world examples, it will be essential reading for all students and researchers of stereotypes.

Perry R. Hinton is a psychologist and professor in the Centre for Applied Linguistics at the University of Warwick, UK. His research is in the area of stereotyping and intercultural communication. His previous books include *The Perception of People: Integrating Cognition and Culture*; *Stereotypes, Cognition and Culture* and *The Psychology of Interpersonal Perception*.

STEREOTYPES AND THE CONSTRUCTION OF THE SOCIAL WORLD

Perry R. Hinton

Routledge
Taylor & Francis Group

LONDON AND NEW YORK

First published 2020
by Routledge
2 Park Square, Milton Park, Abingdon, Oxon OX14 4RN

and by Routledge
52 Vanderbilt Avenue, New York, NY 10017

Routledge is an imprint of the Taylor & Francis Group, an informa business

British Library Cataloguing-in-Publication Data
A catalogue record for this book is available from the British Library

Library of Congress Cataloging-in-Publication Data
A catalog record has been requested for this book

ISBN: 978-1-138-63753-5 (hbk)
ISBN: 978-1-138-63755-9 (pbk)
ISBN: 978-1-315-20553-3 (ebk)

Typeset in Bembo
by Newgen Publishing UK

To Anna, Anthony and Emma

CONTENTS

PREFACE

We all feel we know what stereotypes are. The word is often used in conversation and in the media. Frequently a stereotype is described as a rigid or discriminatory view of a person, in terms of their social category membership (such as their ethnicity, age or gender), undermining their capabilities and ignoring the diversity of the group. For these reasons we are sometimes told that we should stop stereotyping – and certainly stop using negative stereotypes. The problem for the psychologist is why people use stereotypes if they are so wrong, both in terms of accuracy, as an incorrect view of a person, and morally, in that they unfairly discriminate against the person. In both these cases we would expect that people would be better off being 'right' rather than 'wrong'. Why would people employ a 'faulty' or 'biased' view of others? For example, in everyday conversation we may hear someone say that 'accountants are boring' or that 'Germans are efficient but humourless' or that 'teenagers are moody and irresponsible', and there might be widespread agreement about these views in a particular culture, given that these ideas often appear in the media in that society. However, particularly if we are an accountant, a German or a teenager, we might claim that these are (unfair) stereotypes. The statements seem to imply that every, or any, accountant is boring, every German is efficient but humourless and every teenager is on 'an emotional roller coaster' – which really cannot be the case. Now accountants, Germans and teenagers may disapprove of these descriptions but to some degree they have to tolerate them, as there is not much pressure in society at this time to make such statements illegal. However, these descriptions could potentially lead to discriminatory behaviour: the exciting accountant, the really funny German comedian, and the calm and responsible teenager might all be denied opportunities, for which they are eminently capable, with other less able individuals chosen instead. Yet there are times when these types of descriptions (referred to as stereotypes) are deemed to be so offensive that using them can lead to formal social sanction. Discrimination concerning ethnicity, gender and sexuality, age, religion, disability are the subject of specific concerns in Western liberal democracies, with laws enacted to punish offenders. Stereotypes associated with these categories will typically result in censure if publically expressed. Not all instances will result in legal sanction but it is generally clear that they are the subject of societal disapproval (even if the only 'punishment' is Twitter outrage). The disapproval of such stereotypes is that they are viewed as a public expression of an underlying belief. For example, in a society that disapproves of racism, the expression of a racist stereotype implies an underlying racism that needs to be stamped out. Now it is hard for a society to police an individual's private thoughts but it can regulate public behaviour and expressed opinions. In penalizing the use of racist stereotypes, the society expresses its rejection of racism.

Not surprisingly, people have argued that if racist or sexist stereotypes are bad, then all stereotypes are bad, and we should stop using stereotypes in referring to any social group. Presumably, this would include stereotypes about accountants, Germans, teenagers and every other stereotype, such as the owners of certain dog breeds and makes of car as well. This provokes a number of questions. Here are just a few. What makes a description about a group of people a stereotype? Is it possible to have a 'correct' view of a social group? Are stereotypes always negative? Are stereotypes always discriminatory? Does stereotype use always imply an underlying prejudice? Finally, is it even possible to never use stereotypes? Each of these questions poses a problem for a simple definition of a stereotype, particularly if it is argued that people should stop using them. Consider the description 'nurses are caring': is this a stereotype or not? Now, we could (for the sake of argument) claim that nurses only engage in caring behaviour because that is a requirement of the job. Nurses might not have any essential caring nature and their caring behaviour could result from simply doing the job properly. If the description 'nurses are caring' fits into a definition of a stereotype – which it might – then it does not seem to be related to discrimination in society. And you might even claim that the description is true because 'caring people' deliberately choose to go into the 'caring professions'. Furthermore, is the use of a stereotype, in whatever context, always indicative of an underlying prejudice? What about an African American comedian describing certain stereotypes to illustrate the aspects of racism that they have encountered? What about a German commentator using the stereotype of German efficiency ironically to a British or North American audience? Clearly, in these contexts the people using a stereotype are revealing and criticizing discrimination against a group – so the meaning of an expressed stereotype appears to depend on the context and purpose of its expression. Indeed, social context might be the most important aspect of a stereotype. Also, stereotypes do not arise randomly, but *in a culture*. The idea of German efficiency did not emerge in other nations simply by chance. Germany as an industrial powerhouse in the centre of Europe has been a dominant theme of much of the media reporting about Germany throughout the twentieth century; and in the twenty-first century it remains Europe's largest economy. Stereotypes arise in a culture and they are communicated and shared in a culture. I started by considering 'boring accountants', 'efficient Germans' and 'moody teenagers'. Not only do the stereotypical descriptions tell us something about how these social categories are viewed in a particular culture (such as the United States or Britain) – which requires explanation – but also which social groups are relevant in those societies today. Social categories are not fixed, permanent or (necessarily) enduring. In the past there were no such people as accountants, Germans from a nation state called Germany or teenagers. Modern accountancy began in Scotland in the early nineteenth century and the formal organization of the profession in other countries followed. Before 1871 there was no such place as Germany. Being German was not about where you lived but having German as a first language and in this sense a German could be living in Bavaria, Prussia, Alsace, Romania, Austria-Hungary but definitely not 'Germany'. Teenagers are a product of the mid-twentieth-century culture of the United States. While the term has been disseminated around the world, there was a time when 'teenagers' as a social category did not exist, and there are still cultures around the world where the concept is not used. The question then becomes one of: How can you have fixed descriptions of social groups (called stereotypes) when the social categories themselves are not fixed, but have been created at a certain time in history and in a social culture? What we call 'stereotypes' are therefore intimately linked to the social meanings of the different categories of people in a society. What we can say is that stereotypes (whatever they are!) are intimately linked to the way people in culture have constructed their social world. This book therefore examines the concept of 'the stereotype' from its invention nearly 100 years ago to its use in modern twenty-first-century Western society.

I am a psychologist so you will not be surprised that I am interested in the way people make sense of the world around them. Some 20 years ago I wrote a book called *Stereotypes, Cognition and Culture* (also published by Routledge), where I endeavoured to present the different ways psychologists have examined stereotypes, both from an individual mental (cognition) explanation to that of the person in culture. I thought I had produced quite a good balance between them, but on reflection, maybe not. While I am still pleased with the book as a clear account of the topic, my ideas have changed over time. In particular, the implication that individual minds are 'faulty' or 'biased' has increasingly concerned me. The human brain has developed over millions of years of evolution, so it seems rather presumptuous for researchers to consider it in some sense 'flawed'. This seems to me to have resulted from the idea that individuals seek an objectively correct judgement of the social world rather than focusing on people in interaction making sense of the social world. In my view there has historically not been enough of a focus on culture (or social networks) in the psychological analysis of stereotypes. While this current book presents a detailed and comprehensive analysis of the psychological research into the individual use of stereotypes, it also presents this research within its ideological and historical context, revealing the important sociocultural factors in what we mean by 'stereotypes'. We are all cultural beings able to navigate successfully in our culture, learning about the meaning of the different social groups within it. But this does not mean that we accept everything about it. Different groups and different generations learn about the ways of their culture and often seek to change it. And do.

ACKNOWLEDGEMENTS

I would like to thank Guida de Abreu and Helen Spencer-Oatey who have both taught me so much about the importance of culture to human psychology. I cannot thank them enough. My grateful appreciation also goes to my co-author Isabella McMurray and my colleague Troy McConachy for listening patiently as I spent our coffee breaks talking about this book. I owe them lots of coffees. Thanks also to Jo Angouri and Katharina Lefringhausen and all my other colleagues and students in the Centre for Applied Linguistics at the University of Warwick who have made my time there so academically stimulating and personally rewarding.

1

WHAT ARE STEREOTYPES?

Introduction

In Western English-speaking societies we commonly hear the word 'stereotype' spoken and written about in the media, usually in a situation where it is claimed that someone is being treated in a discriminatory way. Indeed, a reference to a stereotype is often a criticism of the view of another person ('you are making stereotypical assumptions about me', 'don't fall back on those hackneyed stereotypes', 'don't stereotype me!' or 'you are just employing a discriminatory stereotype'). In most instances, we are assumed to know why the use of stereotypes is bad but, when explained, it is indicated that the stereotype of a group of people (for example, women, African Americans, Muslims, migrants, the unemployed) presents them in a rigid, negative way that undermines their diversity and also their competence. Stereotypes are viewed as pejorative descriptions that support prejudice against a social group and its members. Using a stereotype is considered objectionable, and when people are presented as acting in a counter-stereotypical way this is viewed positively ('Susan is not a stereotypical mathematician', 'these elderly marathon runners have challenged the stereotype of the frail old person'). And the media frequently report on a person triumphing against a stereotype, particularly when they have fought against some form of discrimination to achieve a goal. Indeed, during the 50 years between the 1950s and the 2000s, the use of the word 'stereotype' in English communication more than trebled (according to Google Ngram) and it is quite likely that it is even more popular now in social media and other forms of Internet communication. This frequent use implies that we all know what the word means – that we have a shared understanding of a stereotype. For example, a news reporter does not need to define a stereotype before presenting a positive message of a person successfully challenging it. Yet the purpose of this book is to interrogate that shared meaning – if indeed there is one – and to examine the assumptions made about stereotypes and the role they play in the way people understand the social world.

The dictionary definition of a stereotype

The first place to look for a definition of a 'stereotype' is in a dictionary. To give a good range of definitions I have chosen six freely available online dictionaries. According to these popular reference sources, a 'stereotype' is:

A very firm and simple idea about what a particular type of person or thing is like.

Macmillan Dictionary[1]

A belief or idea of what a particular type of person or thing is like. Stereotypes are often unfair or untrue.

Longman Dictionary[2]

A set idea that people have about what someone or something is like, especially an idea that is wrong.

Cambridge Dictionary[3]

A widely held but fixed and oversimplified image or idea of a particular type of person or thing.

Oxford Dictionary[4]

A fixed general image or set of characteristics that a lot of people believe represent a particular type of person or thing.

Collins Dictionary[5]

Something conforming to a fixed or general pattern; especially: a standardized mental picture that is held in common by members of a group and that represents an oversimplified opinion, prejudiced attitude, or uncritical judgment.

Merriam-Webster Dictionary[6]

These definitions appear similar but they are not the same. A stereotype is an idea (claim four of the dictionaries) but it could also be an image (state two of them) or a belief or a mental picture. The four 'idea' dictionaries do not exactly agree on what type of idea a stereotype is: just an idea, a set idea, a firm and fixed idea or a fixed and oversimplified idea. Maybe this is why stereotypes are viewed as a bad thing: they are fixed and simple ideas. Yet a fixed idea is not necessarily a bad thing: I am firm in the idea that the earth goes round the sun, and not the other way round (and I am not likely to change my mind about it). A simple idea implies a lack of complexity, but again we can find a simple idea that is not necessarily problematic: stand in the rain and you will get wet. There is more or less the same degree of consistency on a second point, with four dictionaries agreeing that stereotypes are about types of people and things. By this definition, as well as stereotypes about librarians and the French, we can have stereotypes about other things such as makes of car, cats or types of vegetable. However, for the purpose of this book, I am going to focus on stereotypes of types of people (rather than things). Consequently, we can try to summarize the definitions as follows: stereotypes are fixed ideas about types of people. Again we can ask why that is a bad thing? A person might have a fixed idea that physicians are intelligent or nurses are caring and these might be considered generally valid.

The key point about a stereotype appears to be contained in a third aspect of the definitions (although they disagree on terminology, and again only four out of the six definitions mention it): a stereotype is often unfair or untrue, an idea that is wrong, an oversimplified opinion, prejudiced attitude or uncritical judgement. This appears more insightful as to why stereotypes might be viewed negatively – they are often not fair or not true or prejudiced (although these are only mentioned in one definition each). Maybe stereotypes are a bad thing because they are fixed and unfair ideas about people. Furthermore, the *Cambridge Dictionary* introduces an entirely new aspect of stereotypes, that the set idea is held by more than one person ('a set idea that people have'), which is supported by the *Merriam-Webster Dictionary* ('held in common by members of a group'). The *Oxford Dictionary* definition also makes the point that a stereotype is widely held. In these definitions, a stereotype is social: it cannot be a stereotype if it is only held by a single person or even a few people, such as my family, but has to be held by a lot of people – presumably, a specific social group (although this is not stated).

To recap, we can compile a composite definition across the dictionaries about what a stereotype is: it is a fixed (or oversimplified) idea about a type of person that is often unfair or untrue, but widely held (by a particular group of people). But in order to achieve this generalized view I have had to do quite a bit of intellectual work – deciding which features are important and which are not, teasing out the consistency and glossing over the differences. It is quite possible to look at my statement and claim that none of the definitions are actually stating this. I have had to ignore the fact that three of them make no mention of the people using the stereotype, or that while two definitions use the word 'oversimplified' four definitions do not, or that an image or a general pattern might not be the same as an idea. Only one definition claims that stereotypes are untrue and only one says they are prejudicial. There does not seem to be a consistent view of a stereotype in these definitions (unless I impose one upon them).

Some textbook definitions of a stereotype

There is clearly some variety in which features the different dictionary definitions focus on. One way to resolve this is to examine the definitions supplied in academic sources, as these technical definitions may be clearer and more explicit about what a stereotype actually is. While a number of different academic disciplines discuss stereotypes I will focus on the definitions from the social sciences: social psychology, sociology, communication and cultural studies, and applied linguistics. Not all sociology textbooks contain a definition of a stereotype but it is clear how it is viewed. For example, in their definition of sexism, Fulcher and Scott (2011, p. 834) explicitly state that 'stereotypes play a central part'. Elsewhere in the book they cite the media as having 'reinforced racial as well as class and gender stereotypes'. A number of other sociology textbooks assume that a specific definition of a stereotype is not necessary (e.g. Punch et al., 2013). However, the underlying assumption is that stereotypes are a societal problem as they are related (in particular) to racism and sexism. This is made clear in three definitions from sociology textbooks that specify a negative quality to the stereotype:

> [Stereotypes are] fixed and inflexible characterizations of groups of people based on little or no evidence.
>
> *Giddens and Sutton, 2017, p. 1016*

> Stereotype. A prejudicial, exaggerated description applied to every person in a category of people.
>
> *Macionis and Plummer, 2011, p. 354*

> Stereotypes are oversimplified or untrue generalisations about social groups.
>
> *Haralambos et al., 2013, p. 185*

These definitions mirror the dictionary definitions but are more explicit in indicating that stereotypes are fixed and inflexible, exaggerated and oversimplified and these sociology textbook definitions also make it clear that stereotypes are based on little or no evidence, prejudicial and untrue. They are fixed, simplistic and wrong. However, it is worth noting here, that the focus on stereotyping in the sociological textbooks has been in the context of discrimination in society, particularly in associating stereotypes with racism and sexism. While these stereotypes form a major feature of the current book, it is worth noting at this point that a definition of stereotype also needs to be able to encompass all those other stereotypes circulating in a culture, that are not so obviously linked to societal discrimination, such as stereotypes of accountants, Californians, cat lovers, computer gamers, Ford owners, Japanese people, librarians, mothers (or moms), Parisians, sailors, sci-fi fans, Texans, teenagers, wrestlers and vegetarians.

Social psychologists have shared the concern of sociologists about the negative and prejudicial aspects of stereotypes that link them to discrimination in society. However, psychological definitions often assume within them a particular theoretical position, which offers an explanation of why stereotypes arise in the first place (Schneider, 2004), giving variety to the psychological definitions, unlike the common agreement of the sociology textbook definitions mentioned above. One of the most important psychology books about stereotypes is *The Nature of Prejudice* by Gordon W. Allport in published in 1954 (Allport, [1954] 1979). He defined stereotypes as follows: 'Whether favourable or unfavourable, a stereotype is an exaggerated belief associated with a category. Its function is to justify (rationalize) our conduct in relation to that category' (p. 191). Notice that this is the first definition that has indicated that stereotypes can be positive as well as negative, such as the French viewed stereotypically as sophisticated and cultured. This implies that not all stereotypes lead to negative discrimination in society. It opens the possibility that a positive stereotype, such as middle-class people are competent, could lead to positive discrimination in society. Yet the crucial feature of Allport's definition – which is notably absent in the ones considered so far – is contained in his final sentence. Stereotypes are not simply errors of judgement: a person does not stereotype the members of another group by mistake. In Allport's view, the *function* of a stereotype is to provide a justification of the stereotype user's conduct. Consider a discriminatory society where one group has control over the educational resources that they use to favour their own children. A second equally intelligent but discriminated against group will suffer in their education due to the poor facilities they are offered. Consequently, the second group does not generally achieve as good grades at school and, relative to the first group, few members gain entrance to university and rarely obtain high status jobs. By stereotyping the second group as unintelligent, the first group can attribute the failure of the second group to do well educationally to a lack of intelligence, rather than acknowledging the discrimination in the society. In this way the stereotype serves as a justification – or rationalization – by the people using the stereotype for the poor educational performance of the second group rather than their own discrimination. This allows the dominant group to view themselves as blameless in the discrimination in society, yet still benefit from it. (This issue of the justificatory function of stereotypes will be considered in detail later in the book: see especially Chapters 5 and 6).

However, it is interesting to note that modern social psychology textbooks do not tend to focus on the justificatory function of stereotypes (or patterns of societal dominance) in their definitions, in favour of mental explanations of stereotype formation and function, employing terms such as 'cognitive structures' and the 'processing of information' in the mind of the person, that is, in explanations focused on the nature of human psychology and the decision-making of the individual. For example, the following definition was proposed by Hamilton et al. (1990, p. 36) but is also cited 25 years later by Hewstone et al. (2015, p. 607): 'We define a stereotype as a cognitive structure containing the perceiver's knowledge and beliefs about a social group and its members.' This is a more technical definition than the ones we have considered so far, containing the idea of a cognitive structure (which will be examined in Chapter 3), with the implication that stereotypes are linked to the 'structuring' of information (knowledge and beliefs) in the mind of the individual person or 'perceiver'. This theoretical concept is once again emphasized in the following definition: '[Stereotypes are] beliefs about social groups in terms of the traits or characteristics that they are believed to share. Stereotypes are cognitive frameworks that influence the processing of social information' (Branscombe and Baron, 2017, p. 458). Here, again, stereotypes are defined as cognitive 'frameworks' but this time the definition indicates that stereotypes influence 'the processing of social information'. Clearly stereotypes are linked here to something going on in the mind of the person (which will be examined in Chapter 3). Only some of these academic psychology definitions explicitly link stereotypes to prejudice and discrimination: '[S]tereotypes are … the cognitive culprits in prejudice and discrimination … One can see stereotypes as a particular kind of role schema that organizes people's expectations about other people who fall into certain social categories' (Fiske and Taylor 1991, p. 119). Now this definition clearly links stereotypes to prejudice and discrimination but considers it as a cognitive phenomenon, in this case a 'role schema'.[7] This emphasis on stereotypes as 'cognitive culprits in prejudice and discrimination' is made clear by later definitions from Fiske and Taylor:

> Stereotypes are the cognitive side of intergroup bias, beliefs about groups.
>
> *Fiske and Taylor, 2013, p. 457*

> Stereotyping is the cognitive aspect of bias – most frequently studied for gender, race, and age – and it comes in both blatant and subtle forms, a difference that matters in both practical and theoretical terms.
>
> *Fiske and Taylor, 2017, p. 332*

These definitions introduce a social cognitive explanation of stereotypes. Stereotypes are about cognition and bias, which, presumably, leads to prejudice and discrimination. By referring to stereotyping as a cognitive 'bias' there is the implication that an unbiased view of a social group is possible. This is a question examined in some detail later in the book. There is also a specific statement in the Fiske and Taylor (2017) definition that there are two types of stereotype – not mentioned in the other definitions – either blatant or subtle, which has practical and theoretical importance, which other definitions do not mention (see Chapter 3). Stereotyping is considered a mental phenomenon by these psychologists, which bears little superficial resemblance to the dictionary (or sociological) definitions mentioned above.

It is interesting to contrast the definition of a stereotype from sociology and psychology to that which is given in the field of communication and cultural studies:

> [A stereotype is an] oversimplified definition of a person or type of person, institution, style or event; to stereotype is to pigeonhole, to thrust into tight slots of definition which allow of little adjustment or change.
>
> *Watson and Hill, 2015, p. 307*

> [A stereotype is a] biased assessment of a person, group, or idea … Stereotypes are oversimplified assessments applied as generalizations, constituting a form of biased prejudgment.
>
> *Danesi, 2009, p. 277*

> [Stereotypes are] vivid but simple representations which reduce persons to a set of exaggerated, usually negative, character traits.
>
> *Barker and Jane, 2016, p. 313*[8]

Notice that these definitions are quite similar to the dictionary and sociology definitions. However, Barker and Jane (2016, p. 313) provide an explanation of why this reduction to exaggerated traits is occurring, arguing that 'this points to the operation of *power* in the process of stereotyping'. Different groups have different amounts of power in any society and stereotyping others is a way of seeking to maintain power. While this definition is quite different to a number of the other definitions that have been examined so for, it opens up a wider range of explanations for the construction of stereotypes, rather than being simplistic, fixed views or mental (cognitive) biases. Stereotypes are deliberately constructed: they are tools for maintaining power in society. As Barker (2004, p. 188) argued, stereotypes present a binary division between social groups: 'Stereotyping thus simultaneously establishes who "us" is and who is "them"', indicating the role of stereotypes to the relationship between social groups.

Finally, in an introduction to an applied linguistics text, Holliday (2010a, p. 134) selects a typical definition of a stereotype ('a preconceived and over-simplified idea of the characteristics that which typify a person or thing') but thereafter refers to it as a 'cultural stereotype'. Jackson's (2014) textbook on intercultural communication employs a similar definition to Holliday and also emphasizes the cultural aspect of stereotypes in intercultural communication. The idea that stereotypes are *cultural* is absent in many of the above definitions, particularly the psychological ones that emphasize its cognitive qualities. However, here it is explicit that stereotypes arise within a culture, not just 'in the head' of an individual. Holliday (2010a, p. 134) gives an example of a stereotype from a culture that he is familiar with: 'Iranian businessmen put family loyalty before business'. He emphasizes that stereotypes establish fixed notions of what people are like, particularly a cultural group, in language and communication where they are expressed, presenting the following definition: 'Cultural stereotypes are in the main overgeneralizations which are based on the describer's imagination of an inferior Other[9] rather than with objective information about what the people being described are really like' (Holliday, 2010a, p. 134). He concludes by picking up a point from Kumaravadivelu (2007) about intercultural dynamics and cultural stereotypes in political terms: 'cultural stereotypes which are believed to be egalitarian by their users are an influential underpinning of US notions of cultural assimilation which in turn impose ethnocentric cultural viewpoints' (Holliday, 2010a, p. 134). Clearly, in Holliday's view stereotypes are cultural and political. They are employed for purposes of intercultural relations, echoing Barker and Jane's (2016) point about power and intergroup dynamics.

How can all these definitions be summed up? One answer is that they are all telling us something important about stereotypes and this examination of a variety of definitions rather than indicating confusion about what they are, illustrates how complex the concept of a stereotype actually is. Like the ancient Buddhist parable of the blind men seeking to describe an elephant, with their descriptions depending on which part of the animal they are touching (such as the trunk or a leg), maybe the different authors are examining different aspects of the complex concept of a stereotype? Yet, it can be argued that, from these texts, we can infer that stereotypes are viewed as fixed, simplistic overgeneralizations linked to prejudice and discrimination. They may be rationalizations or justification for prejudice. They are associated in some way to the way the mind works – to its cognitive structure – that potentially influences behaviour. There are also important elements in the way that different groups construct their perceptions of each other in order to maintain or challenge power relationships in society. This is particularly important when we consider intergroup or intercultural relations. However, we should also consider stereotypes as 'cultural stereotypes', expressed in language, and it is in culture and intercultural relations that we can examine their origins and the motivation for their use. Stereotypes may be all these things.

The cultural context of the research into stereotypes

Before continuing with the attempt to define stereotypes, it is worth noting a very significant feature of the academic research on stereotypes over the last 100 years. First, much of this research has taken place in the United States, and most of the research has focused on stereotypes of race[10] and gender. For example, I did a quick Internet search of academic articles on stereotypes and of the more than a million articles that were found, well over 90 per cent examined stereotypes of either race (ethnicity) or gender. This is a very understandable focus as, first, the United States has some of the best and most active research universities in the world (during both the twentieth and twenty-first centuries) and, second, issues of racism and sexism have been two of the most important social issues within American society during that time. It is just half a century on from two of the most important developments in the society of the United States in the second half of the twentieth century: the Civil Rights Movement and the Women's Liberation Movement. Examining the influence of stereotypes in these two areas of American society has been of considerably greater social concern, than the American stereotypes of, say, the English, librarians or soldiers for example. In the context of a society with a Declaration of Independence claiming equality and human rights, the issues of racial and gender inequality have a particular significance (see Chapter 6). Before moving on to a further consideration of the definition of stereotypes it is worth briefly examining the cultural context of the majority of the stereotyping research, into two specific stereotypes, of Black people and women in American society.

Race and stereotypes in the United States

Slavery has existed in many human societies. Yet, slavery in the United States, however, was different in that the slaves were exclusively of African origin and the slave owners of European origin (see Chapter 6). Thus, the racial designation of 'White' and 'Black' people was also a distinction between social groups based on power and dominance in the society. In 1790 there were just over 680,000 Black slaves or just below 20 per cent of the population, concentrated in the Southern states, where they constituted 34 per cent of the Southern population. The slave population rose to nearly 4 million by 1860 (Bourne, 2008). In 1863, during the Civil War (1861–1865), Union President Abraham Lincoln issued the Emancipation Proclamation freeing the slaves. Effectively, this meant that any slave escaping the South to the North would immediately become free. The 13th Amendment to the Constitution, passed in 1865, at the end of the war, confirmed the abolishment of slavery throughout the United States. However, 90 years later, in the mid-twentieth century, discrimination against African Americans remained endemic in the society, with segregation of the 'races' in many aspects of life, from schooling to the workplace where discrimination was common. In the South, the Jim Crow laws of 1896 (which were only removed in 1965) formalized segregation in some states. Between 1910 and 1930, 18 states maintained or instituted 'one-drop' laws of racial designation, that is, any African ancestry made a person legally (racially) Black (regardless of their actual skin colour). Anti-miscegenation laws (banning marriage between the 'races') were enacted by 41 states at one time or another, and only repealed for the final 16 states in 1967. It was at this time in the mid-twentieth century that Allport ([1954] 1979), in his major work, drew on the idea of the stereotype to seek to explain why some people developed prejudicial stereotypical views – considered to be rigid, simplistic, inaccurate and illogical beliefs about other social groups – particularly the negative views held by White people about Black people in American society. This developed the hope that if only these stereotypes could be eradicated, prejudice – and its consequent discrimination – would be reduced.

Discrimination against African Americans in the United States continued to be a major social issue throughout the second half of the twentieth century. On 28 August 1963, Dr Martin Luther King Jr made his famous 'I have a dream' speech at the Lincoln Memorial in Washington, DC, where he referenced the passage of a century since the Emancipation Proclamation, and highlighted the then current situation of the African American in his country:

> still sadly crippled by the manacles of segregation and the chains of discrimination … lives on a lonely island of poverty in the midst of a vast ocean of material prosperity … still languishing in the corners of American society and finds himself an exile in his own land. So we have come here today to dramatize an appalling condition.
>
> *King, 1963, n.p.*

The Civil Rights Acts in 1964 and 1968 outlawed racial discrimination in employment and housing. Subsequent laws have strengthened the antidiscrimination legislation. However, despite the election of an African American president in the early twenty-first century, many issues of discrimination, such as inequality in education and in the criminal justice system, remain current (Borowczyk-Martins et al., 2017; Reskin, 2012). In the twenty-first century stereotype researchers acknowledge that the public expression of negative stereotypes of Black people has been reduced, yet are now concerned that these may still be having a subtle effect on the citizens of the country (Fiske and Taylor, 2017). It is this historical and cultural context of racial discrimination in a society professing egalitarian values that makes the stereotype of African Americans so important to the American academic stereotype researchers, as 'race' has been such a highly significant social categorization in their society, and explains the desire to eradicate such stereotypes.

Gender and stereotypes in the United States

At its foundation, women in the United States did not have the right to vote. In the nineteenth century, campaigners such as Susan B. Anthony and Elizabeth Cady Stanton, fought for women's suffrage and, in 1890, the pressure groups were combined into the National American Woman Suffrage Association. Yet it was only in 1920 that the Nineteenth Amendment to the Constitution was ratified giving women the vote. However, during the twentieth century, women remained discriminated against in numerous ways, particularly in the workplace and in positions of power, as acknowledged by the Presidential Commission on the Status of Women, created in 1961. Crucially, Friedan's (1963) million-selling book *The Feminine Mystique* argued that, after the opportunities for women outside the home during the Second World War, women were once again restricted by the pervasive idea of the feminine mystique: 'fulfillment as a woman had only one definition for American women after 1949 – the housewife-mother' (Friedan, 1963, p. 38). Yet Friedan argued this idea was corrosive to women's health and genuine fulfilment. 'The feminine mystique has succeeded in burying millions of American women alive' (Friedan, 1963, p. 325). Critically, this restricted representation of women could be considered in terms of the stereotype concept: a negative gender stereotype, presenting a rigid, simplest and prejudicial view of American women that denied them opportunities outside of a historical gender role (Eagly and Steffen, 1984). By associating aspects of character ('femininity') to the traditional role, women are stereotypically viewed as more communal – self-less and concerned about others – and less agentic – self-assertive and action-oriented – than men (Eagly and Wood, 2012), which constructed a false representation of women, supporting various forms of discrimination and denying women access to non-traditional roles that they were capable of fulfilling. In particular, women were restricted in their opportunities by the oppression of a patriarchal system of societal dominance that presented them as a lower-status 'Other' (e.g. Bennett, 2006; see Chapter 6). Women obtained legal protection against discrimination in the workplace by the Civil Rights acts of the 1960s, and the Women's Liberation Movement of the 1960s and 1970s fought against the prejudice and the restricted view of women that continued to deny them diversity of opportunity and undermine their competence. It was argued by American psychologists that a key element in the continued discrimination against women was the stereotype of them present in the workplace (Fiske and Stevens, 1993); and, in a landmark ruling in 1989, the Supreme Court decided in favour of a female employee who, contrary to Civil Rights legislation, had been discriminated against by her employer on the basis of gender stereotyping (Fiske et al., 1991). A key point that Fiske and Stevens make is that gender stereotypes are not just descriptive but also *prescriptive*: presenting a model of how people *should* be. Underlying this prescription is a set of ideological beliefs about the 'nature' of men and women (see Chapter 6). For example, Prentice and Carranza (2002) asked student participants to identify these prescriptions for American society. The results identified the following characteristics specific to women and men. (I have selected the top ten categories of the 'should' results.) Women *should* be warm and kind, have an interest in children, be sensitive, friendly and clean, pay attention to their appearance, be patient, polite, cheerful and cooperative, and *should not* be rebellious, stubborn, controlling, cynical, promiscuous or arrogant. Men *should* have business sense, be athletic, have leadership ability, be self-reliant, be ambitious, have high self-esteem, be assertive, decisive, have a strong personality and be rational, and *should not* be emotional, approval-seeking, impressionable, yielding, superstitious or shy.

Thus, the stereotype of women has been considered a central element in the discrimination against them (particularly in the workplace). It is easy to see, with the prescriptive stereotypes listed above, how a highly effective woman leader might be labelled as 'unladylike' – and so discriminated against – which was a term used for the female employee who was denied promotion and the subject of a workplace discrimination case considered by the Supreme Court in 1989 (Fiske et al., 1991). The National Women's Law Center (NWLC) presents four examples of these derogatory stereotypes of women in the workplace: 'women aren't breadwinners', which undermines women's working lives in that their work is not considered as valuable as that of men; 'there's something called "men's work" and women cannot do it', which restricts women's opportunities and reinforces misconceptions of gender, even to the extent of placing women store assistants in the domestic goods department and not in hardware; 'women are supposed to act like ladies', showing that women are judged against a stereotype expectation of 'femininity' and may be evaluated harshly if they do not meet this expectation; 'women aren't committed to the job as they are busy being caregivers', again drawing on stereotypical expectations about women (NWLC, 2013). The NWLC argued that these stereotypes are both harmful, in that they unfairly impede the progress of women in the workplace, and illegal as they contravene the Civil Rights Act of 1964. Thus, it is not surprising that activists for equal rights have argued for the eradication of these stereotypes of women in American society.

Sociocultural aspect of stereotypes

While racism and sexism are features of many societies, the specific features of American culture, such as its history of Black slavery, are absent in other cultures, such as in the Russian Federation or China for example, with histories of serfdom in their societies but not based on race. Even where there is a common history of slavery, as in Brazil, where slavery was abolished later than in the United States, there are also differences in the cultural history; for example, miscegenation was a feature of the society. While racism existed in the country, Brazil developed its own culture of 'racial democracy' (e.g. Hanchard, 1999) which, although often considered as mythical, has resulted in a large proportion of its citizens (well over 40 per cent) being neither Black nor White, due to their mixed-race heritage, which is an integral feature of Brazilian identity (e.g. Eakin, 2017). Brazilian census designers have typically employed the categories of White, Brown ('*pardo*') and Black, yet many people from 'White' to 'Black' are happy to self-identify as the more fluid multi-racial term '*moreno*' (Bailey and Telles, 2006). To take a second example, while it is easy to list the negative features of the Soviet Union (1922–1991), women had equality in principle (if not in practice) from the 1920s and were playing a significant role in the workplace throughout the twentieth century (Dodge, 1966; Lapidus, 1978; Mandel, 1971), and hence the context of their lives was materially different to that of women in the United States. While the oppressive regime and its ultimate economic demise had a major impact on its citizens, there were differences in gender issues between the United States and the Soviet Union during its existence: for example, since the 1950s, 70 per cent of medical practitioners in Russia have been women (Ramakrishnan et al., 2014). Indeed, Eveleth (2013) writing in the *Smithsonian Magazine*, noted the greater prevalence of women in STEM (science, technology, engineering and mathematics) professions in the Soviet Union than in the United States (see also Mandel, 1971). In the early 1960s women obtained 40 per cent of chemistry PhDs in the Soviet Union, compared to only 5 per cent at the same time and 35 per cent in the 2010s, in the United States. One explanation was the general focus on mathematics and science for girls as well as boys in Russian schools, parental support and the girls' own ideas of prestigious occupations for themselves in their culture (Eveleth, 2013).

The focus of stereotypes of race and gender within American society is understandable, but these are not the only stereotypes employed in that society and, in other cultures, different stereotypes have emerged with different social issues. In other cultures the historically important relationships between powerful and discriminated-against groups in society are not necessarily based on race, as in the United States, but on geographical, tribal and religious differences (such as the 'troubles' in Northern Ireland or the conflict in the former Yugoslavia in the late twentieth century). Also, there are stereotypes in other cultures that may not be familiar in the United States, such as the stereotypes of people from the different provinces in China (Brown, 2014; Young, 1988), and there will have been stereotypes in the past of people and occupations that no longer exist in modern everyday society (such as the village blacksmith, town crier or fletcher). Thus, the focus on a specific stereotype or a specific culture might influence the understanding of what a stereotype, as a general concept, actually is. Consequently, this book, while acknowledging the importance of the social issues of race and gender in American society, will seek to examine what is meant by a stereotype in its diversity of uses.

Commonly held beliefs about stereotypes

From the above definitions, and the specific focus of the research on stereotypes of race and gender in American society, there has emerged a set of commonly held beliefs about stereotypes (Perkins, 1979). To illustrate this, I have extracted seven points from the dictionaries and a further three from the focus of the research. This set is a variant of the list constructed by Perkins (1979) but captures the same common views about what people typically believe that stereotypes are.

1. A stereotype is a fixed (as in rigid and overgeneralized) idea about the members of a social group.
2. A stereotype is a fixed (as in unchanging) view of the members of a social group.
3. A stereotype is a simple (simplistic) representation of the members of a social group.
4. A stereotype is an inaccurate view about people.
5. It is clearly wrong to believe a stereotype.
6. People believe a stereotype or they do not.
7. Someone who believes a stereotype will act in a discriminatory way towards the members of the stereotyped group.
8. A stereotype involves negative or pejorative terms …
9. … about other people.
10. … who are a minority or oppressed group in society.

We can apply this to the well-known stereotype of 'the poor are lazy'. The stereotype appears to attribute the characteristic of laziness to the poor without exception, rigidly fixing the quality to them. It generalizes, or rather overgeneralizes, the quality of laziness seemingly to all poor people. Furthermore, it is an idea that we can easily trace back to the nineteenth century (and beyond), so is a long lasting view (Fuchs, 2005). We can argue that labelling the poor as lazy is a very simplistic way of viewing them, ignoring the complex and diverse factors that have resulted in people being poor. The 'poor are lazy' stereotype must be wrong as we can easily find a poor person who is not lazy. For all these reasons it is wrong for a person to believe the stereotype. If we examine the evidence from the socio-economic environment, we will find many poor people working extremely long hours for very little pay. For certain reasons (which will be explored in Chapter 2) it is assumed that some (mistaken) people believe in the stereotype and other people (with more realistic views) do not. The stereotype users are a societal problem (in an egalitarian society) as it is assumed that someone who holds a stereotypical view will act in a discriminatory way towards the group based on the stereotype, such as not wishing to provide the poor with social support based on the stereotypical belief that 'the poor are lazy': that their poverty is 'their own fault', they are essentially lazy or 'born lazy'. Thus, not only is the stereotype highly prejudicial but it is used to justify discrimination against the group. Stereotypes present people in negative and derogatory terms, with traits like laziness or ignorance applied to the members of a social group. By attributing the negative quality of laziness, the stereotype denigrates poor people. As Perkins (1979, p. 144) pointed out, 'pejorativeness has become almost built into the meaning of the word "stereotype"'. In our consideration of stereotypes so far, we have seen that the stereotype of Black people is held by White people, the negative stereotype of a women in the workplace is typically held by men (who have discriminated against them). We can be sure that the stereotype of the 'poor are lazy' is held by other – wealthier – people, rather than the poor themselves. Finally, we have seen that stereotypes are ways of seeking to 'justify' the injustice or discrimination applied to lower status groups, like the poor, to 'keep them in their place' and allow the rich to exploit them. Stereotypes are intimately linked to the discrimination against oppressed groups in society.

Commonly held beliefs about stereotypes – which may be misleading

The above ten points are familiar to us, as they are common beliefs about the nature of stereotypes that are frequently circulated in the media. However, there is just one problem: every one of these assumptions about stereotypes is almost certainly misleading (Perkins, 1979). This is not to say that these points do not apply to certain stereotypes but, as Perkins pointed out, when examined in more detail, each of the statements is itself a simplification, which further analysis demonstrates is not so easily applied to all stereotypes. It is like making assumptions about all trees based only on oak and beech trees rather than considering pines or redwoods as well. In fact, each of these points may be an overgeneralization or, as Worchel and Rothgerber (1997) suggested, a stereotype of the stereotype! These ten points are now considered in more detail.

1. A stereotype is a fixed (as in rigid and overgeneralized) idea about the members of a social group.
2. A stereotype is a fixed (as in unchanging) view of the members of a social group.

To claim that an idea is fixed or rigid, we need to be able to distinguish it from an idea that is flexible or changeable. Take, for example, the generalization that birds fly. Is this a fixed idea? Certainly, it is often taken as a defining feature of birds. Also, on learning that an ostrich or a kiwi does not fly – and they are both birds – people do not abandon their belief that birds fly. People are often happy to acknowledge exceptions. Similarly, people are often quite willing to admit exceptions to their stereotypical beliefs, such as learning that a specific English person is extroverted rather than stereotypically reserved. Stereotypes may be no more fixed than other ideas. Furthermore, Perkins (1979) pointed out that most people do not change their 'ordinary' concepts in the face of just a few counterexamples. Consequently, it may be misleading to see all stereotypes as particularly rigid overgeneralizations, rather than simply generalizations (see Chapters 2 and 3). In generalizing (birds fly, the English are reserved) we may be presenting (what we believe to be) the generic properties of a category rather than a rigid belief that an attribute applies to every member of it (see Chapter 5). Finally, all people have concepts fundamental to their belief systems (such as a belief in God, democracy or gender equality) which they do not lightly change, so may appear fixed. Thus, certain stereotypes cannot be divorced from the ideology underlying them. One person's ideological belief may conflict with the fundamental beliefs held by other people, so may be viewed as wrong or false (Perkins, 1979; see also Chapter 6). Indeed, Perkins (1979) pointed out that stereotypes of race and gender may be special cases of stereotypes, particularly when compared to other stereotypes, such as of science fiction fans (as nerdy) or surfers (as laid-back).

We only need to look at the social world of 50 or 100 years ago to realize that people's views of social groups can radically change over time. Just because people know the stereotypes of the past does not necessarily imply that those stereotypes are current or commonly believed in modern society. Indeed, the stereotype of a social group is related to its position (and role) in the society (see Chapter 4). When that position – and its related role – changes so the stereotype will also tend to change. For example, as women's roles have changed in a society so the stereotypical views of women have also changed (Bosak et al., 2018; Diekman and Eagly, 2000). Even in a short period of time stereotype change is possible. A well-known example of stereotype change in twenty-first-century Western popular culture has been the shift in the stereotype of the intelligent and scientifically minded person – the geek – from socially isolated and odd (a nerd) to popular and sexy, commonly referred to as 'geek chic' (Inness, 2007; McArthur, 2009). The suggestion that stereotypes are fixed and enduring may be more related to the methods of studying them than their defining qualities (as will be examined later in the book).

3. A stereotype is a simple (simplistic) representation of the members of a social group.

As Perkins (1979) argued, in order to make a stereotypical claim – such as 'the poor are lazy' – it typically requires quite a complex understanding of the social world. It is rare to hear someone claim that '*all* poor people are lazy' (i.e every single one of them): often the speaker is targeting a highly selective subgroup in their criticisms that they label, for example, as 'welfare fraudsters' or 'benefit scroungers'. In this case, a person has to know something about the state welfare system and the people claiming it. Also, depending on the specific welfare system (in a specific country) the stereotype about the people on welfare is focused on specific topics: for example, that they are 'too lazy to look for work', that they 'squander the money they are given by the state'. These may be false claims but they are not simplistic. The application of the 'poor are lazy' stereotype is specifically focused on certain people who are viewed as the *undeserving poor*, based on an ideological moral position (Romano, 2017; Wacquant, 2009; see also Chapter 6). Crucially, a person who complains about welfare fraudsters might also readily agree that there are genuine deserving poor who should be looked after by a state benefit system, such as the elderly poor or war veterans, so does not stereotype the poor as all the same. Rather than being simple, stereotypes indicate an ideological framework of beliefs about certain groups within society. For example, Alesina et al. (2001) analysed the results of a World Values survey, and compared respondents from the United States and Europe. They found that 60 per cent of Americans say that the poor are lazy, compared to just 27 per cent of Europeans, which might be associated to the relatively smaller state welfare system in the United States compared to European countries (see Fong et al., 2006). Thus, the view that the 'poor or lazy', which may initially appear to be a straightforward example of a fixed and simple stereotype, turns out, after further analysis, to be a much more complex representation, associated with ideology and political beliefs about the deserving and underserving members of society.

4. A stereotype is an inaccurate view about people.
5. It is clearly wrong to believe a stereotype.

There is a tendency to view all stereotypes as inaccurate, on the basis of the dominant research into stereotypes associated with societal discrimination. It is clearly wrong to claim that all Black people are athletic, all women are emotional or every poor person is lazy. However, as noted above, occupational roles can be influential in the creation of stereotypes, as in the stereotype of librarians and accountants, which may reasonably accurately reflect aspects of the occupational role. As Eagly and Steffen (1984) argued, gender stereotypes correspond to the traditional division of men and women into specific roles in a particular society. Thus, the stereotype may have a 'kernel of truth' (Eagly and Steffen, 1984, p. 751) in reflecting the descriptive, statistical distribution of people into certain roles and the characteristics associated with their role requirements. As Eagly and Steffen (1984) pointed out, gender stereotypes may reflect the sexist roles people are required to undertake in a sexist society, and as such provide a descriptively accurate account of that culture. Stereotypes about many, if not all, occupations, may reflect common understandings about the role requirements. Arguably, these may have some degree of descriptive accuracy; for example, Lapidus and King (2019) found that librarians tended to be introvert and conventional (along with other characteristics). As Jussim (2012a) has argued, a stereotype might provide a degree of predictive accuracy, without which we might have no information at all. Consider an American who is about to meet an unknown Englishman for the first time. With nothing else to go on except a general knowledge of the English, the stereotypical expectation that this Englishman will be reserved might be confirmed on first meeting him. In this case, the stereotype has provided a useful and accurate prediction. (However, this does not mean that the American believes that *every single* Englishman is reserved, and might willingly accept that the prediction was wrong if the Englishman turns out to be highly extroverted.) Thus, on a descriptive level stereotypes may not be 'inaccurate'. The problem of gender stereotypes (Fiske and Stevens, 1993, as noted earlier) is that they are employed by some people (who seek to maintain specific gender divisions in society) prescriptively to make a claim about what men and women should do, based on an ideological belief about gender. Critics of this stereotype do not deny that the culture is structured in gender terms (the descriptive stereotype), but challenge the explanation in terms of masculinity and femininity (the prescriptive stereotype).

As we have seen already in this chapter, other stereotypes, such as those of the English and French, and of librarians and accountants, often reflect aspects of social experience. It may not be that English people are inherently reserved or the French inherently sophisticated but that their culture has an effect on its members and their identities, who may act as if it is so. As we shall see in Chapter 5, the impact of culture on shaping our identities – whether it is national cultural or workplace culture – can lead people to act as group members, rather than exclusively as individuals, which leads other people to perceive them in terms of social categories as, say, English or a school teacher. Much of our knowledge of the social world comes from our culture – and what other people tell us – whether through socialization and education (see Chapter 5) or via the media and social media (Chapter 7). Stereotypes may reflect the structure of that culture, and hence can be considered as part of a person's cultural knowledge rather than necessarily a set of false beliefs.

6. People believe a stereotype or they do not.
7. Someone who believes a stereotype will act in a discriminatory way towards the members of the stereotyped group.

At first glance, it seems obvious that some people believe a stereotype and others do not, such as a racist believing a racist stereotype and a non-racist not believing it. However, as we shall see in Chapter 2, even highly prejudiced people are willing to acknowledge exceptions to a stereotypical view, indicating that their beliefs may be more complex than a simple belief that a stereotype is always valid. An added complication is that much of the psychological research into the topic of stereotypes has asked participants to give stereotype descriptions *even if they do not believe them* themselves (see Chapter 2). This means that a person might employ a stereotype because they have been asked to do it by the researcher, not because they believe it or use it in their daily lives. The result of this research therefore may reflect common knowledge rather than a personal belief (see Chapter 3). A further complication is that people are now aware that stereotypes were viewed negatively in society and so may choose not to publicly state their beliefs (Brown, 1965). Indeed, Fiske and Taylor (2013) argued that only 10 per cent of the population (in a Western democracy such as the United States) are willing to overtly express negative stereotypes. As we shall see in Chapter 3, psychologists have adopted different techniques to determine if participants hold stereotypes 'implicitly', but there still remains the question of whether this research is demonstrating personal beliefs or simply common knowledge. There are also many reasons why a person might express a stereotype in language that does not necessarily correspond to a personal belief, when stating a stereotype for a rhetorical purpose. This is particularly the case when we consider the speeches of politicians and the use of stereotypes in their rhetoric of persuading the electorate to support them (see Chapters 6 and 7). There is a question of whether the politician is expressing a personal belief or stating a viewpoint that they hope will get them elected.

Even if we assume that the expression of a stereotype indicates an underlying belief, to argue that it will have a direct effect on behaviour may not be the case. It seems reasonable to assume that a person who believes a racist stereotype will act in in a racist way. However, as we shall see in Chapter 4, this is rather a simplistic view of the relationship between beliefs and behaviour. There are a number of influential factors on a person's behaviour as well as their beliefs about stereotypes. For example, a person's general (negative) stereotype belief about a social group may not influence their specific behaviour when faced with an individual group member. This will be examined in Chapter 4. One of the key elements in determining human conduct is the social expectation about appropriate behaviour in a particular context, a social norm (see Chapter 5). Whereas in the early twentieth century expressing negative racist or sexist stereotypes about people was accepted in American society – in certain circumstances it was normative to do so – by the second half of the century the norm had shifted to this being unacceptable. Furthermore, civil rights legislation and employment law has made the expression of certain derogatory stereotypes illegal in the workplace and thus a prejudiced person (who believes the stereotype) might not express the stereotype in public nor act upon it in the workplace for fear of sanction. Thus, a stereotypical belief may simply be one of many influences on a person's behaviour.

8.   A stereotype involves negative or pejorative terms …

With a research focus on societal discrimination, there is a tendency to view all stereotypes as negative, as is the case with 'the poor are lazy' stereotype. However, this is not necessarily true of all stereotypes. In a paper on stereotypes and nationality published in Japan, Toyama (2006, p. 19) stated: 'We identify French people with sophistication.' This stereotype of the sophisticated French is not only held by people who have never been to France or have only observed them from a distance. Consider the following description by the author Lawrence Durrell (1969), who had lived in France for over a decade, in a British television programme about Paris:

> Really, the French get you absolutely mad with envy. Wherever you go, you find them engaged in some intellectual pursuit: reading recondite books, painting, cooking, playing the harp or writing sonnets. Damn them! It is unfair that the whole country is creative, or trying to be.[11]

Durrell is clearly expressing a stereotype, yet at the same time it is highly complementary and something that makes him, a British writer, envious. Indeed, he was probably exaggerating for effect, yet it still fits the definitions of a stereotype: 'wherever you go, you find them engaged in some intellectual pursuit', 'the whole country is creative'. Yet at the same time, we know what he means: bringing to mind the famous works of French writers such as Voltaire and Descartes, or Sartre or Camus, the famous nineteenth-century French impressionists Renoir, Monet, Cezanne, Gaugin and so on, to representations of French cooking, with cordon bleu chefs and Michelin stars indicating culinary excellence. Even restaurants outside of France print their menus in French to look sophisticated! Thus, this stereotype of the French taps into a complex of cultural knowledge that Durrell is assuming that the viewer will know. The image of the sophisticated French is a commonly known stereotype, whether a person believes it or not. For example, an analysis of British stereotypes of the French had 'sophisticated' as one of the key attributes (Larrivée and Longhi, 2012). Rosenthal (1999, p. 897) pointed out that, for Americans too, French things convey 'an aura of style, culture and prestige'. Yet rather than being simplistic, this, highly positive, stereotype of the French requires some knowledge of French culture. Consider, as a second example, the stereotypically romantic Frenchman. In the 1995 romantic comedy *French Kiss*, an American woman played by Meg Ryan discovers that a charming (but crooked) Frenchman played by Kevin Kline has used her to smuggle a diamond necklace. Yet she still falls for him, and they are together at the end of the film living in a lovely French vineyard: a romantic image of the French lifestyle. Arguably the enjoyment of this film is that, aware of the stereotype of the romantic Frenchman, the audience knows and enjoys knowing that the love match will win out in the film. This is not to say that the only stereotype of the French is positive. The French are also stereotypically viewed as rude, arrogant and lacking in hygiene (Larrivée and Longhi, 2012) with Frenchmen viewed alternatively as effete and decadent (Rosenthal, 1999). However, this simply adds to the complexity of the stereotypical representation of the French by other nations. There appears to be a positive or negative view of the French for any occasion. This certainly challenges the view that stereotypes are rigid or fixed or simplistic.

9.   ... about other people.

There is a tendency, from the negative stereotypes linked to racism and sexism, and 'the poor are lazy' stereotype, to assume that all stereotypes are about other people, specifically created by a powerful social group to derogate them. However, in many cases the members of a social group will self-stereotype, and accept a stereotypical view of their own group, such as the Scottish as tough, the English as reserved or the French as sophisticated. Even a negative stereotype employed by others, such as Scottish meanness or English standoffishness (or rudeness) can be adopted in more positive terms, as Scottish thriftiness or the phlegmatic English, by the group themselves and can become a feature of a group member's own identity (e.g. Burris et al., 2000; Marín and Salazar, 1985; see Chapter 4 on social identity theory). For example, the character Groundskeeper Willie in the US television cartoon comedy series *The Simpsons* is portrayed as a stereotypical Scotsman, rugged and tough, dour and with wild ginger hair who we occasionally see wearing a kilt and a tam-o'-shanter hat. Yet, if you visited Scotland you are unlikely to see a man wearing a kilt on an ordinary day in Glasgow or Edinburgh, there are not many ginger-haired people to be seen and fewer people wearing tam-o'-shanter hats. However, this is a stereotype that Scottish people embrace affectionately in sporting events, with

Scottish fans donning kilts, ginger wigs and tam-o'-shanters to support their national team at international events. A stereotype of one's own group can be also used to help explain aspects of one's life. For example, Sharleen Spiteri, the lead singer of the Scottish popular band Texas that formed in 1989, pointed out in a 2017 interview that women have to be tough in a male-dominated music business and drew on the Scottish stereotype to reflect on her own strength: 'Yes, you have got to be tough. [I am] Scottish; what can I say? I am from Glasgow. It's ingrained into my very being.'[12]

10. … who are a minority or oppressed group in society.

Stereotypes may be employed to oppress people in society, such as using the 'poor are lazy' stereotype to restrict welfare aid to the poorest members of a community. However, there are also well-known stereotypes of librarians and accountants, which are both perfectly respectable professions that are not normally associated with minority groups or oppression. Dickinson (2003) charted the history of the librarian in the academia of the United States. While originally mostly male, librarianship gradually became a female-dominant profession, as female staff could be employed at lower pay and kept at lower grades. By 1900 some 75 per cent of all librarians were women. Subsequently, the stereotype of female librarians developed as 'drab spinsters peering over the rim of their glasses and ready to "shush" a library patron for the offense of talking too loudly' (Dickinson, 2003, p. 97). With the majority of librarians as female, the men who became librarians then tended to be stereotyped as meek and conservative (Newmyer, 1976). While we can see the influence of sexism and the denigration of occupations that were seen as 'women's work' in the stereotype, there also exists the popular view that the traditional activities of a librarian are fairly mundane: checking books in and out, organizing the shelves and the catalogues, working in a quiet space with little opportunity to talk to other people. The job appeared to require an introverted person to survive the work, and so the stereotype bears a relationship to the perceived activities of the role (see Chapter 5). This is particularly the case with accountancy, an occupation that is commonly associated with sitting in an office poring over spreadsheets. The popular (cultural) view is that this is rather a dull activity, famously emphasized by Michael Palin's portrayal of an accountant, in *Monty Python's Flying Circus* comedy show,[13] who visits a vocational counsellor (played by John Cleese) seeking a new profession. He complains that accountancy is not exciting: 'It's dull, dull, dull … It's dull, and tedious and stuffy and boring'; to which the counsellor (Cleese) responds by saying 'Yes, but you see, your report here says that you are an extremely dull person' and hence he is perfectly suited to being an accountant. While this is a humorous skit, it gains its humour by picking up on the well-known stereotypical view of accountancy. Indeed, the stereotype of the accountant has been well-documented: as a 'dull and grey suited bore' (Jeacle, 2008, p. 1296), a 'bean counter' who is 'introverted, cautious, methodical, shy, timid, and boring' (Albu et al., 2011, p. 669) and 'a beancounter stereotype being dull, dry, unimaginative, precise and abiding to rules' (Hung, 2014, p. 256).

In the popular conception, accountancy is viewed as working all day in an office with numbers (just as the librarian is assumed to be spending all days sorting out books in silence), which is not contradicted by a description of the accountancy role from Davis (2015): 'An accountant performs financial functions related to the collection, accuracy, recording, analysis and presentation of a business, organization or company's financial operations.' When children are asked which jobs they would like to do, librarianship and accountancy do not often feature in their lists. According to one study, the 15 most popular jobs children favour are dancer, actor, musician, teacher, scientist, athlete, firefighter, detective, writer, police officer, astronaut, pilot, veterinarian, lawyer and doctor (Bureau of Labor Statistics, 2016). In a 2016 interview with the famous Italian dancer and choreographer Bruno Tonioli (a judge on the television programme *Dancing with the Stars* in the United States and *Strictly Come Dancing* in the UK), he said that his parents wanted him to become an accountant.[14] Presumably his parents wanted him to have a good career and saw accountancy as a stable and secure profession. Yet, neither the interviewer nor the listeners (of the interview) are likely to question why Tonioli chose to be a dancer. We can see from the children's choices that it is considered much more exciting to be a dancer rather than an accountant. Indeed, as Dickinson (2003, p. 108) notes 'when the work was dull, so were the stereotypes'. In many ways the stereotypes of the librarian and accountant are reflecting widespread (cultural) views about the job. Modern librarians and accountants may wish to change the stereotypes of their professions to reflect the interesting aspects of the activity, which has clearly changed with technological developments, and they may endeavour to do so (Jeacle, 2008; Mosley, 2003), but how concerned should society be about these particular stereotypes? Librarianship and accountancy are clearly occupational choices and so there is a degree of personal selection in joining the profession. It is unlikely that librarians and accountants face genuine societal discrimination (as discussed in terms of race and gender above) or oppression, as the terms are typically defined.

The problem of the definition of a stereotype

What the analysis of the ten assumptions about stereotypes tells us is that there has been a tendency to focus on specific stereotypes in seeking to define them rather than examining the concept in its diverse usage. Claiming that all stereotypes are either good or bad or that all members of a social group have or have not got an attribute, and even the suggestion that all stereotypes are 'both evil and erroneous and represented flawed thinking' (Worchel and Rothgerber, 1997, p. 73) presents a 'stereotyped' view of the stereotype that does not stand up to scrutiny. We should also not forget that one person's stereotype might be another person's common sense (see Chapters 5 and 6). When one person expresses the view that bankers are 'greedy, out for themselves, with little concern for others', one listener (who believes that bankers make an important contribution to the capitalist, consumer society) might consider this an objectionable stereotype, yet a second listener might strongly agree with it, claiming it is not a stereotype at all.

This implies that public concern about stereotypes is (not surprisingly) focused on those social groups that have suffered specific discrimination in society, rather than stereotypes more generally. There are no social movements to protect bankers from being stereotyped as greedy or the likelihood of *Schadenfreude* at their misfortune (Cikara and Fisk, 2012). Bankers, like politicians or lawyers, are not considered as disadvantaged in society and so are not seen as needing legal protection from prejudiced stereotypical statements about them, such as 'bankers are greedy', 'lawyers are crooked', 'politicians are self-interested'. Thus, not all stereotypes are publically viewed in the same way, indicating their political role (see Chapter 6). Furthermore, as Schneider (2004) has pointed out, a definition of a stereotype includes within it theoretical assumptions about both people (how they think) and the social world (how it is or should be).

Therefore, there is more to stereotypes than simply being inaccurate fixed beliefs. As Perkins (1979) has shown, stereotypes are not always erroneous in content, not always pejorative; not always about minority groups or groups we know little about and may be about our own group (which we accept as valid and true). Stereotypes are not necessarily simple or unchanging. Perkins (1979) also questioned the view of stereotypes as solely a psychological, mental 'cognitive construct', as this can shift the focus of explanation away from structural (social and cultural) factors; which also questions the assumption of a direct link between a person 'holding' a stereotype and that person's behaviour towards a stereotyped group member. The analysis of Perkins (1979) showed that, outside of a narrow range of specific stereotypes, the dictionary definitions may well be wrong.

Alternative definitions of stereotypes

In many instances, modern academic stereotype researchers have abandoned some of the features that are commonly thought of as key aspects of stereotypes in the dictionary definitions: a fixed idea, simplistic, an overgeneralization, inaccurate (by definition) or always negative. Some textbook definitions now take account of these problems and are more circumspect in what they claim a stereotype is and does. For example, Jones and Colman (1996, p. 843) hedged their definition with the terms 'usually', 'relatively' and 'generally': 'Stereotypes are usually defined as relatively fixed and oversimplified generalizations about groups or classes of people. In practice, they generally focus on negative, unfavourable characteristics, although some authorities include in their conceptions of stereotypes positive social overgeneralizations as well.' Stangor's (2009, p. 2, my italics) definition also includes hedges ('with some exceptions', 'generally') but left out the contentious points (overgeneralization, simplification, negative characteristics):

> With some exceptions, I'd say that we generally agree that *stereotypes represent the traits that we view as characteristic of social groups*, or of individual members of those groups, and particularly those that differentiate groups from each other.

In short, they are the traits that come to mind quickly when we think about the groups.

Other definitions tend to be reduced versions of the ones previously cited, leaving only what they regard as the key features. On the American Psychological Association website the following definition is available from Gerrig (2013, p. 466): '[Stereotypes are] generalizations about a group of people in which the same characteristics are assigned to all members of a group.' And a similar one is found in a recent psychology textbook: 'A belief or association that links a whole group of people with certain traits or characteristics' (Kassin et al., 2017, p. G6).

With the debatable characteristics removed, we are now left with rather anodyne definitions of a stereotype, which is quite different to the ones considered earlier from the dictionaries. Here is a definition from a comprehensive psychological review of stereotyping, and one from a sociology dictionary, which just state the basic agreed feature of a stereotype:

> [S]tereotypes are qualities perceived to be associated with particular groups or categories of people.
>
> *Schneider, 2004, p. 24*

> The characterization of a group of people as sharing the same behaviors and features.
>
> *Bell, 2013, n.p.*

These similar definitions identify a stereotype as the characterization of, or the way we view, a social group. In the psychology definition, it specifically focuses on traits (qualities such as intelligence, laziness, warm-hearted, introverted or kind), whereas in the sociology definition it only specifies their sharing of behaviours and features. If we interpret a 'feature' as an 'attribute' then these could be considered as traits too. But notice that there is nothing about these characterizations being fixed or simplified. The social quality of stereotypes is implied, but there is no explicit statement that stereotypes are widely shared by a particular social group. Furthermore, they do not make any claim about them being wrong, unfair or untrue, and even the idea that a stereotype refers to 'all' members of the group is not explicitly stated. Schneider (2004) is well aware that this definition is a 'stripped-down' version of the ones normally presented:

> This definition has a 'vanilla', even gutless, quality in its refusal to take stands on many of the traditional issues that have animated the stereotype literature. As I have argued, this is probably all to the good. On the other hand, it does embody one strong assumption – namely, that stereotypes involve associations between categories and qualities – and this focuses our attention on the mental representation of stereotypes in terms of memory structures.
>
> *Schneider, 2004, p. 24*

Here we have the one solid aspect of the stereotype definitions: an association between categories (social groups) and qualities. Yet, despite Schneider's claim that this is a 'vanilla' definition, notice that he is arguing for a specific psychological explanation of stereotypes in terms of 'memory structures', rather than examining the sociocultural or political aspects of them. While the definition may be 'vanilla', Schneider is arguing for a cognitive explanation of stereotypes, which will be examined in Chapter 3.

Stereotypes as a construction of researchers

Some academics reject the concept of the stereotype completely for three main reasons. First, given that the social history of one stereotype is very different to that of another, such as the negative stereotype of African Americans (in American culture) and the positive stereotype of the French (in British culture), there exists the question of whether employing the concept of a 'stereotype' – as a set of attributes associated with a social group – is useful in understanding the complexity of social relationships. This is not to deny the existence of discrimination in society (such as racism and sexism), rather the argument is that there are better ways to explain it than by proposing a hypothetical psychological concept called a 'stereotype', which is very difficult to define satisfactorily. Moscovici (1993, p. 9) put this point as follows: 'My mistrust in the paradigm of stereotypes concerns its mistrust in the power of beliefs and languages, its indifference toward the deep complexion of the social fabric.' The relationship between stereotypes and culture will be considered in Chapter 5.

A second area of criticism comes from the study of the interpretation of meaning within language, which will be examined in Chapter 7. People express themselves through talking and writing, and the meanings contained in their discourse can be subtle and complex. When researchers take a variety of statements from different people and make an inference that that they are all referring to the same 'underlying stereotype', they might be undermining the diversity and detail of the individual accounts and constructing the concept of a 'stereotype', rather than demonstrating its psychological existence (Condor, 1988; see Chapter 7). Third, the proposal of a 'stereotype' of a social group implicitly reinforces the cultural categorization of a diverse collection of people as (uncontentiously) members of the same social group: thus, implying that currently constructed social groups are 'normal' or 'natural' rather than acknowledging the social origins of human categories. By proposing 'stereotypes' of Black and White people it emphasizes – and continues to reinforce – a categorical difference between people labelled as 'Black' and 'White', rather than focusing on the way that the society constructs and maintains racist categories through language and political activity (see Chapters 6 and 7).

So what are stereotypes?

The problem of defining a stereotype still remains. Should we abandon the concept as Moscovici and Condor argue? To do so at this point would be wrong in a book solely about stereotypes. Furthermore, if ultimately it is difficult to define, it remains a common term in everyday discussion in the twenty-first century, and so has sociocultural, and in certain instances, legal significance. At this point, however, it is useful to take stock of the issues discussed so far and bring about some sort of synthesis, before moving on to a more detailed analysis in the following chapters. There are three key aspects that need to be considered.

1. Who is being stereotyped?

Stereotypes are about a social group (and its members)

All the definitions we have considered so far have agreed that stereotypes concern the members of a social group, such as African American, English, French, accountant or librarian: indeed, any social group, including fans of the Real Madrid soccer team, surfers, Texans, YouTubers, wrestlers and so forth. An important point to note is that stereotypes concern meaningful groups in a society. Furthermore, they are ways of distinguishing between these groups. For example, in most countries there are stereotypes of people from different regions, such as northerners and southerners in England and Italy, who are viewed as distinct social groups, and have different stereotypes (Jost et al., 2005). However, most English or Italians, familiar with their own regional stereotypes may not know the stereotypes of people from the different regions of the other country. Furthermore, certain groups are socially relevant at some times in a particular community, but not at other times. Modern societies do not have stereotypes about postilions or stagecoach drivers; although I am sure there were stereotypes of them in the past. Thus, stereotypes should not be abstracted from the social and cultural history that constructed both them and the social group they refer to. To understand a stereotype we need to examine how it came about, and the historical and political context that has identified the distinct social group it refers to. This cultural background will be examined in this book.

2. What is the stereotype?

Stereotypes are about the attributes associated with the members of a social group

When we consider social groups, there are a range of attributes stereotypically associated with them, such as: Scotsmen wear kilts and are tough but miserly; the English drink tea, love the Royal family and are reserved; Japanese salarymen wear dark blue suits, dedicate their lives to the company at the expense of their families and are reserved as well. However, academic research has typically focused on the 'personality' characteristics attributed to a group (see Chapters 2 and 3). This is partly a result of methodology, where, in the research, people have been asked to choose attributes associated with a social group from a list of such personality characteristics. However, by focusing on personality characteristics, rather than English tea-drinking and Scottish kilt-wearing, a stereotype has tended to be viewed as a psychological rather than a sociocultural phenomenon, and can also be considered as fixed or rigid, because personality is often regarded as stable and enduring (McCrae and Costa, 1982; Roberts et al., 2007; although see Srivastava et al., 2003). Thus, the stereotypes of the tough Scot and the reserved English imply a general personality characteristic that is assumed to be demonstrable across a variety of situations and individuals.

Attributes are associated with social groups for a reason: stereotype attributes are not randomly attributed to the group, but serve a purpose, which may be to provide an ideological basis for discrimination. However, this may not be the only role of a stereotype. A stereotype may be used to share common understandings – social knowledge – with other members of a culture or social network and predict how group members will behave. A person taking a friend on a romantic trip to Paris, or to a comic book convention, does not have to explain about 'French sophistication', or 'geek culture', which contain stereotypical beliefs and expectations about the people they expect to meet. A stereotype might be used to predict what a person is like when you know little about them except their social group membership. For example, a person, about to meet a friend's brother for the first time on his birthday (and knows only that he is an engineering student) might on the basis of the engineering stereotype choose to buy him a newly published science fiction novel as a present. The stereotype might be considered 'accurate' – it has served its purpose – if it turns out that the friend's brother likes the book. Consequently, although we can agree that stereotypes are about social groups and the attributes associated with them (in a culture), a stereotype as a concept is a complex thing. It is quite possible that a stereotype is used for a number of different reasons. In some cases the attributes may be viewed as 'inaccurate' and in others 'accurate', and the reasons for this will be explored in this book.

3. Who is doing the stereotyping?

Stereotypes are held by a social group about a social group

Stereotypes are about intergroup relations. This is often only implicit in the definitions of stereotypes considered so far but it is a key point. It is important to decide who is doing the stereotyping (see Chapter 2). A stereotype might be widely held but it is constructed within a particular social group. For example, it has been argued that it was Europeans who labelled Africans as 'Black' (as a social category) and themselves as 'White' (as a different social category) (Tsri, 2016). The Japanese changed from being viewed by Europeans as 'White' at one time (that is, like themselves) to being labelled as 'Yellow' at another time (that is, different to themselves) (Keevak, 2011; Kowner, 2014). The construction of social groups occurs within a culture – by a particular set of people who themselves can be identified as a social group – for a particular reason. These reasons relate to the way they make sense of the social world. Stereotypes may be about specific group relationships, such as fans of sporting teams in a major city stereotyping their rivals in negative terms. It can be more insidious, as a way of oppressing social groups in a society. Thus, stereotypes are about intergroup relations, and it can be argued that, as intergroup social relations change, then so will the stereotypes. While a social group may stereotype another to identify and make sense of them, they may also do this to their own group. Thus, a social group may develop a self-stereotype of their own common characteristics (Marín and Salazar, 1985). Throughout this book there will be an examination of the important questions of who is creating a stereotype and who decides if a particular description is a 'stereotype' or not.

The rest of the book

Prior to the early twentieth century, the word stereotype was simply a term in typesetting, and Chapter 2 examines the co-opting of this term metaphorically for a description of people. By the mid-twentieth century there was a generally agreed view about stereotypes in what can be referred to as the 'classical model' of stereotypes. In this model, stereotypes are considered to be 'faulty', rigid overgeneralizations about people and reflect a simplistic view of them. Consequently, stereotypes were considered something to be avoided or eradicated. However, problems of this model led psychologists to conceive of stereotypes as a feature of 'ordinary' cognition, and Chapter 3 examines the detailed research in social cognition. Within this literature, it is shown that stereotypes have been considered both a 'cognitive tool' and a 'cognitive bias'. Chapter 4 examines the importance of intergroup relations to stereotype formation and use, moving from the entirely cognitive analysis of the previous chapter into a consideration of their social function. This is further developed in Chapter 5 where the cultural aspects of stereotypes are considered in detail. This leads to Chapter 6, where it is argued that underlying stereotypes are ideological beliefs that have emerged within particular cultures. It is also argued that, from different ideological positions, different stereotypes will be identified. Chapter 7 examines the ways in which stereotypes are employed in language, within a culture and within the media, with a particular focus on how they are used rhetorically for a purpose within an argument. Finally, Chapter 8 draws the various ideas together to present an overall conclusion to the academic research into stereotypes.

Notes

1 www.macmillandictionary.com.
2 www.ldoceonline.com.
3 https://dictionary.cambridge.org.
4 https://en.oxforddictionaries.com.
5 www.collinsdictionary.com.
6 www.merriam-webster.com.
7 Fiske and Taylor (1991, p. 119) define a role as a 'set of behaviors expected of a person in a particular social position' and a role schema as 'the cognitive structures that organizes one's knowledge about those appropriate behaviours'.
8 Previously presented in Barker (2004).

9 See Chapter 5.
10 There is a discussion of what is meant by 'race' in Chapter 6.
11 *Omnibus*, Season 2, Episode 26, first broadcast 11 May 1969, BBC1.
12 *Saturday Live*, 13 May 2017, BBC Radio 4.
13 Series 1, Episode 10, first broadcast on the 30 November 1969, BBC1.
14 *Saturday Live*, 24 December 2016, BBC Radio 4.

2

THE INVENTION OF THE STEREOTYPE

Prior to the early twentieth century, the only people who used the word 'stereotype' were workers in the printing industry. To create a page of text, the individual metal letters (type) with metal spaces, line dividers and so forth, were composed in a wooden frame, and the page was printed by inking the surface and pressing the blank paper to it. However, this meant that the type, the frame and all the other bits and pieces could not be used for other work until all the required copies of the page were printed and, once broken up, would require the whole thing to be recomposed if further copies were required. The solution was to make a mould of the composed page (usually with papier mâché) and create a metal plate from the mould. Now the page could be printed from the metal plate, called a stereotype, and the frame and all the rest of the expensive equipment could be used immediately for a different page. The creation of the stereotype was a more efficient way of printing as it could be stored away and used to print the page when required without the time, effort and expense of composing the whole thing again. But, of course, the text on the stereotype was fixed and, unlike the individual type in the frame, could not be altered or rearranged to correct any errors.

It was not surprising, therefore, that the American journalist and political commentator, Walter Lippmann (1922), when he was looking for a metaphor for a fixed idea when writing his book called *Public Opinion*, thought of the word 'stereotype', which was familiar to him from the traditional typesetting of newspapers. By selecting this particular metaphor it contains within it the implication that there exists a distinctive set of ideas that are fixed and unchanging, *as if they were etched on a metal plate*. Metaphors may be fundamental to human thinking (Lakoff and Johnson, 1980) but they can also strongly influence the way we view a concept. Consider, for example, the description of immigrants as providing an 'injection' of 'new blood' to 'stimulate' the economy and improve the 'health' of the nation. This medical metaphor of the effect of immigration providing a 'shot in the arm' of the 'body' of the nation, presents a positive interpretation of immigration. However, if immigrants are considered in terms of an inundation metaphor, then they are described as a 'wave' washing over the country, 'flooding' in and 'swamping' communities, which presents them as a destructive force, requiring 'barriers' to 'protect' the nation (see Chapter 7). As we shall see throughout this book, there arises the important question: Is the stereotype metaphor a useful way of understanding a certain type of human idea or is it a distortion of the way people actually think? Just as the inundation metaphor presents a different view of immigration to the medical metaphor, presenting certain human ideas as 'stereotypes' has led to them typically being viewed as particularly rigid and fixed throughout the following century of academic research.

Pictures in the head

For five chapters of his book, Lippmann (1922) expounds his views about stereotypes, using the concept to comment on a range of social and political issues of his day, particularly the peace negotiations in Paris after the end of the First World War, of which he was highly critical. He summarized his ideas in one key statement:

> For the most part we do not first see, and then define, we define first and then see. In the great blooming, buzzing confusion of the outer world we pick out what our culture has already defined for us, and we tend to perceive that which we have picked out in the form stereotyped for us by our culture.
>
> *Lippmann, 1922, p. 81*

The important idea contained here is that we tend to perceive in terms of pre-existing cultural categories. Thus, stereotypes are fundamentally cultural and are used by the perceiver to make sense of an otherwise confusing and complex world. The rest of Lippmann's paragraph is not commonly quoted but it provides a very interesting illustration of his view of stereotypes. By the end of the First World War, Germany had, for nearly 50 years, been run by a coterie of Prussian landed noblemen (referred to as Junkers), in particular Chancellor Otto von Bismarck, who had gained the reputation of being very authoritarian, conservative, religious, disciplined and duty-bound. The image of the German Junker was very familiar throughout Europe and the United States at that time. The defeat of the Germans in the War had brought forward a new generation of German leaders: liberal and democratic, seeking to implement new ideas of government. Lippmann considered rhetorically how the victorious leaders, particularly the French Prime Minister Georges Clemenceau, viewed the Germans in the post-war treaty negotiations:

> Of the great men who assembled at Paris to settle the affairs of mankind, how many were there who were able to see much of the Europe about them, rather than their commitments about Europe? Could anyone have

penetrated the mind of M. Clemenceau, would he have found there images of the Europe of 1919, or a great sediment of stereotyped ideas accumulated and hardened in a long and pugnacious existence? Did he see the Germans of 1919, or the German type as he had learned to see it since 1871? He saw the type, and among the reports that came to him from Germany, he took to heart those reports, and, it seems, those only, which fitted the type that was in his mind. If a Junker blustered, that was an authentic German; if a labor leader confessed the guilt of the empire, he was not an authentic German.

Lippmann, 1922, pp. 81–82

Notice that Lippmann here refers to the 'great sediment of stereotyped ideas' as being ideas that have been perpetuated for years and become fixed in the mind, but should now be changed, according to Lippmann's political opinion. It is not that a stereotype is 'inaccurate' – it has a basis in social history – but it is wrong now in the current context (according to Lippmann): outdated and old fashioned, and does not flexibly take into account the present situation. He argued that Clemenceau had not moved on to listen to the new Germans, and was stuck in the old stereotyped ideas of the German leaders as Junkers, which was no longer appropriate to the new circumstances. To Lippmann, this would have a detrimental effect on the treaty negotiations. Not surprisingly, Lippmann was a critic of the severe conditions placed on Germany in the Treaty of Versailles.

To explain why these stereotyped 'pictures in the head' had such an influence on the way people viewed the social world, despite potentially being out-dated and inflexible representations, Lippmann (1922) proposed three reasons. First, economy of effort, that is, they provide a cultural ready-made image and save the time and effort of thinking carefully about a member of the social group being stereotyped. Thus, the German leaders were stereotyped as Junkers, rather than considered carefully as democrats who repudiated the past actions of their countrymen. Second, stereotypes provide a defence of a position in society. By seeing the post-war German leaders stereotypically, this validated the position of Clemenceau and the other allied negotiators as right and proper in their views, and justified in their actions as the victors. Third, stereotypes create blind spots, that is, contrary evidence is ignored or not properly considered, such as Clemenceau not seeing the new German leaders as different to the Junkers who had preceded them.

Economy of effort

Rather than being a confusing world that we must try to understand in all its complexity, stereotypes provide ready-made cultural ways of structuring and understanding the social world. As Lippmann (1922, p. 88) pointed out: 'The attempt to see all things fresh and in detail, rather than types and generalities, is exhausting and among busy affairs practically out of the question.' Essentially, Lippmann argued that stereotypes are cognitively 'efficient': they save us the time and effort of thinking carefully. This means that with a complex world and a busy daily life they offer a quick answer to making sense of the people and events we face. He described how stereotypes are involved in person perception:

> [M]odern life is hurried and multifarious, above all physical distance separates [people] who are often in vital contact with each other, such as employer and employee, official and voter. There is neither time nor opportunity for intimate acquaintance. Instead we notice a trait which marks a well known type, and fill in the rest of the picture by means of the stereotypes we keep in our heads. He is an agitator. That much we notice, or are told. Well an agitator is this sort of person, and so *he* is this sort of person.
>
> *Lippmann, 1922, p. 89*

On identifying a person by a particular characteristic, a stereotype makes that unknown person 'known' by attributing to them the learnt stereotypical qualities. Lippmann explained that stereotypes are cultural products. He pointed out that an inhabitant of Florence in the medieval period could imagine a saint by looking at the frescos in a church 'standardized for his time by Giotto' (Lippmann, 1922, p. 91). Other ideas come from fairy stories, schoolbooks, novels and plays, which provide preconceptions that we pick up. He cited newspapers and films as providing these cultural representations about what types of people are like. He argued that, using the notorious portrayal of the Ku Klux Klan in the 1915 film *Birth of a Nation* as an illustration, with respect to a media image: 'historically, it may be the wrong shape, morally it may be a pernicious shape' but it tends to be a vivid and highly memorable image (Lippmann, 1922, p. 92). Consequently, members of a social group and a specific set of characteristics may become stereotypically associated.

Defence

The second function of a stereotype is 'defence'. For the individual, stereotypes serve the social psychological function of protecting a sense of who we are and where we fit into society: 'They are an ordered, more or less consistent picture of the world, to which our habits, our tastes, our capacities, our comforts and our hopes have adjusted themselves' (Lippmann, 1922, p. 95). Yet they are more than this as they also have a moral connotation: 'At the core of every moral code there is a picture of human nature, a map of the universe, and a version of history' (Lippmann, 1922, p. 122). They support a person's social identity and provide an explanation of the status quo (for the people in the culture). A member of a dominant group is in a privileged position in a society, but is faced with others in society who are less powerful and of lower status. Rather than accepting that their status and position are arbitrary or, worse, unjustifiable, stereotypes provide an explanation for the status quo and a defence against threats to it (such as demands for social change). For example, Lippmann argued that, in a slave-owning society, an awareness that masters and slaves are fundamentally the same could threaten the power of the masters. However, a stereotype, created in the culture, that slaves are less rational and more emotional, as well as being more brutish than the masters, provides a defence against the threat to the institution of slavery. Rather than admitting that the slavery is due to their oppression, for the masters, the stereotype locates the 'cause' of the slavery in the character of the slaves themselves. It provides an explanation for the social position of the two groups. Hence the masters can even believe that they are being kindly in patronizing their 'childlike' slaves, and maintain the view of themselves as good people. Lippmann suggested that this is the 'perfect' stereotype in that it seeks to justify the unjustifiable in a defence of the status quo.

Blind spots

Lippmann (1922) argued that stereotypes preserve us from the bewildering effects of attempting to see the social world in its totality and diversity, which can lead to confusion and inaction. Stereotypes simplify the world and give it a focus in terms of culturally defined categories and their associated meanings that provide explanations of, and justifications for, certain conduct. Stereotypes structure social perception and influence the interpretation of the behaviour of people. Also, if a person's experience corresponds to the expectations of the stereotype, then it reinforces the stereotype. The cost of this process, however, is that there will be contradictory evidence that cannot be explained. Unfortunately, he argued, the efficiency of stereotypes in making sense of the world may also block people from seeing the world as it is, and how it has changed over time. These are the blind spots of the stereotyped perception. When faced with such evidence, the person may interpret a contradiction as simply 'the exception that proves the rule', and ignore it or even view multiple examples of counter-stereotypical people as not 'authentic' members of the group. Finally, Lippmann (1922, p. 112) argued that the discrepancy between the stereotyped perception and the evidence can become so great that it cannot be ignored: 'the blind spots come from the edge of vision into the center'. It is at this point that there is an opportunity to abandon the stereotype and seek new perceptions. If critics are listened to, leaders are open to change and people are tolerant, then the contradictory evidence may lead to a modification of the 'picture' of a social group and its associated characteristics, and lead to a rejection of the 'out-dated' stereotype. However, he argued that this may not happen for the following reasons.

> A pattern of stereotypes is not neutral … it is the projection upon the world of our own sense of our own value, our own position and our own rights. The stereotypes are, therefore, highly charged with the feelings that are attached to them. They are the fortress of our tradition, and behind its defenses we can continue to feel ourselves safe in the position we occupy.
>
> *Lippmann, 1922, p. 96*

What Lippmann had done was to establish the psychological concept of a stereotype, explaining how and why individuals hold fixed ideas about the social world, which they are reluctant to change. Despite the assertion of the cultural construction of these stereotypes, the stereotype as a fixed mental idea (analogous to the fixed metal plate) 'in the head' of the individual became the dominant idea in the subsequent research.

The experimental study of stereotypes: the Princeton trilogy

There are many ways in which stereotypes have been studied after Lippmann. However, within academic psychology there was, and is, a strong focus on experimental methods. In order to study a concept experimentally, a number of compromises have to be made. The most important is that the concept has to be *operationally defined*, in terms of what can be tested in the psychological laboratory. This is what Katz and Braly (1933) sought to do. Unlike Lippmann, who drew on the socio-political world around him for his analysis of stereotypes, Katz and Braly endeavoured to identify the stereotypes of Princeton University students. Princeton University is one of the oldest and most prestigious universities in North America, established in the eighteenth century as the College of New Jersey, changing to its current name in 1896. In his book *This Side of Paradise* (1920), F. Scott Fitzgerald portrays the loves and life of his protagonist Amory Blaine, an ambitious Midwestern Princeton student among the upper class and wealthy who formed the Princeton type. Between the First and Second World Wars, Princeton students were a specific – homogenous – group of privileged young men, forming their own eating clubs and developing their own clothing style (Clemente, 2008). Princeton had a 'reputation as a haven of the elite' (Clemente, 2008, p. 23).[1] It was with these young men that Katz and Braly undertook their seminal study of stereotypes in 1932 (Katz and Braly, 1933). They asked 100 students to complete a checklist of 84 attributes (adjectives such as intelligent, musical, impulsive, conservative) for ten groups (eight nationalities including American, English and German plus two additional groups, Jew and 'Black'.[2] The participants were asked to select the characteristics from the list (and add additional ones if they wished) associated with the social group. A key point to note here is that the instructions asked the students to select 'those [attributes] which seem to you most typical of the [group]'. Then they were asked to go back and mark the five most typical attributes of the group from their selection. At the end of the study, the researchers combined the results of all the participants and calculated the frequency with which each attribute was selected in the top five and listed the top 12 attributes associated with each group in order. Listed below are the attributes achieving a frequency of 20 or more (well above chance) for Americans and English, with the frequency in brackets,[3] to illustrate the findings.

Americans
Industrious (48), intelligent (47), materialistic (33), ambitious (33), progressive (27), pleasure-loving (26), alert (23), efficient (21), aggressive (20)

English
Sportsmanlike (53), intelligent (46), conventional (34), tradition-loving (31), conservative (30), reserved (29), sophisticated (27), courteous (21), honest (20)

Katz and Braly argued that their method had identified the stereotypes of the Princeton students. However, these stereotypes cannot be an accurate description of the members of a social group, as they argued that nationality or 'race' have no relationship to a person's character. Katz and Braly (1933, pp. 288–289) stated:

> Stereotyped pictures of racial and national groups can arise only so long as individuals accept consciously or unconsciously the group fallacy attitude toward place of birth and skin color. To the realist there are no racial or national groups which exist as entities and which determine the characteristics of the group members.

They later went on to say that a stereotype is 'a fixed impression, which conforms little to the fact it pretends to represent' (Katz and Braly, 1933, p. 181). Thus, Lippmann's 'pictures in the head' were both wrong and irrational. Katz and Braly's use of the term 'group fallacy attitude' strongly located the explanation of the stereotype in the psychology of the individual, shifting the explanation from the culture to locate it in an individual perceiver's 'faulty' reasoning. This shift can, in part, be considered in terms of a wider argument between psychologists and sociologists at the time about explanations for social psychological phenomenon. The term 'group fallacy' had been employed by the psychologist Floyd Allport (1924) in criticizing sociological explanations of behaviour at the group level, such as in Durkheim's studies of crowd behaviour, rather than seeking an explanation at the level of the individual. Critically, in proposing that a stereotype is an individual's attitude 'error', Katz and Braly (1933) were locating stereotypes 'in the head' rather than in intergroup relations or culture.

In particular, the stereotype of the 'Black' group was highly negative, with the characteristics superstitious (84) and lazy (75) producing among the highest frequencies in the study, followed by happy-go-lucky, ignorant, musical, very religious and stupid. Yet it was not just the students who had these 'group fallacy attitudes'. In the same decade, Bruce Wright had been accepted by Princeton University as a student. However, when it was discovered that he was Black, the Dean wrote to him on 13 June 1939 claiming the university 'does not discriminate against any student on the basis of race, color or creed' and that he, the Dean, personally had 'very pleasant relations with your race'. Yet he rejected Wright, claiming 'he would be happier in the environment of others of his race' (Armstrong, 2015). While the Dean had claimed to be non-discriminatory, there were no Black students in the institution at the time and the rejection of Wright could only have been based on race. Subsequently, Wright went to Lincoln University and the New York Law School. He became a distinguished New York judge and 60 years later was made an honorary member of the Princeton class of 2001 (Armstrong, 2015).

The replications

The Katz and Braly methodology was undertaken twice more in a period spanning 35 years with a student group from Princeton University: first in 1950 (Gilbert, 1951) and again in 1967 (Karlins et al., 1969), allowing the analysis of the longevity of the stereotypes to be examined. Below are listed the attributes selected by at least 20 per cent of the participants, for all three studies for the two national stereotypes considered above.

Americans

1932   industrious (48), intelligent (47), materialistic (33), ambitious (33), progressive (27), pleasure-loving (26), alert (23), efficient (21), aggressive (20)
1950   materialistic (37), intelligent (32), industrious (30), pleasure-loving (27), individualistic (26), ambitious (21)
1967   materialistic (67), ambitious (42), pleasure-loving (28), industrious (23), intelligent (20)

English

1932   sportsmanlike (53), intelligent (46), conventional (34), tradition-loving (31), conservative (30), reserved (29), sophisticated (27), courteous (21), honest (20)
1950   tradition-loving (42), reserved (39), sophisticated (37), intelligent (29), conventional (25), conservative (22), sportsmanlike (21)
1967   conservative (53), sophisticated (47), reserved (40), practical (25), intelligent (23), sportsmanlike (22), tradition-loving (21)

It can be seen that broadly speaking a similar set of attributes have been selected in all three studies of the Princeton trilogy. A very similar characterization of the two nationalities appears to be present in all three sets of results across the 35-year period, indicating a (relatively) fixed and enduring stereotype of the groups: a result that supported the view that stereotypes are fixed (over time). However, Gilbert (1951) noted that the increased negative view of the Germans and the Japanese in his study compared to Katz and Braly could be explained by the effects of the Second World War, which had ended only five years before. Gilbert also suggested that the lower frequencies, in his study, might indicate a fading of stereotypes. He noted that there was some reluctance on behalf of the students to make these stereotypical generalizations, possibly reflecting societal changes (and a reduction in the acceptability of expressing negative views of other social groups). Not all these conclusions were supported by Karlins et al. (1969): in some cases the frequency values of an attribute went up – confounding the view that stereotypes were fading. For example, 'materialistic' rose to 67 per cent for the Americans in 1967 (compared to 33 per cent and 37 per cent in the previous studies), which may be related to the cultural circumstances of the time, at the birth of the hippie movement and a questioning of the spiritual and materialistic balance in American society. The increase in the attribute of 'conservative' for the English rose to 53 per cent (from 30 per cent and 22 per cent). The variation in the Japanese stereotype also appeared to reflect cultural factors, as a strong industrial power of the 1920s and 1930s, an enemy during the Second World War to the rising economically powerful ally of the 1960s: with 'industrious' and 'intelligent' as the two highest selected attributes in 1932, replaced by 'imitative' and 'sly' in 1951, and returning to 'industrious' and 'ambitious' in 1967. However, as Karlins et al. (1969) pointed out, despite the changes, the stereotypes of 1967 looked very similar to those of 1932.

Karlins et al. (1969) also found a continued reluctance on the part of some of the students to perform the task, and acknowledged that the participants may have been responding in terms of generalizations they did not believe in themselves. They also found that in many cases the percentages were reduced (particularly for certain negative attributes). For example, the stereotype of the 'Black' and Chinese groups became more positive over the 35-year period. By the time of the 1950 study, Princeton University had a small number of African American students and, while there were still only seven such undergraduate students in 1962, University President Robert F. Goheen sought to encourage the diversification of the university, admitting more African American students and opening the university to women in 1969 (van Rossum, 2010). Karlins et al. (1969) found a very different stereotype for the 'Black' group compared to 1932 (Katz and Braly, 1933) with 'musical' (at 47 per cent) the most popular attribute. Most of the negative attributes from 1932 had fallen steeply in 1967 ('superstitious' dropped from 84 per cent to 13 per cent, 'lazy' from 75 per cent to 26 per cent and 'ignorant' from 38 per cent to 11 per cent), possibly reflecting significant social change.

The impact of the Princeton trilogy

The Princeton trilogy had a major impact on the subsequent stereotyping literature. The importance of these studies is that they established a psychological research methodology for the analysis of a stereotype as a set of character attributes associated with the members of a social group, thereby limiting the definition to just this aspect of the concept (Ehrlich and Rinehart, 1965; van den Berghe, 1966). The psychological research subsequently focused on stereotypes as individual attitudes towards social groups (and their associated characteristics), such as the English as conservative and reserved, rather than behavioural aspects, such as the English drink tea and play cricket, or the cultural conditions of intergroup relations and group-based representation (see Chapters 4 and 5). Crucially, Katz and Braly (1933) made two key claims. First, stereotypes were 'fixed impressions' and, second, they were irrational, so a realist would not employ them. Thus, there was the implication that a specific group of people irrationally accept stereotypes – the stereotype users employing a fallacy – and another group of people – the realists – who think more rationally and do not use stereotypes (which is clearly better). Furthermore, the results of the Princeton trilogy indicated that stereotypes may endure over a long period of time and the 'problem' of stereotypes was not fading away (as Gilbert, 1951, had hoped).

Stereotypes as overgeneralizations

The idea that stereotypes are irrational and inaccurate aspects of individual cognition, as proposed by Katz and Braly (1933) was further elaborated by Gordon Allport, the brother of Floyd Allport, in his well-known book *The Nature of Prejudice* (Allport, [1954] 1979) at the start of the second half of the twentieth century. For Allport ([1954] 1979) a stereotype was defined as an *overgeneralization*: that is the application of an attribute to *all* individual members of the group, which, by definition, is false. Importantly, Allport strongly emphasized the relationship of a stereotype to prejudice, which he defined as 'an antipathy based upon a faulty and inflexible generalization' (Allport, [1954] 1979, p. 9). He did not deny the existence of actual group attributes (which he refers to as 'group traits') or genuine conflict, but these were not viewed as stereotypes or prejudice as such (Bramel, 2004). If the people of another nation are attacking your country then it is not unreasonable to be antagonistic towards them. Prejudice involves an irrational overgeneralization about a group who do not have the attributed characteristic in all its members, and a stereotype is an 'exaggerated belief associated with a category' (Allport, [1954] 1979, p. 191). Hence, the 'problem' of a stereotype is not that people are identified as members of a social group but the fixed characteristics associated with them:

> A stereotype, then, is not a category, but often exists as a fixed mark upon the category. If I say, 'All lawyers are crooked', I am expressing a stereotyped generalization about a category. The stereotype is not in itself the core of the concept. It operates, however, in such a way as to prevent differentiated thinking about the concept … The stereotype acts both as a justificatory device for the categorical acceptance or rejection of a group, and as a screening or selective device to maintain simplicity in perception and in thinking.
>
> *Allport, [1954] 1979, p. 192*

As Allport argued, the idea of the category of lawyer, as someone who deals with the law, is independent of the stereotype that is applied to the category. In applying the stereotypical attribute of 'crooked' to the category of lawyer it provides an explanation of why a person has an (irrational) antipathy to lawyers. Also, Allport claimed (like Lippmann) that a stereotype simplifies the mental task of making sense of people. Rather than dealing with the actual complexity of what lawyers are like, viewing them *all* as crooked provides a simple (and fixed) opinion of lawyers that can be used in the complex decision-making process of perceiving other people and interacting with them. In reality, there might be evidence of *some* crooked lawyers (from reports of cases of malpractice), but perceiving them *all* as crooked is clearly an irrational overgeneralization, as – if we choose to look – we can find plenty of evidence of honest lawyers. Furthermore, as Allport ([1954] 1979, p. 194) pointed out, prejudiced people will even employ contradictory (irrational) stereotypes to 'justify' their prejudice. He cited research showing that the same people who claimed that Jews were seclusive (keeping themselves separate from the rest of society), at the same time claimed they were intrusive (integrating and seeking rapport with Christians). For Allport ([1954] 1979, p. 204) 'Stereotypes are not identical with prejudice. They are primarily rationalizers', which supports Lippmann's view that stereotypes are used as a defence of a person's view of the social world. For example, a person might rationally acknowledge that they and their group are in a privileged position in society compared to another social group and, if they believe in fairness and equality, then seek to redress the discrimination. Alternatively, they might simply refuse to acknowledge the issue (denial), or defend their own position (as Lippmann suggested too) and seek to justify the discriminatory position of their group. A person might blame a discriminated-against group for their own disadvantaged social positon, by the use of a stereotype (such as 'the poor are lazy') rather than acknowledge the unfairness in the society (Allport, [1954] 1979).

While Allport focused on the psychological aspects of stereotypes, he also acknowledged that stereotypes 'manifestly come from *somewhere*' (Allport, [1954] 1979, p. 189) and discusses the influence of the media in reinforcing stereotypes. However, while there may be a 'grain of truth' to some stereotypes through cultural factors, and he cited the historical Christian–Jewish relations here as an example, he argued that stereotypes are by definition fixed overgeneralizations and can emerge even when there is no evidence for them. He gave the example of Armenians being stereotyped negatively (as dishonest and deceitful) at one time in Fresno, California, despite documentary evidence of their good credit rating. Thus, the (false) stereotype can be considered as a rationalization of a prejudice against outsiders. Despite his wide-ranging and insightful account of prejudice, stereotypes were primarily located in individual 'irrational' cognition. According to Allport, a key implication followed.

> We come now to what is perhaps the most momentous discovery of psychological research in the field of prejudice. To state it broadly: the cognitive processes of prejudiced people are *in general* different from the cognitive processes of tolerant people.
>
> *Allport, [1954] 1979, pp. 174–175*

He went on to state that the prejudiced person dichotomizes and is uncomfortable with differentiated categories: 'thus his habit of thought is rigid … He has a marked need for definiteness; he cannot tolerate ambiguity' (Allport, [1954] 1979, p. 175).

The prejudiced person

Theodor Adorno was born in 1903 in Frankfurt, Germany, of a Catholic mother and Protestant father who had converted from Judaism. He became a philosopher, sociologist and composer, and a leading member of the Frankfurt School of social theory. Else Frenkel-Brunswik was a Polish-Jewish psychologist, who had completed her doctorate at the University of Vienna in 1930. Both had had to flee to the United States from the Nazis during the 1930s. Working with adult psychologist Daniel Levinson and social psychologist Nevitt Sanford, in the immediate aftermath of the Second World War, they sought to understand the personality characteristics of individuals who developed anti-Semitic and fascistic beliefs, an issue of major importance given the recent horrors of the Holocaust that had been revealed under the Nazi regime in Germany. Their central tenet was that 'the political, economic, and social convictions of an individual often form a broad and coherent pattern, as if bound together by a "mentality" or "spirit", and that this pattern is an expression of deep lying trends in his personality' (Adorno et al., 1950, p. 1). They refined their own research to look at one specific type of personality, the 'potentially fascistic individual', who would become more widely known by the title of their 1950 book, *The Authoritarian Personality*.

The initial phrase of the research, carried out in 1945–1946, involved distributing questionnaires to over 2,000 adults, both men and women, White and mostly middle class and from the San Francisco region (but also including male inmates from the St Quentin Prison and women from a University of California psychology extension class). From the results of their questionnaire, the authors constructed a new scale, which was revised after testing, called the Fascism or F-Scale, containing questions about society, gender, children, 'proper' behaviour, dealing with criminals and sexuality. This research was followed up with detailed interviews with participants who had scored in the highest or lowest 25 per cent on the questionnaire study. In examining two interviewees in detail, Mack who was high on ethnocentrism and Larry who was low on ethnocentrism, Sanford argued that the results supported their view of a coherent 'mentality' across the interview:

> This seems strongly to suggest that we are faced here not with a particular set of political convictions and a particular set of opinions about a specific ethnic group but with a way of thinking about groups and group relations generally.
>
> *Adorno et al., 1950, p. 51*

Levinson argued that the anti-Semitism found in the questionnaire findings, and with interviewees such as Mack, indicated that anti-Semitism was not simply an antipathy but part of an integrated ideology, a belief system about social groups characterized by stereotypy. This was illustrated by the use of overgeneralized statements, such as 'Jews are …' or 'The Jews do not …', and the perception of, and reaction to, any individual Jew as a generalized category member with all the inferred (negative) attributes of the group. This is irrational, Levinson pointed out, as: 'the specific characteristics comprising the imagery reveals a basic contradiction in that no single individual or group as a whole could have all these characteristics' (Adorno et al., 1950, p. 94).

Levinson argued that a rigid differentiation of groups (often presented as a strict difference of 'race') identified in the anti-Semitism findings – with the anti-Semitic interviewee presenting their in-group as, in some way, under threat from the stereotypically imagined out-group – tended to be generalized to the perception of other out-groups. The ideology that characterized Jews in this way also represented Black people in a similar way, as distinctive and different, implying a general ideology of ethnocentrism – an ethnocentric frame of mind – which comprised a general rejection of out-groups (Jews, Blacks, communists, for example) and a representation of the out-group as 'alien' (Adorno et al., 1950, p.147; see also Chapter 6). Further, Levinson argued that anti-Semitism and ethnocentrism was also correlated with the political dimensions of left–right, supporting the view that there was an underlying set of consistent ideological beliefs making up the psychology of the prejudiced person. Sanford sought to widen this developing model of the authoritarian person by considering religious beliefs, concluding that it was not any particular religious denomination that was related to ethnocentrism but conventionalism and strict submission to the teachings and authority of the religion the person belonged to (Adorno et al., 1950, p. 221).

Frenkel-Brunswik examined the attitudes expressed in the interviews in terms of the 'clinical data' about the interviewee: their family background, family figures (such as their parents), childhood, sex (their orientation and experience), social relations (such as friendships), school, political attitudes and opinions about minorities and race. The results indicated that the upbringing of prejudiced individuals tended to involve relatively harsh parental discipline and a greater focus on roles and duties than expressions of affection, indicating an authoritarian regime in the home (Adorno et al., 1950, p. 386). The prejudiced man tended to have traditional views of sexuality, which were linked to status in terms of an ideal of masculinity, and, in both genders, authoritarian individuals tended to separate (dichotomize) sex and affect. This isolation of sex from affect indicated an underlying disrespect or resentment against the opposite sex, with gender relations more concerned with power than affection. In their attitudes to people, in general, prejudiced individuals tended to be more moralistic (a belief in their own high moral values), ready to blame others and viewed the world as a jungle, leading to a distrust and suspicion of others. Consequently they focused on the hierarchical (power) relations between people (rather than viewing others in terms of equality and mutuality) and material success. Possessions were seen as an extension of the self. Frenkel-Brunswik interpreted the results in terms of Freudian psychoanalytic theory that associated adult personality to childhood development. She argued that authoritarian people tended to repress their fears and anxieties, using the defence mechanism of projection (such as blaming others) and a lack of introspection. They were conformists to external values (social status or religious) and held conventional views of people in society. Frenkel-Brunswik wrote that:

> In order to keep the balance under these conditions [of engaging in the social world], a simple, firm, often stereotypical, cognitive structure is required. There is no place for ambivalence or ambiguities. Every attempt is made to eliminate them, but they remain as potentials which might interfere at any

> time. In the course of these attempts a subtle but profound distortion of reality has to take place, precipitated by the fact that stereotypical categorizations can never do justice to all the aspects of reality.
>
> *Adorno et al., 1950, p. 480*

Thus, the social thought of the prejudiced person is rigid and intolerant of ambiguity. 'The tendency to impose preconceived and often stereotypical categories upon experience may thus be envisaged as a more general trait in subjects scoring extremely high on Ethnocentrism' (Adorno et al., 1950, p. 481).[4]

An individual with a strict upbringing was constantly coping with the unconscious hostility resulting from repressed frustration. Rather than dealing with the real cause of the frustration — the childhood factors influencing their adult personality — their underlying hostility is projected on to other social groups. Even meeting counter-stereotypical members of these groups does not lead to the abandonment of stereotypical views. 'The prejudiced subject is dimly aware that the content of the stereotype is imaginary and that his own experience represents truth. Yet, for deeper psychological reasons, he wants to stick to the stereotype' (Adorno et al., 1950, p. 628). Thus, stereotyping is conflated with prejudice as both originate from the same psychological cause. In contrast, the low scorers on the questionnaire, in their interviews, showed evidence of non-prejudiced thinking. They were self-reflective and viewed issues of discrimination in terms of their historical and social contexts. Adorno argued that they were 'emphatically rational' (Adorno et al., 1950, p. 644) and rejected the stereotypical imaginary ideas projected upon others. Crucially, prejudice against certain groups in society violated their belief in equality and justice.

Allport ([1954] 1979) made it clear in his own account of the prejudiced personality that he identified the same character as the authoritarian personality. The prejudiced person was ambivalent towards their parents, held rigidly moralistic views, viewed the world in terms of dichotomous categories, had a need for definiteness (that is, was intolerant of ambiguity), projected (externalized) on to others the actions of the social world (lacking in self-reflection), liked order and was devoted to institutions, such as, school, church, nation (Allport, [1954] 1979). This was the person who thought in a rigid way and employed stereotypes. Allport ([1954] 1979, p. 396) was unreserved in his description of the prejudiced personality:

> The individual cannot face the world unflinchingly and in a forthright manner. He seems fearful of himself, of his own instincts, of his own consciousness, of change, and of his social environment. Since he can live in comfort neither with himself nor with others, he is forced to organize his whole style of living, including his social attitudes, to fit his crippled condition.

He went further and distinguished the surface, conscious self, of the prejudiced person from the deeper, unconscious mind, citing the example of the women psychology students studied by Frenkel-Brunswik and Sanford (1945) who had expressed anti-Semitic statements.

[They] appeared on the surface to be charming, happy, well-adjusted, and entirely normal girls. They were polite, moral, and seemed devoted to parents and friends ... But probing deeper ... underneath the conventional exterior there lurked intense anxiety ... buried hatred ... destructive and cruel impulses.

Allport, [1954] 1979, p. 397

The tolerant person

In many ways the tolerant personality – who does not think rigidly nor use stereotypes – is explicitly the opposite of the prejudiced personality, according to Allport ([1954] 1979), who noted that the tolerant person has been referred to, in the literature, as democratic, mature, productive and self-actualizing (engaging in a process of self-discovery). The tolerant personality has had a less restrictive upbringing: 'Tolerant children, it seems, are likely to come from homes with a permissive atmosphere. They feel welcome, accepted, loved, no matter what they do' (Allport ([1954] 1979, p. 426). They have not developed the sense of threat, which must be repressed in the prejudiced person, so do not have a psychodynamic need to project their fears on to others. Unlike the prejudiced child, the tolerant child's love of their parents is not superficial so they can be critical of them without fear. They are able to deal with moral issues without adhering to rigid rules of conduct: 'Good companionship and fun are regarded as more essential than good manners and "proper" behaviour' (Allport ([1954] 1979, p. 426). They are flexible in their thinking, not separating topics into dichotomous categories of right or wrong, or strong and weak, but for the tolerant person 'there are shades of gray' (Allport ([1954] 1979, p. 426). They are tolerant of ambiguity and take their time in making categorizations. They can handle frustration and do not blame others when things go wrong. As adults, tolerant people 'are so habitually democratic in their outlook that for them there is neither gentile nor Jew, neither bond nor free. All men are equal' (Allport, [1954] 1979, p. 428). The tolerant person is tolerant of ambiguity, which influences both their cognitive approach to social issues and their ability to empathize with others, which is then reflected in their personal values. Tolerant people have 'an inclusionist style of living' (Allport, [1954] 1979, p. 441). Consequently, the tolerant person is unlikely to employ stereotypes in social perception. Finally, Allport associates the tolerant person (and prejudiced person) with political viewpoints, claiming that the tolerant person 'is very likely to be liberal in his political views. Prejudiced individuals are more often conservatives' (Allport, [1954] 1979, p. 431).

The classical model of stereotypes and stereotype users

By the mid-1950s, in the United States, a model of stereotypes and their use was becoming established in the academic psychological research, as a consequence of the body of work that had emerged with Lippmann's book, the experimental work of Katz and Braly (1933) and the prejudice studies of Adorno et al. (1950) and Allport ([1954] 1979). I am going to refer to this model as the *classical model* of stereotypes and the stereotype user (after Pickering, 2001), as it has been extraordinarily influential on both the academic literature and the public perception of stereotypes and stereotype use. The model can be briefly summed up by five key assertions:

1. Stereotypes are irrational overgeneralizations (or *all* judgements) associating members of a social group with character attributes, and as such are, by definition, false. A person employing a stereotype is viewing group members in a simplistic and fixed manner rather than perceiving them accurately or in a nuanced way.
2. Prejudiced people – projecting their inner repressed hostility on to others – perceive and engage with the social world in terms of rigid, dichotomous thinking. Intolerant of ambiguity, they have very strict ideas of good and bad (which tend to be based on institutional values) and can be characterized by the word 'authoritarian'.
3. Stereotypes provide the fixed and, generally, negative views of others, which are used by prejudiced people to present a (spurious) justification for their prejudice.
4. Prejudiced people may appear on the surface to be 'normal' and 'nice' but psychological techniques[5] can reveal the 'buried' prejudice 'lurking' within them.
5. Prejudiced people are likely to be conservative in their political views.

As a corollary to this view of stereotypes and who uses them, the model also provides an image of the tolerant person (who does not use stereotypes), that can be summed up in the following three points:

1. Tolerant people are flexible in their thinking and tolerant of ambiguity; they differentiate between individuals and appreciate the diversity of others.
2. Tolerant people do not think rigidly or employ fixed stereotypes of others.
3. Tolerant people are likely to be liberal and democratic in their views.

To Allport ([1954] 1979) prejudice was displayed in both the social structure (of intergroup discrimination) and also personality structure (of individual attitudes). He argued that remedial programs should be in both areas to create more tolerant people: for example, changes to the law to influence the social structure, and education and training to influence individuals. In conclusion, he characterized the 'target' tolerant person:

> The maturely democratic person must possess subtle virtues and capacities: an ability to think rationally about causes and effects, an ability to form properly differentiated categories in respect to ethnic groups and their traits, a willingness to award freedom to others, and a capacity to employ it constructively for oneself.
>
> *Allport, [1954] 1979, p. 515*

And, finally, 'It is part of the democratic faith that the objective study of the irrational and immature elements of human behaviour will help us to counteract them' (Allport, 1954, p. 515).

Implications of the classical model of stereotypes

The classical model of stereotypes was unequivocal: stereotypes are bad as they are irrational generalizations, which makes them wrong. This definition means that all stereotypes are inaccurate and indicative of fixed ideas and rigid thinking. Worse than that, people who express stereotyped views, however nice they might seem, harbour unpleasant prejudice. It also distinguishes between two very distinct types of people, the prejudiced personality and the tolerant personality, each described in detail in their own chapter in Allport's ([1954] 1979) book, establishing the idea that stereotypes are a 'problem' of the prejudiced person, which the tolerant person avoids. Finally, the implication emerged from this model that, in the cause of tolerance, stereotypes should be eradicated from society (Brigham, 1971; Taylor, 1981).

The wearers of the black hats and the white hats

'Stereotypes wear the black hats in social science', wrote Schneider (2004, p. 1) in his review of the psychology of stereotypes. It is easy to see why this is, given the establishment of the classical model. They are wholly bad, like the villain who, in a 1950s cowboy B-movie, usually wore the black hat. Yet this quote can offer a deeper insight into the views of the psychology researchers of the time. A generation earlier, within academic psychology in the United States, John Watson had proposed a behaviourist view of psychology, where a person was fundamentally a 'blank slate' and human behaviour was essentially a result of the pattern of environmental reinforcement. Optimistically, the radical behaviourist Skinner (1948), in his novel *Walden Two*, argued that, by employing the right sort of training based on the principles of behaviourism and controlling the patterns of reinforcement, a utopian society could be engineered. However, for other psychologists, this optimism was not shared. The devastation of the Second World War, and in particular the horrors of the Holocaust, had revealed the darkness within the human psyche. Post-war social scientists in the United States were often European emigres, like Adorno and Frenkel-Brunswik, with a Freudian view of psychology, who sought to reveal the unconscious psychological dynamics of prejudice. Yet within the American context, the classical model, although based on a Freudian aetiology, contained within it the optimism of American psychology that there was an answer to the problem of prejudice (and stereotyping). Within its cultural context, there was still a way of psychologically engineering a better world. Developing more tolerant systems of upbringing, developing good companionship and reducing the feeling of threat, encouraging a tolerance of ambiguity and the promotion of liberal and democratic values, could be employed to create a world free from prejudice. The tolerant non-stereotype-using people, such as the psychologists driven by their 'democratic ideology' (Allport, [1954] 1979, p. 516) could transform the prejudiced people (the stereotype users and 'black hat' wearers). Through the activity of the tolerant people, prejudice could be reduced and stereotypes eradicated. Like the heroes of the cowboy stories of the 1940s and 1950s, it is easy to identify the good and bad guys (from their hats or stereotype use); and, in the stories, the good guys won, like the white hat-wearing Lone Ranger, played by Clayton Moore, in numerous television episodes of the 1950s, who rode into town to solve the problems of the honest townsfolk and rid them of the evil black hat wearers. There was little ambiguity in these shows. The viewer knew the good guy and the bad guy (from their hats) who acted consistently. The stories ended very satisfactorily for all concerned, with the bad guy vanquished and the good guy triumphant. Schneider's (2004) comment about stereotypes wearing the black hats in social science was very apposite in the context of the classical model of the 1950s. If we follow the analogy to the end, then it is up to the good guys to ride into town and sort things out – to turn the prejudiced people into tolerant people. Allport ([1954] 1979) discussed a range of educational programs and other training opportunities to bring this about. The goal of this training is clear: it should seek to educate the prejudiced person to become like the tolerant person, in rationality and democratic and liberal values.

The problems of the classical model of stereotypes

The classical model has been extremely influential in the popularization of the concept of the stereotype and its negative connotations in the public domain. Yet, as indicated in Chapter 1, many of the common assumptions about stereotypes (that derive from this model) do not stand up to more detailed academic investigation (Perkins, 1979). Subsequent researchers do not deny the evils of racism or anti-Semitism, but have challenged the classical model both in the way it has defined the concept of the stereotype and, second, in making a distinction between stereotype users and stereotype non-users as separate categories of people; the latter with a 'faulty' way of thinking. The methodological issues identified by the academic critics (considered below) are not simply technical concerns but challenge the fundamental assumptions of the classical model. It is therefore important to consider these criticisms of the classical model in some detail.

Finding or constructing stereotypes?

Imagine yourself to be a liberal, egalitarian, tolerant Princeton University student of 1932. You are asked to take part in a study on social groups, about whom you are open-minded, and well aware of the variety of people within them. In the study you are asked to select a set of attributes from a list that you are required to decide 'seem' to be associated with the group. None of the attributes are necessarily ones you would personally use, but you do your best to follow the researchers' instructions, so you think about the people you have met and the representations circulating in the media that you can remember – such as the English are often portrayed as having a 'stiff upper lip', prefer to drink tea – including popular media representations of the English gentleman, such as the characters played by actor Ronald Colman in films such as *The Dark Angel* (1925) and *Bulldog Drummond* (1929) (Hinton, 2017). Unfortunately none of these attributes are on the list, but you are a clever, helpful person and decide that 'sportsmanlike', 'intelligent' and 'conservative' are the best you can do in the situation to perform the researchers' task. Thus, for even the most tolerant, liberal-minded student, the research method gave them no option but to tick a set of attributes associated with a social group, which was then used to claim that they had a 'group fallacy attitude' and an erroneous, fixed 'stereotype' as a result of their irrational thinking. This is not a necessary and logical outcome of the study but, potentially, an artefact or bias of the method employed by the researchers (Brigham, 1971). The study may not have revealed anything about individual 'stereotypical' thinking but simply widespread cultural knowledge.

The possibility that the participants were drawing on media representations, rather than their own personal views, is supported by statements made by Katz and Braly (1933, p. 289), who noted: 'The characterization of the English savors more of the English "gentleman" than of the general stereotype of John Bull.' Furthermore, Katz and Braly (1933, p. 285) acknowledged: 'The traits most frequently assigned to the Germans seem consistent with the popular stereotype to be found in newspapers and magazines. Their science, industry, ponderous and methodical manner, and intelligence were pointed out by over one-fourth of the students.' There is also further evidence from the paper that the results may not have reflected the students' personal attitudes. In the introduction to their paper, Katz and Braly (1933, p. 281) noted that some students had argued that their own views disagreed with the institutional culture of their fraternity and boarding houses, which discriminated against groups such as Poles and Jews. This is particularly of interest, given the negative stereotype of the 'Black' group found in the study. The students could not report on their personal experiences of Black students as there were no Black students at Princeton at the time, so may have simply drawn on common media representations. Indeed, Katz and Braly (1933, p. 286) noted the similarity of the characteristics of the 'Black' stereotype to the picture 'furnished by the *Saturday Evening Post*: highly superstitious, lazy, happy-go-lucky, ignorant, musical, and ostentatious'. Rather than demonstrating evidence of a group fallacy attitude, the results might simply have indicated the students' knowledge of the popular media in their culture. Even more problematic is the distinction of the 'Black' category from the American category in the experimental setup. As Philogène (2001, p. 411) has pointed out, the Princeton methodology presented African Americans as 'a race apart' from other Americans. Methodologically, in such experimental work, non-overlapping groups should be employed, such as White and Black, or European American and African American, rather than American and 'Black' as separate categories. One possible interpretation of this categorization was that the study was reflecting social distinctions typical of the time, leaving the students with no option but to reinforce the researchers' cultural groupings.

Eysenck and Crown (1948) supported these criticisms. They undertook a study of national characteristics using the Katz and Braly paradigm. Nearly a fifth of the participants said the task was meaningless or impossible, so refused to do it. Of those that did the task, half of them reported that they were being required to give stereotyped answers that were not their own views. Eysenck and Crown (1948, p. 31) reflected: 'when we look for stereotyped views, and give the subject no chance to reply in any non-stereotyped fashion, we should not be surprised that the answers we get are stereotyped ones'. They concluded that nothing about the participants' actual views could be inferred from this methodology. Brown (1965, p. 179) was equally strong in his criticism of the Katz and Braly paradigm: 'Remember that Katz and Braly and many other investigators of ethnic stereotypes did not give their subjects the opportunity to be sensible … May not their subjects have been making the best of a bad task?' (We will further examine the stereotype as a consequence of the research methodology in Chapter 7.) This changes the interpretation of the studies. If participants are drawing on their cultural knowledge rather than their personal views to undertake these tasks, they are not behaving irrationally nor employing a fallacy. Further, to claim that their judgements were fixed and inaccurate is wrong, as they are simply reporting well-known representations present in their culture, which had a cultural 'reality': they were actually circulating in the society. Bramel (2004, p. 52) echoed this criticism: 'Katz and Braly were suggesting that even Princeton students' views of nationality groups, often consensual and confidently expressed, had very little relation to reality.'

Later, psychological researchers sought to address some of the issues arising from the Princeton trilogy. Devine and Elliot (1995) argued that the instructions to the participants in the studies were ambiguous, in that they had not been asked specifically for their personal views. There was also no measure of the participants' own degree of prejudice against any of the groups in the study. In their own research, Devine and Elliot (1995) focused on the Black stereotype. The participants were 147 White students from the University of Wisconsin, who completed the 84-item checklist from the Princeton trilogy. However, an additional nine adjectives were added to the list, which were descriptive terms commonly used with reference to the Black stereotype at the end of the twentieth century, and not on the original list. The participants were first asked to complete the checklist specifically in terms of a *cultural stereotype* of the Black category, with the instructions making it clear to the participants that they are being asked to report a generally known cultural view that was not necessarily their own. Second, they were asked to complete the checklist but this time they were told to indicate the adjectives that they 'personally believe' characterized Black people. Finally, they completed a 7-item Modern Racism Scale (MRS).

A well-known cultural stereotype was identified in the results. The most frequently selected attributes were: athletic (74), rhythmic (57), low in intelligence (46), lazy (45), poor (45), loud (40), criminal (35), hostile (25), with only lazy and loud from the original Princeton list. As it had been made clear that the participants were not indicating their own beliefs but a cultural stereotype, they may also have been more willing to perform the task. However, 31 participants refused to complete the personal beliefs checklist – 30 of whom were low prejudiced – arguing that they felt that they could not make such group judgements. When the results were divided into low-prejudiced individuals and the high-prejudiced individuals on the basis of the MRS, there was a high degree of similarity of the cultural stereotype from the two groups, indicating that both groups were equally knowledgeable about it. However, the personal beliefs showed a very different pattern for the low-prejudiced and high-prejudiced participants. The beliefs of high-prejudiced individuals tended to match the cultural stereotype – which contained mostly negative attributes – but the low-prejudiced people tended to select different, and more positive, attributes such as kind, honest and straightforward, for their beliefs about Black people. Devine and Elliot (1995) had demonstrated that, regardless of their personal level of tolerance or prejudice, all participants had knowledge of the cultural stereotype circulating in their society, but it was only the prejudiced ones who personally believed it.

A second problem with the Katz and Braly methodology was that the 84-item checklist was idiosyncratic, including 'extremely nationalistic' but not 'nationalistic', and potentially influencing the apparent 'fixity' (over time) of the stereotypes. Stereotype variation (rather than rigidity) may not be shown up when using the same checklist. For example, Madon et al. (2001), in their study, found a degree of stereotype similarity when using the original Katz and Braly checklist, but completely different stereotype attributes when participants were given 406 choices on the checklist. They also found differences in the stereotype produced from European Americans and non-European American participants,[6] implying cultural variation rather than cognitive factors in stereotype attribute selection. Both Madon et al. (2001) and Devine and Elliot (1995) found evidence of cultural stereotypes for Black people (as determined by this methodology) but both their modern stereotypes were different to the ones identified in the 1930s. Thus, the argument that stereotypes are fixed over time could simply be a reflection of the checklist items and not any 'fixed' views of the participants.

Again, using the Princeton methodology, Philogène (2001) showed that Black student participants and a non-Black group tended to select similar characteristics for the Black stereotype, although not necessarily with the same frequency, indicating that the stereotype is widely known across a variety of social groups (in the same society), including the group members themselves. This indicates a general knowledge of the cultural stereotype, without requiring any inference that an individual's thinking is biased, rigid or irrational. In a revealing additional study, Philogène (2001) contrasted the stereotype of the category Black with that of African American, using attributes from the Katz and Braly checklist, with 265 participants, who were students in New York, approximately evenly split between African Americans and other Americans (who were mostly European Americans). She found that positive characteristics (such as courteous, progressive, kind) were applied to both groups, showing a change since the initial Princeton trilogy. However, negative characteristics (such as ignorant, arrogant, rude) and boisterous characteristics (talkative, loud, quick-tempered) were applied less to the African American group than the Black group, indicating that a change of categorization can result in a change in the stereotype. This conclusion was supported in research by Hall et al. (2015), who found that the African American stereotype was more positive than the Black stereotype: an exclusively White participant group perceived a person presented as an African American more positively than one labelled as Black. Thus, both the stereotype (as a set of attributes) and the meaning of a social group (to which these attributes are associated) can change over time.

Stereotypes as irrational or cultural thinking?

As Asch (1952, p. 61) argued: 'Most social acts have to be understood in their setting, and lose meaning if isolated. No error in thinking about social facts is more serious than the failure to see their place and function.' For example, Campbell (1967) proposed that stereotypical views can be considered to some degree as habits, and are expressed normatively[7] (i.e. are socially acceptable) within a community. In the middle-class households in 1940s California, the expression of anti-Semitic stereotypes by the 'well-adjusted' and 'normal' female American psychology students (Frenkel-Brunswik and Sanford, 1945) may have reflected the societal norms of that culture (see Chapter 4) rather than any personal repressed hostility lying buried in the psyche of the individual women. Indeed, in a study by Siegel and Siegel (1957) female students were randomly allocated to sorority housing with liberal norms or with more conservative norms. At the start of the study the groups were not distinguishable in terms of personality, yet after a year the students in the more conservative dormitory had become more conservative than those in the liberal dormitory, showing a significant situational or cultural effect on the students' views. An explanation of hidden, buried hostility lurking within these women was simply not required by the evidence. There is further evidence of stereotype use that disputes the Freudian personality explanation. In the highly racist society of apartheid South Africa from the 1940s to the 1990s, the expression of racist stereotypes was socially acceptable; that is, normative. In an examination of authoritarianism and prejudiced attitudes in South Africa, Colman and Lambley (1970) argued that lower values for an authoritarian–prejudice relationship had been found in South African studies (e.g. Pettigrew, 1960) compared to the high correlations found in the United States (e.g. Adorno et al., 1950). In their own study with White South African psychology students, they found a very low correlation between prejudiced attitudes (towards non-White groups) and authoritarianism, that is, participants low on authoritarianism were expressing negative stereotypes. Colman and Lambley (1970) argued that, in this case of low-authoritarian students in a racist society, the expression of prejudicial attitudes serves a utilitarian function of 'going along' with the norms of society, rather than being an outcome of a personal psychological defence. Hence, the expression of a stereotype does not always necessitate proposing an underlying personality cause. In a modern Western society, the opposite might happen: a person who holds racist views does not express racist stereotypes overtly, as they know that this is not socially acceptable (Fiske and Taylor, 2017). The assumption that the expression of a stereotype is an outcome of a fixed and rigid personality type is not required by the evidence, when people are expressing socially normative statements.

Stereotype users as prejudiced and simplistic thinkers?

An important feature of the classical model is that there are two sorts of people: prejudiced stereotype users and tolerant stereotype non-users. Yet Adorno et al. (1950) deliberately selected the extreme high-scoring individuals on their prejudice scale and the extreme low-scoring individuals and then sought to find differences between them. The 50 per cent of the participants in the middle were not considered. The methodology had constructed the dichotomous groups. This was then followed up by a post hoc analysis to explain why these groups are different. The identified characteristics – fixed thinking, intolerance of ambiguity assumed to underlie stereotype use – were not diagnostically examined. For example, making the inference that 'prejudiced people use stereotypes' is not logically the same as the inverse: 'stereotype users are prejudiced'. This is what is known in logic as the inverse fallacy. Just because prejudiced people use certain stereotypes, it does not logically mean that stereotypes are not used by other people or that stereotype use indicates a prejudiced person. Similarly, Allport ([1954] 1979, p. 431) referred to Adorno et al. (1950) to support his assertion of an association of prejudice with political conservatism and tolerance with liberalism. Yet to say that a prejudiced person tends to be conservative in their political views does not logically imply that conservatives tend to be prejudiced. Allport acknowledged the rigid dichotomy of the high- and low-prejudiced individuals in the Adorno et al. (1950) research and the failure to test the reverse associations, such as identifying people 'intolerant of ambiguity' first and then seeing if they are prejudiced or use certain stereotypes, but he dismissed the methodological weaknesses as being 'due largely to the youthfulness of this area of research' (Allport, [1954] 1979, p. 408). However, as more research was undertaken the more obvious it became that this methodological problem could not be dismissed.

Critically, the classical model separated people dichotomously (and artificially): the prejudiced person is 'all bad' (rigid of thought, inaccurate, irrational, fixed in their view of others, projecting their inner hostility on to others, undemocratic and immature and who uses stereotypes) and the tolerant person is 'all good' (mature, rational, democratic, able to deal with ambiguity, flexible and able to see the world in all its complexity and avoids using stereotypes). There is a very clear moral implication in the identification of a 'bad guy' and a 'good guy' in these descriptions. As Gergen (1973, p. 311) pointed out: 'Most of us would feel insulted if characterized as … cognitively undifferentiated, authoritarian … or close-minded.' He argued that this value-laden outcome demonstrated that the social psychologists were not acting as dispassionate scientists but incorporating their personal values into the model (which does not emerge unquestionably from their data). While they appear to be describing a scientific outcome, in fact they are prescribing what they consider to be desirable. For example, Allport ([1954] 1979, p. 515), as noted above, stated that: 'It is part of the democratic *faith* that the objective study of the irrational and immature elements in human behaviour will help us counteract them' (my italics). While this appears to be a plea for rationality, as we see in Chapter 6, this also has a political dimension to it, particularly in terms of who decides what 'irrationality' and 'immaturity' involves. The criticism of the model was even more explicit in Brown's (1958, p. 366) rhetorical questions: 'Is it possible that the social psychologist has used the word *stereotype* to stigmatize beliefs of which he disapproves but which he does not know to be false? Has he perverted his science to achieve a moral purpose?'

Brigham (1971, p. 31) pointed out that the 'problem' of a stereotype as represented in the classical model is that it is considered 'unjustified by an observer'. Yet this 'observer' is not necessarily an objectively determined viewpoint, but is actually the researchers' (and their beliefs), which may not have been made explicit (Brigham, 1971). Thus, the researchers – presumably liberal and seeking to be fair – are placing themselves as the 'observer' who identifies the unjustified stereotypes and then argues that other people should stop using them. This is a political judgement rather than an exclusively psychological judgement, if the assumptions of the psychologists can be challenged. As Taylor and Porter (1994, p. 85) point out, 'We would prefer to believe that only racists and bigots stereotype other groups' (see Chapter 4). Also Brigham (1971) was particularly concerned that, with the focus on stereotypes associated with ethnocentrism and authoritarianism, the model ignored the wide variety of stereotypes present in a culture, such as those of accountants and librarians (discussed in Chapter 1), claiming that 'little has been done towards the construction of a unified theory of stereotyping' (Brigham, 1971, p. 30). Also the expression of different stereotypes might serve different functions, from conformity to social norms, to making sense of the social world or arguing from an ideological position, rather than being indicative of fixed thinking (Brigham, 1971). Crucially he made the point that: 'the term [stereotype] is usually applied by someone to *someone else's* generalization … It is the observer who makes the decision that the beliefs [of others] do not meet his criterion of acceptability and hence are stereotypes' (Brigham, 1971, p. 31). It is critical, therefore, according to Brigham, for observers to provide explicit justification for their labelling of a particular generalization as 'a stereotype'.

Brigham (1971) also criticized the claim that the prejudiced person engages in an 'inferior process' of thought. According to Adorno et al. (1950) and Allport ([1954] 1979), the prejudiced person is fixed and rigid in their thinking, in contrast to the tolerant person, who has a more flexible thinking process (which is clearly viewed as a 'superior process' of thought). A criticism is that the model ignores the evidence of complex arguments that prejudiced people use to support their views (regardless of how offensive others may find them). In the interview research of Adorno et al. (1950), anti-Semitic individuals, when faced with counter-evidence for their views, did not ignore it but engaged in complex arguments to explain it yet still maintain their views. Exceptions to the stereotype were accepted but were claimed to be not typical of the group. When more counter-evidence was given, such as widespread Jewish generosity, the prejudiced people constructed a distinction[8] in their argument between this group (as a social category, referred to as 'good Jews') and 'other' Jews ('bad Jews') who were stereotypical. Hence, the prejudiced interviewees were anti-Semitic but not simplistic or rigid in their thinking (Billig, 1996). Indeed, in his own research on right-wing extremists Billig (e.g. Billig, 1978) showed that prejudiced people were not engaging in an inferior thinking process, but used complex arguments to support and maintain their prejudiced views. Billig (1985) argued that racists are not simplistic in their thinking – they are simply racists – and will employ stereotypes to defend their racist views in argument. Indeed, as noted earlier, Allport ([1954] 1979) showed that prejudiced individuals will even draw on contradictory stereotypes in order to defend their prejudiced views, so it is not indicative of a rigid acceptance of a particular stereotype but a rhetorical technique of supporting an argument (see Chapter 7). The difference between the prejudiced and tolerant person is not in the complexity of their thinking (and may not even be in their use of stereotypes – see below) but that they draw on different arguments to defend opposing ideological beliefs (Billig, 1985; see Chapter 6). Indeed, if stereotypes are attributes associated with social groups, then the idealized tolerant person who does not employ stereotypes may simply not exist. Rather, people with different ideological beliefs may use different stereotypes in their arguments. For example, Chambers et al. (2013) found that when they compared conservative and liberals on their impressions of different groups they found a strong association between political ideology and the opinions about the social groups. For example, liberals had a higher positivity rating of, for example, gays and lesbians, feminists, young people and poor people compared to conservatives; whereas conservatives had a higher positivity rating of both Protestants and Catholics, businesspeople, wealthy people, elderly people and the military compared to the liberals. The use of a particular stereotype may indicate a person's political orientation, rather than simplistic thinking or any underlying psychological hostility. For example, a conservative politician might deliberately refer to opponents stereotypically as 'bleeding-hearted' liberals and a liberal politician might label conservative opponents stereotypically as 'hard-hearted' conservatives, in attempts to diminish them in the public eye. The expression of a stereotype in this case is not indicative of a fixed thinker but a statement in an argument about the social world (see Chapter 6).

Stereotypes or group traits?

Allport ([1954] 1979) proposed that stereotypes, as inaccurate overgeneralizations about social groups, can be distinguished from group traits, which are valid generalizations about social groups. This distinction is crucial because, as Jussim (2012a) points out, if it is not possible to distinguish a stereotype from a non-stereotype, then it is not possible to claim that stereotypes are a special class of 'cognitive structures' and, consequently, they are no more rigid or inaccurate than any other 'ordinary' generalization. There are two reasons for Allport's distinctiveness argument. First, as 'all' judgements, stereotypes are more rigid (or fixed) than other generalizations, in that every group member, without exception, is assigned the stereotypical characteristics. Second, they are inaccurate as they do not correspond to ('objective') social reality. Allport ([1954] 1979) specifically presented the example of 'all lawyers are crooked' as a stereotype (see earlier), which is clearly a fixed overgeneralization (according to the classical model) and undermines the diversity of the group. Furthermore, according to the classical model 'all' statements are indicative of irrational or fixed thinking. However, we can question the view that stereotypes are 'all' judgements, for two reasons. First, when people make 'all' statements, such as 'women are …' or 'the American public are …' they may be exaggerating for rhetorical effect, rather than because they actually believe that every single member of the category are included. For example, a person might state that 'everyone in Spain is so friendly' after an enjoyable holiday in Spain, which we do not interpret as implying that they believe rigidly that every single Spaniard is friendly. Similarly, the author Lawrence Durrell's statement about the French in Chapter 1 that 'the whole country is creative' is eulogizing them for a purpose – to express his love of the French – not because he rigidly believed it literally. Second, Allport ([1954] 1979) argued that overgeneralization creates a belief in the *essence* of the category, such as all lawyers have the quality of 'crookedness' within them. Yet, even a generic claim of essence does not mean that the entire category exhibits the characteristic (Leslie, 2017; see Chapter 5). People may believe that lawyers are predisposed to be dishonest but accept that only some actually are and some are not, just as female mammals are predisposed to give birth but not all of them do. Indeed, people who make generic claims such as 'birds fly' (that is, birds have a defining quality of a potential to fly) are willing to accept that some birds – ostriches, rheas, kiwis, cassowaries and so forth – do not fly. Generic claims are not simplistic overgeneralizations; and the presence of exceptional members of the category, which are accepted as genuine category members, does not lead to a rejection of the generic property. As Lippmann (1922) argued, and Adorno et al. (1950) showed, when prejudiced people employ stereotype 'all' statements, they are often willing to acknowledge exceptions, claiming that an exception does not deny the general case, indicating that, while their views may be offensive, they are not necessarily irrational overgeneralizations.

As Brigham (1971) pointed out, a large number of subsequent authors have argued that stereotypes would be better expressed as just 'ordinary' generalizations, referring to typical members of a category. Therefore the statement that 'all lawyers are crooked' may not be indicative of fixed thinking but a claim about typicality. Like any generalization it may or not be accurate. Both tolerant and prejudiced people know that some lawyers are honest, with Abraham Lincoln and Barack Obama as famous examples, and also that some crooked lawyers exist: for example, the *Wall Street Journal* reported on a lawyer convicted of acting fraudulently (O'Brien, 2018). The question is therefore whether a generalization is valid or not as a typicality judgement, not that the speaker has a 'fixed' belief that every single lawyer is crooked. The problem now becomes one of deciding whether a typicality judgement is an accurate or inaccurate generalization, in terms of the 'true' state of the social world.

Even after time-consuming research, there might still be questions about the genuine proportion of honest and crooked lawyers in the society, even if we can agree on a method for finding this out. This is a problem for the classical model that assumes a benchmark of 'true' social reality. Indeed, as Pickering (2001) pointed out, even the claim that there is an objective reality is an issue of philosophical debate. It then becomes a matter of argument, not of objective reality, but about the state of the social world. One person claiming that 'all' lawyers are crooked (i.e. typically crooked) and a second person claiming that they are typically honest are disagreeing on the state of the social world and the balance of honest and crooked lawyers within it. The second person might cite professional standards keeping lawyers honest and argue that the prosecutions for dishonesty are minimal compared to the total number of lawyers. The first person, who holds the 'crooked lawyer' belief, might claim that the second person is being overgenerous or naive in their view of lawyers and that there are a lot more crooked ones, who just don't get caught, than the second person is willing to accept. This is not simplistic thinking but a complex argument, and the claim of lawyer 'dishonesty' (or 'honesty') might be considered a (false) stereotype or a (true) group trait by the different sides of the argument (see Chapter 7). A key point here is that we may not have detailed or complete data about the social world. Ordinary generalizations – that are not normally referred to as stereotypes – often arise from 'hearsay, rumor, and anecdotes' (Klineberg, 1951, p. 505) so it is quite possible that they are sometimes inaccurate and sometimes accurate. Furthermore, a stereotypical association based on social history – the social reality of the culture – may even be accurate. For example, a study of English social history shows that their culture has encouraged English people to keep their emotions in check – so the English do tend to be 'typically' reserved (Geddes, 2016), which can be considered as a group trait (as well as a stereotype). Vinacke (1957, p. 285) argued, with respect to national stereotypes, that 'they nevertheless generalize some actual cultural traits'. For example, people do not claim that the Japanese are laid-back or that the Brazilians are reserved. Therefore, stereotypical generalizations might descriptively reflect the state of the social world to some extent, i.e. how group members act. Consequently ('inaccurate') stereotypes – as generalizations – may be impossible to distinguish from ('accurate') group traits.

The persistence of the classical model of stereotypes in popular culture

These criticisms explain why academic psychology researchers in the final third of the twentieth century abandoned the classical model and considered stereotypes in terms of 'ordinary' generalizations, to produce alternative psychological explanations of stereotyping, which are examined in Chapter 3. Even at the time of its proposal in the 1950s (e.g. Vinacke, 1957) and certainly by the 1970s (Brigham, 1971) it was very clear that there were serious issues with the classical model of stereotypes. Stereotypes were not fixed and unchanging ideas employed by 'inferior' thinkers. Indeed, the apparent rigidness of stereotypes and their particular association with prejudiced people can be explained by the research methodology employed. The expression of a stereotype was not necessarily an indication of 'faulty' thinking (or unconscious hostility) but could be the expression of a normative description of a social group, common within the culture. Prejudiced people do not think in simplistic ways in comparison to tolerant people, but argue for different beliefs, which the tolerant people may strongly disagree with. However, at the same time, the classical model of stereotypes was gaining public awareness beyond the academic institutions. The impact of the classical model was such that it established an orthodox view of stereotypes that has continued to be maintained through to the present day within Western popular culture. In many ways, the modern dictionary definitions of the stereotype continue to reflect this model. Media commentaries, highlighting examples of stereotyping, will almost certainly frame the discussion in terms of the assumptions of this model. Its persistence may be because of its optimistic implication that there is a method for turning prejudiced individuals into tolerant people, with liberal democratic values, and hence undermine societal discrimination.

This has led to a difference in the general public understanding of 'stereotypes' (as defined in the dictionaries) and 'stereotypes' as represented by the psychological models of social categories and generalizations about them, that emerged from the criticisms of the classical model, which are discussed in the next chapter. Indeed, Vinacke (1957) argued that stereotypes might serve the same cognitive functions as any generalization – to make sense of the social world around us – and hence reflect social learning rather than faulty thinking or repressed hostility (Brigham, 1971; see also Chapter 5). How people learn and employ generalizations about social groups is the critical issue in the understanding of stereotypes. This does not deny the role that stereotypes play in constructing and maintaining prejudice against social groups in a society. An important point to note is that the critics of the classical model are not disputing that a nasty or demeaning statement about a person, on the basis of their social group membership, is a nasty or demeaning statement, and that it has implications for the speaker (demonstrating an antipathy towards the group), the group member (who may be hurt or offended) and society (where discrimination against social group members may be taking place). A society, for reasons of fairness and equality, may choose to legislate against the use of offensive speech about members of certain social groups, and discriminatory practices with respect to them. The problem for the stereotype theorists is the construction of a model that not only explains the use of socially sanctioned stereotypes, but also statements about the polite but boring Canadian (Lenard, 2018) and the inferred characteristics of 1950s car owners in the United States (Wells et al., 1958). As Brigham (1971) pointed out, there are many stereotypes that are not (obviously) linked to societal discrimination, such as the tough Scot and industrious German, which all need be included within the same theoretical model of the concept called a 'stereotype', if a complete understanding of stereotypes is to be achieved. The classical model fails to do this.

Notes

1 It was only after the Second World War that African American (male) students were admitted to the university. In 1969 women were admitted for the first time and, by the early twenty-first century, there were equal numbers of male and female students at Princeton.

2 They used the common term of their time ('Negro'), which is no longer acceptable.

3 The frequency is also the percentage as there are 100 students.

4 Frenkel-Brunswik argued that the prejudiced individual was usually conservative in their political orientation, but she did also identify a subgroup of low scorers on ethnocentrism (assumed to be liberal thinkers) who also showed rigidity in their views.

5 Frenkel-Brunswik and Sanford (1945) used the *thematic apperception test*.

6 This comprised '30 African Americans, 101 Asians, 38 Latino/as, and 19 participants who coded their ethnicity as "Other"' (Madon et al., 2001, p. 1002).

7 Norms are discussed in Chapter 4.

8 A particularization – see Chapter 7.

3

STEREOTYPES IN MIND

Stereotypes and 'ordinary' cognition

Vinacke (1957) argued that stereotypes are concept systems, which could be positive or negative and that organize experience in the same way as other concepts. He contrasted his view with the dominant research of the time that focused on a very narrow set of highly negative stereotypes.

> From this point of view, the characteristics of stereotypes which students of prejudice have been interested in can be placed in proper perspective, as representing part of the total picture, rather than all of it. Thus, for example, it is probably not the fact of stereotyping per se, which marks the prejudicial person, so much as the content of the stereotypes and how they are used.
>
> *Vinacke, 1957, pp. 229–230*

This introduced the idea that the process of stereotyping was not, in itself, a distinctive aspect of cognition, so to understand stereotypes we should look at the 'ordinary' working of the mind. However, Tajfel (1969) pointed out a stark difference in the ways social psychologists had portrayed the human mind in comparison to the cognitive psychologists. The mind, for psychologists studying the perception of the physical world, 'works within the limits imposed by the capacities of individual human minds, and within the socially determined processes of the diffusion of knowledge. It is essentially a rational model, however imperfect the exploring rationality often appears to be' (Tajfel, 1969, p. 79). The human mind had developed, though evolution, for people to make sense of the world around them and pragmatically engage with it (see Hinton, 2016a). People can track the flight of a ball and catch it, negotiate their way through complex terrain, predict the weather and the behaviour of animals from learning associations and relationships, manufacture tools and communicate with each other using language. This indicates complex mental abilities uniquely designed for solving human problems. Yet, in contrast, in academic social psychology, '[o]ur image of a social man is that of a man who has lost his reason' (Tajfel, 1969, p. 80). Tajfel argued that we should look to the 'ordinary' working of human cognition (the rational cognitive model) to understand what is happening in social perception. While he agreed with Allport ([1954] 1979) that stereotypes are related to the categorization of people as social group members, he emphasized that categorization and generalization are important to ordinary, everyday perception, including social perception, particularly when we have to make judgements in an uncertain world. Rather than inferring that the person who describes the Germans as scientifically minded[1] has a 'faulty' mind or repressed 'hidden' hostility, we could examine how a person learns this association (or generalization) from its (consistent) presence in their culture.

Perception and social perception: categorization and generalization

For the psychologist Jerome Bruner, '[p]erception involves an act of categorization' (Bruner, 1957, p.123). The concepts we employ categorize the world around us: a particular pattern of light falls upon our eyes but we perceive a chair. The act of categorization allows us, in Bruner's term to 'go beyond' the initial identification and infer other characteristics of the object, which in this case, from our knowledge of chairs, is that we can sit on it (Bruner, 1957). Importantly, perception prepares us for action – helping us decide how to behave towards the perceived object. Now there is a huge diversity of chairs from antique chairs made by Thomas Chippendale, Shaker-style chairs, to Eames moulded-plastic chairs, and many more of different colours and styles, yet we generalize the attribute 'can be sat on' to all of them, not because we are rigid simplistic thinkers but because we have learnt that this is their general purpose. However, this does depend on context and, if we were in a Wild West saloon and a fight broke out, then a chair could be categorized as 'something to use as a weapon' and picked up (rather than sat on). Perception has developed through evolution with an ecological validity, serving a pragmatic function (Gibson, 1979), so we should not expect it to operate according to some form of philosophically defined objective measure of judgemental 'accuracy'. Consider for a moment a simpler primate, the vervet monkey. Vervet monkeys give different alarm calls identifying different predators, e.g. leopard, snake and eagle (Seyfarth et al., 1980). Calling out the vervet equivalent of 'leopard' has them running up high in the trees, 'snake' and they stand up and scan the ground and 'eagle' has them hiding in dense foliage. Treating each individual (i.e. a particular leopard) as a group member with a shared characteristic (they eat vervets) is pragmatic (it leads to a specific avoidance behaviour) that has survival value. The monkeys might make a 'mistake' in that one particular leopard has just eaten and is not on the hunt but it is not worth the risk – it is better to give a false alarm than be eaten. We can argue that human evolution followed the same principles. Learning what is edible and what is dangerous requires perception, classification, association and generalization. Knowledge of a category only has to be pragmatically useful, not objectively accurate or even very detailed. The purpose of perception for vervet monkeys, and for people, is to function successfully in their environment.

Bruner also argued that perception has a representational function; that is, it provides a model of the external world. Perceptual learning is 'learning the relations that exist between properties of objects and events that we encounter, learning appropriate categories and category systems, *learning to predict what goes with what*' (Bruner, 1957, p. 128) This is not to say that perception is always an 'accurate' representation of the external world, although it can be. A key point about Bruner's view of perception is that we learn categories, and certain categories can become more readily accessible than others, due to experience and context. When we are ill, we are ready to act towards a person identified as a member of the category 'doctor'. By categorizing a person as a friend, we will expect them act towards us in a friendly way (as that is what we believe 'friends' do). A key point about categories is that they are not fixed or universal (although we might believe that they are) but are employed in a context for a purpose. Bruner et al. (1956) argued that the categories we use are human inventions, not the discovery of a 'natural order' (see Chapter 6). We have invented the categories we use, such as tomatoes, lions and snobs (to give Bruner et al.'s examples), as they help us make sense of the world and function successfully within it. Even a category like a typical modern chair is a consequence of the society that invented it: a culturally constructed category. It would have been unfamiliar in traditional Japanese society where people sat cross-legged on comfortable tatami mats. This also means that the categories (and attributes) people use to guide their actions in their everyday lives will change when they cease to be pragmatically useful. Human thinking about the social world, in this cognitive sense, is no different in kind from thinking about the physical world (Hinton, 2016a). It is important to note that a person can be categorized in multiple ways and which social category we choose depends on experience and the context in which we encounter them (Crisp and Hewstone, 2006). To explain this, Tajfel (1969) proposed three elements to the perception of people, as a rational model of sense-making in contrast to the faulty thinking model he criticized: categorization, assimilation and coherence. In categorizing a person as a social group member, we are identifying them in terms of a known category, which we have learnt (assimilated) through our culture (see Chapter 5). Thus, while categorization is a universal cognitive process, the specific system of categories is related to the meaningful groups in a particular society. A modern person is unlikely to categorize another person as a serf, villein or freeman, as these are not relevant categories in twenty-first-century societies, yet in feudal Europe they were highly significant. The application of assimilated (learnt) cultural categories to people provides coherence; that is, it includes a meaningful explanation of the structure of society. This person is a 'lord' (and has these characteristics), and that person is a 'serf' (and has those characteristics). Similarly, any person making sense of the modern social world around them will apply the currently meaningful social categories present in their culture.

In terms of human cognition, stereotypes may be indistinguishable from other categorizations and generalizations. For example, at a basic level there are two dimensions by which we can categorize other human beings in terms of our own survival. First is distinguishing friend from foe (friendly or unfriendly) which we can label as 'warmth'. It is not a characterization we want to get wrong as there could be severe consequences. Second is a judgement of competence. An angry toddler might lash out but they are not competent to cause any harm to an adult carer (usually) but an angry large man carrying a baseball bat might be someone we choose to avoid. Cuddy et al. (2007, 2008) argued that these two dimensions of warmth and competence are central to the content of stereotypes that emerge from the relationship between social groups. A friendly competent group of people could be of great assistance in helping us achieve our goals (like the members of a traditional family or tribe). And we often support a friendly incompetent person (such as bringing up children or looking after the sick or elderly in a family). However, an unfriendly competent person could be a great threat to our survival and so appropriate actions have to be followed (such as preparedness for fight or flight when another tribe or nation acts in a hostile way). Finally, unfriendly incompetent people might wish us harm but they offer a lesser threat than competent people and we may tend to treat them with disdain.

To test this idea, Cuddy et al. (2007) conducted a telephone survey asking American adults to rate different social groups in terms of their warmth and competence in terms of 'how they are perceived by Americans'. The overall results were then mapped on to a chart of warmth and competence. Different clusters emerged of the social groups. Groups viewed as high in both warmth and competence were housewives, Christians, the Irish, the middle class, Americans and Black professionals. In the low warmth and high competence were Whites, the British, Jews, Asians and the rich. In the high warmth and low competence were the elderly, 'mentally impaired' and the disabled. Finally, in the low warmth and low competence were the poor, welfare recipients, Turks, feminists and Arabs. Thus, the stereotypes of different social groups can be seen as reflecting how they were perceived in American culture. These stereotypes then influence the emotional and behavioural tendencies of the person employing them, such as admiration for a warm and competent group, pity for a group viewed as warm but low in competence, envy for a group viewed as competent but low in warmth and, finally, contempt for a group low in both warmth and competence (Cuddy et al., 2007). This *stereotype content model* (Cuddy et al., 2007, 2008; Fiske et al., 2002) provided a rational explanation of why specific broad categories of stereotypes might emerge in a culture. Hence, both the process of stereotyping and the content of stereotypes can be considered as arising through a 'normal' processes of cognition (which is explored in the rest of this chapter) and the relationship between groups (examined in Chapter 4) in a culture (see Chapter 5).

The human mind in academic (cognitive) psychology

The ancient Greek philosopher Aristotle distinguished between humans and other animals on the basis of the former's reasoning ability (the rational principle). According to Aristotle (and also Plato) the good life or the virtuous life was the well-thought-out life, of considered choice and purpose (e.g. Bertman, 1973). This is not to say that animals do not behave intelligently or that humans do not sometimes behave irrationally, but the critical difference is that people have the ability to give reasons for their choices. Throughout Western history, humanity has been characterized by its reason and ability to reflect. For the seventeenth-century philosopher John Locke (see Chapter 6), consciousness is essential to thinking (Fuller et al., 2000). It is through conscious awareness that we know ourselves, and can plan and reflect as rational beings, which allows people to make sense of the world around them and their own lives. Human reasoning is a 'self-conscious, self-directing activity … in the case of theoretical reasoning, when we are constructing a scientific account of the world, and in the case of practical reasoning, where its characteristic manifestation is choice based on deliberation' (Korsgaard, 2018, p. 297). In the nineteenth century this was examined in psychology in terms of the concept of *attention*. As the famous psychologist William James ([1890] 1950, p. 403–404) explained, when we pay attention, it involves '[t]he focalization, or concentration, of consciousness … It implies withdrawal from some things in order to deal effectively with others'. Teachers will tell children to 'pay attention' in class in an attempt to get them to focus (their conscious mind) on an academic task in the lesson, such as writing an essay. Yet it was only in the 1950s that psychologists began to study attention in the laboratory. A key early finding was that our ability to pay attention (consciously concentrate) to a task was *limited in capacity* (Broadbent, 1958), that is, the time to perform a task was related to its complexity. Furthermore, a complex task can take up 'all' of our conscious mental 'capacity', meaning everything else has to be ignored. We cannot write an essay and have a detailed conversation at the same time. We can switch our attention from one to the other but not do them together (Broadbent, 1958; Treisman, 1960). However, we can do some things at the same time: for example we are able to carry on a conversation at the same time as dealing out playing cards; as the second task is a simple, routine activity, allowing us to concentrate on the conversation.[2] Kahneman (1973) explained this by arguing that different tasks require different attentional 'resources' and, while we might have an overall limit on capacity, we can do more than one thing at a time if the combined tasks do not 'overload' these attentional resources.

A really clever feature of the human mind is that *practice* can lead to skilled performance that no longer requires the attentional resources necessary on first encountering the task (Kahneman, 1973). For example, when first learning to juggle it requires a person's full concentration but still they will often drop the balls. Gradually, as skill develops they find it becomes easier to keep the balls in the air. A highly skilled juggler can easily carry on a conversation at the same time as juggling. The same experience occurs when learning to read or drive. Practice with certain tasks leads to *automaticity*, that is, with repeated experience, routine elements of the task no longer require conscious control. Habits are practised routine elements of action (James, [1890] 1950) but we can also develop automatic 'habits' of thought through practice. In a seminal experiment, Shiffrin and Schneider (1977) illustrated the effect of practice on a decision-making task. A person looked at a 2 x 2 grid on a screen. From one to four letters would appear in the grid. As fast as they could, the participants had to press one button if a specific target letter appeared on the screen and another button if it did not. The responses or *reaction times* were measured. The participants performed the task thousands of times. At first it was very clear that the number of letters on the screen influenced the reaction times: the more letters the slower the times, indicating a conscious check of the letters one by one. In one variation of the task, the target letters changed throughout the study, so than an M might be a target at one time but not at other times when it appeared in the grid. Despite lots practice this variation continued to required conscious attention (as shown by the reaction times). However, in a second variation, a particular letter was consistently a target: if it appeared at any time in the grid it was always the target and never not. Here, the more practice the participants had the faster their target detection became. After a lot of practice the reactions were unaffected by the number of letters in the grid and the participants reported the target letter 'popping out' from the grid as soon as it appeared. The target detection had become automatic with practice. While the benefit to the outcome of developing automaticity is clear, there is a cost. After thousands of trials of practice with consistent target letters, Shiffrin and Schneider (1977) surprised the participants by changing them! Now a well-learnt target letter (say, M) had to be ignored (as it was not a target any more). Suddenly performance was far worse than at the beginning of the whole study and the participants often made mistakes. It was only after a long period of additional practice with the new target letters that they began to unlearn the old association. Practice did lead to automaticity but, if the situation changed, it was extremely hard to change an automatic response (as with any habit). The crucial feature of this finding was that practice led to automaticity when there was *a consistent association* between two elements (the letter 'M' and 'a target'). This study showed that experience leads us to detect associations present in the world, which, if consistent over time, become well-learnt and automatically activated.

The importance of this research (see Posner, 1978), is that, with experience (practice), we no longer have to pay attention to the regularities of daily life, once we have learnt them. It becomes a 'habit' of thought. This indicates that a considerable amount of mental processing takes place outside of conscious awareness as a result of this *associative learning*, which may be a fundamental process of human learning (e.g. Morewedge and Kahneman, 2010). A young child learns the consistent relationship between words (as a pattern of letters) and their meaning, which later, as a skilled reader, occurs automatically. As a result of many such studies, it was argued that there are two modes of human thought (Shiffrin and Schneider, 1977). We do have the capacity for rational thought and reflection, but this mode of thought takes time and concentration (attention), and limits our ability to think about other things: yet it allows us to flexibly deal with complex or novel problems that we may not have encountered before. If we overload it – by trying to do too many complex things at once – we will no longer be able to deal with all the information and probably make mistakes. However, we have a second mode of thought that employs (automatically) the familiar and routine associations we have learnt through experience. When walking and talking we only have to concentrate on the latter as the former (normally) is a well-practised skill that we perform automatically. We can characterize this type of fast mental processing as habit or 'running on autopilot'. Bargh (1994) characterized automatic activation as occurring outside awareness, not involving intention, operating efficiently and outside of conscious control, but is inflexible so hard to change. This model of the mind indicates that we are likely to (automatically) learn the consistent associations present in the social world as well as those in the physical world.

The organization of knowledge in the mind

Probably the most important automatic system of the human mind is the operation of a person's knowledge system called *semantic memory* or knowledge memory (Jones et al., 2015). Crucially, it is definitely not like a dictionary or an encyclopaedia storing accurate or objective information.[3] It is a complex interconnected structure of concepts and information that a person has learnt – be it from personal experience, other people, school or the media (see Chapter 5). For example, consider a British person's knowledge of the police. While the term 'police' technically refers to a civil force responsible for law and order, which is known globally, British knowledge will include a wide range of additional information – as consistent associations – for example, that the police do not usually carry guns; the policemen (but not the policewomen) wear domed helmets, they are sometimes referred to as 'bobbies' (from the name of the founder Robert Peel), and were traditionally believed to be helpful (as represented in numerous books and films). These and many other things will comprise British people's common knowledge of the police, which will come to mind when they think or talk about the police. Yet this information may not be accurate for any individual British police officer (who may be wearing a flat cap or even carrying a gun). Also people from different cultures will have a different knowledge of the police, such as a resident of Los Angeles and their experience of the Los Angeles Police Department (LAPD). Bartlett (1932) argued that semantic memory is organized in terms of schemas. A schema is an organized collection of knowledge about a concept, 'an active organization of past reactions or experiences' (Bartlett, 1932, p. 201), so there will be a schema, or network of learnt associations, in semantic memory for 'the police'. Crucially, as illustrated above, this knowledge will be cultural (Saito, 2000). Making sense of a person or an event involves both the information before us (this particular police officer), and our knowledge and expectations about the world (knowledge of the police) in an active and constructive process, which Bartlett referred to as the 'effort after meaning' (Bartlett, 1932, p. 44). Perception or sense-making involves a cognitive effort after coherence (see Tajfel, 1969, earlier). People tend to interpret new experiences through their schemas, with a tendency for conventionalization, which involves making sense of new, unusual or confusing information by interpreting it in terms of one's cultural knowledge (Bartlett, 1932). For example, in contrast to the Japanese understanding of Zen, the British meaning of Zen includes the attribute of 'Eastern religion' (Saito, 1996). Knowledge – the content of semantic memory – is a vast network of these interlinked schemas, through which we understand the world and the people within it. While the schema concept has become less popular in the twenty-first century as it has been considered hard to define in detail (see Hinton, 2016a) and now semantic memory – our personal knowledge memory – is often considered in terms of an *associative network structure* (Fiske and Taylor, 2017). However, the two can be linked by assuming that each small part of the network surrounding a specific concept can be considered a schema (Payne and Cameron, 2013). In thinking about the British police, the stereotype of the British bobby might automatically come to mind, learnt from its consistent portrayal in the media at a particular time in the culture (e.g. McLaughlin, 2005).

Collins and Loftus (1975) proposed that concepts in semantic memory were organized by the relationship between them, that is, connected by associative links. The association of these links can be characterized in terms of 'distance', with two highly associated concepts being considered 'close together' and more unrelated concepts further away, or 'strength', where related concepts have stronger associations. Both metaphors are seeking to capture the same idea of degrees of association. When a concept, such as 'doctor', is activated, for example when we are reading a book that mentions a doctor, then that activation spreads, like a drop of water on a tissue, to the surrounding area of semantic memory, partially activating related concepts, like nurse or patient, making them more readily accessible. Thus, by the activation of semantic memory, we are able understand a story about a hospital, involving doctors, nurses and patients. Similarly, when we walk into a real hospital we are already prepared for the people we will meet there and how we expect them to behave. The associative network model can be extended dimensionally, in that Rosch and Mervis (1975) argued that concepts are organized hierarchically, or 'vertically', in terms of specificity of concept. At the top of the network are general concepts like 'health worker', with subordinate concepts, such as 'doctor' and 'nurse' below it, and below each of these further subordinate more specific concepts, such as types of doctors or nurses. The attributes of higher-level categories, such as 'health worker', are applicable to all the lower objects in the hierarchy. Rosch and Mervis (1975) argued that some concepts are at a *basic level*, which are the most useful in everyday life, such as 'doctor' or 'nurse' rather than the higher-level 'health worker' or the more specific 'orthopaedic surgeon', although usefulness can be influenced by context. We can consider person categories (or social groups) as 'nodes' in the semantic network, with 'doctor' a basic-level category close to 'nurse' in the network (Cantor and Mischel, 1979). Thus, semantic memory is a complex network of associated concepts and attributes.

There has been some debate as to how we categorize a new object or person by locating it in semantic memory, as the nature of this network means that there are no hard and fast boundaries between local networks (or schemas). Rosch and Mervis (1975) suggested that we use *family resemblances* to make a categorical judgement. From experience, we create a typical or average category member, called a prototype. This explains why stereotypical attributes are included within our knowledge of a category of people, such as the typical British bobby being 'helpful' or the typical nurse as 'caring'. While the prototype theory has been supported in the research (Minda and Smith, 2011; Smith and Medin, 1981), some authors have argued that we categorize people based on exemplars rather than prototypes (Nosofsky, 1986, 2011). Rather than comparing any new example to a prototype, it is located among a space of the examples of the category. Where it is located in this space depends on the context of the judgement. Even though a typical nurse might be female, in a particular context a male nurse might be considered a most relevant exemplar of the nurse category. It is possible that we might use prototypes for some judgement tasks and exemplars for others. Abstract prototypes – which can be considered as stereotypes – might guide judgements when there is very little information available and exemplars may be useful when there is not a developed prototype, or more detailed information is available or the perceiver is motivated to make a more refined judgement (Hinton, 2016a). Thus, in cognitive terms, stereotypes are part of the organized information in semantic memory that people use to make sense of the social world. In our 'effort after meaning', learnt associations will be used to make expectations about people and events. Hence we might be surprised when we meet an outgoing, individualistic and talkative Japanese person. That sense of 'surprise' (a noting of the unexpected) has nothing to do with the individual Japanese person (who just happens to be outgoing, individualistic and talkative) but derives from our semantic memory – of the association of the Japanese with 'quiet' and 'reserved' – from their representation in our culture. An important point about the automatic activation of semantic memory is that we are not consciously aware of its operation, only its outcome. Therefore, learning associations can be considered as a fundamental aspect of human cognition, an automatic system that operates quickly and efficiently, creating our knowledge and expectations about the world. The structure of semantic memory, based on the strength of the associations developed through practice (experience), explains why we might think of helmets and truncheons when reading about the British police and not guns and sunglasses, which might occur when thinking about the LAPD.

Human judgement: heuristic rather than logical or statistical decision-making

People can learn to reason logically or statistically: for example, these are often part of philosophical or mathematical education. However, logical or statistical reasoning usually require time and effort and are very inefficient in dealing with the ordinary predictable everyday problems of life. However, there has been a tendency in philosophy and modern psychology to present logical and statistical reasoning, the *scientific method*, as a 'gold standard' of reasoning (Andersen and Hepburn, 2015), compared to which, human everyday associative judgements are viewed as substandard or erroneous. As we shall see below, there are two difficulties with this view. First, people simply do not have the conscious capacity (or can afford the time or the effort) to pay careful attention to every minor decision of life. Second, humanity – usually relying on common-sense knowledge (see Chapter 5 and below) – has been a hugely successful species, so the idea that human thinking does not meet artificial standards of logic or statistics might ignore the pragmatic success of associative decision-making in an uncertain world. Indeed, numerous studies giving people logic problems to solve have shown that 'ordinary' human thinking 'fails' to get the logically correct answer in such circumstances (Robertson, 2017; Wason, 1966). For example, there is a logic problem called a syllogism, which involves two premises followed by conclusion. A person is asked to decide if the conclusion logically follows from the premises. According to the rules of logic it can be determined if a conclusion logically follows from the premises. If the premises and conclusion all start with 'some' then the conclusion does not logically follow from the premises. In the 1930s, Sells presented participants with a syllogism of the following form: premise (1) some Black people are A; premise (2) some As are B; with a conclusion of (3) some Black people are B (see Allport, [1954] 1979, p. 168). Note that this syllogism is always illogical, regardless of what is given as A and B, as a conclusion stating 'some' will never be a logical, or necessary, outcome from two premises stating 'some' (see Hinton, 2016a). However, Sells presented one positive syllogism (about athletes and heroes) and one negative syllogism (about sex offenders and syphilis). White student participants, with pro-Black attitudes, argued that the positive syllogism was logical and the negative syllogism was not, whereas other students, with anti-Black attitudes, claimed the reverse. Thus, the participants' beliefs about the state of the world influenced their answers about the validity of the conclusions, and not the rules of logic. It therefore appears that people have a tendency to make 'ordinary' judgements based on associative or common-sense knowledge, rather than following the rules of logic in their decision-making (e.g. Robertson, 2017).

As well as 'failing' to solve problems logically, people are not very good at statistical decision-making. Like logical reasoning, statistical reasoning provides a benchmark or criterion for 'correct' thinking. Using probabilities in decision-making can lead to a greater understanding of the relationship between possible causes and effects, such as smoking and cancer. Given that some people do understand statistical reasoning (such as statisticians and the employees of insurance companies) we can ask if participants in psychology experiments typically use statistical reasoning in their decision-making. The answer to this question – no – was revealed in the groundbreaking work of Daniel Kahneman and Amos Tvesky, who investigated people's use of probability in a number of well-known studies. In one investigation (Kahneman and Tversky, 1973, p. 241), they gave a description of a man called Jack to the participants who had to decide if Jack was a lawyer or an engineer:

> Jack is a 45-year-old man. He is married and has four children. He is generally conservative, careful, and ambitious. He shows no interest in political and social issues and spends most of his free time on his many hobbies which include home carpentry, sailing and mathematical puzzles.

The participants were told that Jack was one of 100 men in a room, where 70 of them were lawyers and 30 were engineers. The researchers argued that the description, which is a stereotype of an engineer, does not actually give any specific information about Jack's occupation so is less informative than the number of men of each occupation in the room. The *base-rate probability* that Jack is a lawyer is 0.7 (as there are 70 out of the 100 men) and only 0.3 (30 out of 100) that Jack is an engineer. Statistically, Jack is more than twice as likely to be a lawyer as an engineer. However, participants typically said that Jack was more likely to be an engineer. Kahneman and Tversky (1973) argued that the participants ignored the probabilities and employed a strategy based on the stereotypical description, which they called the *representativeness heuristic* (where a heuristic is a strategy). Jack was representative of a stereotypical engineer – he was the sort of person the participants associated with an engineer – so they inferred strategically that he was one.

In another study, Tversky and Kahneman (1982) presented participants with a description of Linda that matched the feminist stereotype, and then asked them to order a number of statements referring to her, from most likely to least likely. There were two statements that the researchers were interested in. The findings showed that participants judged the statement that 'Linda is a bank teller active in the feminist movement' to be more likely than the statement that 'Linda is a bank teller'. However, the category of 'bank teller' must be larger than the category of 'bank teller active in the feminist movement', so *must* be more probable. Tversky and Kahneman (1982) referred to the participants' heuristic solution as the *conjunction fallacy*, the illogical claim that a conjunction of two attributes is more likely than only one of them. The participants appeared to be using the feminist stereotype to make their decisions about Linda. Stereotypically, she was unlikely to be a bank teller and more likely to be active in the feminist movement and this influenced their judgement, which was both logically and statistically incorrect. In a wide range of similar studies, the researchers demonstrated that people's judgements were typically heuristic rather than logical or statistical (Kahneman et al., 1982). For example, people would often rely on what readily came to mind when thinking of a problem – the *availability heuristic* – or overemphasize first impressions in their judgements – the *anchor-and-adjustment heuristic*. Thus, the research into statistical reasoning complemented that on logical reasoning. People typically do not employ either in their judgements but rely on heuristics, that is, learnt associations (or beliefs) about the state of the world.

Kahneman (2011) argued that heuristic thinking, which people often employ even when they have the time to think carefully and deliberately, indicates how pervasive it is in everyday life. He argued that these learnt heuristics were part of, what he termed, *System 1* thinking, a fast mental processing system operating automatically, requiring little or no effort or voluntary control, with answers appearing in consciousness even when the person is unable to explain the reasons for thinking them (Haidt, 2001): a development of the automatic processing system discussed earlier. *System 2* is the attentional system that we employ when we have the time and inclination to engage consciously with complex or novel tasks, which Kahnman (2011) associates with agency, choice and concentration. People are only able to multitask because System 1 can do the familiar, practised tasks leaving System 2 to deal with any complex decision-making. System 2 is explicit, analytic and reflective and is considered a uniquely human mode of thought and newer in evolutionary terms than System 1 (Evans, 2008). The problem is that people may think that they are thinking rationally (logically and statistically) but they are actually thinking heuristically. Indeed, Kahneman won the Nobel Prize for Economic Sciences in 2002, for the invention of the field of behavioural economics, demonstrating that business and investment decisions were often based on heuristic 'biases' when set against logical or statistical methods.

There is a temptation to believe that System 2 is 'better' than System 1, as it seems to involve the type of reasoning (e.g. logical, rational) that traditionally has been presented by philosophers from Plato to Kant as the 'proper' way of thinking, that will produce 'right' answers. It is also what is encouraged in academic and scientific study, in a Western educational system: such as considering different perspectives on a problem and creating abstract models to solve it. However, this ignores the importance of System 1, without which we would be 'strangers in a strange land', with nothing familiar and having no expectations, and forced to apply our limited consciousness to every one of the thousands of mundane problems of daily life (see Chapter 5). Without System 1 we would be functionally incapable. Haidt (2006) describes this by the metaphor of a rider on an elephant. The System 1 'elephant' is our evolutionarily developed system of engaging in the world (with all our animal needs and emotions). It can survive very well without the 'rider' (System 2), and is much more powerful. Though weaker, the rider or System 2 (rational consciousness) can make complex decisions and guide the elephant and, over time, train it to change its behaviour. However, we should remember that in everyday life the two systems work together to perform the variety of tasks that the person is required to perform. Indeed, some authors argue that there may simply be two modes of processing relying on the one underlying mental system, rather than two separate systems (Kruglanski and Orehek, 2007).

Tools in the cognitive toolbox: heuristics make us smart

Despite the various studies identifying human logical and statistical 'failings', some researchers began to question the assumption that logical or statistical methods were the appropriate criteria for producing successful answers in human judgements. First, with the research identifying a long list of human thinking errors and biases, it is a wonder that human thinking is successful at all. Yet it is. Humankind is the most successful species on the planet. Other researchers argued that human thinking should be considered in terms of its functionality not in terms of its failure to match up to some arbitrary criteria of logic or statistics (Fox, 1992). Fox (1992) argued that prejudgement – relying on learnt associations and experience – is not the same as societal prejudice against certain social groups. As he noted to illustrate his point, in the famous *Star Trek* science fiction stories, it is the quick-thinking and 'irrational' Captain Kirk who usually saves the day rather than the logical Mr Spock. This is because many problems people face in their everyday lives involve uncertainty, such as those facing a doctor working in A&E (accident and emergency), who may not have the luxury of time and detailed information to come to a logically 'correct' judgement but must make a rapid decision or else the patient will die. With such time constraints it is only the doctor's skill (experience and quick heuristic thinking) that can save the patient's life (Gigerenzer et al., 1999). Gigerenzer and Gaismaier (2011) argued that rather than heuristics being 'errors' or 'biases', they are what make human beings smart. Most human decisions have to be made rapidly. The limitations of the human (conscious) mind plus the uncertainties of the social environment mean that people seek workable, practical solutions to problems that are satisfactory rather than perfectly or logically accurate. In the real world (outside the artificial constraints of the logic problems in the psychology laboratory), heuristics allow people to make quick decisions, which are not guaranteed to be always 'right' but in situations of uncertainty can be surprisingly, and pragmatically, accurate. In fact, Gigerenzer and his colleagues argued that human thinking is adapted to the environmental circumstances of human existence; taking into account other actors (such as friend or foe) and past experience. Human thinking is not a poor or 'faulty' version of 'proper' reasoning but, in the human environment, heuristics are faster and more successful than other decision-making methods, and often more accurate. The mind can therefore be described as *an adaptive toolbox* of heuristics (Todd and Gigerenzer, 2012).

Logic problems in the psychology laboratory do not have the same personal significance as practical problems in everyday life. For example, a psychologist studying logical reasoning asks a rural farmer to solve the following simple logic problem: 'You need a horse and a cart to take your produce to market. You only have a horse. Can you take your produce to market?' Logically, the answer is 'no' but the farmer answers 'yes'. When asked to explain this 'illogical' answer the farmer explains that they would not leave their produce to rot but borrow a cart to get it to market. This is a perfectly reasonable and pragmatic answer to the practical problem of having no cart but needing to take produce to market. The farmer has not accepted the artificial restriction of the abstract question and answered in terms of the practical everyday knowledge of getting farm produce to market (Scribner, 1977). The answer has *ecological validity* (Gigerenzer et al., 1999). Thus, in ordinary life, human thinking is pragmatic. Human decisions rarely can draw on a fixed or exhaustive set of logical possibilities, with a set of agreed assumptions, which are required for a logical or statistical analysis. The problems of everyday life are not *bounded*, like an abstract logic problem, but 'fuzzy', with ill-defined terms and a lack of general agreement on the way to approach them. In such circumstances heuristics may provide more successful solutions than logic or statistics.

(Gigerenzer et al., 1999) argued that human heuristic thinking is typically 'fast and frugal', heuristic and pragmatically successful. People are not seeking logical or objective correctness in their decisions but a useful answer in the circumstances. Examining practical problems in everyday life, where people draw heuristically on their cultural knowledge (rather than some 'objective' criterion) demonstrates a high level of skilled decision-making. Strategies are never *always* correct, but in the complex human environment, they are often the most accurate method of judgement (Gigerenzer and Gaissmaier, 2011). One of the most useful heuristics is the *recognition heuristic* (Goldstein and Gigerenzer, 2002). German and American participants were asked to decide which of two American cities had the larger population. It seems reasonable to assume that the Americans, with their greater knowledge of their own cities would be more likely to get the answer right. However, the American participants (who did have greater knowledge) had various reasons for deciding that one rather then the other city was the larger. They had a problem of deciding what information was most diagnostic. The German participants, however, had no such information. In fact some of them had only heard the name of one of the cities before. They simply made their decision using the recognition heuristic: which city name was the most familiar. The results showed the German participants to be more accurate than the American participants.

Even a simple question such as 'what are engineers like?' has no logically 'correct' answer. Recall that, implicit in the Kahneman and Tversky (1973) study above, the stereotype of engineer was assumed to be wrong (i.e. uninformative and not diagnostic) compared to the statistical information. However, this assumption, that stereotypes are always wrong, is open to question (Jussim, 2012a). Despite some searching through the research literature, I have not been able to find any information about how many engineers enjoy the hobbies of carpentry, sailing and mathematical puzzles, and how many do not (see above for the description of Jack the engineer). It is not possible in a reasonable time to work out logically or statistically if these attributes are correct or not. But these appear to be typical hobbies of engineers familiar in the culture (and in the media), such as the engineer Howard Wolowitz in the US television show, *The Big Bang Theory* (2007–2019). We know that engineering involves mathematics and construction and someone interested in these activities might (reasonably) like making other things (carpentry) and learning about the complexity of the movement and control of vessels in wind and water (sailing). The working life of a lawyer is very different, with different skills such as speaking persuasively in a courtroom, and they are likely to have different interests. Thus, if the stereotype reflects the structure of the culture then it is not necessarily irrational or a bias to strategically predict – by relying on cultural knowledge – that Jack is an engineer (Hinton, 2017). Indeed, stereotypes can be viewed as 'energy-saving devices' in the cognitive toolbox (Macrae et al., 1994). Macrae et al. (1994) asked participants to perform two memory tasks, learning geographic information and a personality description. The participants were better at both tasks when they were given a stereotypical label for the personality characteristics. The stereotypes could be processed quickly (as they rely on learnt associations) and freed up more cognitive resources for the other task (of remembering the geographic information). Also, heuristics as learnt cultural associations, or cultural stereotypes, such as Brazilians are laid-back, Australians like sport, librarians are bookish and art students are creative, may provide heuristic information to guide social judgements when little or no other information is available (Jussim, 2012a).

The predictive brain

From the above analysis, it can be argued that the human unconscious mind operates on simple but highly effective automatic procedures. It develops expectations by learning the associations present in the physical and social world, which it employs to make predictions about an uncertain world. Evidence for this idea comes from the psychology of object perception, where it has been suggested that the (unconscious) brain operates as a 'prediction machine' (Clark, 2013; see also Bubic et al., 2010). Therefore the unconscious mind can be labelled *the predictive brain* (Clark, 2016). It operates by mechanistically learning the associations present in the world, and using past experience to make predictions about the current situation. Repeated experiences influence the learnt probabilities and the unexpected presents new possibilities. For example, on meeting their neighbour's dog for the first time a person will expect that it will bark, as they have learnt an association (with a high probability) of dogs and barking. The predictive brain operates by the simple principle of maximizing predictive success and minimizing *surprisal* (making an unsuccessful prediction). This can be specified mathematically by Bayes' theorem (which also underlies many machine-learning, artificial intelligence systems). Essentially, predictions are based on the frequency of associations, which are used to create *prior probabilities* – an expectation – which guide predictions at any moment. It is a dynamic process that is constantly and incrementally being updated by experience.

The model of the predictive brain can be applied to the social world too (Clark, 2013; Hinton, 2017). A child will learn the association between medical doctors and white coats, stethoscopes, surgeries, examinations and medicines. However, much of what they have learnt does not come from personal experience but from other people telling them about doctors, and doctors in the media (see Chapter 5). Yet to the predictive brain, each occurrence, such as seeing a doctor with a stethoscope in a picture book, will provide one more instance to subtly increase the probability of the doctor–stethoscope association.

A crucial point is that the predictive brain is not picking up the attributes that are logically correct or socially important: it is simply unconsciously applying probabilities to all potential attributes and, through repeated experience, certain attributes gain a diagnostic probability (that they are more likely than not) and can be employed for successful prediction. The operation simply involves updating probabilities based on associations present within the culture. There is a constant learning cycle of prediction, feedback (confirmation or surprisal) and the adjustment of probabilities to minimize subsequent surprisal. If 90 per cent of the nurses experienced in a culture are women, then the predictive brain will develop an association between nurse and female, purely on the probabilities, as this high probability is diagnostic and leads to the prediction that an unknown nurse will (probably) be female.[4] However, if it encountered 50 per cent male and female nurses then gender is no longer a diagnostic attribute for a nurse and would not be learnt as an association with nurse. The predictive brain is neither sexist nor non-sexist; it is simply probabilistic, picking up on the associations learnt about the social world from the culture the person inhabits.

Heuristics such as the representativeness heuristic (Kahneman and Tversky, 1973; see above) are only considered a 'bias' or an 'error' as the stereotype was assumed to be false (i.e. uninformative) by the researchers. Yet Kahneman (2011) acknowledged that where an association is present in the culture, and he cites the relationship between basketball players and height, then the representativeness heuristic produces the same result as a Bayesian analysis – that is a statistically valid prediction. Thus, the unconscious mind, rather than being illogical or ignorant of probability, is actually undertaking a dynamic statistical analysis based on cultural information. This model also explains cultural differences in heuristic decision-making. For example, Puddifoot and Cooke (2002) showed that students in a university in the southern United States associated guns with personal freedom, independence and protection from crime, but students in a British university associated guns with violence, madness and the cause of crime. Hence, the predictive brain model argues that people's implicit (learnt) associations reflect the culture they live in (see Chapter 5) and the prevalence of those associations in that culture.

The automatic activation of cultural stereotypes

If the definition of a stereotype is restricted to the agreed 'attributes associated with a social group' (Schneider, 2004; see Chapter 1) then, in terms of the research in cognitive psychology, stereotypes are learnt associations no different to other associations acquired from the culture, such as 'dogs bark', 'cowboys wear Stetson hats' and 'the French make wine'. A crucial point made by Devine (1989) is that personal beliefs and knowledge of stereotypes are conceptually distinct. A person may know a stereotype just as they know many things (from learning about their culture) but this does not mean that they endorse the stereotype, and may even vehemently disagree with it. To make this point clear, she specifically referred to stereotypes as *cultural stereotypes*. This was demonstrated in a study where she asked 40 White participants to list the cultural stereotype of Black people and subsequently fill in the Modern Racism Scale to measure their anti-Black prejudice (Devine, 1989). The same stereotypical characteristics of the social category 'Black' were produced by both low-prejudiced and high-prejudiced participants. Also independent judges, presented with the stereotypical descriptions, could not predict the person's level of prejudice from them. This led Devine to conclude that people learn the associated attributes of different social groups from their culture during socialization and, importantly, these particular cultural stereotypes are frequently encountered (in the media for example) and become extremely well-learnt. Drawing on the two systems or dual processing model described above, she argued that this repeated experience of cultural stereotypes can result in the automatic activation of a stereotype on encountering a stereotyped group member, regardless of the prejudice of the individual. Knowing a stereotype and an antipathy towards a social group are not the same thing.

In a second study, Devine (1989) asked White participants to perform two apparently unrelated experiments. In the first phase, they were asked to rapidly detect words appearing either on the left or right of a screen, by pressing a 'left' or 'right' button. In the second phase, they read a 12-sentence paragraph about a person called Donald who performed ambiguously hostile behaviours, such as demanding his money back in a store or not paying his rent until his apartment was repainted. They then rated Donald on 12 personality scales, 6 of which were related to hostility. However, the relationship between the two phases was the key aspect of the study, which it was later confirmed the participants had not detected. In the first phase the words were specifically selected (for some participants) to be related to the Black stereotype (which the participants did not spot) that were assumed to automatically activate the Black stereotype (and its cultural association with hostility). It was then predicted that, for these participants, this stereotype would influence their ratings of Donald, which would be more hostile than for participants who had only experienced neutral words in the first phase. The prejudice level of the student participants was known from a previously administered Modern Racism Scale. The results showed that the automatic stereotype activation did result in higher hostility ratings of Donald but this was not affected by the students' prejudice level. The activation and influence of the stereotype was assumed to have occurred outside of the participants' awareness or conscious control. The implication of the study is that everyone, regardless of prejudice level, could be influenced by the automatic activation of a known cultural stereotype.

In a final study, Devine (1989) examined White participants' personal beliefs as well as their knowledge of a cultural stereotype. Participants performed the task anonymously. Initially, they were asked to generate as many word labels for Black Americans that they could think of. Subsequently, they were given ten minutes to write down their own thoughts about the social group. All participants completed the Modern Racism Scale. The results showed no difference between the prejudiced and non-prejudiced participants in their reporting of known pejorative labels for Black Americans, indicating common cultural knowledge. However, there were clear differences between the prejudiced and non-prejudiced participants in their listing of thoughts. High-prejudiced individuals listed more negative thoughts (e.g. 'Blacks cause problems') and trait thoughts (e.g. 'lazy'), whereas the non-prejudiced individuals listed more positive thoughts (e.g. 'friendly') and more belief thoughts (e.g. 'it is unfair to judge people by their color'). Devine argued that when given time to exercise conscious control, despite the automatic activation of the stereotype, the non-prejudiced people suppressed it in their (conscious) judgements. Devine (1989) argued that the non-prejudiced individuals were motivated to exercise conscious control and sought to suppress the stereotypical associations, which they knew but did not agree with. She characterized this activity as being like breaking a bad habit.

Subsequent research has argued that cultural stereotypes are not always activated in the presence of a stereotyped group member, as they have to be viewed in a socially relevant context (Devine and Monteith, 1999; Devine and Sharp, 2009; Macrae et al., 2002). Also, for any person, there are alternative possible stereotypes, and which is activated depends on the social context. For example, the Black stereotype was automatically activated in the context of 'prisoners' but not in the context of 'lawyers' (Wittenbrink et al., 2001). Also different attributes of the cultural stereotype might be automatically activated in different contexts, as shown in a study comparing Blacks and Asians in a basketball and classroom context (Barden et al., 2004). Therefore the automatic activation of specific cultural knowledge will be context dependent. However, the importance of Devine's (1989) research was that it shifted the research focus within cognitive psychology from the overt expression of stereotypes by prejudiced people (as in the 1950s research) to the automatic activation of cultural stereotypes in both prejudiced and non-prejudiced individuals.

The problem of implicit stereotypical associations in American culture

It is clear that the majority of the research into stereotypes has been driven by concerns about discrimination in American society, as noted in Chapter 1. Myrdal (1944) referred to this as the *American dilemma*: a culture based on egalitarian ideals yet containing societal discrimination against African Americans. Devine explicitly cited this dilemma as an influence on her work (Devine, 2003). Devine and Sharp (2009, p. 62) made this point clear by associating racial stereotyping with the 'negative effects that run counter to the guiding principle on which our nation was founded (i.e. that all people are created equally and deserve equal treatment)'. Wide-ranging changes in the culture, civil rights legislation and workplace regulation has meant that the American society of the twenty-first century is very different to that of Myrdal's time. This has resulted in a significant reduction in the public expression of discriminatory stereotypes (Fiske and Taylor, 2017). Yet, despite these changes, it is also clear that societal discrimination has not disappeared. Consequently, the psychologists have shifted their interest from the overt expression of stereotypes, such as racists expressing racist views, to the implicit cultural stereotypes (or subtle stereotypes as Fiske and Taylor, 2017, refer to them) as identified by Devine (1989). Even well-meaning, liberal-minded people in American society expressing a belief in fairness and equality, and seeking to behave in a non-discriminatory way, will have still learnt negative cultural stereotypes that might have an automatic (or implicit) effect upon them (Devine and Sharp, 2009).

Unfortunately, Bargh (1999) was less optimistic than Devine (1989) in people's ability to consciously control automatically activated cultural stereotypes, referring to these automatically activated stereotypical associations as a 'cognitive monster'.

> Hoping to stop the cognitive monster by trying to control already activated stereotypes is like mowing dandelions; they just sprout back again. As with dandelions, the only way to kill stereotype effects is to pull them up by their roots – by removing their capabilities for automatic activation, or (better still) by preventing the seeds to take root in the first place, through eradication of the cultural stereotype itself.
>
> *Bargh, 1999, p. 378*

The problem with the 'monster within' idea is that it resonates with the hidden 'monster' of the classical model, considered in Chapter 2, but the meaning here is different: having learnt the stereotype, it may not be possible to unlearn it. Switching his metaphor to dandelions, he talks of 'preventing the seeds to take root', which can be considered as people not acquiring the stereotype in the first place. When a discriminatory association, which is learnt from the culture, is no longer present in that culture then that particular stereotype will no longer be learnt, or potentially, automatically influence future generations.

While the cognitive model of the mind considered above is universal in terms of its conscious and automatic components (Kahneman, 2011), the automatically activated learnt associations, such as stereotypes, will be cultural. People are brought up in different societies so will (implicitly) learn different sets of associations due to their different cultural histories. Indeed, the Black stereotype related to African Americans in the United States may be unknown in Mali or Mongolia, who will have learnt their own cultural associations – and stereotypes of culturally relevant groups – due to the history and structure of their own societies (Hinton, 2017). However, in the twenty-first century, the research demonstrated an increasing role of unconscious processes in everyday decision-making (Bargh and Morsella, 2008; Dijksterhuis and Nordgren, 2006). Indeed, North and Fiske (2012) represented the human thinker as an *activated actor*. Fiske and Taylor (2017, p. 16) argued that 'social environments rapidly cue perceivers' social concepts, without awareness, and almost inevitably cue associated cognitions, evaluations, affect, motivation, and behaviour'. Ferguson and Bargh (2004, p. 33) argued that 'there is now a general consensus that people's understanding of the world is automatically shaped by previous experiences and knowledge'. The problem of cultural stereotypes, for the American researchers, was not that the human mind is 'faulty' but that people in their culture will have learnt negative stereotypes (as implicit associations) about social groups (such as African Americans) that might subtly influence even the most egalitarian of people in their decision-making and perpetuate the American dilemma (see Chapter 6).

The implicit association test and unconscious 'bias'

The development of the *implicit association test* or IAT (Greenwald and Banerji, 1995), further led to the dominance of implicit stereotyping research in the psychology of stereotyping during the early twenty-first century. The IAT is a reaction time test that examines the strength of association between different pairs of concepts, such as flowers and insects, and pleasant and unpleasant (Greenwald et al., 1998). The technique works for any two pairs and therefore it is a general test of learnt associations; that is, of implicit associations in semantic memory.[5] The test can be used to examine implicit stereotypes by examining the stereotypical attributes associated with a social group. Typically, a socially meaningful bipolar contrast is studied, such as men and women, with a stereotyped attribute, such as science and liberal arts (Greenwald et al., 1998). The results showed faster response times to the stereotypical associations, indicating that stereotypical attributes are implicitly associated with the social group by the participants in memory. The IAT is assumed to be an independent measure of the strength of an implicit association in contrast to the overt (conscious) expression of a person's views about a group, and is therefore a test of implicit stereotypes. In the implicit association test, the participant sits facing a screen, a keyboard before them, with their left index finger on a left-hand key, such as the A key, and their right index finger on a right-hand key, such as the 5 key on the numeric pad, as in the set-up of Greenwald et al. (1998). Stimuli, typically words or pictures, appear on the screen that participants have to classify as either one of two categories, as fast and as accurately as they can, by pressing the designated key. In the first part of the test, the participants classify items appearing on the screen according to the first category pair, for example female and male, pressing (for example) left for female and right for male. Typical male words could be man, son, father, boy, uncle, grandpa, husband, male and female words could be mother, wife, aunt, woman, girl, female, grandma, daughter. In the second part, the classification is done on the second category pair, for example science and liberal arts, pressing left and right accordingly with, for example, astronomy, maths, chemistry, physics, biology, geology, engineering as the science words and history, arts, humanities, English, philosophy, music, literature as the liberal arts words. In the third part, the participants now have to classify items as either female or science by the left key and male or humanities by the right key. In the fourth stage, the first category pair is swapped to the opposite keys, to control for response biases, and the participants practise categorizing items this way. Finally, the participants now classify items as either male or science with the left key and female or liberal arts with the right key. The order of categories, the pattern of the keys and the order of category combinations, can all be balanced across the experiment, to control for all other factors except the strength of association (in terms of the speed of the response). Finally, the mean reaction times are calculated from the results in the various parts of the study to find the strength of association between men and science, men and liberal arts, women and science and women and liberal arts.

At the outset of the research Greenwald and Banaji (1995, p. 15) made it clear what they meant by implicit stereotypes: '*Implicit stereotypes* are the introspectively unidentified (or inaccurately unidentified) traces of past experience that mediate attributions of qualities to members of a social category.' Now that there was a way of measuring implicit stereotypes (as these learnt associations were termed) the use of the test grew phenomenally (Greenwald and Nosek, 2001; Nosek et al., 2007), specifically as a measure of implicit associations about social groups facing discrimination in the society of the United States. A website[6] was set up for anyone to test their own implicit associations on a range of social issues (Nosek et al., 2007), such as race, gender, sexual orientation, disability and so forth. Nosek et al. (2007) found that stereotypical associations consistently led to faster reaction times (which were unrelated to explicit beliefs as shown on a questionnaire). While there was variation in the findings between individuals, the dominant result was that there was a widespread reaction time preference (i.e. faster reaction times) to stereotypical associations about the social groups across thousands of participants (Nosek et al., 2007).

Critically, the IAT results were acknowledged as having a social cause yet the focus has often been on a (hidden) 'bias' in individual minds (Banaji et al., 2015). The implication of this is that a participant's individual results (as an implicit bias) can be (mis)interpreted as a personal mental 'failing' (Hinton, 2017; see also Gergen, 1973). While this issue of terminology could be considered an academic discussion between university psychology researchers, the success of the IAT has led it to be used in the public domain, specifically in the area of anti-discrimination training and employed with individuals to reveal their *personal* biases, rather than the general learning of cultural associations. For example, it has been presented to a popular audience as detecting the 'hidden biases of good people', as in the subtitle of Banaji and Greenwald (2013)'s book. Other researchers (e.g. Hinton 2017; Tetlock and Mitchell, 2009) have challenged this interpretation of the IAT results as an unconscious bias of the individual. First, we know that an 'ordinary' citizen of the United States seeking to be non-prejudiced, fair in their judgements and respectful of diversity, will *almost certainly* find that they are unconsciously biased if they take all the tests on the Harvard website. With a bank of, say, 20 tests, a person will demonstrate some reaction-time preferences (even by random chance) and the probability of showing no preference across the tests is negligible. While the test of a particular stereotypical 'bias' may appear individually diagnostic,[7] as a cultural association it is revealing a group-based (i.e. cultural) bias rather than necessarily requiring any claim about any individual (except that they are a member of a culture). The test is a general test of implicit associations so my prediction is that people will show a reaction time 'bias' in favour of members of Gryffindor compared to Slytherin (from the Harry Potter stories by J. K. Rowling) and they do show a preference for flowers over insects (as in Greenwald et al., 1998). Claiming that individuals have a 'hidden bias' against Slytherin or insects appears an unnecessary inference given that these are both associations that have been learnt from the culture. Yet the focus on societal discrimination and unconscious bias can be understood in terms of the researchers' concerns about the American dilemma.

In a series of articles Tetlock and his colleagues criticized the implicit 'bias' interpretation of the IAT (e.g. Tetlock and Mitchell, 2009), specifically in the interpretation of the White–Black IAT differences. Arkes and Tetlock (2004) included the rhetorical question 'Would Jesse Jackson[8] "fail" the Implicit Association Test?' in the title of their paper. Critically, they claimed that the data reflected known cultural associations rather than any individual or personal antipathy towards a social group, arguing that the use of the word 'prejudice' or 'bias' for the IAT findings is not the same as the traditional definition of the word 'prejudice' linked to behavioural discrimination in society (e.g. Allport, [1954] 1979). For example, a White participant may show a preference (i.e. respond more quickly) to Betsy (labelled a 'White' name) compared to Laytona (labelled as a 'Black' name) but this does not necessarily indicate any hostility or prejudice towards African Americans. In support of this, van Ravenzwaaij et al. (2011) performed an IAT on White students in the Netherlands, comparing Dutch names and Moroccan names on positivity. There was a preference for Dutch names. Van Ravenzwaaij et al. (2011) rejected an explanation of 'racial bias' (of the White Dutch against Moroccans) by including a third group, Finnish names, in their study. They found a similar Dutch preference over Finnish names, but no difference between Moroccan and Finnish names, indicating that the effect was simply an in-group preference, and not due to 'hidden' racial prejudice. Tetlock and Mitchell (2009) suggested that to refer to the responses as individual 'bias' ignores the possibility that the findings may reflect the actual relationships between groups in the culture. They concluded that a reaction-time measure such as the IAT may be appropriate for examining the workings of human memory but less so for exploring the political questions of prejudicial behaviour in society.

A crucial issue of the debate that developed was whether the IAT was diagnostic (i.e. predictive) of individual discriminatory behaviour. Jost et al. (2009) robustly countered the arguments of the Tetlock and Mitchell (2009) study, citing evidence of studies showing a correlation between IAT measures and behavioural responses.[9] In an increasingly technical debate, Greenwald et al. (2009) argued, from an analysis of 184 different studies, that the IAT was shown to have predictive validity of behavioural outcomes across a range of different topics of study. Yet in critiquing the Greenwald et al. (2009) analysis, Oswald et al. (2013) argued that the correlations of the IAT with other measures of discrimination (based on race) were small, and the IAT was a poor predictor of the behaviours normally associated with prejudice; concluding that the IAT 'provides no more insight than explicit measures of bias' (Oswald et al., 2013, p. 188). Greenwald et al. (2015) critiqued the analysis of Oswald et al. (2013) and argued that statistically small effects can still result in significant effects in society. However, they acknowledged the problems of employing the test to predict the behaviour of specific individuals, arguing that the IAT has social significance in examining the general bias within a social group, such as the implicit bias (of ethnicity) of a community of police officers (see Chapter 4). This was supported by Hardin and Banaji (2013, p. 23) who argued that 'locating the problem of prejudice in a few problematic individuals … is missing the point', and argued that the focus should be on exploring prejudice across individuals, i.e within social groups or cultures. The debate continued (e.g. Oswald et al., 2015) but a key point of agreement can be drawn from it. The optimistic idea that the IAT is some sort of precise measure of an individual person's 'hidden' prejudice – predicting discriminatory behaviour – has been strongly challenged. There are both theoretical and practical problems with this view. Indeed, the supporters of the test as a measure of implicit bias (e.g. Hardin and Banaji, 2013) accepted that it may be a more appropriate technique for looking at the associations aggregated across a group of people rather than as a test of the individual.

One such broad based study was undertaken by Axt et al. (2014) using data from the Harvard IAT website, which restricted the participants to American citizens or residents yet still had over 97,000 participants, who provided their own ethnic group identification. Participants undertook a number of IATs online, comparing the ethnic groups, White, Black, Asian and Hispanic. The results showed a degree of in-group bias, favouring their own group, but a consistent pattern of preference was discovered across all participant groups: White, Asian, Hispanic and Blacks (from high to low preference). In a second study on religion, with just over 350,000 participants, they again found an in-group bias, but, once more a consistent pattern of preferences for all participant groups: Christianity, Judaism, Hinduism and Islam, or Christianity, Judaism, Buddhism and Islam (dependent on whether Hinduism or Buddhism was included in the categories). In a final study, with just under 50,000 participants, they found a consistent age hierarchy across all participant groups: young adults, middle-aged adults, old adults. Axt et al. (2014) concluded that the hierarchies can be related to the social structure of the culture, and suggested that the implicit associations reflected the accumulation of experience (in that culture). The results indicated that citizens of the United States, regardless of their ethnicity, religion or age, have all learnt the social hierarchies existing within the structure of their culture. Consequently, Hinton (2017) argued that rather than referring to IAT results as an unconscious or implicit 'bias' these learnt patterns of association should be more appropriately termed 'culture in mind' (see also Shore, 1996).

Replacing 'biased' people with 'fair' artificial intelligence systems

The view that even 'good people' have 'hidden biases' (Banaji and Greenwald, 2013) presents a difficult problem for society. In a modern democratic society, it is hoped that people in positions of responsibility, such as doctors, teachers or judges, are all good people. Indeed, complex systems are set up in recruitment and employment to select and monitor the chosen individuals so that they are suitable for their roles and continue to carry them out appropriately and uphold the values of the society. However, despite their allegiance to these values and their dedication to undertake their tasks according to principles of fairness and equality, if these people are subject to 'hidden biases' that they themselves are unaware of, then their competence is called into question. There are two ways of dealing with this. The 'biased' human beings can be replaced in their decision-making by computerized artificial intelligence systems that are assumed to be fair. Alternatively, attempts can be made to train the 'biases' out of the individuals (see below).

Artificial intelligence (AI) systems operate by using standard procedures, called algorithms, so that they always operate in the same way, according to clear principles. Furthermore, they can engage in *machine learning* using Bayesian statistical methods. Once the system has been set up, and fed the appropriate data, it will make decisions according to what it has learnt. By definition, an AI system has no hidden biases and, if allowed to make the decisions, this removes the 'biased' human completely out of the process. Taking the human decision-maker out of the system is assumed to make the system fairer. This was precisely what was done by the introduction of an AI system in the US criminal justice system to predict risks of reoffending and advise on sentencing. Unfortunately, it did not turn out as expected. Angwin et al. (2016) undertook an analysis of 7,000 Florida arrests where the AI system had been used to provide sentencing decisions. While the AI system drew on 137 different measures to make its decision, and was not given any information on the defendant's ethnicity, the sentencing decisions demonstrated a racial bias against Black defendants (Angwin et al., 2016). The AI system appeared to have developed an 'unconscious' or 'implicit' racial 'bias'.[10] Indeed, Dressel and Farid (2018) also showed that the same criminal justice AI system made similar judgements to ordinary people (i.e. untrained in legal decision-making) on 1,000 cases examined. How is it that a fair AI system can be as 'biased' as people? Claiming that the algorithms are in some way 'faulty' implies a post hoc interpretation of systems designed to follow clearly defined procedures. However, if we look at what a good AI system does, it learns associative patterns in the data given to it to make predictions (according to Bayesian principles). It makes decisions based on these learnt patterns of association. An AI system is simply picking up the associations present in the data. Just as the people in the Axt et al. (2014) studies demonstrated their learning of the social hierarchies in American culture, the AI system was picking up the patterns of association from the data (culture). In fact the AI system was operating like people do – or people are operating like AI systems (Dressel and Farid, 2018). These results indicate that the 'bias' is not in the people (or the AI system) but in the data they are given: the bias lies in the culture. To make the AI system 'fair' (i.e. operate according to egalitarian values – see Chapter 6), it would have to be specifically programmed not to employ the associations present in the culture that has societal discrimination within it.

Training to remove unconscious 'bias'

An alternative to replacing 'biased' people by 'fair' AI systems is to seek to train the 'bias' out of the people. Not surprisingly this has generated an industry of anti-bias training. However, the model of the mind outlined in this chapter indicates that short-term training may well be ineffective. Devine (1989) suggested that it is hard to change learnt associations, like changing a habit, and Devine et al. (2012) argued that any interventions, to be effective, must be intensive and long term to have any effect. However, recall that Bargh (1999) argued that while you can cut back the dandelions they will keep growing back until they are ripped up by their roots. That is, as long as discrimination exists within the culture, people will continue to learn about it. It is only when the discrimination disappears from the culture that the associations will no longer be relevant to a person's cultural knowledge. Unfortunately, evidence supports this pessimistic view of short-term training. For example, Lai et al. (2016) examined nine different interventions to try and change the 'racial' IAT results of their participants, such as exposure to counter-stereotypical examples or priming multiculturalism, and even deliberately trying to manipulate the IAT to produce contrary results. In one example, the participants read a vivid story imagining walking alone at night and being violently assaulted by a White man and rescued by a Black man. Overall, the various techniques all had some effect, with the story more effective than some others; but the most important finding was that subsequent testing demonstrated that any beneficial effects (reducing the implicit 'bias' on the IAT) had disappeared within a day or two.

In a meta-analysis of 492 intervention studies to change implicit bias, Forscher et al. (2019) found that most studies involved single-session manipulations that tended not to be particularly effective. Indeed, the overall conclusion to the meta-analysis was that implicit measures can be changed but the effects are weak. More importantly they did not find any change in explicit measures of behaviour, consequent on changes in implicit measures. This leads to the question as to what is most effective in workplace training to bring about less bias, and a more diverse workforce. In a study examining 30 years of data from 800 US firms employing a broad range of methods for promoting diversity, Dobbin and Kalev (2016, p. 60) were very clear: 'strategies for controlling bias – which drive most diversity efforts – have failed spectacularly since they were introduced to promote equal opportunities'. They argued that '[t]he positive effects of diversity training rarely last beyond a day or two, and a number of studies suggest that it can activate bias or spark a backlash' (Dobbin and Kalev 2016, p. 54). Voluntary training was significantly more effective than mandatory training. Effective strategies to encourage a reduction in bias, and an increase in diversity, involved greater engagement with the issues, promoting social accountability, mentoring, developing self-managed teams, cross-training (across departments) and targeted recruitment strategies. Specifically a number of these factors relate to the encouraging of positive contact between diverse groups (Dobbin and Kalev, 2016, 2018; see also Chapter 4 on the contact hypothesis).

The risk of psychologizing culture

It is completely understandable that American psychologists wish to explain – and ameliorate – the social ills of their society. Over the last 100 years, the psychological construct of the 'stereotype' has been the centre of their work on prejudice related to societal discrimination, focused on the workings of the individual mind. The classical model presented overtly expressed stereotypes as seemingly diagnostic of a hidden hostility lurking beneath the conscious surface – of even 'well-adjusted' and 'normal' female psychology students expressing negative stereotypes at a time when it was socially acceptable to do so. Major political struggles have taken place over that same century to bring about wide-ranging changes to the culture along with civil rights legislation in support of discriminated-against groups. This cultural change has brought about a significant reduction in the public expression of overt negative stereotypes concerning discriminated-against groups in the society. Yet issues of societal discrimination remain current. In the twenty-first century the focus of the psychological research into stereotypes turned to implicit stereotypes, revealed by the implicit association test, which appeared to be diagnostic of a hidden bias lurking beneath the conscious surface – of the even the most egalitarian and non-prejudiced individuals (seeking to behave fairly according to their egalitarian beliefs). Both these psychological models have presented the human mind as problematic (faulty or biased) in the explanation of stereotypes. In seeking to understand stereotypes through a focus on the individual mind, and on stereotypes related to societal discrimination, there has been a tendency to remove the focus from the structure of the culture in the formation of associations between social groups and attributes. However, what the cognitive research has demonstrated is that people are cultural beings, learning the myriad associations and social relationships present in their culture. As cultural associations, stereotypes have a social significance within a particular culture. They are constructed in a society by a particular group of people for a particular purpose at a particular historical time (Pickering, 2001) and they can subsequently be widely circulated in the communication of that culture, as will be explored in the rest of this book. By seeming to distil the complex fabric of culture into an individual cognitive 'problem' (a fault or a bias), the historical, sociological and political significance of these learnt cultural associations, or generalizations labelled as 'stereotypes', is potentially diminished.

Notes

1 Selected by 78 per cent of the participants in Katz and Braly (1933).
2 Although occasionally, in an animated conversation, we lose track of the dealing and have to stop and focus on it to recover our place.
3 Plato argued that 'real' knowledge involved justified true beliefs. For example, the belief that Lyons is the capital of France is a false belief. The belief that Paris is the capital of France is true but unjustified if the explanation is that it is the largest city in the country. Only Paris as the capital, as the seat of the French government, is a justified true belief. A person's semantic memory may contain any of these three forms of 'knowledge'.
4 If 90 per cent of nurses in a culture were men then the predictive brain will learn an association between nurses and men.
5 The IAT has also been employed to examine attitudes by the association of a bipolar concept (e.g. Black and White) with an evaluation (such as good and bad). These implicit attitudes are discussed in Chapter 4.
6 http://implicit.harvard.edu.
7 One criticism of the test's individual diagnosticity is that it may not be reliable: Lopez (2017) reports taking the test online and producing different results on different days.

8 The famous African American civil rights leader.

9 Underlying the debate was also a liberal–conservative ideological argument in the United States as to the state of racial discrimination in that society, with Tetlock and Mitchell (2009) critical of a 'static interventionist' view, which, they argued, has produced an ideological bias in the interpretation of the IAT. Jost et al. (2009, p. 54) identified the static interventionist view as referring to a liberal political viewpoint, and explicitly described a member of the Tetlock group as an 'outspoken conservative'.

10 Further evidence showed that 'biases' were emerging in other AI systems employed to replace the human decision-maker: for example, an employment AI system demonstrated bias against women and in favour of men (e.g. Dastin, 2018).

4

STEREOTYPES, PREJUDICE AND SOCIAL GROUPS

Prejudice and discrimination

Allport ([1954] 1979, p. 20) acknowledged that prejudgement based on categorization is a normal feature of human cognition: 'The human mind must think with the aid of categories (the term is equivalent here to *generalizations*). Once formed, categories are the basis for normal prejudgement. We cannot possibly avoid the process. Orderly living depends upon it.' Indeed, Bodenhausen et al. (2007, p. 123) argued that 'categorization lies at the heart of social perception'. Placing a person into a social category provides a basis for prediction. If we did not have prejudgement the world would be a confusing and dangerous place that it would be almost impossible to navigate through. For Fox (1992) our evolutionary history has led us to develop prejudgement, the ability to predict how the physical and social worlds operate, so we can act pragmatically. This can be considered as the ability to generalize, to learn associations present in the environment. Thus, many of our prejudgements about the social world will involve cultural knowledge and beliefs about the behaviour of the members of social groups according to their societally determined roles (see Chapter 5): we expect nurses to care for the sick and teachers to educate the young. Therefore, understanding the social world is about discriminating between people, usually on the basis of a social group membership, to determine what goes with what; that is, what attributes are associated with the group in this culture. For example, we categorize one person as a doctor and another as a plumber, and then expect them to behave according to our expectations. If we have a medical problem we contact a doctor (and not a plumber) and if we have a problem with a domestic water supply we will call a plumber (and not a doctor). However, in learning the social categories present in their culture, a person acquires more than simply facts about the groups (such as doctors prescribe drugs and plumbers repair pipes) but they also acquire additional cultural associations concerning the social group present in their culture, such as stereotypes of doctors and plumbers: such as doctors are confident, decisive and dedicated but arrogant (Carpenter, 1995) and plumbers are sometimes viewed as unprofessional (turn up late, wear dirty clothes and don't keep their promises).[1] Indeed, the stereotype that plumbers are male may be learnt by children from their own experience, as a gendered phenomenon in their society where plumbers are typically men (Liben, 2017). This learning from culture about social groups may or may not involve accurate generalizations (for example, if most doctors are not arrogant or most plumbers are professional) but they are clearly commonly known representations of the social groups in the society.

The problem of certain cultural stereotypes with negative associations is that, in a society seeking accuracy and fairness, it is argued that these stereotypes can lead to negative discrimination – people being *discriminated against* in areas in which they are perfectly capable, i.e. they face unfair restrictions in the society. In a simple case, a householder might choose to attempt a plumbing repair themselves (which they are not competent to perform) and not employ a plumber (who is competent to undertake the repair successfully) due to a negative stereotypical belief about plumbers. Or, a householder employs a male plumber and not a female plumber on the cultural stereotype that plumbing is a 'male job' (see Chapter 1). Thus, what is typically referred to by the term 'prejudice' is not simply a prejudgement, but a negative view of the members of a specific social group that (presumably) leads to discrimination against them in the society. For Allport ([1954] 1979, p. 6) prejudice, as an issue of social concern, is an irrational antipathy, a negative attitude without proper justification: 'thinking ill of others without sufficient warrant'. For example, a person who has a negative opinion of welfare claimants might also express the stereotype that they are lazy. Thus, the negative attitude (prejudice) and the stereotype combine to justify discrimination against the group – which can be argued is both inaccurate – the group is not typically lazy – and unfair – these are some of the most disadvantaged people in society (see Chapter 1). Not surprisingly, therefore, academic analyses of prejudice – against a specific social group – (e.g. Allport, [1954] 1979; Brown, 2010) usually includes a detailed examination of the stereotypes about them.

Allport ([1954] 1979) argued that prejudice concerns a social group ('others'), so one person's dislike of another individual for idiosyncratic reasons is not normally considered prejudice. Prejudice involves an antipathy against a social group, such as holding racist or sexist attitudes. A key point here is that prejudice is directed against a social group typically by members of another social group. As Allport ([1954] 1979) also pointed out, people tend to favour groups that they belong to and are prejudiced against groups to which they do not belong. This explains why Brown (1965, p. 181) argued that stereotypes are not objectionable because they are generalizations, or because they might be false, or even because we have learnt them from other people rather than through direct experience. He argued that they are objectionable due to their ethnocentrism: they are group-centred and the stereotyped group is viewed as inferior on a relevant characteristic pertinent to a social judgement, by the members of a group stereotyping them. Thus, the stereotype is employed by a specific group of people to deny the members of another social group equal status, and stereotyping (and the intergroup prejudice) can be considered an intergroup phenomenon. Traditionally in psychology, prejudice has been viewed as an aspect of personality (the prejudiced or authoritarian personality: see Chapter 2). Brown (2010) challenged this view for three reasons. It ignores the social context of people's attitudes, which are typically similar to other members of a social group. It ignores the broader cultural context where certain attitudes are acceptable or not acceptable in a particular society at any one time. It also ignores the historical changes in prejudice with changing sociocultural (and political) circumstances: prejudice against social groups can change over time within a culture. Brown (2010, p. 7) argued for a more general view of prejudice as 'any attitude, emotion or behaviour, towards members of a group, which directly or indirectly implies some negativity or antipathy towards that group'. He also argued that the term 'prejudice' should not be restricted to a purely cognitive phenomenon but that terms such as racism and sexism can be included within the umbrella term of 'prejudice'. Prejudice therefore may not be a 'fixed' concept and, furthermore, there may be different forms or degrees of prejudice (Brown, 2010). Thus, the question of attitudes as an individual or group phenomenon will be discussed in this chapter.

In modern Western liberal democratic societies, based on values of equality and the universal rights of adult citizens (see Chapter 6), the expression of prejudice against a social group is seen as violating those basic values, and related to societal discrimination. Consequently, employment legislation has been enacted to outlaw this form of discrimination and in, some cases, the expression of related negative stereotypes. This has been done by distinguishing between unlawful and lawful discrimination. Unlawful discrimination is about treating members of one group less favourably than members of other groups based on a certain designated personal attributes. For example, in the United States, Civil Rights Acts specify that advantaging a member of one social group over another based on *protected classes* (ethnicity, religion, national origin, age, sex, familial status, disability status, veteran status and genetic information), in areas such as employment, is unlawful discrimination. Thus, the rejection of a candidate for a job simply on the basis of their membership of one of these categories is illegal. Underlying unlawful discrimination is that it is based on negative attitudes and stereotypes (see Chapter 1 on gender stereotyping). However, other characteristics can be the basis of lawful discrimination, as these are considered justifiable on reasonable grounds, such as health and safety or competence. For example, a child, a blind person or an unqualified pilot are not allowed to fly passenger airplanes. In all other cases of discrimination in the workplace, such as choosing a candidate for a position, the selection has to be directly based on justifiable criteria, such as qualifications and relevant performance measures to avoid unfair discrimination. Just as Fiske and Taylor (2017) argued that overt stereotypes are rarely expressed in modern Western societies but subtle (implicit) stereotypes continue to influence people (see Chapter 3), Brown (2010) also pointed out that indirect aspects or subtle forms of prejudice may be more difficult to determine, and potentially more problematic, than the obvious negative expressions of prejudice that were more common in the past, and less so today. This means that in the United States and other Western liberal democracies there is considerable concern about 'hidden' forms of unjustified discrimination (in employment practices for example) particularly if this involves protected class discrimination. Consider the following illustration. An orchestra recruits new members and each candidate is tested on their musical skill by playing a particular piece. This is a reasonable (i.e. justifiable) assessment for such a role. However, it is observed that the orchestra is predominantly men and over a significant period of time mostly men are recruited. It is theoretically possible that the male candidates are generally better musicians, but this appears to be a case of gender discrimination, violating the equality assumption. This can be easily tested. If, instead of the selection panel observing the musician performing the piece directly, the judgement is made with the candidate behind a screen, then any anti-female prejudice in the musical judgement will be avoided as the candidate's gender is no longer discernible. Now if more female candidates are selected, this provides evidence that the previous judgements did involve gender discrimination. The inference that follows is that the panel (whether they were aware of it or not) were discriminating against female candidates. While it might be a case of overt prejudice – the male panel members do not want women in their orchestra – it could be some form of subtle prejudice or implicit 'bias' (see Chapter 3) based on a musician stereotype associating gender to musical competence.

Attitudes, stereotypes and prejudice

Greenwald et al. (2002, p. 5) presented the following definition of a stereotype: 'A stereotype is the association of a social group concept with one or more (nonvalence) attribute concepts.' This is identical to Schneider's (2004) definition – see Chapter 1 – but including the term 'valence', which in psychology refers to an emotional reaction. Liking and attraction are positively valenced emotions, and disliking and antipathy are negatively valenced emotions. Thus, a stereotype is an association but not the emotional reaction associated with it. Associating old age with frailty can be considered a stereotypical association; however, viewing old age negatively (compared to youth), is a valenced judgement: it is an attitude. 'An attitude is the association of a social object or social group concept with a valence attribute concept' (Greenwald et al., 2002, p. 5). Typically it is assumed that there will be a degree of consistency, that is, a psychological tendency or learnt disposition, in a person's reaction to the attitudinal object or social group (e.g. Eagly and Chaiken, 1993; Fishbein and Ajzen, 1975). An attitude is not a one-off judgement but a generalized evaluative opinion about a person, object or event, that we expect to be exhibited consistently in their talk and behaviour. Therefore an attitude, as an association and an evaluation, can be considered as a general tendency to act in a particular way towards the attitudinal object. An American might have enjoyed speaking to a French person at a party, but this does not reveal their attitude towards French people *in general*, as there are numerous reasons why the conversation went well, such as discovering a shared interest in a music genre. However, if the person consistently seeks out French people, and has many French friends, we are more likely to assume that they have a positive attitude towards French people (as a social group). Thus, for prejudice to occur, there must be an attitude (towards a social group) related to a belief (about the social group). For example, a person has an antipathy towards members of a certain political party. This involves both an attitude ('I don't like them') and a belief statement ('they are a bunch of crooks').

Attitudes and behaviour

There is a common assumption that attitudes are reflected in behaviour. This is why the expression of negative stereotypes is considered such a bad thing, as it is assumed that the person will have a tendency to act in a discriminatory way towards the stereotyped social group. There is the assumption of attitude–behaviour consistency (e.g. Smith and Terry, 2003). However, this may be quite complex to determine. Consider the person who expresses a positive attitude towards physical exercise: they claim that is good for you. They say that they like to exercise, and they go regularly to a gym. This association of an object (exercise), a valence (the person likes it) and behaviour (they do it often) led to the three component model of attitudes: an attitude has a cognitive, affective and behavioural component (Eagly and Chaiken, 1993; Rosenberg and Hovland, 1960). This model implicitly assumes that an attitude will be manifested in all three components; which has happened with this case. However, for various reasons people may act in ways that are not concordant with their expressed views (Fazio and Olson, 2003), making the determination of a person's 'attitude' potentially difficult. Consider a person who says that 'exercise is good for you', as they know, by learning from their culture, of the positive health benefits of exercise, the value of exercise for children and importance of a healthy workforce. However, they actually never exercise themselves. In this case, the person is expressing a socially approved-of attitude but not one that is consistent with their own behaviour.

We can see this issue in a seminal study about attitudes towards the Chinese in 1930s California. At this time, it was socially acceptable to express anti-Chinese sentiments. Throughout the second half of the nineteenth century, the Californian state legislature had passed a number of anti-Chinese laws. In 1882, the national Chinese Exclusion Act prohibited all Chinese immigration (repealed in 1943). A 1906 Anti-Miscegenation Law prohibited Chinese marrying non-Chinese (nullified in 1948) and the 1913 Alien Land Laws prohibited their ownership of land (ruled as unconstitutional in 1947). Thus, in the 1930s there had been over 80 years of institutional anti-Chinese discrimination in Californian society. In a well-known study, LaPiere (1934) examined the relationship between anti-Chinese attitudes and the behaviour of people in the hospitality trade in California. For example, he booked into 'the "best" hotel in a small town noted for its narrow and bigoted "attitude" towards Orientals' (LaPiere, 1934, p. 231) with two Chinese companions, a foreign-born Chinese graduate student and his wife. They were accommodated without demur. Two months later, he contacted the hotel and asked if they would accommodate 'an important Chinese gentleman. The reply was an unequivocal "no"' (LaPiere, 1934, p. 231). Over a period of two years, he and his Chinese companions travelled the Pacific Coast and visited 66 places of accommodation (mostly hotels) – being refused only once – and 184 restaurants without complaint. LaPiere concluded that, in these encounters, ethnicity was less important than other factors. His companions were well dressed, socially skilled and spoke unaccented English. Six months later, he sent questionnaires to the establishments asking if they would accept 'members of the Chinese race'. He received over 120 responses, with over 90 per cent stating that they would not. LaPiere's study had showed that the expression of a negative and, at that time, socially acceptable attitude (in the questionnaire) by a hotel or restaurant staff member – presumably associated with a stereotype of the Chinese – was not predictive of the actual behaviour of the restaurant or hotel staff when he and his Chinese companions visited them.

Wicker (1969) examined a wide range of studies that showed discrepancies between expressed attitudes (often determined by questionnaires) and behavioural measures of interaction with group members (as in LaPiere's study), including studies of White employees with respect to Black employees and White college students with respect to Black college students. This analysis revealed the complexity of the attitude–behaviour relationship: questionnaire measures might be revealing accurate assessments of a generalized attitude but this may only be marginally influential in predicting actual behaviour in a specific situation, where a wide range of other factors may be more dominant (Wicker, 1969). There are personal, social and situational factors that influence behaviour as well as a particular attitude. For example, a hotel clerk's sense of responsibility for good customer service might dominate any general antipathy towards a particular social group, especially if they are well dressed and well mannered, as LaPiere's companions were. Thus, the expression of an attitude (inferring a negative stereotype) does not necessarily predict behaviour in a particular context. Wicker (1969) argued that caution should be exercised when making untested claims about the social significance of attitude findings (from questionnaire-type studies). While the topic of the study – the object of the attitude research – may be socially significant, the results of the study might not be, in terms of behavioural predictions. Second, attitude measures (such as questionnaires) need rigorous testing to make sure that they are genuinely associated with the behaviours of interest, rather than simply measuring a particular type of verbal response. Finally, researchers need to focus more on the different influences on behaviour, their variety and importance, rather than assuming a simple direct attitude–behaviour link.

This is what Fishbein and Ajzen endeavoured to do. They argued that attitudes cannot predict what people actually do (specific behaviour) but, rather, what they intend to do (behavioural intentions); as specific actions may depend on very specific circumstances (Ajzen and Fishbein, 1980; Fishbein and Ajzen, 1974). For example, a person may intend to give to a poverty-relief charity appeal but suddenly realize that they have left their wallet at home, so cannot contribute. However, behavioural intentions are not influenced by just attitudes but also the person's subjective norms;

that is, what they believe to be the socially appropriate behaviour in the situation (Ajzen, 1991). Finally, their attitude towards the behaviour itself also influences the behavioural intention, such as a positive attitude towards charitable giving. These factors combine to form a behavioural intention (that they will give to the charity), which may result in the actual behaviour. However, as Ajzen (1985) pointed out, people's behaviour is also influenced by beliefs about their ability to perform certain actions or not. Ajzen (1991) referred to this as perceived behavioural control, such as their ability to get to the appeal location. These factors are combined in the *theory of planned behaviour* (Ajzen, 1991). The success of the model has been shown in a number of areas, in such as predicting when charitable donations will be made (Kashif et al., 2015; Smith and McSweeney, 2007). Its importance to prejudice research is that, while accepting a link from attitudes to behaviour, it emphasizes that this is not a simple direct relationship. Expressed attitudes – associated with particular stereotypes – may predict behavioural intentions, but actual behaviour may also reflect other factors, such as an awareness of socially approved of attitudes that they may or may not hold themselves.

Explicit and implicit attitudes

The theory of planned behaviour argued that behavioural intentions are conscious and worked out 'reasonably' from attitudes, subjective norms and subjective control. But as we saw in the last chapter, conscious mental processing takes time, effort and motivation, and learnt stereotypical associations can be activated automatically. With the advent of experimental techniques such as the implicit association test (IAT; see Chapter 3), there was the possibility of revealing 'hidden' implicit attitudes as well as implicit associations. Just as the IAT can be used to examine stereotypical associations (such as young–old with healthy–unhealthy), it can also be used to examine implicit attitudes by associating social groups with evaluations (such as young–old with good–bad). Whereas an explicit statement of a person's attitude may be consciously thought out, such as when filling in a questionnaire, in other circumstances an implicit attitude might be more influential on behaviour (Fazio, 1990; Greenwald and Banaji, 1995). Fazio (1990) argued that people may have well thought out beliefs about a social group, which leads to the rational, conscious expression of their attitude towards its members, indicating how they intend to act (resulting in attitude–behaviour consistency). This agrees with the theory of planned behaviour (discussed above). However, the person has to be motivated and have the opportunity to engage in conscious deliberation for this consistency to arise. When this is not the case, implicit attitudes, like other learnt associations, might be automatically activated in the presence of the attitudinal object. Fazio (1990) argued that when there is no opportunity for conscious processing there may be a direct relationship between implicit attitudes and behaviour either as an immediate reaction (Fazio and Olson, 2014, give the example of a 'yuk' reaction) or indirectly, acting as 'a filter through which the object is viewed' (Fazio and Olson, 2014, p. 155). This model is referred to as the MODE model, from *Motivation and*

Opportunity in DEtermining the attitude–behaviour link. This is another example of a dual process cognitive model (Chaiken and Trope, 1999; see Chapter 3). However, Fazio and Olson (2014) do not see them as independent systems, but the two processes operate together and the dominance of one over the other depends on the motivation and opportunity for conscious processing. Fazio and Olson (2014) agree that attitudes are often learnt associations, as discussed earlier, but point out that attitudes can also develop through conscious reasoning. Furthermore, they argued that attitudes differ along a continuum of their accessibility. Some highly learnt attitudes may be automatically activated, such as a negative view of cockroaches compared to puppies (Fazio et al., 1986), especially in the context of spotting one in a restaurant (Ewoldsen et al., 2015). At the other end of the continuum there may not be an established attitude at all (maybe towards unfamiliar groups, such as actuaries or Greenlanders). Other attitudes might require cognitive effort to access (such as a person's attitude towards government funding of space exploration). Consequently, an attitude can only influence behaviour once it has been activated.

Other researchers have also made a distinction between implicit attitudes and explicit attitudes (Gawronski and Bodenhausen, 2006, 2007). Implicit attitudes are learnt associations between an attitudinal object with an evaluation. For example, if a social group (e.g. migrants) is always represented negatively in a person's experience (in news reports, other media information and in the communication more generally in their culture) then a negative evaluation, associating migrants with negative consequences of immigration, will be learnt as an implicit attitude. Explicit attitudes are conscious (reasoned) evaluations of the available information such as weighing up the costs and benefits of immigration to a society. Clearly the two types of attitudes are not independent as they may influence each other and also depend on the information available to the person. Indeed, Fazio and Olson (2014) argued that there is often a high degree of consistency between explicit and implicit measures in attitudinal situations. People may consciously hold the same attitudes as those commonly expressed – and learnt implicitly – from their culture. However, this is not necessarily the case. Ewoldsen et al. (2015) identified the issue as concerning attitudes about socially sensitive topics (such as racial attitudes) and whether implicit attitudes influence social responses (see also Echabe, 2013). When a person is able to exert conscious control, then 'individuals with racist attitudes are often motivated to mask their true feelings so as to not appear prejudiced' (Ewoldsen et al., 2015, p. 324). A prejudiced individual, aware of the social undesirability of their personal attitude, may be able to supress to it in explicit attitudinal responses (such as a questionnaire) to avoid social disapproval but – so it is argued – not in an implicit measure, such as the implicit association test (see Chapter 3); with the implication that the IAT is revealing the 'hidden' or 'real' attitudes of the individual. However, as pointed out in Chapter 3, this tendency in the literature to represent implicit associations as an individual's 'real' beliefs may not be the case. An implicit attitude may reflect a learnt cultural association between a social group and evaluation (such as 'terrorists are bad') rather than an individual's attitude towards a particular revolutionary group. Furthermore, in the LaPiere (1934) study it was socially expected that the hotels and restaurant workers would show anti-Chinese prejudice. Yet they only did this in their questionnaire responses (assumed to be under conscious control) and not when the Chinese couple were standing in front of them. This highlights the fact that attitudes towards social groups need to be contextualized by the prevailing political ideology of the culture. In 1930s California there were laws institutionalizing anti-Chinese discrimination so, in that context, the expression of anti-Chinese feeling was a socially accepted view. In the twenty-first century the expression of anti-Chinese feeling is not socially approved of, and discrimination that was once legal is now illegal, and this will be reflected in the learnt attitudinal associations (see Chapter 6).

Thus, there is a genuine question as to whether implicit or explicit attitudinal measures reflect a person's 'true feelings'. There is also the methodological question of what is actually being examined by the different assessment techniques. Echabe (2013) criticized the distinction between implicit attitudes and explicit attitudes, arguing that there are structural differences in the assessment formats; for example, the participants often do not know what is being tested in the implicit measures, which can appear ambiguous and require rapid responses, whereas the measures of explicit attitudes are unambiguous and are not time constrained. The experimental methodology may influence the implicit response, such as the particular contrast set up in the experiment. Comparing contrasting groups (such as White–Black or men–women) on the good–bad dimension are often interpreted as indicating evidence of an implicit attitude in line with known societal discrimination. However, consider an English person living in France and genuinely loving all things French (such as author Lawrence Durrell mentioned in Chapter 1). They might show faster reaction times for English–good and French–bad due to a learnt preference for their own nationality. However, this does not indicate that they have a 'hidden' implicit anti-French attitude. Inferring that a reaction-time difference (associating a social group with good or bad) indicates a 'real' personal attitude can be problematic for other reasons, as the association is not necessarily a 'personal' antipathy but a reflection of the known social hierarchy of privilege in a culture. For example, a social group might be classified as good as they are favoured in the society (high status) and a second group is classified as bad are they are clearly not favoured in the society (low status). As Axt et al. (2014), pointed out, these results might simply show knowledge of the social relationship (advantage or disadvantage) between social groups within society. For example, a culture that is constantly representing Muslims in a negative way is likely to result in a person learning an implicit cultural association of Muslims and negativity, regardless of their own views about the religious group (Echabe, 2013).

This leads to the question of how relevant it is to know about people's attitudes, either implicit or explicit, and the stereotypical associations supporting them, in combatting societal discrimination that has potentially brought about those associations. By locating the cause of expressed attitudes in individual psychology, it may underestimate the role of social institutions in maintaining societal discrimination (Chaiklin, 2011). To reduce discrimination it may be more effective to change society (and people's behaviour) by institutional means (such as legislation), rather than seeking to change commonly held attitudes first. To illustrate this, Chaiklin (2011, p. 47) quoted Dr Martin Luther King Jr, who pointed out: 'The law cannot make an employer love me, but it can keep him from refusing to hire me because of the color of my skin.' Furthermore, rather than behaviour being determined by attitudes, attitudes may follow from behaviour (Bem, 1972). Changing the structure of a society (by changing legislation and social practices) may result in a significant change of attitudes in that society (Chaiklin, 2011; Weber and Crocker, 1983; see also Diekman and Eagly, 2000). For example, there has been considerable social change throughout the twentieth century in Western societies, and current social attitudes are very different to those of 50 years ago (as shown by evidence such as the General Social Survey in the United States and the British Social Attitudes survey).

Implicit prejudice

In the second decade of the twenty-first century, a topic of public concern in the United States was the shooting of unarmed young Black men by police officers. To examine whether there was an implicit bias in police officers' rapid interpretation of an ambiguous situation, Correll and his colleagues (2002), in a series of studies, employed the following laboratory reaction-time set-up, similar to a first-person shooter task in a video game. Participants sat before a screen showing a realistic everyday street scene empty of people. An image of a man would appear on the screen either holding a gun or another object (such as a cell phone). The participant's task was to press one key – labelled the 'shoot' key – if he was holding a gun and a second key – labelled the 'don't shoot' key – if he was not. Speed and accuracy of responding were measured, and after each trial the participants received feedback – points for accurate and rapid responses (within a certain brief period) or penalty points for inaccurate or slow responses. Participants were given less than a second to respond, either 850 milliseconds or, in another study, 630 milliseconds (Correll et al., 2014). The results were clear. The participants, American undergraduates and adult non-students (Correll et al., 2002) and police officers (Correll et al., 2007), regardless of their own ethnicity showed a consistent tendency to press 'shoot' more quickly for a Black gunman and 'don't shoot' more quickly for an unarmed White man. Mistakes were also consistent: they pressed 'don't shoot' more for a White gunman, and 'shoot' more for an unarmed Black man. Crucially, this demonstrated that the implicit bias was not a specific attitude of a few prejudiced individuals but consistent across the different groups tested within the culture.

Even though there is the question of assuming that this form of laboratory task can be associated with the 'real-world' context of police activity, it did show a consistent result for the various participants that required explanation. Correll et al. (2014) concluded that the participants employed a more lenient criterion to shoot for Black targets. Obviously, given the social context of the research, the performance of police officers was of specific interest. However, as Correll et al. (2014) point out, the police may be less biased than other citizens due to their firearms training and experience or more biased due to their occupational socialization and focus on criminal activities, often associated with minority groups. Indeed, in a comparison of police officers and adult members of the community (Correll et al., 2007), the police officers were more accurate in their decisions, and less biased in their errors than other participant groups, although still influenced by a 'racial bias' in their response times. Practice improved the performance of the community participants, which tended to make their results more like those of the police. Correll et al. (2014) argued that all participants are influenced by the negative stereotype associating Black men with guns (more specifically, with gun crime in US culture). However, the effect of this implicit bias can be mitigated (to some extent) by conscious control. Interestingly, they found that 'beat cops' (those who patrol a familiar location), such as those in their 2007 study, did not show a bias in their errors but 'special-unit' officers showed the same bias as community members (Sim et al., 2013). Correll et al. (2014) explained this difference by arguing that the beat cops deal with a wide range of people in a wide range of circumstances, both perpetrators and victims of crime as well as other citizens, which developed their knowledge of the diversity of people on their beat, which can be interpreted as training their conscious control. However, special-unit police take a proactive approach to street crimes, such as conducting drug raids, or stop-and-search of suspects, which often means that their work involves a very specific minority of the population.

While this evidence showed the positive effect of training, with non-police participants reducing their bias by training and performing similarly to the beat cops, the effects of training for the community participants tended to be short lived (Correll et al., 2014, see also Chapter 3). More importantly, there are a range of factors that make conscious control much harder to exert in the real-world context, such as stress, fatigue or when performing an additional task (referred to as a cognitive 'load'). In a study by Correll et al. (2014), one group of participants – the expert group – were given practice on the task to reduce their implicit bias, whereas another group – the novice group – were not. The expected difference in performance was found, with less bias in the expert group. However, when the participants had to perform an ongoing memory task with numbers, the expert performance deteriorated. With a high cognitive load, an expert was no better than a novice in the no-load condition. Correll et al. (2014) argued that the research revealed that, when people are in a position where they are required to respond quickly, in what may be an ambiguous situation, the influence of other cues in the environment, such as race, may result in a response bias due to learnt stereotypical associations, linking these cues to the expectation of threat. In the laboratory situation, the beat cops tended to be more accurate than ordinary citizens, but it is also important to note that the laboratory is different to the ordinary working environment of the police. Correll et al. (2014) noted that sleep deprivation is an issue for police officers who may be dealing with incidents in the night-time. In addition to fatigue, fear and arousal may also be present in a real-life incident; with all these factors having a negative effect on the ability to exert conscious control of automatic responses. As they point out, training in calm conditions may be ineffective in actual events, where these factors are present. They concluded that training may be required in more realistic situations to be effective. They also argued that being aware of the stereotypical bias, and employing conscious thought to exert control over these automatic associations, referred to as 'implementation intentions' can also improve accuracy. However, despite these attempts to undermine this implicit prejudice through training, the significant finding of this research is that the 'racial bias' was a widespread learnt association rather than an individual antipathy.

Unwitting racism: the police investigation of the murder of Stephen Lawrence

The issue of implicit stereotypical expectations about race was starkly revealed in the police investigation in Britain of the murder of Black teenager Stephen Lawrence in 1993. Stephen and his friend Duwayne Brookes were waiting for a bus in South London, on their way home. Stephen was 18 years old and was hoping to train as an architect. They were attacked by a group of five young White men who stabbed Stephen to death. The attackers and victims were completely unknown to each other and the only possible explanation was that it was an unprovoked racist murder. The following day the police received, anonymously, the names of the suspects. However, as time passed there began to be concerns about the police investigation. Suspects were arrested but charges were dropped, and there were no convictions. In 1997 the British government ordered an investigation into the police investigation, headed by retired judge Sir William MacPherson, with a focus on the question of racism in the police. The report was published in 1999 (MacPherson, 1999), accusing the police of institutional racism, and presenting 70 recommendations for change. The report noted how police officers had treated Duwayne Brooks not as a victim and witness but in terms of their negative stereotypes of young Black men, with one officer assuming that there had been a fight at the scene, not a murder. The report stated: 'Mr Brookes was by some officers side-lined and ignored, because of racist stereotyping particularly at the scene and at the hospital. He was never properly treated as a victim' (MacPherson, 1999, 46.28vi). Importantly, the report drew on the concepts of 'unwitting', 'unconscious' and 'unintentional' racism (MacPherson, 1999, 6.12). The report rejected the view that the explanation of the problems of the investigation was due to a few 'bad apples' in the police. It argued that there was widespread 'unwitting' racism – which might now be referred to as an 'implicit bias' – resulting partly from the 'racist stereotype of black people as potential criminals or troublemakers' (MacPherson, 1999, 6.17). In seeking to explain this unwitting racism, the report noted that the primarily White police officers may only 'meet members of the black community in confrontational situations' (MacPherson, 1999, 6.27 and also 37.18). Thus, the primary experience of the White police officers of Black citizens was in the highly distorted situation of potential crime. Furthermore, this experience was shared, and appeared to be confirmed, by fellow officers within their 'canteen culture' (MacPherson, 1999, 6.17, 37.24), where the consensus view appeared to validate the negative stereotypical association of Black men and criminality, which was then learnt by new members of the community. To counter this, the report argued for better training of the police, greater and wider community engagement, and more recruitment of police officers from a variety of ethnic backgrounds.

The murder of Stephen Lawrence had revealed two aspects of racism and racist beliefs, the witting and the unwitting. The perpetrators, in the most extreme way, acted out their overt racist views in the appalling murder of an innocent and unknown young man simply on the colour of his skin. Eventually, two of the five perpetrators were convicted of the murder in 2012. Yet the unwitting racism identified in the police by the MacPherson report was of a different order. The police officers were (presumably) endeavouring to carry out their job of the collection of evidence for a criminal conviction, which, in this case, they failed to do appropriately. It was not their individual motivations that were particularly the focus of the report, but the way in which their collective, cultural experiences had led to the acquisition of common racial stereotypical associations that had undermined their performance. Whereas the early work on prejudice had focused on the 'bad apples', the minority of people whose overt views transgressed the values of the majority of society (e.g. Allport, [1954] 1979), the later work on implicit prejudice and such instances of police behaviour has led to much of the research into prejudice focusing on the ways in which cultural group members acquire, and are influenced by, their 'common knowledge', or cultural stereotypes, of the different social groups in the society (see Chapter 5).

In 2018, the British Prime Minister Theresa May instituted a Stephen Lawrence commemoration day on the 22 April every year.

Implicit prejudice: 'bad apples' and 'rotten barrels'

Psychologists in the study of prejudice have often focused their research on the psychology of individuals, such as identifying the authoritarian or prejudiced personality (Adorno et al., 1950; Allport, [1954] 1979). Thus, prejudiced people are often regarded as the 'bad apples' in the 'barrel' of society (Fiske, 2004). This has been a popular metaphor to represent prejudice, with the implication that something needs to be done about the (psychology of the) 'bad apples' to keep the rest of the 'barrel' from going rotten. However, the modern research on implicit prejudice challenges this view. For example, Roets and van Hiel (2011) acknowledged that the open-minded (non-prejudiced) person can automatically 'succumb' to stereotype influence in rapid decision-making (although they will seek a more measured judgement in situations when they can allocate the time and attention to do so). This has resulted in a shift in the focus of the prejudice research more towards the 'barrel' (the group).

The primary implication of the old view was that prejudice is best addressed by changing the hearts and minds of individuals, for good-hearted people will think well of others and behave accordingly. However, research in recent years demonstrates that the old view is incomplete, even dangerously so.

Hardin and Banaji, 2013, p. 13

This was supported by Fiske (2004, p. 119), who stated, 'Unfortunately, for this comfortable account that isolates the problem [of prejudice] in a few bad individuals, the accumulated evidence suggests that most of us are perfectly capable of behaving badly in the relevant context.'Yet this quote evokes two immediate questions: who are the 'most of us' (including presumably Fiske herself) and what does 'behaving badly' mean in this context? An answer to the latter is given by the implicit cognition researchers Hardin and Banaji (2013, p. 15): 'Research ... suggests the ubiquity with which common prejudice and stereotyping operates among all kinds of people along lines laid down by extant social relations on a variety of dimensions.' Thus, implicit prejudice reflects the learnt pattern of social relations, social organization and organizational hierarchies within a culture. The 'us' are members of that culture.

In most aspects of life, learnt associations about societal relations and social organization can be considered as pragmatic and successful cultural knowledge guiding a person's understanding of the social world, such as when to call a doctor or a plumber, or which political party to vote for. The issue of implicit prejudice is when learnt associations are related to the 'socially sensitive topics' (Ewoldsen et al., 2015). For example, there is little or no public concern (in a Western democracy) about the influence of other stereotypical associations, such as that between bankers and greed.[2] This appears to provide the answer to what 'behaving badly' means. From the work of Allport ([1954] 1979) through to the work of Hardin and Banaji (2013), the psychological research has been prefaced with stories of racism in American society. The motivation of the researchers is clear throughout the work: an understandable desire to reduce racism in their culture and bring about a fairer and more egalitarian society. Thus, the problem of implicit prejudice is that people – even those wishing to behave in a fair and egalitarian way – may be influenced in their judgements and behaviour by the (discriminatory) associations that they have learnt from their (discriminatory) society. This shifts the focus of the explanation of implicit prejudice from the individual to the culture. Hardin and Banaji (2013, pp. 22) make this explicit: 'egalitarian societies elicit egalitarian-minded people', and 'we believe that culture-wide changes in implicit prejudice will require culture-wide changes i.e. in social organization and practice' (Hardin and Banaji, 2013, p. 21). They concluded with a plea for greater equality in society:

It is our contention that locating the problem of prejudice in a few problematic individuals and designing solutions to the problem around this view is to miss the point. The profound implication of the discovery of implicit prejudice is that anybody is capable of prejudice, whether they know it or not, and of stereotyping, whether they want to or not. Therefore, given the implicit operation of prejudice and stereotyping and its ubiquitous nature, we believe that solutions should focus on identifying the enabling conditions that call out prejudice and stereotyping across individuals rather than focusing on identifying the rotten apples. Once identified, we must focus on the enabling conditions that promote egalitarianism and healthy individuation.

Hardin and Banaji, 2013, p. 23

Thus, implicit prejudice (as a 'bias') is a not a cognitive 'failing' of the individual (who has learnt about the discriminatory structure of their society), but of a society whose social organization discriminates against specific social groups. The conclusion is a political call for a fairer and more egalitarian society (see Chapter 6).

Implicit prejudice and the problem of intention

In Western societies, a person has legal responsibility for their own actions, except in certain specific circumstances. Indeed, in these individualistic societies, the person is typically viewed as the primary cause of their own behaviour (Ross, 1977; Triandis, 1995). A person overtly behaving in a racist way, such as chanting racist slogans at a political rally, is assumed to be well aware of what they are doing. Any subsequent punishment is based on the assumption that they meant to perform this illegal act (in a society where it is illegal). Legally, responsibility assumes intention (Krieger, 1995). However, how should the legal system deal with a person who claims to be egalitarian in their conscious decisions (and we believe them), but acts in a discriminatory way due to unconscious prejudice ('bias')? A number of authors (such as the MacPherson Report, above, and Hardin and Banaji, 2013) have used the word 'unwitting' to describe this unconscious influence on behaviour, of which people are unaware and do not intend. To what extent can a person be considered as responsible for unwitting behaviour based on implicit learnt cultural associations? In a study by Cameron et al. (2010) participants were given the following situation: a White employer, who consciously wished to be fair in making employment decisions, 'unwittingly' discriminated against African Americans. When told that it was due to a 'gut feeling' that the employer was consciously aware of but found difficult to control, the participants maintained that the employer had responsibility for their actions. However, when it was presented as an unconscious bias, that the employer was unaware of, the attribution of personal responsibility by the participants was lower. A question, therefore, arises as to how a legal system should deal with a case of real-world discrimination that arises from implicit prejudice that the perpetrator was neither consciously aware of, nor intended to occur (Krieger and Fiske, 2006).

Social attitudes: the person and the group

Eysenck (1961) viewed authoritarianism (see Chapter 2) as one form of tough-mindedness (Eckhardt, 1991; Ray and Bozek, 1981) which was assumed to be the personality of the stereotype user in the classical model in Chapter 2. In a study of social attitudes, Eysenck (1961) found extraverts and members of the working class to be higher on tough-mindedness than comparison groups. Whereas, the first result associated a social attitude (tough-mindedness) to personality (extraversion) the second finding related the social attitude to a social group (the working class). How can an attitude be a group-based phenomenon? For Lipset (1960), working-class authoritarianism was brought about by their circumstances, and not predictable from psychological dispositions. Social attitudes are a group-based phenomenon rather than (exclusively) psychological in origin. The combination of deprived or harsh family circumstances, poor education, geographic and employment isolation and especially the economic threats and insecurities (particularly financial) of their lives, all contribute to produce these common social attitudes, in Lipset's view. While Lipset's ideas have been examine and criticized (e.g. Eckhardt, 1991; Houtman, 2003; Napier and Jost, 2008), the key point here is that unlike the early views of Floyd Allport and Katz and Braly (see Chapter 2) that attitudes – particularly those related to stereotypes – resulted from individual psychology (personality), alternative social psychological – and sociological – research indicates that social attitudes are group-based phenomenon (be it police canteen culture or the working class, for example). The importance of the person (who employs a stereotype) *as a member of a specific social group* has been implicit in the stereotyping research, but not always explicit (Allport, [1954] 1979; Brown, 2010) At any time a person is a member of a one social group (referred to as the *in-group*) and not a member of another (comparison) social group (an *out-group*). In fact, we are all members of many social groups: which social groups are relevant, such as nationality or age, at any one time will depend on the context (Crisp and Hewstone, 2006). As Allport ([1954] 1979) pointed out, societal prejudice is a form of out-group rejection, where one group discriminates against another. Representing the individual thinker (in psychology) as (personally) having either a rational and logically 'correct' perception of a social group, or alternatively a 'faulty', 'biased' or stereotypical perception of people, may be ignoring a significant aspect of human psychology: social group membership. Achieving perceptual accuracy may be of considerably less importance than other – social – factors in the motivation of an individual *as a social group member*. As the stereotype content model proposed, stereotypes are closely associated with intergroup relations (see Chapter 3).

Fiske (2003) argued that there are five core social motives guiding people in their social decision-making. First, people are motivated by belonging. People are members of groups to which they wish to belong and so they conform to group norms (see Chapter 5) and are loyal to the group. Second, group membership also provides shared understandings of people and events. Hence, group membership also involves a third factor, a motivation to make sense of the world in terms of shared group meanings, as this supports the sense of identity as a group member. As group members, people are mutually controlling of each other, this provides a motivation to learn the group norms and expectations to exert control on the outcomes of one's own and others' behaviour. Fourth, people are motivated to enhance their sense of self. We all wish to see ourselves positively, and one key way of doing this is in terms of the national, cultural or religious groups to which we belong. Finally, people are motivated to trust others to make life operate cohesively. Trust is strongly associated with group membership, in deciding who to trust (fellow in-group members) and not to trust (out-group members). People are not therefore motivated to produce a rationally accurate judgement of others, when motives of belonging, understanding, control, self-enhancement and trust may be dominant. Crucially, these motives explain why group members refer to the group as providing explanations of the social world. How groups construct these common understandings and communicate their social attitudes among their members will be discussed in the later chapters.

Social groups and social identity

Tajfel (1969) argued that the specific (cognitive) act of categorizing a person as a social group member has an effect on social perception: within-group differences tend to be minimized and between-group differences accentuated. For example, Tajfel et al. (1964) asked Canadian students to select attributes of people from India and Canada. The most popular attributes were considered stereotypical traits, and two distinct stereotypes were produced for the two nationalities. They also observed two Indians and two Canadians being interviewed, after which they rated the characteristics of the interviewees. The two Indian interviewees were rated as more similar on stereotypical traits than on non-stereotypical traits. The within-group similarity effect was similar for the Canadians (the group to which the participants belonged) but less pronounced. Tajfel argued that a second aspect of social categorization is *in-group favouritism*, that is, a person will tend to make a social judgement that favours members of the in-group (Tajfel, 1970). Tajfel (1970) showed that this effect can occur even with arbitrary categories, using a method referred to as the *minimal group paradigm* (MGP). A group of 48 14–15-year-old British schoolboys were told that they had been allocated to groups based on their preference for particular abstract paintings (although the allocation was actually randomized). They were then asked to select a pattern of rewards (points indicating a financial reward), from a list of options, for an in-group and an out-group member. The results showed that the boys' selections demonstrated a strategy of maximizing the difference in reward in favour of their own group. While other options would have given the in-group member more money, these other choices would have also given the out-group member a similar or larger amount. Moghaddam and Stringer (1986) followed the same methodology, with similar participants, 10–12-year-old British schoolboys, and divided the groups on a trivial criterion (based allegedly on a number-of-dots estimation task) or on a more meaningful categorization (their membership in the school house system). The results showed the same effect of in-group favouritism, regardless of the category criterion. Thus, even the most trivial of group differences can be effective in bringing about in-group favouritism. Indeed, it is an in-group effect, as advantaging the in-group member appears to be more important than disadvantaging an out-group member (Hornsey, 2008). In a review of MGP studies, Pechar and Kranton (2017) showed that emphasizing the importance of group membership, loyalty to the group, intergroup competition and representing the out-group as immoral all increased the intergroup differentiation. When group membership is emphasized, people are motivated to view the in-group positively, in comparison to out-groups.

We are all members of multiple socially defined groups: family, nationality, age group, ethnicity, occupation, for example. Some groups we choose to be a member of, such as occupational groups, but others are assigned to us by other people, such as teenager or old person. The act of categorization is also an identification of difference. Furthermore, making a categorization that locates ourselves in a group is an act of social identity. According to *social identity theory* (Tajfel and Turner, 1986), a person's sense of self is intimately bound up with their group memberships, such as their religion, nationality or occupation. This is not to say that people do not have an idiosyncratic personal identity, but that much of social behaviour and experience occurs in terms of a person's social identity. The explanation of in-group favouritism is that people are motivated to have a positive social identity, which is enhanced by viewing their in-group favourably (Hogg and Sunderland, 1991). Group members will acknowledge that another group is better on certain characteristics, such as arts students acknowledging the superiority in mathematics of science students, but will claim in-group superiority on other characteristics, such as arts students' creativity and freedom of expression, important to their own social identity (Mummendey and Schreiber, 1984). Positive stereotypical characteristics will tend be accepted by a social group and negative aspects of a stereotype might be reinterpreted in positive terms, to enhance their self-esteem: such as Scottish people reinterpreting the negative stereotypical attribute of 'miserliness' to the positive 'thriftiness' (Spears, 2011). Identifying people as group members (categorization) and making social comparisons (with other socially relevant groups), emphasizes intergroup differences and leads to a tendency for people to view social groups, including their own, stereotypically.

In a development of social identity theory, *self-categorization theory* examined in more detail the way that people employ their group membership in their self-perceptions and social behaviour (Turner et al., 1987). While a person has multiple social identities (such as doctor, parent, town councillor, house owner), the context is a major determinant of the specific social category employed in a particular encounter (Hewstone et al., 2006). At work in a hospital, the doctor identity is salient (for the above person) but when visiting their children's school, parent is more relevant. Turner (1991) argued that the selection of the relevant category can be determined by a number of factors. First, the category has to be accessible: a person cannot employ a category they have not learnt or is not relevant in their experience. Second, the categorization is influenced by the ratio of the intergroup differences compared to the intragroup differences, called the meta-contrast ratio. The larger the meta-contrast ratio, the greater the likelihood of this categorization being relevant in the context. For example, there is little difference between students and professors when they are watching the college sports team, but a large difference between them and the fans of the opposing college. However, in the lecture room, the student–professor categorization is most salient. Finally, a categorization is considered salient if it predicts the behaviour of the participants, called normative fit. For example, in the lecture room, the student–professor categorization predicts and explains the behaviour of the people in the room. Furthermore, there will be specific contexts where a person acts exclusively as a group member, called *depersonalization*. For example, a government ambassador or a hospital doctor being interviewed in the media will act and respond *as an ambassador* or *as a doctor*, with no reference to their personal opinions. Thus, according to self-categorization theory, in a specific context, a stereotype (or stereotypical judgement) can reflect the perceived understanding of the situation by the people involved. While social identity and self-category theory can explain how categorization can lead to stereotypical perceptions, it has been criticized as implying that this is a mechanistic consequence of the context and social relationships – potentially underplaying the possibility of people challenging the currently employed social categorization (Sindic and Condor, 2014; see Chapter 7).

Balanced identity theory

Greenwald et al. (2002) brought together the social identity concept with the structure of social knowledge, as learnt associations (discussed in Chapter 3), in *balanced identity theory* (Cvencek et al., 2012). By placing a 'me' node at the centre of social knowledge, the self-concept can be identified in terms of associations of this node with non-valenced attributes, such as roles (parent, neighbour, teacher) and attributes (responsible, intelligent, conservative), and, second, self-esteem can be identified with the associations of the components of the self-concept with a valence (positive or negative). These exist within the social knowledge structure, which includes stereotypes (as associations between social groups and attributes) and attitudes (as associations of a social object or group with a valenced attribute). The theory also draws on consistency theories within psychology (Festinger, 1957; Heider, 1958), arguing that people seek consistency in their cognitions and behaviour, such as a person who believes in green issues supporting sustainable development and recycling their garbage. Furthermore, these theories propose a motivation to maintain consistency and reduce inconsistency in their cognitions. Balanced identity theory employs consistency, or balance, to explain the dynamics of associative strengths in memory (see Chapter 3). Consider the following triad: a person (the self or 'me' node), a social group (northerners) and an attribute (friendly). A particular person may identify with the group ('I am a northerner'), which forms a strong association in their knowledge memory. The person also believes that northerners are friendly, a strong stereotypical association between the group and the attribute. They also believe that they themselves are friendly, which is a strong association between the self and the attribute. As friendliness is a positively valenced attribute, the link between the self and the attribute can be considered as a self-esteem association, and the link between northerners and friendliness is a positive attitude towards the social group. This is a balanced triad of associations, so will be maintained and, if any one of these associations was initially relatively weak, it would be strengthened to bring about consistency, according to the consistency (or *balance-congruity principle*) underlying the theory.

Balanced identity theory can explain how stereotypical associations are linked to social group membership and social knowledge (Dunham, 2013; Greenwald et al., 2002). It is also able to integrate social identity research with the research on implicit associations. In a typical study, three implicit association tests are used (Greenwald et al., 2002; see also Chapter 3). Self-esteem is examined using the contrasts 'self' and 'other' and a valence (positive and negative). Group identification (comparing self and other) is tested with a group comparison (such as age: young and old). The attitude to the group is found by the comparisons of the groups (young and old) and a valence (good and bad). Finally, the participants' reaction times can be put into a statistical regression analysis to examine the three relationships. The results showed evidence of balance: the associations were correlated. For example, a positive attitude to 'female', strongly identifying as female and high self-esteem[3] were highly correlated, in support of the balance-congruity principle. However, one problem lay in the identification of people with low valence groups, such as older people and the categories of young and old, where the latter is viewed less positively than the former (Dunham, 2013). Balance was found with young participants (around 20 years old): strong identification as young, high self-esteem and a positive view of young (people) all went together (Mellot and Greenwald, 2000, cited in Greenwald et al., 2002). However, the researchers expected that high-esteem older people (aged around 75 years) would have a positive attitude to old age. However, the opposite was found. The results showed that they had a more positive association (attitude) to young than old, and a stronger group identification with young rather than old (Mellot and Greenwald, 2000, cited in Greenwald et al., 2002). The researchers attribute this to the influence of culture that 'consistently and pervasively values youth over old age' (Greenwald et al., 2002, p. 24). This indicates that, while a person may seek and achieve a positive view of their group, they cannot ignore the associations present in their society. However, social identity theory suggests that people are aware of when they are members of a (stereotypically) low valued group and may seek to present the group more positively (Spears, 2011) or simply not identify with the group (Ellemers et al., 1988). Despite this complexity, balance identity theory does offer an explanation of why promoting positive attributes of lower status groups (such as old age with wisdom and personal freedom) could both reduce the negative stereotyping of the group and enhance the self-esteem of its members.

Stereotypes and intergroup relations

Tajfel (1981, p. 224) quoted social anthropologist Robert LeVine: 'Describe to me the economic intergroup situation, and I shall predict the content of the [intergroup] stereotypes.' It is important to remember that stereotypes come from the social history of intergroup relations. Implicit in the ideas expressed in the above section on social identity is the assumption of social comparison (Tajfel, 1981): in identifying one group and its members there is also the identification of another group as not-members. Thus, stereotypes – as the identification of group differences – are constructed in the relationship between groups, which in many cases can be viewed in terms of intergroup conflict. This was examined by Sherif et al. (1961), who argued that when groups are competing for resources – particularly economic resources – the conflict can be termed *realistic conflict*, as the groups are in a genuine conflict situation. One consequence of this is the development of a negative view of the out-group by the in-group. As we saw earlier, even the minimal group paradigm produced in-group favouritism. In their own well-known Robber's Cave study, carried out in 1949, Sherif and his colleagues randomly allocated 12-year-old boys in a summer camp to two groups. Initially separated, the boys developed their own group names (the Eagles and the Rattlers) and engaged in group activities. They were then brought together for competitive activities, such as tug of war and baseball. The groups became very competitive with conflict developing outside the organized activities, such as the Eagles burning the Rattler's flag and Rattlers ransacking the Eagles cabin. The conflict between the groups resulted in a negative attitude towards the out-group, with name-calling and the attribution of unfavourable attributes. In a test of intergroup perceptions, the boys rated the two groups on six attributes (brave, tough, friendly, sneaky, stinkers and smart alecks) in terms of how many of the group members had the characteristic. The results showed a strong negative out-group stereotype, with an extremely positive stereotype of their own group. In the final stage of the study, the groups were given joint tasks that required cooperation, such as recovering a stalled truck. Over a number of days, cooperation continued to be required to achieve superordinate goals, and the groups developed more positive attitudes towards each other.

A key point about the Robber's Cave study is that the boys were selected specifically for being 'ordinary' lower middle-class (White) boys – and hence not expected to have any particular biasing psychological or personality factors, and randomly allocated to the groups. Hence, the subsequent animosity between the groups that resulted in negative stereotype formation was attributed to the group identification (in the first stage of the study) and the subsequent intergroup conflict. This group-based argument explains why Gilbert (1951), in the Princeton trilogy after the Second World War, found that the American stereotypes of the Japanese and the Germans had become much more negative in comparison to the earlier study of Katz and Braly (1933). While Sherif et al. (1961) sought to bring the boys together at the end of their study to reduce the negative attitudes between the groups, the serious consequences of real-life conflict may mean that stereotypical attitudes persist for a considerable period after a conflict has ceased.

Intergroup contact

Despite all societies being made up of multiple groups, the degree to which these groups interact is highly variable. When there is a history of institutionalized group segregation in a society, anti-discriminatory and civil rights legislation can revoke the formal legal structures of segregation, but social and economic discrimination may continue between groups that results in continued segregation. Even in a society where groups suffer a similar degree of discrimination, there may still be a cultural separateness and a high degree of rivalry between the groups, such as the Irish and Italians in nineteenth-century New York (Moses, 2017). Allport ([1954] 1979) considered the argument that, in such a situation, people in one group, particularly members of a dominant group, form an unrealistic and stereotypical view of the other group (particularly a discriminated-against group). Hence, learning more about the other group should (in theory) lead to a more realistic understanding of them and a repudiation of negative stereotypes about them. He rejected a simplistic form of this *contact hypothesis*, as there are plenty of historical examples of groups in constant contact, so know each other well, but due to the state of intergroup relations maintain stereotyped views of each other. However, when the conflict ceases, or the discrimination is removed (at least at a formal level), what are the circumstances where the intergroup contact might break down stereotypes and foster greater understanding between members of the different groups? Allport ([1954] 1979) argued that the contact had to be more than superficial, at least at the level of acquaintanceship. A crucial factor was that the members of the different groups had to pursue a common goal, essentially operating as a team, working together as equal status members. Contact also had to be normative, as otherwise social expectation (of associating only with fellow group members) would encourage group separation. Finally, Allport ([1954] 1979) argued that, for the contact to be successful, it required institutional and legal support. For example, in the Sherif et al. (1961) study, the researchers institutionalized the team working in the latter part of the experiment. If all these conditions are implemented then the contact hypothesis predicts that people will gain a more realistic view of out-group members and view them less stereotypically in discovering that 'they are no different to us'.

The practical application of the contact hypothesis to real-life prejudice was supported by studies by Williams (1964) in four US cities, where lower prejudice towards minority groups (by the White majority) was associated with greater contact (reports of personal acquaintanceship with minority group members). Pettigrew (1971) argued that, for contact to succeed, the situation had to be one fostering trust. Where contact occurred in a context of distrust (prejudice and conflict) antagonistic relations could be reinforced. Forbes (2004) also argued that while the contact hypothesis may have a positive effect at the personal level (of individuals in interaction), when analysed at the level of the group greater levels of contact can lead to greater antagonism rather than a reduction in prejudice (as a clash of cultures). However, the contact hypothesis has been shown to have a significant effect in a range of practical situations, such as reducing racial prejudice among sailors, the police and students (Pettigrew and Tropp, 2006). Pettigrew et al. (2011) emphasized the importance of intergroup friendship as a significant factor in reducing prejudice, and argued that this form of contact can gradually undermine ingrained historical intergroup antagonism. The benefits of such contact may extend to other groups beyond those interacted with, in reducing prejudice towards out-groups, with even imagined contact having a positive effect on the attitude towards an out-group (Hewstone and Swart, 2011; Miles and Crisp, 2014). This research has led to the contact hypothesis underlying many prejudice reduction interventions. However, simply putting different groups together, such as in a school or university, may not result in the groups associating with each on campus, unless all the conditions suggested by Allport are implemented (Hewstone and Swart, 2011).

Stereotype threat

Consider a situation that satisfied the requirements of the contact hypothesis: a mixed group of Black and White students are in a class in a school in the United States. They are all of equal status, the school has anti-discrimination policies and social practices respecting all backgrounds and cultures, which is clearly supported by the teachers. Despite the positive learning environment set up in the school, there is still the risk of negative stereotypes influencing the experience of the students. This is the problem of *stereotype threat*, which Steele (1997, p. 614) defined as 'the social-psychological threat that arises when one is in a situation or doing something for which a negative stereotype about one's group applies'. He identifies stereotype threat as a general situational pressure that can be experienced by any group where a relevant negative stereotype about them is known, such as an intelligent Black student aware that they risk confirming a stereotype of lower intelligence if they fail to demonstrate their potential in an examination. Importantly, the person themselves may not believe the stereotype but knows that others in the situation are aware of it. Furthermore, regardless of disconfirming evidence, every new relevant situation becomes another instance of stereotype threat. While acknowledging that there may be many reasons (economic and cultural) that can influence a group's performance in the educational system, Steele (1997) argued that stereotype threat can account for why African Americans tend to underperform in the US schooling system. An important aspect of any performance is a sense of identification with the domain of the activity, such as the identification of the self (feeling 'at home') in the academic domain. Stereotype threat disrupts this, and when it becomes chronic it can lead to a dis-identification from the domain and the abandonment of the activity (Woodcock et al., 2012). Thus, a student, capable of high achievement, underperforms due to stereotype threat and disengages with the academic domain. However, Steele (1997) argued that stereotype threat can be ameliorated in a number of ways. For students within a threatening situation – such as African Americans engaged in traditional education – stereotype threat can be reduced by affirming the group members' belongingness in the system, with relevant role models (such as African American teachers and academics) demonstrating group members' success in the activity, with clear evidence that different cultural and academic viewpoints are valued. For disengaged students, a non-judgemental strategy of the teachers along with building self-efficacy (competence and confidence) can lead to greater identification, of the self with the domain. Steele (2010) presented a range of examples illustrating stereotype threat in a number of different domains for groups negatively stereotyped in those domains, along with interventions to reduce its effect, following the above guidelines.

One insidious aspect of negative stereotypes is that they can appear to be confirmed in what has been referred to as a *self-fulfilling prophesy* (Snyder et al., 1977). Imagine a teacher who holds a stereotypical belief that a particular social group is not as intelligent as other groups. The teacher, with low expectations of the group members' performance, may not encourage a student from this group as much as the others. The student, disillusioned by the situation, may underperform against their potential. Consequently, the teacher observes that the student has performed as they expected, in accordance with the stereotype. However, the cause of the low achievement is the negative environment for the student, not their lack of ability. Hence, stereotype threat is the constant pressure of feeling that no matter how hard one tries, any failure will be attributed to the stereotypical attribute of the group of which one is a member (see Chapter 5). One way to break this seemingly vicious cycle is to challenge the simplistic view of intelligence as a fixed internal trait (Dweck and Sorich, 1999). Aronson et al. (2002) showed that, in their study, when African American students were encouraged to view intelligence as malleable, complex and responsive to engagement rather than fixed and unalterable, they not only performed better but also showed greater engagement and enjoyment of academic activity. Techniques such as this undermine the negative expectation of the stereotype by removing it as a fixed 'measure' (and stressor), against which group members feel judged.

Changing the categorizations

We are all members of multiple social groups, so one way of seeking to ameliorate the effects of negative stereotypes and out-group discrimination is to change the groups that are relevant to the domain of activity. For example, dividing children into boys and girls can result in stereotypical gender expectations of performance and also stereotype threat. Deschamps and Doise (1978) showed that, if a second categorization is used – a *crossed category* that cuts across gender – then gender expectations can be undermined. When a group of boys and girls were equally divided into mixed-gender groups, labelled 'blue' and 'green', the gender expectations of performance were removed. However, in many instances the creation of a new category is not possible, so an alternative is to focus on a superordinate category that unites both groups. This is the basic concept of the *common in-group identity model* (Gaertner and Dovidio, 2000), which predicts that, if people accept this new categorization then the intergroup bias is reduced. For example, rather than emphasizing differences (by categorizing people into Black and White, for example), identifying people by their common group membership – as all Americans, for example – can have a positive influence on interpersonal relations. Subsequent research has shown that, in many situations, this is an effective way of breaking down intergroup boundaries, reduce intergroup bias and form a new common identity (Crisp, 2006; Hewstone and Swart, 2011). However, group recategorization does not always result in a reduction in discrimination between the original groups. This is due to in-group identification (Crisp, 2006). According to social identity theory (above) some group identities are more important (high identification), such as nationality, than others (low identification) such as homeowner. In a study with British high school students, Turner and Crisp (2010) examined their perception of British people and French people with the group categorizations focusing on nationality or emphasizing a common European identity. The results showed that participants who strongly identified as British showed more intergroup bias in the common identity condition. While the recategorization reduced the intergroup distinction, this was not something that the high identifiers wanted. Hence, not all groups are the same, or are equally interchangeable, as meaningful groups that people accept as relevant to their own identity. For many people, certain group memberships (their religious group or nationality) may be fundamental to their identity. A recategorization can be rejected if it creates an identity threat to a person in a number of different ways: it may not be a categorization that they agree with or accept, it may diminish an important distinction that they wish to maintain, it may be viewed as a threat to their values and, finally, it might undermine their (privileged) position in the society (Branscombe et al., 1999). A recategorization, and the creation of different social groups, may not be meaningful to the people involved, as culturally meaningful groups are associated with the structure of society.

Stereotypes and the politics of intergroup relations

Sidanius and Pratto (1999, p. 31) claimed that: 'all human societies tend to be structured as systems of *group-based social hierarchies*'. Furthermore, discrimination, prejudice and oppression are built into this structure. This forms the basis of their *social dominance theory* (Sindanius and Pratto, 1999, 2012). By the construction of a particular social structure, a dominant group (or groups) are able to secure a disproportionately larger share of the society's resources than other, subordinate groups. Typically, dominant groups are age-based (with middle-aged people having greatest power), gender-based (with men having more power than women), with other groupings also used to stratify a society (such as race, religion, nationality). The system is dynamic as there are competing social pressures for the maintenance of the particular hierarchical system, such as ideologies supporting the system and, at the same time, social pressure for change, such as ideologies of equality (see Chapter 6). The balance of these forces determines the level of discrimination and inequality in the society. Take, for example, a typical European medieval system of aristocrats and commoners. There were legal and institutional systems of aristocratic power. Ideologies of difference are promoted such as stereotypical ideas that aristocrats are superior people to the commoners: described as gentlefolk (gentlemen and gentlewomen) and 'noble', even employing the euphemism of 'blue blood' to describe their distinctiveness from commoners who should 'know their place' and accept the discrimination against them. Such a system may survive for a long period if the forces maintaining it dominate. However, competing forces, such as alternative ideologies (for example, egalitarianism) and widespread discontent (about social conditions) can, in a particular context, lead to a complete upheaval of the system, as in the French Revolution (see Chapter 6). The same dynamics are taking place in the group-based hierarchies of modern societies, with social forces maintaining the current structure of group-based inequality competing with forces for change. While social dominance theory acknowledges the psychological issues of social identity and group membership, it introduces a factor that many psychological explanations of prejudice ignore: intergroup *power*. Power determines who can do what, and with what resources, in areas such as education, occupation and religion. The privilege of one or more social group may be institutionalized (as in the racism of apartheid South Africa) or through more subtle societal intergroup discrimination. However, there is a clear asymmetry in the power balance, with dominant groups able to create institutional structures that better provide for their well-being than subordinate groups, in areas such as housing, income, education and health care (Sidanius and Pratto, 1999). Yet, even though powerful groups have access to more resources than less powerful groups, all groups have some degree of choice and agency in their actions. Power can be expressed in different ways by different groups such as an employers' lockout to gain favourable terms from the workers or workers taking strike action to bring about an improvement in their conditions.

Sidanius and Pratto (1999) argued that 'legitimizing myths' underlie structural discrimination in society, which at a psychological level provide a rationale for the discrimination as fair and desirable. These are commonly held beliefs about the social order, providing ideologies of discrimination: for example, a belief that some people are better than others, as a form of Social Darwinism or even the promotion of meritocracy, provides myths that legitimize discrimination against people and social groups. However, as well as these hierarchy-enhancing myths there are also other alternative hierarchy-attenuating myths such as 'universal rights' or 'all God's children' that promote equality (Pratto et al., 2006; Pratto et al., 1994). Consensually held stereotypes are legitimizing myths. By representing subordinate groups as inferior (such as being less able, less rational or less dynamic), stereotypes provide a justification for the dominant group's position, as well as undermining the performance of the subordinate group by stereotype threat (Pratto et al., 2006). Stereotypes therefore can be considered as ideological constructions supporting the social organization within a culture (see Chapter 6).

It is clear why dominant group members wish to employ stereotypes as legitimizing myths that favour them in a social system, but why would subordinate group members accept these same stereotypes that present themselves as inferior to a dominant group? An answer comes from *system justification theory* (Jost and Hamilton, 2005). System justification is defined as a 'process by which existing social arrangements are legitimized, even at the expense of personal and group interest' (Jost and Banaji, 1994, p. 2). This challenges the view that in-group favouritism, ethnocentrism and self-interest are the sole drivers of stereotype use, with research identifying instances of out-group favouritism (Jost et al., 2004). System justification theory acknowledges that people will seek a positive self-image as an individual, and as a group member, but proposes a third motivation, that is, a general desire to view the status quo as legitimate and good. Stereotypes therefore serve a rationalizing function, of supporting the social system. Jost et al. (2004) argued that implicit measures, such as the implicit association test (discussed earlier in this chapter and in Chapter 3), can reveal system-justifying associations that may not be observed in explicit measures., Nosek et al. (2002) found that both European Americans and African Americans both showed in-group favouritism on explicit measures. However, on implicit measures, the White–Black, good–bad IAT results tended to show a stronger association for White–good (in terms of reaction times) for both groups. Thus, the implicit associations that all groups have learnt from their culture can potentially have a system-justifying influence on them. For example, Jost et al. (2004) cited the work of Correll et al. (2002), discussed earlier in this chapter, showing that African American participants also showed an anti-Black bias in the shoot-don't-shoot task. Jost et al. (2004, p. 897) referred to these implicit cultural associations as 'consensually shared system-justifying biases'.

System justification also explains why stereotypes are both positive and negative. As we saw in Chapter 1, stereotypes of women are not solely negative but contain positive attributes, such as warm and nurturant (Fiske and Stevens, 1993). However, the stereotype is role-defining (Eagly and Wood, 2012), presenting a societal prescription of what women *should do*: that is, justifying the traditional (status quo) position of women. Jost et al. (2004) argued that such stereotypes are a form of benevolent sexism – making positive statements about women that reinforces an ideological belief in the gender divisions in society (Glick and Fiske, 2001). Stereotypes as system-justification explanations may be accepted by the group being stereotyped, particularly when stereotypes are complementary, such as men are agentic but not communal and women are communal but not agentic (Jost and Kay, 2005), as they promote the idea that neither men or women are 'better' but simply different (so are suited to traditional roles). This aspect of system justification can also be seen in the 'rich but miserable' or 'rich but dishonest' and the 'poor but happy' or the 'poor but honest' stereotypes presenting an illusion of the 'positives' of poverty (Kay and Jost, 2003), implying a rationalization that supports the status quo. Ironically, system justification may have a positive effect on the well-being of people being stereotyped, as it disguises the discrimination against the group (Osborne et al., 2018), and can weaken support for social change (Jost et al., 2012; Osborne and Sibley, 2013).

Stereotypes: from individuals to intergroup relations

The focus on the stereotype as a personal cognitive failure of rationality, or a mental 'bias', located in the personality of the individual has tended to undermine the importance of social groups and social relationships in the historical investigation of stereotypes. As we have seen in this chapter, people are members of social groups, and their identity as a group member may be more important than any motivation for 'accuracy' in their social perception. Furthermore, as Tajfel (1969) argued, personal understandings of the social world are shaped (made coherent) by the meaningful groups and the intergroup relations that we have learnt about from our culture. Thus, the relationship between people, as group members, will reflect these common understandings, which may be expressed as stereotypes. As demonstrated in this chapter, stereotypes reflect the structure of the relationships between groups and group members in a society. They are employed to maintain power relationships of dominance and subordination between social groups, and maintain (or challenge) the status quo. The formation and transmission of stereotypes take place within the history of social relations within a society.

Notes

1 Listed on the Big State Plumbing (2018) website as a common stereotype, in contrast to their own professional team.
2 Indeed, Cikara and Fiske (2012) showed that banker misfortune was greeted by *Schadenfreude* rather than sympathy in their study.
3 Or a positive attitude to 'male', strongly identifying as male and high self-esteem.

5

SHARING STEREOTYPES

Learning stereotypes: the person in culture

In the well-known science fiction novel *Stranger in a Strange Land* by Robert Heinlein (1961), humans return to Mars 25 years after the previous mission led to disaster. They are amazed to find a sole survivor of the first mission, Mike, who had been born on the ship and brought up by mysterious and invisible Martians. He agrees to return to Earth, and the novel focuses on his attempts to make sense of American society as an intelligent outsider (the stranger in a strange land of the title). Though fictional, and set in the future, it cleverly presents a critique of a culture, with all its oddities and irrationalities, which the stranger tries to understand. In 2012, the Library of Congress named it one of the 88 novels that shaped the United States. As we shall see in this chapter, for most people, their own culture, with its particular social mores, is often viewed as 'normal' and 'natural'. There is a popular analogy that 'culture is to people what water is to fish'. The point here is that fish are unaware of the crucial importance of water to their lives, and similarly people often ignore culture, which shares a similar importance to their existence. It is only when we encounter another culture that we may consciously reflect on their different expectations and ways of behaving. Furthermore, we may be simply unaware of the numerous ways culture has influenced our thinking. As we saw in the previous two chapters, implicit associations have dominated the research into social cognition. These numerous learnt cultural associations guide our expectations and understandings of the social world, and can be considered as our 'culture in mind' (Hinton, 2017). We learn the *folkways* of our society, as Sumner (1906) put it (see below). We are cultural beings with cultural understandings and cultural expectations. In moving from one culture to another, our expectations may no longer be pragmatic or predictive. It may take many years to learn the ways of another culture. Furthermore, the work on implicit associations indicates that, to paraphrase a well-known saying, 'you can take a person out of their culture but you cannot take their culture out of a person'.[1] Human decision-making takes place in a cultural context of other people and, as we saw from the previous chapter, we may be motivated to accept a cultural interpretation of the social world, for reasons of group cohesion and social identity.

The child making sense of the social world

The debate between models of the person as a rational thinker or as a cultural being has been played out in the major theories of child development proposed by Jean Piaget and Lev Vygotsky. On the one hand, Piaget and Cook (1952) argued that children pass through a number of developmental stages of thought in their progress to adult reasoning capabilities, becoming more sophisticated in their thinking over time. Experience provides continual feedback to the child, aiding their cognitive development and increasing their potential for abstract reasoning. Children are represented as naive scientists seeking to make sense of their world, but limited by their stage of intellectual development. For example, Piaget's daughter Lucienne, at 4½ years old, claimed that it could not be afternoon as she had not had her nap: a learnt association, showing transductive reasoning (Piaget and Inhelder, 1969). A more experienced older child, at a later stage, will not make this mistake, as they are able to think about times of day in a more sophisticated way. Piaget argued that initially the child tends to be egocentric and concrete in their reasoning and it is only when they attain the final stage of intellectual development around the age of 12 that they develop the ability for abstract reasoning. Thus, according to Piaget, the teenager – like the adult – has the potential to think rationally and logically – but they may not employ it, as we saw in Chapter 3.

While Piaget emphasized the developing reasoning abilities of the child, Vygotsky (1978), on the other hand, emphasized the sociocultural aspects of a child's cognitive development. The child can be characterized as an apprentice adult, developing the skills of adult understanding within the context of language and culture. The learning process itself is cultural, with schooling a very different experience at different times and in different cultures. At any point in their development, the child is limited in what they can and cannot do (such as baking a cake or reading a story), but adults can *scaffold* the child's learning, in helping them to develop new skills, such as holding the child's hand as they stir the cake mixture or helping them with difficult words. Learning is a highly social process. Cognition develops socially, with adults teaching the child specific cultural techniques of problem-solving. Even memory involves stories that are constructed in language and structured by culture: for example, understanding the meaning of a 'birthday party' involves telling a story of a cultural practice of celebration. Examining children's performance on logic problems may give the impression that human thinking progresses towards a 'goal' of rational, logical reasoning, but Vygotsky challenges this idea. It has been shown that even mathematics learning in schools is a cultural experience (e.g. Andrews, 2016). While it is clear that adults have the potential to think abstractly, they often rely on learnt cultural practices to make everyday decisions. For Vygotsky, language and culture structure a child's learning experiences, making the development of cognition a process of social interaction. Rather than viewing human learning as a process of thinking development (against an objective measure of logic or other reasoning criterion) it can be considered as a process of *socialization* into the adult community. Vygotsky argued that thinking involves psychological tools, such as language and other forms of symbolism. Tools can be diagrams, signs or works of art (Vygotsky, 1997). Psychological tools essentially are the collective ways of performing cognitive tasks that the individual acquires during cognitive development. Consequently we think in culture. Social relations are internalized by the child and become their way of thinking (Friedrich, 2014).

Knowledge involves learning about the meaningful categories in the culture and the relationship between them: 'Categorization is fundamental to human cognition … organizing and structuring our knowledge about the world' (Bodenhausen et al., 2012, p. 318). In putting things (people, objects) into categories, we are differentiating them, according to their associated attributes. Hence, a fundamental issue for the child seeking to make sense of their world is learning what goes with what (Bruner, 1957). They may get it 'wrong' sometimes (as Piaget's daughter did in associating the afternoon with post-nap) but they are learning associations. While Piaget (1954) emphasized the active and constructive aspect of a child's intellectual development, it is also clear that children will defer to adults in decision-making (Donaldson, 1978). Given that much of the feedback they receive about the world comes from adults, it can be inferred that children have to assume that adults (generally) know better. Thus, the child's understanding of meaningful categories comes from the adults around them, as Vygotsky argued. However, the young child still faces a basic problem of determining what goes with what in terms of categories and attributes (e.g. Jarvis, 2006). That is, a basic problem for the child is learning the generalizations (associations) present in the adult world.

The child must trust that adults are making meaningful distinctions when they identify categories (Harris, 2012): that is, the categories and attributes are not arbitrary but, when adults make categorical distinctions, they indicate some form of basic categorical difference (Rosch, 1978). For example, adults distinguish between dogs and cats but do not make a categorical distinction between big dogs and small dogs. Thus, while individual dogs may be big or small or long-haired or short-haired, they are all *essentially* dogs, which bark, chase sticks and wag their tails. Essentialism is the belief that, underlying the barking and tail wagging, dogs have an *essence* that makes them dogs and not cats. Thus, when adults make distinctions between social categories (such as men and women or Black and White people), it is not surprising that the child assumes that there is an essential difference between the categories. Indeed, Gelman (2003) has argued that, on the basis of her research, young children are *essential*, in that they tend to make essential judgements about the differences between categories. She also suggests that they are not simply picking up cultural associations but actively constructing a folk psychology of the world about them (see later in this chapter on folk psychology): that is, the children are acting like naive scientists trying to work out the relationships between things. Most non-social categories that the child is faced with are based on essential differences, such as dogs and cats or fish and birds, and it have may have evolutionary value to make such judgements (Gelman, 2003). The problem here is that human social categories can be arbitrary, in that they do not refer to differences in *essential* human attributes, and are based on culturally constructed distinctions and attributes, such as nationality or ethnicity. It may be too much to expect that young children are able to distinguish between essential biological categorizations and the socially constructed categories prevalent in their culture.

Young children are able to make generic inferences about categories of things, such as 'lions are dangerous' or 'women give birth'. Leslie (2007, 2008) argued that inferring generic properties is the default, most primitive mechanism of human generalization and is a basic aspect of human cognition. Consider, for example, a generic property of women as 'giving birth' to baby human beings. This is a distinctive quality of women compared to other human categories. It is also inferred to be true despite the fact that some women do not give birth. This appears to create a conundrum: if we imagine a society where most women do not give birth, how could children learn that this is a generic property of women? Leslie (2007) argued that background knowledge (about animals and procreation) supports this property, as a *characteristic property* (of female animals). Therefore, learning that at least one woman has had a baby may be enough to infer a generic property. Why do children not attribute the generic property to 'people' rather than 'women', given that not all women give birth and some people do? Leslie (2007) argued that discovering that men do not have babies is a 'positive counterexample' as they have an alternative property – a male reproductive system – that distinguishes them from women. However, instances of women not giving birth are 'negative counterexamples' (Leslie, 2007) as they do not have an alternative property – they simply have not had babies. Therefore, learning that Susan has chosen not to have babies or Mary cannot have babies, does not affect the categorization of Susan and Mary as women or the generic property that women 'give birth' (Leslie, 2007). This basic generic mechanism looks for a good predictor of a property, which is neither irrelevant ('long-haired people have babies') nor too broad ('people have babies'). Furthermore, it seeks the kind of people (as a category) *disposed* to having the property – women (Leslie, 2017). This basic generic mechanism can make generalizations on very limited information yet does rely on background (cultural) knowledge of categories to do so. Unlike statistical generalizations (which become more probabilistically accurate the more instances experienced) generic generalizations can be false – identifying attributes that are not actually generic – as well as true. Young children may be 'essential' because, in making sense of the world they employ this fundamental generic mechanism to generalize from examples to make inferences as to 'what goes with what'. However, they do not essentialize all social categories, such as sports teams, but do with other categories such as race and gender (Leslie, 2014). This may depend on the way their parents engage with them (and talk to them about such categories). For example, children growing up in conservative families in the United States tend to essentialize race and gender more than those brought up in liberal families (Rhodes and Gelman, 2009). Thus, a basic mechanism of generic generalization (combined with some cultural knowledge) may be one influence in the acquisition of stereotypical generalizations (Leslie, 2017).

Yet children become more sophisticated over time. Taylor et al. (2009) compared 5-year-olds, 10-year-olds and adults on an adoption task, that is, a cow brought up by pigs or a girl brought up by men. They were then asked to predict what the cow or the girl would be like when grown up, physically and behaviourally (such as would the girl prefer traditional male- or female-gender activities). The younger children tended to treat gender and animal species as innate and inflexible concepts showing evidence of essentialism in their thinking. Whereas there was similarity in the physical predictions for all participants groups, the older children and the adults were more differentiated and flexible in their judgements of human gender (compared to animal species) in their consideration of environmental explanations of behaviour. It has also been found that young children hold more rigid stereotypes and will apply these stereotypes more widely to category members than adults (Sherman et al., 2013). Despite the child's initial assumption of essentialism, as they get older they discover the complexities of social categories, and have the ability to appreciate that complexity.

However, adult employment of specific categories can have a powerful influence on children's use of them, as proposed in *developmental intergroup theory* (Bigler and Liben, 2006). Bigler and Liben (2006) acknowledged that categorization is employed to make sense of the social world, but argued that evolution has developed a 'flexible cognitive system that motivates and equips children to infer – from environmental data – which bases of classification are important within a given context' (Bigler and Liben, 2007, p. 163). This means that children are perfectly capable of detecting physical differences between people (such as skin colour, eye shape) but they are not evolutionarily 'hard-wired' to employ them in 'racial' categorizations. It is the social context (as set up by adults) that determines which attributes, related to which social groups, become meaningful to the children. For example, using 6–11-year-old summer school students, Bigler et al. (1997) created different groups by the colour labelling of desks, bulletin boards and activities. They then manipulated the involvement of teachers, who either highlighted the colour labels or ignored them in their communication with the children. Finally, the children were assessed for their behavioural biases and peer preferences. Importantly, the in-group preferences (based on the colour labels) only occurred in the situations where the teachers highlighted the colour groups. Fundamentally, the child is faced with the problem of making sense of (or categorizing) the different people they experience in their social environment. To achieve this, there are three elements to developmental intergroup theory. First is the establishment of which human attributes are psychologically salient. This is influenced by perceptual discriminability (it is easier to detect long hair than reading ability) and proportional group size (minority groups are more distinctive than majority groups as there are fewer of them). However, the relevance of these detected attributes is determined by adult use, which may be explicit or implicit. An example of explicit use of a particular categorization is when parents or teachers frequently refer to it, such as gender in 'good morning, girls and boys' or 'can the boys get the pencils and the girls get the paper'. An example of implicit use is in social segregation, such as placing the boys and girls in different seating areas and undertaking different activities. In seeking to understand the social world, children 'infer that the social divisions they observe must have been caused by meaningful, inherent differences between groups' (Bigler and Liben, 2007, p. 164). It is not that children simply pick up adult categories but they are actively attempting to make sense of the structure of the adult world and seek explanations of why certain categorizations are employed by adults in their society. Observing that adults distinguish between people in terms of, say, race or gender, the children may make inferences about why this is, i.e. that there are 'meaningful, inherent differences between the groups' (Bigler and Liben, 2007, p. 164).

Developmental intergroup theory proposes that these salient dimensions will then be employed by the child in their encounters with group members, such as perceiving a person as a girl, with girl attributes. Furthermore, the child will develop stereotypes about social groups – attributes assumed to be present in the group members – and also prejudices based on these inferred attributes. Thus, the child is not inherently 'biased' in making sense of the social world, but will be strongly influenced by the structuring of the adult world they encounter, as it provides answers to the question of which (of the many possible) categorizations are relevant in their culture, and which attributes (associated with a category) provide an explanation of the different treatment of different social groups in society. Developmental intergroup theory proposes that children learn which social categories are relevant in their society, and which attributes are assigned to different social groups, by a basic desire to make sense of the world, employing a flexible cognitive system, applied within a cultural context. Consequently, children will acquire stereotypes and prejudices about social groups from the adult social world, not because they are seeking to make sense of a social world that has a specific combination of group-attribute associations and intergroup discriminations within it. Like a stranger in a strange land, the child attempts to make sense of the particular social organization they live within, constructed by the adults of their culture.

Learning to be a citizen of a society: socialization

Socialization is about learning the 'right' way of thinking and behaving according to the values of a particular society. It is about learning which behaviours are acceptable or approved of by society and which are not. Sociologist Talcott Parsons ([1951] 1991, p. 143) characterized the situation in the follow way: 'What has sometimes been called the "barbarian invasion" of the stream of new-born infants is, of course, a critical feature of the situation in any society.' While he deliberately puts the term 'barbarian invasion' in quotes, to emphasize its metaphorical status, it is an illustrative metaphor to use. As Parsons pointed out, the newborn child has yet to learn the expected behaviours of a person of their particular status in their society.

He argued that a stable social system involves the individuals within it acting, and interacting, according to each other's expectations. These expectations are related to an individual's role in the system (such as doctor, patient, father, mother, man, woman) and the acceptable interactions with others (such as a child not being rude to adults). While the system involves voluntary action, the individual acting outside of role expectations, that is, not conforming to the norms of their social position, can find themselves under the influence of social control, either from their own sense of 'doing wrong' or from others who may disapprove of this non-normative behaviour. Within a society there is a system of general values, which essentially define the culture and the shared meanings of its members (Gerhardt, 2016). While there may be flexibility within roles, deviance from role expectation is counteracted by social disapproval, which can be a formal mechanism of social control (such as the law and the justice system). There is, however, in some societies, flexibility in the roles individuals can take on and, again in some societies, opportunities for social mobility are available. Thus, socialization is a social learning process of the person appreciating the alternative roles and expectations available to them and also the rewards and punishments associated with alternative behaviours within the different roles. In a general sense, socialization is a process of learning 'one's place in society'. Parsons, like many other social scientists in the mid-twentieth century (such as Adorno et al., 1950) was influenced by Freudian psychology in proposing how an individual internalized the values of their society, and their role within it, emphasizing the importance of the role of parents in the child's socialization. For Parsons, values and norms are central to individual action choices. Hence the importance of socialization, which is essentially a process of enculturation: learning to behave appropriately in a culture.

While Parsons set out the basic ideas of socialization, he has been criticized for presenting a rather conservative version of the social system, as it presents a dominant ideological position, rather than a society made up of competing ideologies, and so his ideas do little to explain the mechanisms of social change (Gerhardt, 2016; Turner, 1991; see also Chapter 6). This was particularly the case with gender. Drawing on Freudian ideas of normative sex roles and their development, Parsons ([1951] 1991) presented an image of gender roles that today would be described as gender-role stereotypes (Eagly and Wood, 2012), which reminds us, as Lippmann (1922) suggested, that one generation's stereotypes can be a former generation's accepted beliefs about social groups. Despite the variety of criticisms of Parsons' work, many of his ideas about socialization remain current, such as the role of parents, school and peers in the development of the socialized individual. In particular, his focus on the importance of cultural values and the consequent norms of behaviour in any society, presents an explanation of social action in terms of common values (Turner, 1991).

Intergenerational transmission of beliefs and values

Much of what the child learns about the 'right' way to behave – what to do, and what not to do – comes from the *primary socializing agent*, the family, which, in most societies, usually involves parenting (Grusec, 2011). Critically, in many cultures, the young child spends most of their early years in the family, which involves both their care and control of their access to resources. Thus, it is within the family that the child's environment is managed. One of the major theories of how the child is socialized within the family is *social learning theory* (Bandura, 1977). Essentially, the child observes the actions of others – particularly adults – and will tend to imitate their behaviour. Thus, the parents, grandparents or other significant caregivers act as models for the child's behaviour. The important aspect of social learning theory is that, rather than patterns of reward being required for learning, observation and imitation are key to the learning process. In a famous series of studies carried out in the mid-1960s with an inflatable clown-like toy, called a Bobo doll, Bandura and his colleagues demonstrated the influence of an adult model on a child's behaviour (Bandura, 1977). In a room containing a Bobo doll, a child aged 3–5 played with finger paint and stickers. In the experimental condition, an adult entered the room and engaged with the Bobo doll in a set pattern: pushing it over, punching it and sitting on it, hitting it with a plastic mallet and saying aggressive phrases such as 'sock it to him!' In the control conditions either the adult ignored the Bobo doll or no adult appeared in the room. The child was then taken to another room with a number of appealing toys but after a few minutes they were told that these toys were 'for other children' and taken to a third room. This procedure was to mildly frustrate the child, as frustration can lead to aggression, and the study sought to observe how they would behave in the third room, where there were a number of both aggressive and non-aggressive toys, including a Bobo doll. In this room, children in the experimental condition tended to imitate the aggressive behaviour of the adult model with the Bobo doll, in both their actions and their speech, indicating that the children had learnt the adult behaviour without any specific reward. An aggressive male model was more influential than a female model, boys tended to engage in more aggressive behaviours than girls, and the children tended to copy a same-sex model more than an opposite-sex model. A second study showed similar effects when the child observed the adult on film rather than being physically present in the initial room (Bandura, 1977). The importance of this research was that the child had not been 'trained' to punch and hit the doll in any particular way through practice and reward. Also, the gender difference indicated that, even at this stage of the child's socialization, the children had learnt the (1960s American) cultural expectations associated with gender and behaviour (that is, what it was considered socially appropriate for males and females to do). Furthermore, even with an adult model who was punished for their actions, the children still demonstrated that they had learnt the behaviour when they were given a positive incentive (juice and sticker books) to demonstrate what the model had done (Bandura, 1977). Thus, other people, specifically significant adults such as parents, serve as models for the child's behaviour. Indeed the theory proposes that social learning is a processing of *modelling* behaviour on significant others.

Social learning theory supports the view that children acquire (through observation) the social categories relevant to their culture (mother, father, doctor, nurse). They also learn that they themselves are members of specific categories, and how to act appropriately as a group member (through imitation). For example, children will learn that gender is a social categorization, and of which category they are a member. Thus, children are in a process of seeking what gender means by detecting the gender cues in their culture (Martin and Ruble, 2004). Socialization is, therefore, also a process of *identification* (Bandura, 1969), where a child learns who they are (the categories they belong to) and how to behave appropriately, in terms of the behaviours associated with these categories in their culture. According to social learning theory, identification is

> a continuous process in which new responses are acquired and existing repertoires of behaviors are modified to some extent as a function of both direct and vicarious experiences with a wide variety of actual or symbolic models, whose attitudes, values, and social responses are exemplified behaviourally, or in verbally coded forms.
>
> *Bandura, 1969, p. 255*

This explains why the children copied the same-sex model more than the opposite-sex model in the 1960s Bobo doll studies. Also, the acceptance of greater aggressive behaviour in males than females – in the culture in which the study was set – meant that the boys imitated the aggressive behaviours more than the girls, indicating that they were aware of the cultural gender-role expectations of behaviour. Thus, social learning theory, along with the research on sex roles in society, has argued that 'gender' is a combination of socialization and identification (Zosuls et al., 2011); that is, learning what it means to be female or male in the culture and how to model that role (or *perform* gender as Butler, 1988, put it: see Chapter 7). The issue of gender stereotypes is that role differentiation is stereotypically associated with inferred attributes, such as male agency and female communality (Haines et al., 2016), which present cultural prescriptions on how the genders should behave. However, cultures are not static and social roles are not fixed, so social change can lead to significant changes in role expectations (Diekman and Eagly, 2000; Eagly et al., 2019; see Chapter 7).

Despite parents telling their children to 'do as I say and not as I do', Bandura showed that social learning is taking place by observation and imitation outside of specific teaching activities. Van Ausdale and Feagin (2001) gave an example of a 3-year-old child making a racist statement in a nursery, which horrified both the parents and nursery staff who both espoused anti-racist attitudes. It was inferred that she had learnt it from another child whose parents expressed such views, simply through observation, which was then imitated. To take a more positive example, van Ausdale and Feagin (2001) also noted how young children dialling 911[2] to report an emergency, are often praised as heroes in the local press, in the belief that this is an extraordinary action. Yet, as van Ausdale and Feagin (2001) pointed out, dialling 911 is common knowledge in the adult world and is something that even a young child may have picked up through observational learning. The authors argued that adult-centric thinking influences views of children and misunderstands how they learn about the social world. As noted above, children are active agents seeking to makes sense of the world around them. First, although they are limited in their experience, children make quite reasonable assumptions about the world (Bigler and Liben, 2006; Gelman, 2003). Second, they can pick up new information quickly from observing other people, particularly adults, as models (Bandura, 1969). While it is likely that parents and other carers provide the most immediate models, social learning can take place with any model, dependent on the circumstances. The crucial aspect of this research for an understanding of stereotyping and stereotypes, is that children learn stereotypes – like other cultural associations – from the people around them, who serve as models, and with whom they identify.

The family, as the primary socializer, transmits moral values, political beliefs and other attitudes to children (see Grusec and Hastings, 2015). For example, Bengtson et al. (2009) reported the findings of a long-term study (over a 30-year period) of the influence of parents and grandparents on the religious beliefs of subsequent generations in families in the United States. They found that there was a stronger continuity of religious beliefs from grandparents to grandchildren than political beliefs over the decades examined, despite there being an increasing number of people indicating no religion (between the 1971 to 2000 period). Also, while grandparental influence is mediated through the parents, there was also evidence of a direct influence indicated, particularly of grandmothers on granddaughters. While the influence of family on religiosity and religious service attendance had weakened over the 30-year period, religious orientation continued to be transmitted to the next generation. Bengtson et al. (2009, p. 342) concluded that their findings 'affirm the continued resilience and relevancy of families for the passing on of religious traditions and beliefs to younger generations'. Jennings et al. (2009), also in a long-term study across three generations (from the mid-1960s to the late 1990s), examined the transmission of political values from parents to children in the United States. Despite societal differences, with one group of offspring labelled 'the Protest Generation' of the 1960s and a later one labelled 'Generation X' of the 1990s, the transmission effects were similar. The strongest effects were found for parents who were both politicized and consistent in their political attitudes. Like the transmission of religious orientation, parents tended to pass on their political orientation to their children. Indeed, parents have been shown to influence their children across a range of social attitudes, such as gender attitudes (Cunningham, 2001). O'Bryan et al (2004) examined the social attitudes of a group of parents and teenage children, the latter attending a single-sex Catholic school in a Midwestern city in the United States. There was a differential parental effect on their children, with mothers more influential in attitudes to race and fathers more influential in attitudes to homosexuality and female sex roles. Also, a general factor of parental intolerance had an effect on their children, but these effects tended to be modest. Carlson and Knoester (2011) supported the view that parents have an influence on children's gender ideology (beliefs about male and female roles). When they examined different family structures, they found that the influence of biological parents was stronger than that of step-parents, but the quality of the relationship was also important. Overall the findings indicate that parents remain the primary influence on their children's social attitudes, but they are not the only influence.

One way of demonstrating the influence of family and the wider culture on the child is to examine immigrant families. Phinney et al. (2000) compared the attitudes of five groups of teenagers on a number of questions about their family obligations (such as whether they should obey their parents or live at home until married). Three groups were from immigrant families to the United States (Armenian, Vietnamese and Mexican) and two non-immigrant groups (African American and European American). These results were compared to their parental attitudes on the same topic. The results of the non-immigrant groups can be considered as representing the dominant cultural values in the wider society, which indicated a lower overall acceptance of family obligations than in the immigrant groups: for example, immigrant adolescents (and their parents) had a consistently higher sense of family obligations than non-immigrants. However, there was a consistent finding across all groups of a lower agreement with family obligations for the teenagers compared to the parents. There was also some evidence, with the Armenian and Vietnamese families, that the longer the residence in the country (with the child born in the United States) the greater the discrepancy. Thus, these results indicate that the values of the children, while influenced by their parents, are also influenced by the dominant cultural values in the society that they are brought up in.

Formal education

For some educational theorists there is no real distinction between socialization and education, except that the latter is undertaken in a formal, institutional structure. As Durkheim (1956, p. 71[3]) argued 'education consists of a methodological socialization of the young generation'. Essentially, education provides the formal means by which children are inducted into the society, by teaching them its ways. The famous educationalist John Dewey agreed that education is intimately bound to its social context, arguing that the meaning of 'education' is constructed within a particular society or kind of society, which explains the title of his key work, *Democracy and Education* (Dewey, 1916). He further argued that where a distinction between education and socialization is made, it is often for a political purpose, such as distinguishing between the 'educated' elite and 'uneducated' masses, where a cultural 'superiority' is claimed for the elite. Furthermore, reducing the concept of education to some sort of vocational skills training is likely to perpetuate societal divisions, and class structures, rather than producing a truly democratic society (Benson et al., 2007; Dewey, 1916). This highlights a distinction between schooling and education, where schooling often refers to a form of instruction or training, such as learning practical skills like reading, writing and arithmetic; whereas education is often presented as the development of personhood, as a rational knowledgeable human adult, in a Western liberal tradition. This latter idea can be traced back through nineteenth-century educationalist Matthew Arnold to Plato's ideas of the well-lived (i.e. reflective and rational) life (Carr, 2003).

The societal importance of this can be seen in that most modern societies require their children to spend a large proportion of their lives in formal and (often) state-run education. Consequently, the school system is an institutional structure, teaching a specific academic curriculum, which can become an ideological issue of public debate (Olneck, 1990). Essentially, a curriculum involves a 'canon' of knowledge, with the inclusion or exclusion of material a political decision. Thus, school textbooks present a socially sanctioned representation of history, literature and culture. Also, different countries will often present their children with very different accounts of history in their school books. Consequently, schooling can be considered as an enculturation (or socialization) into the dominant ideology of a specific society. Images of social groups in schoolbooks at one period may be very different to those at other times or to representations held outside of the dominant cultural group. This means that the content of schoolbooks that, from one ideological viewpoint, are presenting the received wisdom of the culture can, from another point of view, be seen as reinforcing stereotypes (e.g. Allport, [1954] 1979). Within Western society, from the late twentieth century, there has been a debate, along political lines, between the 'traditionalists', wishing to maintain the traditional cultural canon, and the 'multiculturalists', seeking to widen the canon to include other historical 'voices' (e.g. Banks and McGee Banks, 2016; Grant, 1992). Thus, education can be an ideologically contested space of competing cultural values. Schools in promoting specific state-sanctioned ideological values, present a representation of 'knowledge' about the world, and the relationship between social groups within it, incorporating structural elements of the society. Parents and schools may be complementary or competing influences on the children's acquisition of values. Consequently, the culturally structured knowledge that children learn at school about social groups may be, or may not be, different to that learnt in other contexts or by previous generations, aspects of which may be viewed as stereotypes (see Chapter 6).

Peers and media culture in socialization

One effect of a formal schooling system is that it places children in the company of their peers for a large proportion of each day. Adolescents, in particular, are viewed as being at a stage of identity development where they are sensitive to social influence and particularly responsive to peer pressure (Erikson, 1963, 1968; Steinberg and Monahan, 2007). What is learnt in the recess and in peer-socializing may not be the same as that promoted in the classroom or in the family. One specific example that psychologists have examined in detail is that girls perform as well as, if not better than, boys in mathematics yet may not choose the topic for advance study due to a cultural stereotype of mathematics as a 'male' subject (e.g. Keller, 2001). Adolescence is also a time of dating in American culture and, over 50 years ago, Brown (1965) noted that girls did not tell boys that they were good at mathematics (or pretended they were not) as they were concerned that this would make them less appealing as a romantic partner in the culture of the time. More recently, Hyde and Kling (2001) argued that both benevolent sexism (Glick and Fiske, 1997) and stereotype threat (Steele, 2010) may influence women in their engagement with mathematics education. Crosnoe et al. (2008) showed that a key influence on girls taking mathematics courses was their close friends' choices and achievements, with peer influence increasing throughout the adolescent period. Peer support for mathematics was found to be a significant factor in the motivation of girls in studying mathematics; with other factors being the mother's mathematical support, gender-egalitarian beliefs and learning about feminism (Leaper et al., 2012).

While parents, teachers and friends may have an important influence on the attitudes and behaviour of the child, an increasing influence over the last 100 years has been that of the media on the child's knowledge of the social world. Allport ([1954] 1979, p. 200) was unequivocal about the role of the media in stereotype maintenance: 'They [stereotypes] are socially supported, continually revived and hammered in, by our media of mass communication.' A key point that Allport identified here is that the media presents a specific representation of the social world. Rather than viewing this as a reflection of the 'real' world, it can be considered as a construction in terms of the ideology of the programme makers and broadcasters (see Chapter 7). Television channels are commonly identified by a political orientation in their news coverage. In many countries this ideology is determined by the state, in terms of state-run television and radio channels. The importance of media representations of social groups is that the media are considered to be a powerful influence in the socialization process (Genner and Süss, 2017). An individual's direct experience of the social world is limited to a very small proportion of the people and social groups within it. Considerably more may be learnt about the social world from the media, particularly as there had been a consistent rise in screen use by teenagers during the second decade of the twenty-first century, with smartphone usage at six hours per day by 2016 for older teenagers (Twenge et al., 2018). Through observational learning, the structure of the social world may be learnt through the lens of the media. However, media use is somewhat different to family, friends and school as a socialization agent, as the adolescent has greater control over what media sources they engage with (Arnett, 2000). A young person's knowledge of the social world may therefore be mediated by the social media networks they belong to. As Prot et al. (2015, p. 279) argued: 'Through repeated priming and reinforcement of specific knowledge structures, exposure to any type of experience can lead to lasting influences on personality and social development.'

Since the time of Allport ([1954] 1979), there has been the view that the media presents stereotypical portrayals of social groups, which influences viewer perceptions of them (e.g. Bryant and Oliver, 2009). This is often studied by experimental techniques such as *content analysis*, which involves counting up how many times members of one social group perform certain activities or take on particular roles in the media, in contrast to members of a comparison group, such as who plays the hero and who plays the villain in a drama, with the former, in Allport's time, dominated by White male characters (Allport, [1954] 1979). Thus, the argument is that members of a culture learn (through social learning processes) the patterns of privilege and dominance through their media use. Drawing on large-scale survey data of television watching, Gerbner's *cultivation theory* (e.g. Gerbner, 1998) argued that people's beliefs about the world become more aligned with media representations the more time they spend watching the screen. In consistently portraying particular social groups in certain (stereotypical) ways it is inferred that this reinforces the stereotypes of these groups in the minds of the audience (Mastro, 2009). Consequently, media representations have been criticized for two main reasons in the stereotyping of social groups. First, the consistent portrayal of the members of a social group in restricted social roles constructs media stereotypes, which, from an egalitarian perspective, reinforces unfair societal divisions. For example, Ramasubramanian (2011) presented White undergraduates with stereotypical and counter-stereotypical media exemplars of African Americans. The results showed that stereotypical media portrayals increased stereotypical beliefs, in contrast to counter-stereotypical exemplars (Ramasubramanian, 2011). Ramasubramanian concluded that this research indicated that affirmative action to increase counter-stereotypical examples in the media would counter the effects of media stereotyping. Second, the media acts as a socializing agent so, given the first point (above), its influence should be challenged. In modern Western societies this latter has been enacted within the field of media literacy education (Scharrer and Ramasubramanian, 2015). As Scharrer and Ramasubramanian (2015, p. 171) pointed out:

> [T]here is promise for education efforts addressing the media's role in stereotyping to mitigate the effects of exposure to negative or narrow media depictions of social groups and possibly even enhance the positive media influence of exposure to nonstereotypical and favourable media depictions.

In their own study, sixth-grade schoolchildren (approximately 12 years of age) were given television clips and asked to answer questions about them, such as, 'How would you feel if you were portrayed in these limited ways?' 'What messages are producers trying to get across through these depictions?' An emergent theme from the responses was the emphasis on differences rather than similarities, and the positive effects of being exposed to different experiences and diverse points of view. Scharrer and Ramasubramanian (2015, p. 183) concluded that 'media literacy efforts with young people can … promote an appreciation of diversity and multiculturalism'.

The rules of social conduct

All societies are organized by the relationships between social groups and expectations about them. As illustrated so far in this chapter, each new generation is socialized into the ways of their culture. Sumner (1906) referred to the traditional learnt ways of behaving as *folkways*, such as rituals of birth, marriage and death, or everyday activities such as shopping or eating. Folkways represent the underlying 'rules' of social conduct in a society, with prescriptions about how to behave and not to behave (without bringing about social disapproval). Folkways or social mores are usually so well known as to be implicit and unconscious (Sumner, 1906). In any social situation folkways provide the conventional or traditional 'rules' of conduct; that is, collectively agreed social expectations of behaviour that give meaning and order to the social situation: the customs and the traditions of a culture (Manning, 2017). Sumner (1906) saw folkways both as adaptive to circumstances but also fixed in the sense that pre-established folkways are invariably followed without rational reflection. For example, Lemert (1942) cited the English abroad at this time, continuing to follow their customs such as dressing formally for dinner, despite being in the heat of the tropics, where European formal clothes were decidedly unsuitable. As Lemert (1942) pointed out, folkways provide a framework within which social control operates. Whereas Sumner (1906) saw folkways as an adaptation to environmental conditions (and hence as 'naturally' emergent), Lemert (1942) disagreed, arguing that, with technological societies, the social construction of folkways is more evident. For Sumner (1906), folkways can be powerful and enduring. In observing the racial discrimination still present in the Southern states of the United States of his time, 50 years after the abolition of slavery, he considered that legislation had been ineffective in changing folkways. However, 70 years later, Aronson (1976, p. 196) argued that 'stateways can change folkways'. Aronson claimed that it was simplistic to think that you could change deep-rooted prejudiced attitudes simply by abolishing slavery, but changing the relationship between people as indicated by the contact hypothesis (see Chapter 4) combined with changes in legislation can bring about social change. When there is clear authority support, legislation provides a focus for what now *must be* the case, such as fair treatment under the law, which prejudiced people must accept or face sanction. Where cooperation and interdependence are supported by social policy, folkways can change (Aronson, 1976; Taylor, 2000).

Social norms

The 1950s was still a time of racial segregation in Virginia, yet Minard (1952) observed an interesting pattern of social relations between the miners at the Pocahontas coal field in the state. Whereas 40 per cent of the White miners were consistent in their attitudes and behaviour towards the Black miners (20 per cent friendly and 20 per cent hostile), 60 per cent showed friendliness in the mine and discriminatory behaviour in the town. For example, on the mine bus to town, such miners were happy to sit next to a Black colleague, yet in town or on the interstate bus they would avoid them. As Minard (1952) noted, different patterns of group expectations can develop in different social environments (such as in a jitney bus[4]) and different communities (the mine and the town). This demonstrated that it was not just a person's individual attitudes (prejudiced or non-prejudiced) that determined their behaviour, but that the powerful influence was the prevailing social norms. This result also shows that despite close contact between groups, different spatial locations, such as different streets in a town, can set up boundaries of different 'rules' of interaction between groups that can maintain social segregation (Dixon, 2001).

A *social norm* is the more common term for a cultural 'rule' in social science than folkway, which Sherif (1936, p. 3) defined as 'the customs, traditions, standards, rules, values, fashions, and all the other criteria of conduct which are standardized' as a result of contact between people. Norms are constructed in social environments and learnt by new members of a community (such as children during socialization). Social norms provide expectations of behaviour (including the verbal expression of attitudes). They may be formal rules to the benefit of the community (such as a law requiring all vehicles to drive on the same side of the road) or informal expectations (such as saying hello on entering a small shop in certain communities). Norms provide an important influence on social behaviour, with politeness norms guiding much of human communication (Spencer-Oatey, 2008). This indicates that a person's expressed attitudes and behaviour may be based more on learnt expectations (social norms) than just on their individual beliefs. This can be observed in the expression of anti-Semitic statements in American society during the mid-twentieth century. Opinion polls commissioned by the American Jewish Committee showed that in 1946 the majority of respondents (64 per cent) had heard negative statements about Jews (Dinnerstein, 1994). In the social context of their time, the expression of such attitudes was therefore culturally normative. However, the post-war social context rapidly changed and the expression of such attitudes reduced significantly in the 1950s (to around 15 per cent) as they became no longer socially acceptable or culturally normative (Dinnerstein, 1994). The reverse can also occur. Rogers and Franz (1962) showed that White immigrants to Rhodesia (now Zimbabwe), adapted to the (racist) White Rhodesian community of that time, with whom they integrated, adopting their social norms, including the expression of anti-Black attitudes. Hence the acceptability or unacceptability of expressing a specific generalization about a social group (a stereotype) will depend on the prevailing social norms, which are themselves based on an underlying ideology (see Chapter 6).

Social norms can be divided into two forms. First, there is what people actually do, for example, it may be normative to wear a coat when it is cold[5] as most people do it. This is termed a *descriptive norm* (Bicchieri, 2006; Cialdini et al., 1990). It is typical or (statistically) expected behaviour. However, certain other norms, called prescriptive or *injunctive norms* (Cialdini et al., 1990), provide a cultural blueprint for what a person *should do* in any particular social context, such as a social norm of wearing smart black clothes to a funeral. Injunctive norms are societal prescriptions about what a person should or should not do, with the risk of social disapproval through to formal punishment for disobedience. The two norms can serve different functions. Descriptive norms can be considered as typical behaviour – providing a model of 'what goes with what' in the society – but violations (such as wearing a cape on a cold day) do not lead to sanction. However, injunctive norms provide a moral imperative about 'right thinking' and 'correct' behaviour. Laws and other social rules (such as professional standards) provide prescriptive norms of what people should do. Descriptive norms can be learnt by observation and imitation (as part of socialization) and become implicit knowledge of the social group members. However, injunctive norms may require more complex cognitive processing as they involve self-regulation, and may be counter to what we would otherwise prefer to do (Jacobson et al., 2011). Cialdini and his colleagues (Cialdini, 2003, 2011; Cialdini et al., 1990) have argued that seeking to bring about attitude change is greatest when people observe that the attitude (and related behaviour) violates both injunctive and descriptive norms: a person not only knows what they should do (the injunctive norm, such as people should not take drugs) but also see that most other people follow it (the descriptive norm, that people typically do not take drugs). Focusing solely on the injunctive norm may ignore the important influence of descriptive norms on behaviour. Injunctive and descriptive norms can conflict, such as in a community where recreational drug taking is illegal yet common. Similarly, there may be an injunctive norm against the expression of a discriminatory stereotype, due to a societal belief in equality, yet despite this it may be commonly expressed (as a descriptive norm) by a specific social group. For example, ageist stereotypes may be common in young adults with little knowledge of, or contact with, the elderly (Bousfield and Hutchison, 2010; Greenberg et al., 2002). The conflict of norms is particularly the case where there are different cultural groups within the same society – for example, different religious groups – with different beliefs and values. This is also the case when different cultures come into contact. The norms as expressed by one culture, both injunctive and descriptive, may be considered stereotypical by the second culture with a different ideology.

Social roles

While people may wish to view themselves as unique individuals in Western societies, their behaviour is influenced by their group memberships (as we saw in Chapter 4). People perform a number of different roles throughout their lives. These are related to their personal relationships and social group membership. Everyone in society inhabits multiple roles whose relevance depends on the social context (Crisp and Hewstone, 2006). However, each of these roles will also be associated with societal norms, such as what it means to be a 'good mother' (Gorman and Fritzsche, 2002). *Social role theory* argues that the stereotypes of men and women reflect the norms associated with the traditional male and female gender role in a particular society (Eagly et al., 2000; Koenig and Eagly, 2014). There is a descriptive norm (of what men and women actually typically do in the society) along with an injunctive norm (about what they should do). The socialization process teaches children the categorizations relevant to them (in the society) and also the requirements associated with those categories, as social roles. Hence, boys are taught the male role and girls are taught the female role when a gender division of labour is present in a society, which may be transmitted through socialization and supported by economic institutions (Pearse and Connell, 2016). It is here that the concept of norm can be applied. Whereas descriptive norms reflects the actual state of the society, injunctive norms are means of social control, as they maintain and justify that ideology (see Chapter 6), and behaving in opposition to them can be represented as social deviance (see below). Eagly and Karau (2002) in their *role congruity theory*, focused on the example of female leaders. The traditional role of women has created the stereotypical attributes of women (e.g. communality), which, in the society, are incongruous with the stereotypical attributes of a leader (e.g. agency). In particular a good female leader showing agency is violating the injunctive norm of the female role (as represented stereotypically). Consequently she may be evaluated negatively (and unfairly) in contrast to a male leader, either in terms of her leadership qualities (which are underrated) or her deviation from expected female behaviour (which is disapproved of). It is worth noting that, if social change does take place, such as more women becoming leaders (despite these obstacles), this can undermine the leader-gender stereotype association and change the descriptive norm (Weber and Crocker, 1983), then injunctive norms can change. Thus, stereotype change (in terms of normative expectations) can follow from social change. Eagly and Karau (2002) showed that while in 1974 nearly 50 per cent of respondents in a US survey agreed that men were more suited to politics than women, by 1998 this figure had dropped to just over 20 per cent. Yet despite societal changes towards greater gender equality, norms associated with gender can persist. For example, Killewald (2016), using data from the US Panel Study of Income Dynamics, showed that the female homemaker norm in heterosexual marital relationships had diminished but the male breadwinner norm persisted, with the husband's full-time employment positively associated with the stability of the marriage.

Roles and dispositions

Social role theory (Eagly and Wood, 2012; Koenig and Eagly, 2014) provides an explanation of why people develop stereotypical associations between social groups and attributes. When social group members are restricted to certain social roles, such as women in traditional nurturant roles, then the stereotypical association of the group and an attribute (women and nurturance) will tend to develop, regardless of the presence (or not) of the attribute in the group members. One explanation for this involves the process of *attribution*; that is, inferring a cause for a person performing certain behaviour (Kelley, 1973; Shaver, 1983). Broadly speaking we can attribute a person's behaviour to internal causes, such as their personality or disposition, or to external causes, such as the environment or social factors. Attribution theories seek to explain the decision-making process that produces an attribution (Kelley, 1973; Shaver, 1983). Crucially, attribution theories make no claim about the actual dispositions of social actors but seek only to explain what leads social perceivers to make a dispositional attribution, called a *correspondent inference* (Jones and McGillis, 1976) While it has been argued that people will rationally make a correspondent inference when the behaviour is freely chosen and there are no discounting external causal factors, research has demonstrated a *correspondence bias*; that is, people tend to make correspondent inferences even when the behaviour is constrained (Gilbert and Malone, 1995; Ross, 1977). For example, participants inferred that essay writers shared the views presented in the essays even when they (the participants) knew that the writers had been explicitly told to write the essays from a particular perspective (Jones and Harris, 1967). It may be that perceivers are not simply ignoring situation information, but believe that despite situational constraints, actors always have a degree of choice in their behaviour (despite the costs of deviance in some circumstances). Also, perceivers may employ *causal schemas* in their decisions when the person is not known, that is, learnt relationships between dispositions and behaviour, or cultural expectations (Kelley, 1973). Reeder and Spores (1983) showed that, although participants acknowledged the influence of social pressure on a teenager taking part in a robbery, they still attributed a disposition of low morality to the robber. Perceivers may be making quite subtle judgments based on the situation and possible dispositions when attributing causes to behaviour to determine the mental state of the actor as: 'the situational force holds power only to the extent that the perceiver believes the person is motivated to respond to it' (Reeder et al., 2004, p. 543; see also Reeder, 2009). Even when there is an awareness of role constraints, perceivers may view in-role behaviour as, at least partially, dispositional. Thus, a person performing a job that is (culturally) regarded as boring is attributed the quality of 'dullness' (as in the accountant stereotype), or a person spending all day in a quiet space surrounded by books must be an 'introvert' (as in the librarian stereotype). Similarly, patients after a successful hospital stay may regard the nurses who treated them as particularly 'caring' people (e.g. Shattell, 2004; Thomas et al., 2018).

From norms to normal: defining deviance

Semin (1980) argued that people do not need to explain the behaviour of others when they engage in culturally expected behaviour, such as normative and in-role behaviour. However, it can be confusing and disturbing if people engage in non-normative, out-of-role behaviour. For example, Garfinkel (1967) asked his students to act in unexpected ways, such as addressing a professor familiarly by their first name[6] or acting as a guest in the family home. These techniques were referred to by Goffman as 'breaching' studies as they breached (or violated) the social expectations (norms) of the situation. In many cases, the students simply could not do it: the anxiety induced by the prospect meant that they could not address the professor in such a familiar way, and their family members found the unusual behaviour so annoying that they stopped. Even when they explained why they had done it, their families were still annoyed! Conformity to social norms makes the world predictable and comprehensible. However, when someone behaves in a non-normative way, it provokes the question of 'why did they do that?' but also reveals the breach of an implicit cultural association that people have learnt (DiMaggio, 1997). In many instances, unexpected behaviour is also socially undesirable behaviour, and there is a tendency for people to attribute such behaviour to internal dispositional causes (Jones and McGillis, 1976). Consequently, a person who does not follow the social norms may be viewed as personally 'deviant' (Becker, 1963). Conformity to social norms is therefore viewed as an indicator of correct and proper behaviour. This can result in people who do not follow the social norms being stereotyped in terms of deviance: as juvenile delinquents, criminals or agitators, for example.

Social reaction to deviance: labels and stereotypes

The study of deviance has a long history in sociology. In the nineteenth century Émile Durkheim argued that deviance both defines a society and changes it (Downes et al., 2016). The identification of deviance reveals the norms and values of society, which as Garfinkel (1967) showed, may not always be immediately obvious to the members of a culture. Also, deviance can be considered a challenge to the social structure of a society that has to be 'dealt with', either by opposing the deviance to defend the society and its organization – by penalizing or excluding the deviants – or by adapting the norms and developing the values of the society to incorporate the deviance within a changed society. For example, in mid-1960s California, Simmons and Chambers (1965) found that 'homosexual' was the top answer to the question 'What is a deviant?' with 49 per cent of the 180 respondents selecting it. However, 50 years on from the study, through political action and social change, civil rights legislation now enshrines homosexual equal rights under the law and same-sex marriage is legal in the state where the research by Simmons and Chambers was undertaken, with a new categorization of 'marriage' encompassing both heterosexual and homosexual couples.

Yet what defines a deviant? In the Simmons and Chambers (1965) study, there were a wide range of answers, including reckless drivers, movie stars, self-pitiers, liberals, conservatives and know-it-all professors. As Kitsuse (1980, p. 2) noted: 'Everyone is deviant to someone.' However, there are two key aspects to societal deviance. First, the concept of deviance presupposes a social and moral order (of norms and values) concerning social relationships and the language employed to establish them, against which people can be judged (Goffman, 1963). Importantly, the 'agreed' norms and values within a society are those of the dominant and powerful groups within it. Second, in stigmatizing a person or a group it involves creating a (negative) stereotype about them (Goffman, 1963). Hence, a person is identified as a group member (such as criminal, homosexual or mentally ill) and, despite the diversity within the group, is attributed characteristics that lead to their stigmatization and rejection. As Becker (1963) argued, a wide range of people committing a wide range of acts (from spraying graffiti or stealing a bicycle through to domestic assault or murder) result in a person entering the criminal justice system and becoming labelled as an 'offender'. Henceforth, this disparate collection of people are treated as a social group of 'offenders', with various societal rules and sanctions applied to them, such as restriction on employment and other activities – potentially for the rest of their lives (Davies and Tanner, 2003). Thus, the society itself constructs the social category of offender, rather than there being any common attribute of the group members (Becker, 1963). Hence 'deviance' can be considered as that which is labelled as deviance by a specific group of people (such as a dominant group in society). This shifts the balance of explanation from the 'nature' of the 'deviant' (i.e. the attributed stereotypical characteristics) to the ways in which deviance is socially defined and constructed by the people determining the normative standards of a society (Goode, 2016; Goode and Ben-Yehuda, 2010).

This can also be seen in the social construction of mental illness (Scheff, 1999). As Scheff (1999) pointed out, there were a third of a million patients treated for mental illness in US hospitals at the time he was writing, with considerably more former patients in society. The risk to other members of the public from those who had been mentally ill was minimal, yet the stereotype of the violent 'insane' person was continually perpetuated within society, in everyday conversation and the media. For Scheff (1999), in contrast to the medical model of mental illness, many 'symptoms' are actually breaches of social norms, such as not looking at a person, specifically at their eyes, when talking to them. The interpretation of norm violation can then confirm the original labelling: this person is labelled as mentally ill and they have just behaved in a socially inappropriate way so they are mentally ill. Scheff (2010) suggested that normalizing the norm violation can counter the effects of labelling, and he gave an example of this with psychiatrists and mental patients. In one example, elderly depressed male patients would barely speak, whispering one-word answers to questions, considered symptomatic of their illness. Yet, when they were asked about their experiences as young men in the Second World War, they became more voluble and animated. Scheff argued that the awareness of their status as outcasts (deviants) exacerbated their current situation, and the recollection of their time as valued and accepted members of the community counteracted some aspects of their depression. By reinterpreting norm violations as normal, rather than as confirmation of deviance, it is possible to counteract the effects of negative labelling. To illustrate the negative effects of labelling on a person, Scheff (2010) presented an example from his own education. As a young physics student he had been asked to solve a problem in front of the class, which he did, producing the correct answer. He continued:

> My professor was so astonished that he said, 'Did Jim (the star student) tell you that?' That was the beginning of the end of my love affair with physics. He had labelled me as a plodder, and embarrassed me in front of the class.
>
> *Scheff, 2010, p. 6*

In contrast he cites a teacher teaching mathematics to underprivileged elementary schoolchildren who avoided such labelling. When the teacher asked a question, such as the number of sides to a milk carton, no answer was dismissed as wrong. The teacher normalized any response to avoid any labelling associated with ignorance, such as explaining a wrong answer by saying 'your answer is about the visible side' of the carton (Scheff, 2010, p. 6). Like stereotypes, labelling social groups in terms of 'deviance' constructs social relationships based on group identities, and reflect values and norms about who *should* do what.

> Definitions of right and wrong do not drop the skies. They are humanly *produced*, *constructed* as a result of clashes of ideologies, interests – economic, social, cultural, political – the outcome of struggles between and amongst categories in a society, each vying for dominance, or at least acceptance, of the views and behaviors that characterize them as a social entity.
>
> *Goode, 2004, p. 47*

The ways in which deviance is identified and represented is intimately associated with social control (Grattet, 2011). The labelling of deviance identities the 'the good, decent, respectable folk – and 'them' or the 'Other' – the deviants, bad guys, undesirables, outsiders, criminals, the underworld, disreputable folk' (Goode and Ben-Yehuda, 2009, p. 38; see also Chapter 6).

There are occasions when powerful social agents, such as politicians and the media, engage in what Cohen (2002) referred to as *moral panics*, where a social issue becomes exaggerated and distorted, with a deviant group presented stereotypically in reports as *folk devils*, and characterized as embodying a threat to the moral order ('unless something is done') as they are anticipated to continue in their wicked and perverse behaviour. The fear generated in the public about this group via the media representation creates the moral panic. Cohen (2002) identified seven such folk devils in Western societies: youth (particularly young, working-class males), perpetrators of school violence (shootings and bullying), drug users, paedophiles, media sex and violence, welfare cheats and refugees (migrants); all of whom have been the subject of moral panics, where media reports generated fear and hostility in the public based on stereotypical representations of them. Often the moral panic results in the authorities (police, politicians, government) enacting punitive (but potentially ineffective) actions to deal with the problem. Garland (2008, p. 15) suggested that 'a specific group of deviants is singled out for "folk devil" status, in large part, because it possesses characteristics that make it a suitable screen upon which society can project sentiments of guilt and ambivalence'.

Culture: the lived network of meaning

Wilhelm Wundt, often referred to as the father of psychology, wrote as much on cultural psychology, or *folk psychology* as he termed it (Wundt, 1916), as he did on experimental and physiological psychology (Wundt, 1874). Yet, for much of the twentieth century English-speaking academic psychology abandoned the analysis of culture in its focus on individual behaviour and cognition. Cultural psychology only re-emerged in the last decade of the twentieth century, as a subject in its own right (Stigler et al., 1990). This meant that individualist explanations tended to dominate psychological explanations, such as viewing stereotypes as a 'problem' of the individual thinker – who perceives the social world 'irrationally' (see Chapter 2). Yet culture is fundamental to an individual's understanding of the social world in which they live. For Geertz (1973, p. 89), culture 'denotes an historically transmitted pattern of meanings embodied in symbols, a system of inherited conceptions expressed in symbolic forms by means of which [people] communicate, perpetuate, and develop their knowledge about and attitudes toward life'. Hence, people are socialized into a network of meaning.

Anthropologists such as Geertz (1974) and psychologists such as Bruner (1990) argued that we cannot extract ourselves from culture, as culture is like the air we breathe (or like water to a fish) in that it is fundamental to our existence and the meanings we create in order to act. Furthermore, cultural myths are more than simply 'falsehoods' (that 'sophisticated' people have abandoned) but are integral to our understanding of the world (Bruner, 1990), and exist just as much in modern societies as they do in traditional cultures (Barthes, 1972). Consider the mythical beliefs that money makes you happy or that money makes you unhappy. Neither are beliefs that can be proved or disproved but they can be widespread in a particular culture, with most people believing in them. Bruner (1959) identified a Western cultural myth associating happiness with innocence, and the gaining of knowledge (or a loss of innocence) represented in culture as a fall from grace (with the cost of that knowledge involving guilt and unhappiness), or a challenge to the gods (which in Greek myth usually turns out badly for the humans involved). Innocence is represented as an Arcadian ideal, such as a happy childhood or the life of a simple shepherd (Bruner, 1959). Cleverness is associated with competence but artifice and discontent. Nostalgia is a yearning for that lost innocence. As Housman's ([1896] 2017) poem puts it: 'That is the land of lost content, I see it shining plain, the happy highways where once I went but cannot come again.' As the culture changes, so new variants of the myth are created (Bruner, 1959): such as the rise of pollution and environmental destruction associated with technological knowledge, contrasted with a more innocent 'return to nature' and a simpler 'good life'. Bruner (1959) draws on examples from twentieth-century American popular culture to illustrate how films, books and cultural movements have echoed this myth of happiness and loss of innocence. Such myths can exert a powerful influence on the members of the culture in their understanding of their social world (see Chapter 7).

Cultural myths can be legitimizing myths (Sidanius and Pratto, 1999; see Chapter 4), such as a belief that a cultural group, a people or a nation, are special, divinely chosen or exceptional in some way, such as being more civilized or more rational than other groups, which provides a justification for their ownership of land or other resources and dominance over other people. Stereotypes can be considered as common cultural myths. For example, in Japan there is a widespread belief that blood types are associated with personality types, and so are relevant to compatibility in romantic and other relationships (like the association between astrological birth sign and personality in Western countries). Sakamoto and Yamazaki (2004) noted that, while the idea had been proposed in the late 1920s it had been rejected by academic research. However, from the 1970s onwards numerous popular publications included the idea, peaking in 1984–1985, which led to a widespread belief in the idea, which by the turn of the twenty-first century had become a majority view. Sakamoto and Yamazaki (2004) examined an annual survey, between 1978 and 1988, of around 3,000 people between 13 and 59 years old, which included both blood type and responses to personality questions. They found no correlation of blood type and personality before the boom period (1984–1985) but significant correlations thereafter, particularly for blood groups Type A and Type B (which the authors point out are the most well-known personality types). Sakamoto and Yamazaki (2004) suggested that the results indicate a self-fulfilling relationship between the stereotypes and the responses. As the blood group stereotype became more popularized, people were influenced by it in their responses to the personality questions. As Bruner (1959, p. 354) stated: 'Life then produces myth and finally imitates it.'

Bruner (1990, p. 35) argued that with a culture there is a folk psychology as 'a set of more or less connected, more or less normative descriptions about how human beings "tick"', which is one of the most powerful instruments of a culture. People learn this network of cultural meaning in their socialization just as they learn their first language. Consequently, they employ this folk psychology to make sense of the social world around them by shaping their expectations and guiding their interactions. It forms the common-sense understanding of the members of the culture. However, this is not a fixed set of ideas but is changing as the culture changes. New ideas enter the culture, such as the dissemination of Freudian ideas mid-twentieth century (see below) or even blood-type stereotypes (above), and are incorporated and transformed within it. Human psychology, assimilating this network of meaning (including those descriptions labelled as 'stereotypes') is therefore crucially linked to cultural history (Bruner, 1990; Gergen, 1973). The belief that a particular social group has a particular characteristic is constructed in a culture and communicated to its members. Stereotypes are an aspect of this folk psychology or 'culture in mind' (Hinton, 2017; Shore, 1996) that members of the culture acquire from their community.

Social representations as common sense

The dominant approach to stereotypes within both academic psychology and popular culture has been based on two basic assumptions: *positivism*, that there is a 'real' social world 'out there' and *individualism*, that the individual should be the focus of psychological explanation, with a person examined in terms of the accuracy or inaccuracy of their perception of that 'real' social world. Consequently, a stereotype, interpreted as the 'inaccurate' attribution of a characteristic to a social group, is taken to indicate a 'faulty' or 'biased' thinker. As we have seen in this chapter (and is further developed in Chapter 6), the former is challenged by the arguments that there is no philosophically unproblematic 'real' social world 'out there', but that people within a culture co-construct their social world for the purpose of creating shared meanings. From a sociocultural (or Vygotskyan) perspective, social interaction should be the focus of psychological analysis with mental constructs as 'internalized sociality' (Jovchelovitch, 2019). A key aspect of stereotypes is that they concern shared beliefs and social attitudes, an aspect of human psychology often ignored in the focus on individual beliefs and personal attitudes (Farr, 1993, 1998). Yet from the beginning of academic psychology, Wundt (1916, p. 3) identified the importance of collective representations to human psychology: 'those mental products which are created by a community of human life and are, therefore, inexplicable in terms merely of individual consciousness, since they presuppose the reciprocal action of the many'. More recently, Moscovici ([1961] 2008, 1988) has proposed *social representations theory*, a development of the idea of collective representations (Farr, 1998). Ideas about, and descriptions of, the social world are not isolated in the mind of the individual but exist within the communicative interactions of a culture (Moscovici, 1998). Shared knowledge guides social behaviour (Elcheroth et al., 2011). Moscovici (1998) provided the analogy with money to explain his view of mental elements as cultural products, as *social* representations. An individual has their own money but that money only has meaning as constructed as a mode of exchange (social interaction) within the culture. The individual can only buy things with 'their money' as other people agree on its shared value. Physical objects, such as bank notes and coins, are not in themselves 'objectively' valuable and may not even be understood as money outside of that culture.

Moscovici chose the term *social representations* to emphasize the dynamic social nature of these representations, and their plurality and variability in a culture (Moscovici, 2000). Through communication, individuals assimilate social representations but also contribute to their development. Social representations form a cultural system of values, ideas and practices that allow the individual to make sense of their social world and its structures. They also provide a framework of meaning through which the members of a culture are able to communicate with each other (Moscovici, 2000; see also Chapter 7). Yet these are not a fixed set of cultural schema, prototypes or stereotypes 'in the heads' of individuals. Moscovici (1984) locates them in the *consensual universe* of everyday discussion, media and social media communication. This is a dynamic space where social representations are *diffused* from their source into public communication, such as a journalist reporting on a new political or scientific idea.[7] Subsequently, social representations can spread across a social group (*propagated*) through communication. Finally, social representations may conflict, resulting in *propaganda*, where particular social representations are proselytized in support of the viewpoint of a social group (Doise, 1993). In the consensual universe, social representations are not fixed but are negotiated and developed. In his own early research, Moscovici ([1961] 2008) showed that Freudian psychoanalytic ideas had diffused through French popular culture and the way different social groups represented it: the Catholic press tended to favour it, representing it as analogous to the confessional, whereas the communist press saw it negatively, as a (capitalist) American influence. Moscovici provided an explanation of how these social representations are formed. New social representations enter the public domain by the process of *anchoring* (Moscovici, 1984), that is new concepts are associated with known ideas, such as the psychoanalytic consultation with the confessional. A second process, *objectification* (Moscovici, 1984), makes an unknown or abstract concept concrete by giving it a social reality, such as representing climate change by media images of droughts, floods and melting polar ice (Höijer, 2011).

While Moscovici (1993) criticized the term 'stereotype' as ignoring the social fabric of human life (see Chapter 1), when a social group, such as people labelled as Hispanic or Latino, are continuously discussed within everyday communication (the consensual universe) in a specific way, such as in terms of illegal immigration and criminality (Stewart et al., 2011), then a 'stereotypical' social representation of Hispanic or Latino people gains a social reality within that culture, where 'social realities are created, maintained, or transformed by collective practices that uphold shared systems of meaning and mutual expectancies' (Elcheroth et al., 2011, p. 744).

Moscovici (1988) distinguished between three broad categories of social representations. *Hegemonic representations* are social representations that are held by most members of a society (or a cultural group). For example, individualism, the belief that the individual is both the cause of, and has responsibility for, their own behaviour, is hegemonic in Western societies (Farr, 1998; Gillespie, 2008). *Emancipated representations* are open to public debate, such as concepts of health and well-being, with different social representations freely debated and developed in communication (for example, viewing health as 'free from illness' or a sense of personal well-being). Emancipated representations 'have a complementary function inasmuch as they result from exchanging and sharing a set of interpretations' (Moscovici, 1988, p. 221). Finally, there are *polemic representations*, which are 'determined by antagonistic relations … and intended to be mutually exclusive' (Moscovici, 1988, p. 221). Polemic representations arise from social conflict and are not universally held but are employed by competing social groups, such as social representations of capitalism and communism as either the best or worst ('evil') political systems. Specific stereotypes can be considered polemic representations in political arguments: such as representations of bankers as greedy and uncaring or the poor as underserving and lazy.

Common sense, social representation and stereotypes

The importance of social representations theory to the consideration of stereotypes is that it emphasizes the role of the consensual universe (social communication) as the locus of meaning: 'Social representations theory is vital to the study of social stereotypes because it insists on their inherent shared symbolic and collective qualities' (Augoustinos and Walker, 1998, pp. 635–636). Social representations, employed within communication, are neither necessarily fixed nor universally agreed upon (as either 'true' or 'false') but are the culturally shared understandings constructing social meaning and social reality. As Jovchelovitch (2008, p. 12) pointed out, everyday understandings (as opposed to philosophical reasoning) are often represented in psychology and other academic disciplines as 'obstacles, noise, and errors to be removed: the superstitions, mythologies and false beliefs they carry should be replaced with the truth of expert or scientific knowledge'. Like the philosopher Hannah Arendt, Jovchelovitch (2008) argued that in Western philosophical thinking there has been a dichotomy both between common sense and reason and the (thinking of the) masses and the elite, with the latter in both cases represented as superior. Yet, as Jovchelovitch (2008, p. 7) pointed out, it is 'common sense that must sustain a human life and indeed the survival of the species – not to mention the survival of the philosopher. Not accidently then that it is called by many languages the *good sense*.' Common sense 'knits' a community together and links the group members to the lives of others in a common understanding of the social world. Lay knowledge is not simply irrational distortion or error but: '[w]hat may look irrational, or wrong to the observer makes sense to the actors of knowledge' (Jovchelovitch, 2008, p. 15). For Billig (2008, p. 106), 'Common sense, or sense of community, lies at the heart of human nature.' For the majority of people throughout history, certain social representations (often referred in the academic literature to as 'myths'), particularly religious beliefs, have provided essential meaning to their lives (and deaths) that cannot be explained by an appeal to logical reasoning or scientific truth. Yet they are fundamental to people's understanding of their existence (Armstrong, 2004).

By isolating a 'stereotype' from the social fabric, from the culture of the group employing it and ignoring its position within a framework of representations, psychologists have traditionally extracted it from its 'network of meaning' within the communication of the society disseminating and assimilating that social representation (Moscovici, 1993). Importantly, Staerklé et al. (2011) argued that social representations theory provides a framework for analysing competing belief systems (which structure social knowledge) in a multicultural society and leads to opposing ideological views being represented as stereotypes. They also argued that social representations (like social identity theory) explain why widely shared stereotypes that emerge from antagonistic intergroup beliefs 'can be used as strategic tools which political actors draw upon to mobilize ingroups and to delegitimize outgroups' (Staerklé et al., 2011, p. 762). The stereotypes that 'bankers are greedy' or 'the poor are lazy' are not simply 'biased' cognitions, but are social representations held by specific social groups, concerning the distribution of wealth in the society, involving political claims about who is deserving and who is not in that society. As such, stereotypes are cultural products employed in communication. Societies are made up of multiple cultures, and as we shall see in Chapter 6, the social representations held by liberals and conservatives may be viewed as 'common sense' within their own social group but as 'false stereotypes' by their political opponents.

Notes

1 There are numerous variations of this saying, such as 'you can take a Texan out of Texas but you cannot take Texas out of a Texan'.
2 The emergency telephone number in the United States.
3 Originally published posthumously in English in 1922.
4 A form of shared taxi.
5 Rather than wearing a cape or a shawl.
6 Interestingly, in modern British universities students are encouraged to use their professors' first names in class, so would not regard this as a non-normative 'breach'.
7 He distinguishes the consensual universe from the *reified universe*, the space of formal analysis and theory, such as in academia, scientific investigation or technical theological debate.

6

STEREOTYPES AND IDEOLOGY

There is a popular US comic strip called *The Wizard of Id*, about the imaginary kingdom of Id, which has been syndicated in a thousand newspapers worldwide. In one cartoon, the king, speaking to the peasants, declares, 'Remember the Golden Rule!' One of the peasants asks 'What's that?' to which another peasant replies: 'Whoever has the gold, makes the rules!' (Parker and Hart, 1971). In a humorous way this reveals a key aspect of any society: some people, often defined as a distinct social group, have more power than others in the control of social relations. While there is an optimistic view that anyone in a Western liberal democracy can become the country's leader, the process of getting elected costs money. For example, a presidential candidate in the United States needs to have hundreds of millions of dollars of funding for their campaign (Ingraham, 2017). Mills (1956) argued that, in the United States, the economy, the political system and the military are dominated by a *power elite* of six groups: the historically prominent families, celebrities, the chief executives of major companies, the corporate rich, senior military leaders and a political directorate of the government executive. Domhoff (2006) argued that the power elite, particularly in terms of the corporate rich and the political directorate, are still relevant in the United States in the twenty-first century.

Historically military might and control of resources (such as land and wealth), has determined who has the power in a society. For example, when William Duke of Normandy conquered England in 1066 CE he distributed the land among his followers, such that in 1085 CE (as recorded in the Domesday Book) less than 1,400 Norman nobles controlled the entire country of up to 2 million people. A European feudal system divided the population into the aristocrats with power and the peasants who were required to serve the lord on whose land they lived. Medieval Europe was not only dominated by military elites but also by the Christian Church. A religion can gain considerable power, particularly when it becomes associated with the secular power as the state religion. 'Religion gave state authorities and state power its legitimacy, and the government was the protector of the Christian faith' (Nieuwenhuis, 2012, p. 153). A critical role of religion is what Berger (1967) referred to as 'world building'. Religion presents an external power outside of human beings yet related to them, which positions people within a structure of meaning and order. A religion can play a central role in 'world maintenance', explaining and justifying social divisions by providing a legitimizing authority for a particular pattern of social relationships (Berger, 1967). Religious prescriptions about what people should or should not do legitimize the social order. Thus, a key aspect of religious authority is that it provides an explanation of the social order, where the subordination of certain groups may be presented as part of a (God-given) *natural order* of society – a dominant belief in European thought until the eighteenth-century Enlightenment (Jacob, 1981) – which can be employed to justify a hierarchy of dominance and the subordination of social groups (Sidanius and Pratto, 1999; see Chapter 4). In modern times, Karl Marx described religion in a capitalist society metaphorically as the drug ('opium') of the oppressed masses, either giving them succour ('the heart in a heartless world') or masking their oppression (McKinnon, 2005). The Italian Marxist philosopher Antonio Gramsci argued that a revolution of an oppressed majority was much less likely against the hegemonic power of the church and state, than against simply an oppressive state, as the former legitimizes the latter by associating the social structure with a moral and social order accepted by the people (Eyerman, 1981).

Clearly, social groups in subordinate positions are aware of the social dominance of other groups and, despite world-maintaining pressures, there have always been attempts throughout history to change the social structure of a society. Therefore, for the dominant group, holding on to their power comes from exercising *social control* (e.g. Janowitz, 1975). For the eleventh-century Normans in England this meant building a large network of between 500 and 1,000 strategically placed castles to dominate the surrounding lands. Since the Enlightenment, modern governments no longer claim a religious authority, but employ a variety of formal mechanisms of social control, such as the military to defend the country from external threat and suppress rebellion, militia to deal with local disturbances such as riots and the police to maintain order in the society. Social *regulation*, that is, obliging obedience to the formal norms of the society (such as its laws), can be potentially beneficial to citizens, in protecting their human rights, but over-regulation or regulation in an oppressive economic system can result in alienation, which, in Marxist terms, is a lack of control over one's own production in a stratified society (Acevedo, 2005). A legal system is instituted to deal with transgressors, such as a criminal justice system involving the police, lawyers, courts and punishments from fines to imprisonment. All these formal systems of social control are there to avoid deviance and maintain control. Historically this was done rather crudely, with the threat and enactment of severe physical penalties including capital punishment, in public exhibitions of state control. However, Foucault ([1975] 1995) argued that, from the eighteenth century, social control developed into the maintenance of *discipline*, such as the institution of prisons and the technology of surveillance. Power became distributed across disciplinary institutions (such as prisons, schools and hospitals), constructing and controlling individuals, to create 'docile bodies' (or 'normal' citizens) that are distinguished from deviants, which these institutions inevitably create as well (see Chapter 5). Thus, the disciplinary society is one where state power acts throughout the society via the disciplinary institutions to maintain the social organization. However, as well as formal systems of social control, a society can also maintain order by *informal social control* through the socialization process, as described in Chapter 5. Informal social control makes the members of a society complicit in maintaining the power relations of the society by internalizing social norms (e.g. Cialdini, 2007). Thus, all of the cultural factors discussed in Chapter 5, from socialization, schooling and learning the informal norms of society will result in its members acquiring knowledge of their society and its social structure, often represented as the 'proper' structure of society. The socialization process will contain within it explanations of the social relations and power structures in the society. Indeed, since the early sociological analysis of the concept, it has been argued that, in modern Western societies, informal mechanisms of social control can have a more powerful influence over the members of a society than the formal mechanisms, in the maintenance of control over the wider population by the dominant group (Ross, 1901).

Despite these powerful methods of maintaining social control, Berger (1967) argued that all socially constructed worlds are precarious – at risk of upheaval from events and conflicting interests. Religion, as well as supporting a social structure, can have the opposite effect, that of destabilizing the social order, or of 'world shaking' as Berger (1967) termed it; as demonstrated by the effect of Martin Luther's criticisms of the Church in 1517 (resulting the Protestant–Catholic schism in the Christian Church), the religion-led Western anti-slavery movement of the eighteenth and nineteenth centuries, or the role of religion in the anti-apartheid liberation struggle in South Africa (Smith, 1996). Hence, within any society there will be competing forces for both stability and instability. This was examined in a study by Gates et al. (2006), who analysed a dataset of the political systems of all countries with over half a million inhabitants between 1800 and 2000 in terms of their stability, examining autocratic and democratic systems, on the dimensions of executive recruitment (whether leadership was restricted or open), constraints on executive decision-making (from few to many) and political participation (from low to high; such as electoral involvement). The 'low' end of all the three dimensions was characterized as an 'ideal' autocratic system with the 'high' end of all three dimensions, characterized as the 'ideal' democratic system. They found that the most stable systems tended to be ones that were consistently (i.e. self-reinforcing) autocratic or democratic. With inconsistency (such as increasing participation in an autocratic system or restricted executive recruitment from a narrow social group in a democracy) there will be a tendency for the system to change in the direction of the nearest consistent ideal type. Identifying inconsistency in the system will also present a challenge to its stability. For example, highlighting unfairness in a democratic system is to seek to change it in the direction of a more ideal democracy. Thus, in a democracy, labelling the views of one's political opponents as 'stereotypes' (represented as discriminatory and wrong), particularly if they form the power elite, is a political act seeking system change. Hence, highlighting 'stereotypes' of specific social groups can be considered as 'strategic tools' (Staerklé et al., 2011; see Chapter 5) in undermining a dominant ideology, highlighting social inequality and seeking to change the social structure.

Introduction to ideology

There are a variety of meanings applied to the term *ideology*, from the study of ideas to a pejorative term for another person's views, but it is worth starting with the basic idea: ideology is a worldview, for example having a liberal or conservative, left-wing or right-wing political ideology (e.g. Williams, 1977), discussed later in this chapter. The topic gets more complicated when considered from a Marxist perspective. For Marx, each social class has its different worldview, which he referred to as *class consciousness*. However, he argued, the ideology of the bourgeoisie, about capitalism, was a case of 'false consciousness' as their views disguised their 'real' interests in the exploitation and oppression of the working class. In the 1920s György Lukás, working in the Marxist tradition, argued that the irrational structure of the social world (in a capitalist society) results in the need to construct theories of society to explain – or rationalize – why this state of the world has come about. Ideologies are such explanations. Some of these ideologies construct social reality in ways to maintain the status quo. The ideological framework of the bourgeoisie, from economics to art, supports the capitalist system, including its justifications of why there are rich and poor people (Eyerman, 1981). For Lukás, human relations within a capitalist society become defined in capitalist terms (exchange and commodities), and thus produce a false consciousness – a capitalist ideology represented as traditional 'knowledge' – which can influence all social classes. However, excluded from the control of economic resources and political power, the working class have a more direct knowledge of their 'real' situation through their own experiences (Eyerman, 1981). Therefore the development of class consciousness in the workers, that is an understanding of Marxist ideology, is crucial for capitalism to be opposed. In developing their own class consciousness – rejecting the ideology of the bourgeoisie – and recognizing their own exploitation at the hands of the capitalists and bankers, the workers will, according to Marxist theory, seek to change the social order (in a 'class struggle').

This indicates the complexity of the term 'ideology' as it can refer to three concepts: (1) the development of ideas and understandings about the social world, (2) the set of beliefs about the social world held by a particular group of people (such as a social class) and (3) a set of illusory beliefs about the social world; which are 'false' in comparison to an alternative ideological framework that is accepted as 'true' – be it Marxism or scientific method (Williams, 1977). Thus, while one group of people may earnestly hold a set of beliefs, they may be criticized by others (with a different worldview) as being unable to see the 'true' state of the social world, and referred to pejoratively as ideologues, as they are considered blinkered by their doctrinaire ideology. However, believers in any ideology will claim the 'truth' of their views, which creates the problem of finding an agreed truth, independent of ideology, which may not be possible.[1] As Williams[2] (2002) argued, while there may be universal agreement about certain aspects of the social world, such as a person's income for a particular year expressed in terms of US dollars, which can be considered facts or true statements, other aspects are open to debate, such as whether this income is considered adequate to live at an acceptable standard. Therefore, there may be no agreed 'truth' about the definition of 'the poor', with a person considered poor in one social context (or by one ideological group) but not poor in another, such as at a different time or place (or by another ideological group), despite universal agreement on their income and access to resources. More problematic is that the explanation of why people are 'poor' (or not), is embedded in specific constructions of these terms through the ideology of the people proposing them. Consequently, competing ideologies do not deny the existence of facts about the social world but differ in their interpretation of them. An additional problem about the distinction between ideology and the 'true' state of the world is that most people (such as voters in a Western country's national election) simply do not have enough factual information to make a detailed evidenced-based decision based on the 'true' state of the social world (Martin, 2015), even if there is one! People's information about the world is usually partial and often drawn from sources, such as newspapers and news websites, which themselves are associated with particular ideologies (such as conservative or liberal), so will be representing that information in a particular way.

Lukás was influential in the Frankfurt School of social theorists, such as Adorno and his colleagues, whose work was discussed in Chapter 2. These scholars moved to the United States from Europe, at the time of the Nazi threat, and the failure of the Marxist activists to understand the German working class. In the 1930s, members of the Frankfurt School, such as Adorno, shifted away from a Marxist analysis of false consciousness, based on economic relations. In their studies of prejudice in the United States the focus was on personal relations, drawing on the psychodynamic ideas of Freud, and the role of the family and upbringing on adult personality as an ideological explanatory framework, which, it was acknowledged, ignored economic processes (Fromm, [1932] 1982). They were particularly concerned about the development of anti-Semitism, having themselves been forced to flee Europe from the Nazis, but also examined racism within the context of their new society. Adorno and his colleagues represented the prejudiced, authoritarian individual (the stereotype user) as having developed a 'false consciousness' about the social world but this time the explanation was presented in Freudian terms rather than those of Marx. This was picked up by Allport ([1954] 1979) who made the ideological position clearer by associating the non-prejudiced person – the non-stereotype user – with liberal and democratic (American) values (see Chapter 2). Hence the stereotype user was an 'irrational' thinker who had developed an ideology of difference that, in terms of an egalitarian ideology, is a false consciousness. This idea that accepting a contrary ideological position (to the observer[3]) is a sign of 'faulty' thinking has continued within Western thought. For example, Thompson (2015) has argued that false consciousness is an irrational 'defective' social cognition arising through socialization to accept uncritically the dominant values of a social system, and 'false consciousness remains a major problem in modern societies' Thompson (2015, p. 459). He is clear of the standard against which an ideological 'consciousness' should be measured: 'The Enlightenment project of producing autonomous, rationally competent citizens should still be the standard by which to judge the intensity of defective social cognition' (Thompson, 2015, p. 459). The Enlightenment project will be considered later in this chapter.

The failure of the Marxist revolutionary movements in the later twentieth century, the post-Second World War economic success of capitalism and the diminution of traditional working-class employment led to a loss of influence of Marxism in Western political thought in the late twentieth century. However, the Marxist ideas about ideology that dominated the twentieth century still have a legacy in modern thinking about the concept (Freeden, 2003). While it is tempting to see ideology as a system of values, when people discuss ideology, as Marx did, they often focus on certain moral, religious or political beliefs about the social world – and the social order – that are '*idealized, universalized* and *detached* expressions of actual social relations' (Martin, 2015, p. 18). A person's system of beliefs is often characterized as 'their own' (i.e. individually based) in the academic stereotype research, yet ideologies are group-based belief systems, with political ideas constructed within a sociocultural context by a specific social group about what the social relations between people should be. The expression of ideological beliefs links a person to fellow group members (others who share their political views) and distinguishes them from their political enemies. Hence opinions can be considered as deriving from group membership and group-based ideology as the idealized representation of that group in terms of its beliefs about the world (Martin, 2015). This is particularly relevant in Western democracies dominated by political parties, which usually represent ideological positions on issues, which have tended to be associated with class-based groups (Saunders, 1990). The parties exist to achieve power and hence influence social relations, such as using their power to change laws (and other formal norms). However, allegiance to a political party can be considered as an important group membership for a person's identity (see Chapter 4) and hence voting for a particular party may be transmitted across the generations in families and communities (see Chapter 5). Thus, it may be inappropriate to model a person's ideological (political and moral) views, in terms of a 'rational' seeker after an 'accurate' social 'truth', but as a politician acting in support of group interests, such as party, class and social status: that is, cultural group membership (see Haidt, 2001).

Ideology as a cultural system

The anthropologist Clifford Geertz (1973) acknowledged that a popular view of 'ideology' is of a rigid and mistaken set of beliefs, which presents a distortion of the social world (the 'truth' of which can potentially be discovered by scientific methods): a view influenced by Marxist ideas. A contrasting viewpoint, Geertz identified, is ideology as an outcome of a socio-psychological 'strain' of coping with social relations, such as having to fulfil a social role, which has often been considered in psychological, particularly Freudian, terms. The resulting anxiety is ameliorated by adopting a reassuring ideology (see Chapter 2). While acknowledging both interpretations of ideology, and their potential usefulness, Geertz sought to create a less evaluative definition that could be employed by social scientists. He drew on the idea of 'symbol systems'. He argued that human beings are 'suspended in webs of significance' that they themselves have spun. He continued, 'I take culture to be those webs, and the analysis of it to be therefore not an experimental science in search of law but an interpretive one in search of meaning' (Geertz, 1973, p. 5). Understanding culture involves the interpretation of symbols, such as cultural artefacts (such as a crown symbolizing authority), rituals (such as a wedding) and the meanings communicated in language as a symbolic system. For Geertz, ideologies are symbol systems that construct social realities. Ideologies are ways of giving meaning to experience. 'It is thus not truth that varies with social, psychological, and cultural contexts but the symbols we construct in our unequally effective attempts to grasp it' Geertz (1973, p. 212). We may weave new webs but we cannot make sense of the world directly (and perceive the 'true' nature of social reality) but only make sense of it through one web or another. In this sense, all ideologies are false – as there is no universally agreed 'truth' – but they are what influence our actions. Ideologies are constructed in culture, which constructs a social order. 'Culture is the fabric of meaning in terms of which human beings interpret their experience and guide their action; social structure is the form that action takes, the actually existing network of social relations' (Geertz, 1973, p. 145). There will be a social structure based on a dominant ideology in a culture. Competing ideologies will construct different social structures. Hence it is the construction of ideologies, with their 'images of social order' that makes human beings the political creatures that they are (Geertz, 1973, p. 218).

Mumby (1989) agreed with Geertz's definition of culture and ideology and argued that ideology and power are intimately related. The web of culture is also the site of conflicts and competition: 'the production and reproduction of culture is inseparable from the relations of domination that characterize a social system' (Mumby, 1989, p. 293). To Mumby, ideology is not just a system of beliefs but constitutes the 'consciousness of every social actor' (Mumby, 1989, p. 302), and sustains social relations of dominance. Thus, politics can be considered as argumentation in terms of competing ideologies that are employed with expressive power and rhetorical force to maximize their persuasive effect on others, by techniques such as the denial of contradiction, representing group interests as universal, presenting humanly created phenomena as objectified and immutable, and claiming that the goals and values of the dominant group are also the values of subordinate groups (see Chapter 7). The important point about human cultures is their flexibility of meaning-making. Unlike an animal's limited and usually innate responses (to death for example) historically people have reacted in a variety of ways in different cultures in terms of the meanings assigned, to death for example:

the disposal of a corpse may be undertaken in a number of different ways, including burial, cremation or even mummification. Each religion has its own rituals and ceremonies surrounding death dependent on its ideology. Geertz (1973, p. 218) argued that humans are agents of their own realization, creating out of their own 'general capacity for the construction of symbolic models the specific capabilities that define' themselves. People collectively construct the meanings of their own lives, and in times of upheaval or social change this becomes particularly relevant to them. Natural disaster, war, periods of discovery and invention, all may present challenges to the 'web of significance' and lead to the development of alternative interpretations of social reality. Ideologies are not immutable and can be challenged and reconstructed through political action. One such period, critical in the history of Western societies is referred to as the Age of Enlightenment, which will be considered later in this chapter.

Social construction, social groups and ideology

As Bruner et al. (1956) argued, social categories are inventions, not discoveries (see Chapter 3). Indeed, following from Bruner's point, we can conclude that the choice of categories is neither 'natural' nor arbitrary, but is meaningfully chosen, and is intimately associated with the culture and an ideology. Modern genetics informs us that there is only one race of human sapiens, regardless of superficial physical differences (Tattersall, 2009) with skin colour, for example, an environmental adaptation (Tiosano et al., 2016), so the categorization of people into 'races' related to attributes such as 'skin colour' is a social construction. Indeed, there is historical evidence that in societies that do not distinguish between people on the basis of their 'race' such cultural categories do not emerge. For example, Kaufmann (2017) investigated the historical records of hundreds of people of African origin living in sixteenth-century Tudor England. Of particular importance was the sheer number of people who – despite the scant records – appeared to live ordinary lives, working in a range of jobs, marrying and having children, as integrated members of the community, with no evidence of 'racial' discrimination. Hence claims about a specific model of human nature – as 'true' or 'real' – and even the 'evidence' presented in support of it, is challenged by *social constructionism*, which argues that 'taken-for-granted knowledge' (Burr, 2015, p. 2) can be critically examined and shown to be historically and culturally specific. Therefore a specific interpretation of the social world is an (ideological) construction in a context for a purpose and, as such, cannot be divorced from social action and social motives. Also, language is not simply a descriptive medium for describing the 'natural' categories that exist in the world, but it is through language that the social world is constructed and interpreted (Burr, 2015; Gergen, 2015; see Chapter 7). As we saw in Chapter 4, the identification and labelling of 'deviance' is a social construction in language. The choice of social categories (in a culture), the labels selected to refer to them and their associated attributes are all described through language in terms of a particular ideological construction (see Chapter 7). As we saw in Chapter 2, in the

American research, the stereotype of Black people has traditionally been identified in negative terms but more recent research indicates that the stereotype of African American is much more positive (Philogène, 2001). While it may be argued that the two category labels relate to the 'same' group of people, the different terminology reflects a changing ideological construction of them.

Stereotypes as an ideological issue

In 2014, former US President Bill Clinton cleverly commented: 'We only have one remaining bigotry. We don't want to be around anybody who disagrees with us.' The power of group membership, and its accompanying ideological beliefs, often leads to a rejection of an opposing ideological group, rather than any consideration of their views. When the US government published their 2018 annual *Human Rights Report*, which was highly critical of Russia, the Russian Foreign Ministry replied with a statement that the report was based on 'Russophobic stereotypes' and contained 'politicized assessments and blunt ideology-driven clichés' (Khamelyanin, 2018). We can see from this that stereotypes and ideology share at least one characteristic in common: they have both been used in pejorative terms. There have been a number of definitions of stereotypes given in this book (see Chapter 1), and I don't think that a reader would be surprised to read the following description: They 'can be seen as cognitive structures with legitimizing functions. There is no principle or very clear demarcation from other knowledge structures, although there clearly are differences' (Stråth, 2006, p. 23). However, this is not a definition of a stereotype but of ideology. While the word 'ideology' evokes a wider social, cultural and political context than the word 'stereotype', the two words are intimately linked. Stereotypes only gain their meaning when considered in terms of an ideology. A statement about a social group is typically only labelled as a 'stereotype' when it follows from an ideological position that the speaker has rejected in favour of an alternative ideology. Recall from Chapter 2, Lippmann (1922) in his invention of the term 'stereotype' employed the example of the French Prime Minister Clemenceau's approach to the Germans in the treaty negotiations post-the First World War. It is clear that he, Lippmann, thought that Clemenceau was wrong. According to Lippmann's belief system, Clemenceau *should* have thought differently – and treated the Germans more leniently. By claiming that Clemenceau had a 'stereotypical' view of the Germans (and this is a 'bad thing' as it was a fixed outmoded view), Clemenceau was wrong and Lippmann right.[4] Lippmann had employed the term 'stereotype' in his argument to claim a superiority of his view over that of Clemenceau, who I am sure would have disagreed (see Chapter 7). This also explains why a relatively small set of stereotypes have been of major interest in the research in the United States. Negative stereotypes of African Americans are associated with an ideology of difference and social discrimination, which is considered unacceptable in a society professing egalitarian values as its core ideology, which American psychologists studying stereotypes such as Allport ([1954] 1979, p. 331) clearly support:

[I]n the United States, discrimination is … in a profound sense, regarded as un-American. The founding fathers took a strong stand on the matter. And the common people, from the earliest days of the Republic, knew what that stand was.[5]

The influence of the Enlightenment on Western ideology

Geertz (1973) argued that in a society where tradition guides social relations there is less likely to be the creation of new ideologies. The life of the medieval European peasant was governed by the cycles of the season, the diktats of their lord and the rules of the church. While the society remained stable, social changes only occurred slowly, but an occasional upheaval, such as the bubonic plague (Black Death) in the middle of the fourteenth century, had a significant impact on the lives of the people, leading to more radical social change. However, in the late seventeenth century and eighteenth century there arose in Europe (including Britain and its North American colonies), people of the 'middling sort', unaligned to aristocratic landowners or their labourers, but doctors, lawyers, merchants, teachers, military officers and priests, who were neither poor nor rich but intellectually engaged at a time when there were also major advances in science, communication and technology. Uniquely, the social context allowed this middling sort (who later became known as the 'middle class') to be critically reflective about human experience, framed in terms of rational thinking, without presenting themselves as seditious, in Britain at least (Black, 2015). Urban life, particularly in London and other major cities, and the growth of (global) commercial activity provided the framework for new scientific investigations and critical thought. Widespread across Europe, the period became known as the Enlightenment (or the Age of Reason). Human relations were no longer to be constrained by religious orthodoxy or authoritarian leadership but determined by rational thought. Historically, this period is viewed as the beginnings of modernity, and represented in the West as the point in history 'that laid the groundwork for today's hegemonic global culture of liberal democracy and human rights' (Stuurman, 2010, p. 8). The latter half of the eighteenth century saw both the American and French Revolutions introducing the idea of governance based on equality and fairness.

Egalitarianism: equality and fairness

The idea that people have certain 'rights', that is, self-evident expectations about their existence, can be traced back to the philosopher Thomas Hobbes in *The Leviathan*, published in 1651, who proposed that individuals have the 'natural right' of self-preservation. Hence, it was not immoral or against 'natural law' for a destitute and starving person to steal food or for a person to refuse to act to bring about their own self-destruction. However, Hobbes did not see this as fundamentally threatening the authority of the state (or the sovereign) over the citizens (Carmichael, 1990). It was the philosopher John Locke in his two treaties on government, in 1689 and

1690, who argued that it was justifiable to rebel against a state that violated the citizens' 'natural rights' to life, liberty and property (Thompson, 1976). With rights also came duties, such as not violating another person's natural rights. The view that a sovereign had a natural right given by God to rule over the population was also rejected. Consequently, underlying government was a 'social contract' between the citizens and the authority, where the former would give up some of their rights to the latter so that it would act for the general good to protect citizens' rights and promote their well-being. Thus, legitimate government is only at the consent of the people. Drawing on these Lockean ideas, and by representing the British king George III as an autocratic dictator, as did political activist and philosopher Thomas Paine, the American colonists could argue for the legitimacy of declaring their independence in 1776. The fact that decisions on the governance of the colonies, such as taxation, were taken in the British parliament, rather than by the king, was also rejected as illegitimate, on the basis that the colonists themselves had no representation in this parliament, and they therefore had a legitimate 'right' to reject taxation without representation. In the Declaration of Independence, Thomas Jefferson presented these Enlightenment values as the basis for government: 'We hold these truths to be self-evident: that all men are created equal; that they are endowed by their Creator with certain unalienable rights; that among these are life, liberty and the pursuit of happiness' (US National Archives, n.d.).

The idea of egalitarianism as a political philosophy was promoted by Paine in *Common Sense* (1776), which became a best-seller in the 13 rebelling American colonies in that year. Indeed, Paine argued very strongly for government where the sovereignty lay with the people, not a monarch. He was later to develop these ideas into explaining how, in a republic, this is enacted through a democratic process: 'This sovereignty is exercised in electing and deputing a certain number of persons to represent and to act for the whole' (Shapiro and Calvert, 2014). Paine also lived in France in the 1790s during the French Revolution (1789–1799), writing the *Rights of Man* in 1791. Individuals may not have the power to exercise their natural rights, so the government (of collective sovereignty) should act to defend these rights. Thus, governments should act for the good of the people, with their power constrained by the will of the people. These ideas were often represented in the various mottos circulating during the French Revolution, such as the phrase 'liberté, egalité, fraternité', first used by Maximilien Robespierre in 1790, and later adopted by the French state in 1848.

Many of these ideas of Enlightenment philosophy serve as the basis for the modern liberal democracies of the West, promoting 'government of the people, by the people, for the people', as Abraham Lincoln put it in the Gettysburg Address of 1863. However, despite Paine's argument that simple systems were less disordered, the actual process of government (in maintaining the natural rights of people) can be complex due to competing issues related to different rights. Edmund Burke in the *Reflections on the Revolution in France* (1790) (Burke, 2015) argued that natural rights may not be preserved in an uncivil society and, for a civil society, the government should act in terms of the general utility: for example some aspects of individual liberty must be given up to maintain the common good. This creates difficult issues of how to protect the rights of the few as well as of the many, the weak as well as the strong. Indeed, debates in modern political philosophy often revolve around questions of liberty (such as what are valid restrictions of people's freedoms) and on equality (such as what is just and unjust), with political lobbyists arguing that evidence of specific types of discrimination counters a basic belief in equality, and proposing changes to be made in society and to the legal system, to ameliorate the identified inequality, based on fairness (e.g. Rawls, 2007).

Commerce and colonialism

Yet this is not the only story of the Enlightenment period in Western history. In the fifteenth century, Europeans were well aware of the wonderful products of Asia, such as spices and silks, but they were extremely expensive. Their source lay in the 'Far East' (from a European perspective), involving long land trade routes (now referred to as the Silk Road) dominated by powerful intermediaries who determined the price. However, the development of ocean-going ships, particularly in Portugal and Spain, presented an opportunity to change all that. In 1488, Bartolomeu Dias sailed around the Cape of Good Hope, creating a European route to the Indian Ocean and, later, to the South China Sea, making the coasts of Africa, India, the Spice Islands (Maluku) and China accessible to European traders. In 1492, Christopher Columbus' attempt to find a Western route the East Indies (the Spice Islands) encountered the American continent, with its huge potential for exploitation. In 1519, Ferdinand Magellan rounded Cape Horn, crossed the Pacific Ocean, and arrived at the Spice Islands in 1521. The world's oceans were now open to European mariners who could travel both ways to Asia, the source of the prized products – avoiding intermediaries and their costs. Not only were the European ships technologically advanced (ocean-going) but they also carried advanced weaponry in the form of guns (muskets and cannons). Trading routes were opened along with trading stations, often by force or the threat of force, making the European traders immensely wealthy. In the Treaties of Tordesillas (1494) and the Treaty of Zaragoza (1529), with the support of the Pope, Portugal and Spain divided the non-Christian world between them (Coben, 2015; Disney, 2009). This did not please the Dutch (arriving later in the Spice Islands and Japan), or the British and French (arriving in India and North America). Thus, began a period of rivalry between the European powers in their trade with, and colonization of, the rest of the world, throughout the Enlightenment period.

How did the Europeans – claiming to be civilized nations – justify their actions? The Dutch jurist Hugo Grotius (1583–1645), an early Enlightenment thinker of international law, and also a proponent of the idea of natural law, argued that the Portuguese could not claim exclusive rights to the Eastern trade routes, due to the self-evident Law of Nations, that is, 'Every nation is free to travel to every other nation, and to trade with it' (Thornton, 2004, p. 31; see Clulow, 2014). He also proposed that the seas are free for anyone to travel and are not subject to national jurisdiction. This concept of the 'freedom of the seas' (Reppy, 1950) was later supported by Britain and the United States; and has remained a feature of international law. Land ownership could be acquired legally (from a European perspective) in three main ways. First, it could be bought from a local authority, such as a sovereign, providing legal documentation. Second, it could be owned, according to international law, by 'right of conquest' (Korman, 1996), that is, having been taken by force of arms, it became legally the property of the victor (the 'right of conquest' was only completely removed from international law by a United Nations Resolution in 1974). Finally, land could be claimed under the doctrine of *terra nullius* ('empty lands'), that is, land could be claimed that was currently 'vacant' or without ownership (O'Neill, 2016).

While purchasing the land or acquiring it by conquest was costly,[6] claiming 'empty lands' had both a cost benefit and appeared to avoid the charge of being aggressive conquerors. This was the doctrine behind much of the British acquisition of North American lands (O'Neill, 2016). The problem with this doctrine is that these so-called 'empty lands' were not empty of people at all. They might not have had the population density of Europe or may not have had the farms, cities and social structure recognizable to the Europeans but there were people there and the Europeans had to acknowledge the fact. A justification came from John Locke: while God had given the land to all men, it was their duty to God 'to subdue it, to cultivate it, enrich it, and to divide it up into discrete individual tracts of private property', which 'rational' (European) men had done (O'Neill, 2016, p. 22). Thus, the hunters moving across the land, or villagers with no sense of private property, were 'irrational', and wilfully or ignorantly ignoring God's law. This idea was reinforced by their status as non-Christian heathens. Thus, the take-over of the not-empty 'empty lands' was justified as bringing both 'civilization' and the 'word of God' to native peoples who were viewed as 'less than fully equal human beings' in the eyes of the Europeans (O'Neill, 2016, p. 22).

Drawing on the idea of human progression, in the mid-eighteenth century, the philosopher and economist Adam Smith spelt out a popular view of the time: there were four stages of human historical development – hunting, pasturage, farming and commerce. Furthermore, different peoples of the world were mapped on to the stages in terms of their inferred development: from the Native Americans at the first stage; nomads of the Eurasian Steppe at the second; the great civilizations such as Egypt, Rome, China, India and Japan at the third; and finally only eighteenth-century Europeans at the fourth stage of 'commercial society' (Stuurman, 2010). This assumed progression, on the path to civilization and reason, was presented more starkly later in the century by Jean-Jacques Rousseau who characterized the hunters as 'savages', the nomads as 'barbarians' and the farmers and traders as 'civilized' (e.g. Mendham, 2011). The new rational, scientific ideas of the Enlightenment led to a fascination with taxonomy; with Carl Linnaeus classifying plants, animals and minerals, in a systematic way; hierarchically, from kingdoms (such as the animal kingdom), down through families, species and varieties. Each species was given a unique name and, despite its theoretical weaknesses, the terminology still remains influential in the classification of plants and animals today. Unfortunately, Linnaeus sought to apply the method to people, categorizing people in terms of a mixture of physical and cultural differences, essentially based on their continental location, with the inference of European superiority (e.g. Fara, 2004). While Linnaeus did not employ the term 'race' in his classification, others did: such as the German physician Johann Blumenbach, the French philosopher Voltaire and British philosopher David Hume (Harris, 1968). Numerous texts were created, documenting the measurement of superficial human physical characteristics with a variety of pseudo-biological interpretations. The concept of biological degeneracy led to the most outrageous claims about the racial differences between people in what is now termed *scientific racism*, although the different human 'races' were 'created by the scientists, not by nature' (Blakey, 1999, p. 26). It is more properly referred to as 'pseudoscientific racism' (Pickering, 2001) as it is simply racism wrapped up in bad science. Modern genetic evidence shows that *Homo sapiens* as Linnaeus termed them have a common genetic origin in Africa, thus the concept of human 'races' is scientifically meaningless (Tattershall, 2009). Hence, a racial distinction between people is a social construction (Blakey, 1999), but was employed as an ideological justification for colonization.

The legacy of Western Enlightenment history

Stuurman (2010) argued that both these stories – enlightenment and egalitarianism on the one hand and colonialism and European 'civilization' on the other – are misguided and simplistic accounts of history, ignoring the complexity and variety of ideas and activities of that historical period in an attempt to present a preconceived line of argument. It is important to realize that during the Enlightenment period there were a wide variety of opinions: for example, the anti-imperialist views of Denis Diderot (Stuurman, 2010). Yet, with the collapse of the European empires during the upheavals of the twentieth century, the nations of the West in the late twentieth and early twenty-first centuries had to deal with a post-colonial world (McLeod, 2010), and a legacy of former domination (e.g. Hall, 1992). At the same time the ideas of liberal democracy and egalitarianism, deriving from the Enlightenment thinkers, came more to the fore of political discourse, with many Western countries instituting a range of civil rights and equality legislation in the latter half of the twentieth century. Although simplified constructions of history (that can be labelled as cultural myths), these two competing stories of the Enlightenment retain a pervasive influence on Western thought even in the twenty-first century (e.g. Israel, 2001; Pagden, 2013).

Stereotypes and the ideological construction of difference

These two stories of the Enlightenment are relevant to the understanding of what is meant by a 'stereotype', as they identify a fundamental difference between egalitarian ideologies and ideologies of difference. The stereotypes of public concern, the 'socially sensitive topics' (Ewoldsen et al., 2015), are those related to societal discrimination that is related to an ideology of difference. Thus, the 'problem' of stereotypes, from an egalitarian ideological perspective, is that an ideology of difference is employed to justify societal discrimination *that is unfair or unjust*. For example, employing a stereotype as an a priori ideological belief in a social group's 'incompetence' as a reason for restricting their opportunities in society (and maintain societal discrimination) simply denies the group members their equal rights and any chance to demonstrate their actual competence; whereas providing equal opportunities to take on a diversity of roles (and a level playing field in their performance) is likely to demonstrate the stereotype to be false. Thus, an egalitarian ideology does not deny the possibility of differences between people (and groups) but focuses on the ways in which a particular society denies equal opportunities, equal rights or equal treatment under the law. Thus, the vast majority of the research into stereotypes has been focused on those stereotypes associated with discrimination in American society (and other Western societies) which, from an egalitarian perspective, *should not be so*.

Stereotypes and an ideology of racism

Ancient Rome was a society built on slavery, which was not based on race.[7] The Romans regularly freed slaves (by manumission) and so it was possible for a person to be born free, captured in war, enslaved and then freed by a master to live a free life in Roman society (Joshel, 2010; Wiedemann, 1985). Seneca (the Stoic tutor of the Emperor Nero), a rich slave owner, wrote to his friend Lucilius:

> Kindly remember that he whom you call your slave sprang from the same stock, is smiled upon by the same skies, and on equal terms with yourself breathes, lives, and dies. It is just as possible for you to see in him a free-born man as for him to see in you a slave.
>
> *Seneca, 2016, letter 47:10*

Thus, their position (as slaves) was often attributed to fate rather than to a fundamental difference in 'nature'. The situation in seventeenth- and eighteenth-century North America was very different. Slaves were distinguishable by origin and skin colour. The negative characteristics attributed to Africans (what is now labelled as a 'stereotype') was a consistent feature of Europe and American literature during the eighteenth and nineteenth centuries, in stories, cartoons, advertisements and accounts (Pickering, 2001). Pickering (2001) referred to this propaganda output as 'the politics of not belonging', which constructed an ideological difference between the European and the African. This mass media promotion of racial difference (which was strongest in the nineteenth century) put forward a racist argument for social dominance in a social context where other ideologies challenged it, such as the egalitarianism of Thomas Paine, for example. The primary criticism of slavery in the eighteenth century was from devout Christians, particularly the Quakers who believed that all people were equal under God, with the Pennsylvanian Quakers banning slavery among themselves and founding the Pennsylvania Abolition Society in 1775.

The United States was established on a founding ideology of egalitarianism – influenced by Locke's views of a just and liberal society (Pangle, 1988). As noted above, the American Declaration of Independence (1776), in Thomas Jefferson's words, claimed that the creation of all men as equal was self-evident. Yet 41 out of 56[8] signatories, including Jefferson himself, were owners of Black slaves. Five early presidents owned more than 100 slaves each: George Washington (250–350), Thomas Jefferson (around 200), James Madison (over 100), Andrew Jackson (under 200) and Zachery Taylor (under 150), according to Whitney (2006). This is a contradiction. How could a society professing a founding principle of equality support an institutional structure of slavery based on race? The answer is in the social construction of difference between European men and African men that excluded the latter from the equality of the former (an ideology of 'not belonging'). In his *Notes on the State of Virginia* (1785), Jefferson presented the inferred characteristics of Black people: '[I]n reason much inferior, as I think one could scarcely be found capable of tracing and comprehending the investigations of Euclid' (Franklin and Gates, 2001, p. 45). Benjamin Banneker clearly could, and wrote to Jefferson in 1791. Banneker was a free Black man, an astronomer and mathematician who created a series of almanacs. Jefferson replied sympathetically ('no body wishes more than I do to see such proofs as you exhibit'; Ray, 1998, p. 399) but nothing changed in the circumstances of Black people in the country (Cerami, 2002, p. 168). The expression of egalitarian values can only be maintained if an excluded group is viewed as 'not belonging' (Pickering, 2001), i.e. not belonging to the category of people who should be treated equally. Slavery was abolished 74 years later. Yet, post-slavery, the implementation of anti-miscegenation laws, segregation and occupational discrimination continued to support the politics of 'not belonging', maintaining a 'racial' pattern of privilege in the society. At the time Allport's ([1954] 1979) book on prejudice was being published, African American psychologist Claude Steele was learning what it meant to be Black as a young child due to the racist restrictions in access to the local swimming pool (Steele, 2010).

Changing the structure of society, and outlawing societal discrimination based on race in areas such as occupational selection, through the civil rights legislation of the 1960s have had a material effect on that discrimination and, furthermore, there is evidence that the changes in American society have brought about a more positive image of the African American in that society (Philogène, 2001). However, evidence of racial stereotypes persisted, such as that of Black criminality (Devine and Elliot, 1995). Is this indicative of an irrational belief or is it evidence of continuing societal discrimination based on an ideology of difference? From the 2010 census, Sakala (2014) showed that the US prison population is made up of 39 per cent White people and 40 per cent Black people. However, White people make up 64 per cent of the general population and Black people only 13 per cent; meaning that 450 per hundred thousand of the White population are incarcerated along with 2,306 per hundred thousand of the Black population. Pro rata, this means that for every one White person incarcerated, five Black people were incarcerated. This shows that there exists an association between 'race' and crime in the society. Thus, there is a racial disparity in the criminal justice system (Tonry, 2010). From a purely egalitarian perspective, this is clearly a case of societal discrimination that should be corrected to bring about a fairer society. However, as Tonry (2010) has argued, research shows that some White people support policies that maintained racial hierarchies, with the stereotype of Black criminality supporting attitudes to crime that result in Black offenders being treated more harshly than White offenders. Hence, the stereotype of Black criminality is related to an ideology of difference within the structure of society.

Stereotypes and the ideological construction of gender

Enlightenment ideas of egalitarianism influenced both the American Revolution and the French Revolution. Yet in France, the concept of *fraternité* (in the motto '*liberté, egalité, fraternité*') was immediately challenged by Olympe de Gouges in 1791 as ignoring the rights of women (see Hunt, 2016). Gourges made her appeal in terms of the new egalitarian ideology based on human rights, supported by writers such as Thomas Paine. Yet her claims of equality were rejected.[9] While the traditional view of men and women was based on a religious ideology that they differed in their God-given 'nature' by theologians such as Thomas Aquinas (1225–1274), the Enlightenment thinkers behind the two revolutions rejected religious ideology in favour of reason and egalitarianism. So why were women excluded from the political sphere? While Locke argued for women's rationality and education, there persisted an ideology of difference, based on a belief that women's role was in the family rather than in politics (Nyland, 1993). Zaeske (1995, p. 193) argued that this was also the view of Thomas Jefferson: 'Jefferson reflected the common belief that women appealed to the passions rather than to reason and would inevitably corrupt civic virtue if they mixed "promiscuously" at public meetings.' Kukla (2008) also agreed that Jefferson saw women's role in the family, and the purpose of female education was to provide a supporting role for men within that family. Again, the justification of the exclusion of women from the polity (of citizens with equal rights) was by representing them by an ideology of difference, i.e. 'not belonging' to the category of citizens.

Campaigners for women's suffrage were eventually successful in 1920 in the United States and 1918 in the United Kingdom. However, as Friedan (1963) argued, if the ideology of difference persists in a society (see Chapter 1), there is a continued social pressure, combined with structural factors, presenting women's role in the family as 'natural' and other roles as 'unnatural'. Civil rights legislation during the 1960s sought to outlaw structural barriers to equal opportunities, and the United Nations Convention on the Elimination of all Forms of Discrimination Against Women (CEDAW), in 1979, made this an international treaty. A key issue that remained was that women may be denied these opportunities, and continue to be underrepresented in areas of employment, due to stereotypical beliefs (see Chapter 1) based on an ideology of difference. Hence, a capable woman might be judged more harshly than her male peers and denigrated as an atypical women (Fiske and Stevens, 1993). Research shows that when there is underrepresentation in an occupational field (such as politicians being mostly male) then successful women may be subtyped as atypical, but when gender is no longer diagnostic of the category then the stereotype will change: politicians will no longer be assumed to be male (Weber and Crocker, 1983). Thus, social change enhancing women's opportunities has brought about stereotype change over the last 30 years (Diekman and Eagly, 2000, Duehr and Bono, 2006; Eagly et al., 2019).

One contemporary issue is the proportion of women in the STEM (science, technology, engineering and mathematics) professions and in the caring professions (for example, teaching, health care, psychology and social work). The former have traditionally been represented as 'male' and the latter as 'female', according to the stereotypical association of male qualities with objectivity and rationality and female qualities with communality and emotional sensitivity (Eagly and Wood, 2012; Lloyd, 2002). In the World Economic Forum's (2018) *Global Gender Gap Index* (GGGI), many Western countries (such as the United States and United Kingdom) feature well into the 'good' half of the index, indicating greater gender equality than most countries worldwide. Yet female recruitment to STEM professions remains low, with only 20 per cent of engineering graduates being female in the United States (Yoder, 2017), and is both high and increasing in the caring professions, such as female teachers in the United States rising from 66 per cent in 1981 to 76 per cent in 2016 and male psychology PhDs dropping from 70 per cent in 1975 to 30 per cent in 2008, with women making up 74 per cent of early career psychologists in 2010 (Willyard, 2011). Thus, in statistical terms, there is a cultural association of women with the caring professions and men with STEM subjects in the United States in the twenty-first century. Yet, there is greater female participation in STEM careers in other cultures (Stoet and Geary, 2018) and historically in the Soviet Union as described in Chapter 1. Hence there continues to be a genuine (statistical) association between gender and these occupations in the United States, which appears to support an ideology of difference. From an egalitarian ideological perspective, the explanation lies in the culture, such as deep-seated discriminatory practices.

The ideological construction of the teenager

The modern Western stereotype of the vulnerable 'teenager', in the midst of an emotional identity crisis (e.g. Hinton, 2016b), makes little sense when applied to famous historical figures, such as 'teenagers' Princess Pingyang, commanding an army of 70,000 in seventh-century China, Joan of Arc (Jeanne D'Arc) in the fifteenth century, leading the French against the English in the Hundred Years War or British naval officer Horatio Nelson,[10] in the eighteenth century, a lieutenant at 19 (after six years' service), and in command of a warship at just 20. Historically, children were part of the adult social world, often working alongside them. Puberty indicated the change to adulthood, with the age of consent (in countries where it existed at all) reflecting this, at around 12 years (Bullough, 2005; Zhu and van der Aa, 2017). However, it was only in the nineteenth century that the modern concept of childhood was invented, defining its properties. Two key factors influenced this construction: the presence of children in the developing industrialized (factory) economy and a Victorian romanticism about an ideal childhood. Social reformers who saw the long hours and appalling conditions faced by many children (and adults) in the factories sought legal reform, such as banning the employment of children under a certain age leading to child labour legislation in the United States and Britain, primarily at the end of the nineteenth century (Cunningham, 2000). At the same time compulsory education was introduced in the United States (to 14 years) and in Britain to the age of 10 years. Alongside social and economic changes in people's lives, one of the major influences on the perception of childhood was the nineteenth invention of the concept of *childhood innocence*, which was interwoven with implicit ideologies of race and class (Ariès, 1962; Bernstein, 2011; Higonnet, 1998). The depictions of childhood in nineteenth-century art, such as by Mary Stevenson Cassatt (1844–1926) or Pierre-August Renoir (1841–1919), present idyllic scenes of middle-class (White) children 'untainted' by the 'corruption' of the adult world. Children were represented as angels (especially in the depictions of childhood death associated with high infant mortality), as in the photographic work of Julia Margaret Cameron (1815–1879). Ideas of protecting the child developed from stopping economic exploitation to the preservation of childhood innocence as an idealized state (Cunningham, 2006; Higonnet, 1998).

During the early twentieth century, the tightening of child labour legislation, increases in the age of consent (with a consequent delay in marriage) and rises in the age limit of compulsory education in the mid-twentieth century in the United States, resulted in the creation of a group of post-pubescent people, still in education yet with income (from parents) and old enough to drive, yet with no adult responsibilities or expectation that they would marry or enter the workplace. At first defined as a consumer group, the 'teenager' became a feature of American culture (Palladino, 1996), developing their own identity and rituals (such as 'dating'). The cultural position of the group – being adults physically yet not having adult responsibility – led to the stereotypical depiction of the 'irresponsible' teenager. Also teenage 'irresponsible' behaviour was interpreted as deviant, creating the concept (and stereotype) of the 'teenage delinquent' (represented in numerous films of the 1950s and 1960s) with the associated adult concerns about social control (Cohen, 1997). To explain this 'irresponsibility', the teenager was represented as not a proper (i.e. responsible) adult, labelled as an emotional risk taker, explained in terms of an 'immature' brain (Epstein, 2007; Payne, 2012). Furthermore, this description of the irresponsible teenager can be considered a stereotype as many would argue that neither risk-taking nor irresponsibility reflect the lives of the majority of teenagers (Sercombe, 2014).

It is important to note that the 'teenager' – the categorization of 13- to 19-year-old people as a distinct social group – is a cultural construction. It only emerged in

English-speaking Western societies, specifically in the cultural context of the United States, post-the Second World War. It did not emerge as a social category in other non-English-speaking cultures (Hinton, 2016b). Typically other languages begin the teen numbers with 11 (one-teen), so this particular 'teenage' (13–19) group makes little sense in other languages and cultures. However, the world-wide propagation of the concept of teenager throughout the world with the promotion of American cultural products (such as teen movies and teen magazines) led to its knowledge, if not necessarily its use, in other cultures (Hinton, 2016a, 2016b). However, the ambiguity of the teenager as adult-but-not-adult was clarified somewhat when the United Nations Convention on the Rights of the Child in 1989 proposed the age of 18 years as the division between child and adult, to which nation states agreed by signing the convention. Subsequently, the teenager has become located primarily in the 'child' category rather than the 'adult' category in everyday communication and even in psychology textbooks (Hinton, 2016b). However, numerous historical and legal precedents complicate this definition of childhood. For example, in many parts of the world, a person aged 17 years may choose to drive a car, be in employment, marry, have sex, have children and set up an independent home, which are all perfectly legal activities in their country.[11] Yet they are defined as a child, with a range of associated negative stereotypes of teen sex, teen parent (SmithBattle, 2013) and high school dropout (Dorn, 1996) supporting the categorization. Thus, through an ideology of difference (of 'not belonging' to the adult category), the once-adult-teenager has been recategorized as a vulnerable 'child'.

The Other: the ideological construction of difference

In her famous 1949 book, *The Second Sex*, Simone de Beauvoir ([1949] 2010) argued that throughout history humanity has been presented from a male perspective, with man as the norm or the default person in the representations of 'mankind'. This has meant that women have only been understood and interpreted (given meaning) by reference to men and defined by men in terms of difference and sex, summed up in the phrase 'the second sex'. Compared to men, 'She is the Other' (de Beauvoir, [1949] 2010, p. 26). De Beauvoir perfectly captures the concept of the Other (and the process of *othering*) that has gained wider currency in the humanities and social sciences since that time (e.g. Brons, 2015). A dominant group (the in-group) presents themselves as normal, with the Other (an out-group) positioned in opposition and represented as different, not normal, with their social position, opinions and behaviour considered as less important, less valuable and less relevant than that of a dominant group who has constructed them as the Other. Consequently, the Other can become 'invisible' in the power structures of a society. By representing the Other as intellectually or morally inferior a dominant group can justify their dominance over the Other (Pickering, 2001). Foucault ([1961] 2001) argued that othering constructs differences between people, in a binary opposition, such that, in categorizing some people as 'insane' (who then may be rejected from society or incarcerated), it defines the Other (the insane); but by the contrast it also defines what it means to be an in-group member or 'normal' (sane). In many ways stereotyping and othering can be considered as the same process. The traditional psychological focus on stereotyping in the cognition of the individual has tended to ignore the power relationships, the sociocultural, historical and political construction of difference, which the concept of Othering does not do. Othering involves ideology (Holliday, 2010b; Pickering, 2001) – an ideology of difference – and hence may offer a better understanding of the role of 'stereotypes' in discourse, in the ideological construction of social meaning in communication, and in the power structures of society, than a focus on individual cognition. Othering is not unique to the dominant group, but can be considered in terms of intergroup relations, and subordinate groups can equally construct the Other in their representations of out-groups (Brons, 2015). Group membership is associated with social identity and self-esteem (see Chapter 4), so constructing one's own group as superior to another group (in oppositional terms), provides a person (an in-group member) with a sense of moral superiority over the Other (the out-group).

Orientalism: ideology, othering and stereotypes

In his book, *Orientalism*, Edward Said (1978) analysed the way in which 'the Orient' and the 'Oriental' had been represented in Western culture and literature, arguing that 'the Orient' is not a place but a Western ideological construction. Said (1978, p. 42) argued that Orientalism was a library of ideas, both literally (as he cites a range of literary sources about the 'East') and metaphorically, in cataloguing or locating the image of the Oriental in Western discourse: 'These ideas explained the behaviour of Orientals; they supplied Orientals with a mentality, a genealogy, an atmosphere; most important, they allowed Europeans to deal with and even to see Orientals as a phenomenon possessing regular characteristics.' The 'Oriental' was constructed (stereotyped) by these characteristics as different (an Other) compared to the 'Occidental' (the Westerner). In his examples, Said focused on the Middle East. In constructing the concept of the Oriental, Europeans had set up a binary division between the West and the East, defining themselves in opposition to an Eastern Other. The various cultural differences, from architecture to religion, led to a perception in the West of the East as ancient, mysterious, inscrutable, exotic and erotic, within a representation that was essentially feminine. This was contrasted to the rational, technological, advanced and male West. This representation pervaded Western discourse about the East, legitimizing colonialism and political domination (McLeod, 2010). It also made assumptions about 'race' and gender, in the construction of demeaning stereotypes of the immoral and devious Oriental man and the childlike, obedient and erotic Oriental woman (McLeod, 2010). More than this, it represents the East in terms of simplistic images, which commodifies the culture (Holliday, 2010b). The commodified Other can be appealing – such as the 'mysterious' East as a place to visit – yet this both constructs and exaggerates difference ('they are not like us') and generates explanations of it, such as making 'the Orient' the subject matter of Western academic analysis. This can even lead to a 'morality of helping', where modern Western ideology (such as a sense of moral superiority) is employed to seek to overcome 'the imagined deficit Other … rather than appreciating deeper cultural complexities' (Holliday, 2010b, p. 94).

A critical point made by Said (1978) is that Orientalism is not a rigid and simplistic 'stereotype' created by Westerners ignorant of the East, but constructed by 'the experts' production and circulation of cultural knowledge in the service of their colonial and post-1945 empires' (Chua, 2008, p. 1181). Orientalism is historically a construction of Westerners who have often been in close contact with the East. Hall (1992) argued that the ways in which representations of the Orient in Western culture have been structured and mediated through a lens of Western political and economic interests have symbolically constructed the Orient (and Orientals) in the Western imagination. This again can be seen as part of the 'politics of not belonging' (Pickering, 2001) in ideologically constructing an us-and-them binary difference. This is particularly the case with Muslims in Western discourse. To paraphrase de Beauvoir: the Muslim is the Other (Creutz-Kämppi, 2008; Silva, 2017). In an analysis of over 600 *New York Times* articles between 1969 and 2014, Silva (2017, p. 18) argued that the word 'radicalization' 'shifted from a symbol of leftist political and economic conflict to a concept positioning Islam in direct opposition to the values, beliefs, and ideologies of Western countries'. Consequently, the use of the term 'radicalization' is now employed discursively in the mass media to symbolically represent an East–West conflict and construct Muslims as an alien Other (Silva, 2017). Indeed, the research on othering has revealed the narrow focus of the traditional approach to stereotypes (as fixed irrational cognitions).

> The concept of the Other takes us some way beyond the limitations of the stereotype by bringing more closely into the frame both those involved in the process of othering as well as the object of this process, and by grounding stereotypical misrepresentations more firmly in the structures and relations of power which give them their binding force. It does not displace or supersede the concept of the stereotype but renders it rather more complex, opening up for interrogation its ambiguities and contradictions of meaning and effect.
>
> *Pickering, 2001, p. 69*

Modern Western society, ideology and stereotypes: the liberal–conservative dichotomy

William Graham Sumner, whose idea of folkways were discussed in Chapter 5, was an anti-imperialist who introduced the terms 'ethnocentrism' and 'cultural relativism' into sociology. Yet he did not believe in a political ideology based on natural human rights. He wrote:

> Before the tribunal of nature a man has no more right to life than a rattlesnake; he has no more right to liberty than any wild beast; his right to the pursuit of

happiness is nothing but a license to maintain the struggle for existence, if he can find within himself the powers with which to do it.

Sumner, [1913] 1980, p. 234

This idea, referred to as *Social Darwinism*,[12] argues that social life can be characterized in evolutionary terms, as 'the survival of the fittest'. There are no rights or equality in the natural world. In this view, survival in the social world is achieved through hard work and economic success. Sumner described a character that he referred to as the 'forgotten man', the decent, honest, hard-working, organized and responsible man, who lives within his means, pays his debts and his taxes (Shone, 2004). In the social world: '[t]here is no device whatever to be invented for securing happiness without industry, economy, and virtue' (Sumner, [1919] 2007, p. 468). Therefore, taking from the virtuous citizen (the forgotten man) through taxation to give to the profligate and the lazy is punishing the worthy to give to the unworthy. For Sumner, liberty relies on people taking responsibility for their own lives. There is a cost of not doing this, which in the cause of maintaining that liberty should not be rewarded (Shone, 2004). These libertarian sentiments are elements of what is referred to as modern 'conservativism', as opposed to the ideas of equality and rights influencing modern 'liberalism'.[13] Indeed, Wacquant (2009) has argued that the modern neoliberal (i.e. 'conservative') approach to social welfare has operated in a paternalistic way[14] on the principle of punishing the poor. The distinction between conservative and liberal ideologies, for this book on stereotypes, is that there is tendency to refer to one's own ideological position and political views as the 'truth' and that of one's political opponents as false and immoral 'stereotypes' (Graham et al., 2012). Thus, the labelling of certain statements as true or false, accurate or inaccurate, valid or stereotypes, often derives not from the analysis of their objective truth or falsity but from an ideological position of differences in beliefs about political *morality* (Haidt, 2012; Lakoff, 2016).

Allport ([1954] 1979) claimed that stereotype users tended to be conservative and non-users as liberal. Subsequently, this has been disputed in the argument that both conservatives and liberals use stereotypes, just different ones (e.g. Chambers et al., 2013). The negative social perception of poor people by conservatives and wealthy people by liberals can be interpreted as stereotypical perceptions, yet they are also indicative of ideological differences. Lakoff (2016) argued that differences in the moral basis of conservative and liberal views results in them having very different political worldviews (ideologies). The metaphor of the family is commonly applied to society with the government as parent and the citizens as children, and so Lakoff (2016) employed this metaphor to summarize the differences in the two worldviews. For the conservative, the primary motive is survival in a dangerous and competitive world. It is the duty of parents to teach their children to be self-reliant (in this tough world). They do this through discipline (reward and punishment), which will result, in children who acknowledge the moral authority of the parent, in the learning of self-discipline. Consequently, parents are able to protect and nurture children who respect and obey them. This system will create moral people of the next generation, perpetuating the moral order. Being good, such as following religious moral standards, is indicative of moral strength, the primary moral value. This involves self-discipline and self-denial; otherwise people will become morally weak. There is a tendency for undisciplined people to follow their basic desires, become weak in terms of self-indulgence, such as sexual lasciviousness, or develop a lack of self-control (such as drug-taking), which is considered immoral and should be resisted to avoid wrongdoing (or worse doing evil). Hence it is important to maintain the (traditional) moral order that is at risk of corruption by immoral influences. Lakoff (2016) labelled this worldview as *strict father morality*. In contrast, he referred to the liberal worldview as *nurturant parent morality*. The moral goal of nurturance is to produce happy and fulfilled children (who then become nurturant themselves). Children must learn empathy and cooperation in order to become nurturant people. They do this by becoming self-conscious – self-aware, questioning and open – which leads to the development of a social conscience and the nurturance of social ties within the family. Morality is the cultivation of one's happiness (and consequently that of others), and moral strength is directly associated with nurturance. Self-development results in increased empathy and the nurturance of social ties and moral growth. A key aspect of morality is fairness, such as treating each child equally and fairly. This explains why modern liberals argue for a universal egalitarianism.[15] When examined through this lens of universal egalitarianism, famous historical activists, such as Thomas Jefferson, often fall short, as their activism was focused within a particular group of which they were a member, often related to enshrined social distinctions in the society, rather than across all social groups. Thus, stereotypes as indicators of prejudice and societal discrimination (and hence indicative of ideologies of difference) have been of particular concern to American liberals (as in the work of Allport, [1954] 1979).

Lakoff (2016) argued that these parental metaphors help us appreciate why conservatives and liberals misunderstand each other, even on the belief about whether people are basically good or not. These metaphors also help to understand how people engage in the political world and view society. For example, liberals will argue that 'the poor are lazy' is an offensive stereotype. They will empathize with the poor – as equal 'children' of the society – who are not being treated fairly and this discrimination needs to be challenged as it is immoral. Everything should be done to support them and redress the inequalities they face. Liberals will also provide lots of examples of the poor not being lazy to illustrate how false the stereotype is. However, as Lakoff (2016) noted, this evidence is unlikely to convince conservatives to change their views (any more than liberals will change their views to become conservatives). For conservatives, poverty is a failure to protect and support the family. They will acknowledge that there are some poor people who do not seek public assistance, but scrimp and save (depriving themselves of pleasures) to clothe and feed their children. These self-disciplined poor people are morally upstanding and worthy of community support (even though they have not asked for it). However, welfare beneficiaries are showing their unworthiness by asking others to support them. Furthermore, they should be doing everything they can to support themselves to avoid relying on others. If they drink alcohol, smoke cigarettes and take drugs then they are using their welfare irresponsibly and immorally. No matter how much evidence liberals provide showing that the poor are not lazy, the existence of a welfare system supporting large numbers of people is indicative, from a conservative perspective, of its corrupting influence and the encouragement of immoral behaviour.

Differences in society (that is, the existing pattern of cultural associations related to social groups) are viewed differently through these two worldviews (ideologies). Take for example the discovery that one social group appears consistently and disproportionately in the criminal justice system. All members of the society will learn this association – and both liberals and conservatives may accept it as fact – but what it means will depend on the worldview or ideology. Through the lens of the strict father morality, committing a crime is morally wrong (which people must know), so criminals should simply stop committing crimes (which is their personal responsibility to do so). Failure to do so is indicative of a lack of self-discipline. A group that appears disproportionately in the criminal justice system is therefore demonstrating a group-related lack of self-discipline, implying a moral weakness in the group. However, from a nurturant parent perspective, the interpretation of the cultural association as a group-based moral weakness (i.e. a disposition for criminality) is an offensive stereotype, as it is contradicts a fundamental belief in fairness and equality. The explanation lies in a social system that is unfairly discriminating against them: so changes need to be made in society to treat this group equally, such as providing the group with equal opportunities within the society and giving them their fair access to societal resources.

Support for this distinction between liberals and conservatives comes from *moral foundations theory* (Graham et al., 2009; Haidt and Graham, 2007). Integrating ideas from anthropology and cultural psychology showing moral pluralism across cultures (Graham et al., 2013), the theory proposes that all humans have a set of moral foundations, which are then modified through culture. Five key moral foundations have been proposed: care–harm, fairness–cheating, loyalty–betrayal, authority or respect–subversion and sanctity or purity–degradation. Each society constructs its own morality in the way it interprets and enacts these foundations through its cultural history. Thus, differences in morality will emerge between groups that emphasize different foundations. The theory was applied to liberals and conservatives in American society, using the moral foundations questionnaire (MFQ) (Graham et al., 2009, 2011). The results showed that liberals focus more on the first two moral foundations (care and fairness) whereas conservatives more evenly employed all five. Loyalty, authority (respect) and sanctity (purity) were therefore more important to conservatives than liberals. Thus, differences in ideology between liberals and conservatives, such as their beliefs about the rich and poor, can be aligned with their different moral foundations. This idea is associated with Lakoff's analysis (above) as it implies that liberals and conservatives operate within different 'webs of meaning' (Geertz, 1973) based on their different emphasis on the five moral foundations. The importance of this for stereotype research is that, in order to understand what a person means when they make a statement that a description is a 'stereotype' (such as 'the poor are lazy 'or 'the rich are greedy'), rather than seeking an explanation in terms of cognitive irrationality or bias, the meaning of that statement may be more fruitfully sought in the ideology held by the speaker or critical listener. Hence political debates often involve an argument about the state of the social world framed in terms of ideologies about how that social world should be organized. It is the question of stereotypes in language and argument that is considered in the next chapter.

Notes

1 Particularly as the belief that there is a 'truth' out there to find is itself an ideological viewpoint.
2 A different Williams.
3 Recall from Chapter 2 that Brigham (1971) argued that stereotypes are referenced against the views of this implicit 'observer'.
4 There are other instances where Lippmann clearly was not 'right' in his views (see Pickering, 2001).
5 The views of Thomas Jefferson, one of the founding fathers, will be considered later in this chapter.
6 Yet in many cases still hugely profitable.
7 Slavery in Rome was primarily Europeans enslaving other Europeans. Similarly, slavery was also a feature of the Malian Empire (1230–1600), with Africans enslaving other Africans.
8 See www.mrheintz.com/how-many-signers-of-the-declaration-of-independence-owned-slaves.html.
9 In fact, the first election for which women could exercise voting rights in France occurred in 1945. Olympe de Gorges was executed by the revolutionary government in 1793 during the Reign of Terror.
10 Britain's most famous naval commander, with his statue in Trafalgar Square in central London.
11 Graupner (2005, p. 7) referred to the 17-year-old 'child', located in the same social category as a 5-year-old, as 'an absurdity of the later 20th century'.
12 Although Sumner did not use the term himself.
13 As this is a book on stereotypes rather than political philosophy this is no place to go further into a discussion of the complexities and nuances of what is the definition of 'conservatism' and 'liberalism'.
14 See Lakoff's 'the strict father' concept below.
15 Although modern philosophers are debating what is the best way to create the fairest egalitarian system (e.g. Lippert-Rasmussen, 2015).

7

STEREOTYPES AND EVERYDAY STORIES

Stereotypes, metaphors and meanings

When journalist Lippmann (1922) wished to describe what he saw as a fixed idea, he not surprisingly drew on a metaphor from the printing industry he knew well, a fixed metal plate called a 'stereotype'. This metaphor has led to statements about social groups, such as 'the British are reserved' being understood in psychological theories (and dictionary definitions) as indicating a fixed idea ('as if etched on a metal plate'), in a person's mind, a 'cognitive framework' leading to a simplistic, rigid or biased perception of a member of a social group, which is wrong, as a British person may not be reserved. Yet the implication that a stereotype is this underlying 'mental structure' may be a consequence of the metaphor and not due to the functioning of the human brain. Contrast the metal plate metaphor with a stereotype as a well-known social representation or cultural association that people employ strategically in language for a particular purpose, just like any other learnt association circulating within the 'web of meaning' of their culture. The implication from this is that we don't have to rigidly or fixedly believe that the association is objectively true or morally right; and the purpose of its use will vary from context to context: for example, to argue for, or against, a political ideology; to explain an aspect of the social world; to heuristically predict the behaviour of people and events, or to make a joke or ironic comment. Consider the following statements: 'I hate the British! They think they are so superior' (meaning aloof and reserved); or 'The British are so lovely and polite' (meaning charming and reserved); or, to an extravert British friend, with a smile: 'Hey, man! Where is your British stiff upper lip?' (meaning surprisingly not reserved). Is there a justification for claiming that all three speakers have the same fixed 'stereotype' (of British reserve) in their heads, 'biasing' their social perception of the British? Clearly, all three speakers are aware that the British are associated with the attribute of 'reserve' in their culture, so they expect a listener to understand their meaning without requiring any explanation. Yet all three statements convey different meanings, rather than a rigid view of the British. In fact the first and second statements convey opposing meanings. While relying on a well-known cultural association, each of the three statements uses this association to serve a different rhetorical purpose. The first person is employing the known association to express a dislike of the British, the second person is using it to make a positive statement about the British, and the third is making a humorous quip among friends. Hence, the meaning of the utterances is contained within the language employed, rather than an underlying 'stereotype' (with a fixed meaning).

If we abandoned the etched-on-a-metal-plate-in-the-head metaphor, 'stereotypes' might be viewed in an entirely different way. However, why would we do this, given that an extremely large number of experimental studies have found evidence of fixed ideas about social groups and their associated attributes 'in the heads' of their participants? One answer is that the experimental research methodology employed in these studies, far from discovering these 'stereotypes', has actually created them (Condor, 1988). Consider a typical psychology experiment on stereotypes. The researchers present the participants with a fixed set of social groups (determined by the experimenters) that they have to use. The participants are then asked to associate these social groups with various attributes. Again, the particular set of attributes is usually provided by the experimenters. A classic example of this type of this task is the checklist method of the Princeton trilogy (see Chapter 2). Typically, the task set-up gives the participants no choice but to construct a 'stereotype' in their responses (based on the groups and attributes they are given). Indeed, the participants of the Eysenck and Crown (1948) study explicitly stated that that this task was meaningless as it was not how they viewed people. Furthermore, Katz and Braly (1933) noted that the participants' responses matched descriptions present in the media, so the answers could have been drawn from relevant cultural representations in their society, and not the participants' 'fallacy'.

In such a psychology experiment, the method is designed to find consistent or fixed patterns in the data and reduce variation. Consistency in responses is labelled as 'evidence' and variation in responses is labelled as 'error'. Condor (1988) argued that this methodology biases the results in favour of an inferred 'cognitive structure' or psychological 'stereotype' and deliberately ignores the importance of variation in people's descriptions of others. Recall that in the Katz and Baly (1933) study, most people *did not* give the stereotypical responses. For example, while 29 per cent of participants chose the attribute 'reserved' for the category 'English', 71 per cent of the participants – the majority – did not select this characteristic: surely an equally important finding. To put it starkly, in a seminal study about stereotypes, *most of the time most of the participants did not choose* the 'stereotype' attributes in their responses. This variation questions the validity of the metal-plate-in-the-head metaphor. Condor (1988) argued that in everyday communication we see variability of meaning and purpose in language use, all the time. To ignore that variability is to ignore what is happening in everyday life (rather than in the artificial environment of the psychology laboratory, where helpful participants agree to do what the psychologists ask of them). In everyday life variability provides the subtlety of language to convey different meanings (Condon, 1988). As Cauthen et al. (1971) noted, what are referred to as 'stereotypes' are linguistic behaviours: it is within language that meaning is created and ideas are expressed. People talk about social groups (and their historically associated attributes) for a particular purpose, which may be to provide information or speak persuasively in support of an ideological position. Therefore, employing the metaphor of a fixed metal plate to describe a cultural association may be to ignore its flexibility of use in discussion and argument within the shared space of everyday communication.

Talking about people in our group and people not in our group

The people around us are usually the most important to us, such as our family, friends or colleagues. We interact with them on a regular basis and so knowing what they will do or say is significant to us. Consequently, we can refer to these people as psychologically close to us, unlike the people we might see in news reports or travelogues about foreign countries, who we can describe as psychologically distant. The concept of *psychological distance* can refer to people socially, spatially or temporally distant from us (Stephan et al., 2010; Trope and Liberman, 2010). What has been found is that we tend to construe people who are psychologically close to us in a more individuated and concrete way compared to more distant people, who we construe more categorically and abstractly (Trope et al., 2007). This makes sense, as it allows us to predict their actions more subtly, and it is therefore worth the effort to think about them carefully, but it also means that psychologically distant people are construed more categorically, or stereotypically. The fact that a close friend, José, is from Brazil is one aspect among others: he is a doctor, plays the saxophone, likes climbing and reads detective novels. The abstract idea of 'Brazilian' may hardly influence our judgement of him. However, in a newscast from the Rio de Janeiro carnival, the people may be construed as stereotypically Brazilian. We can see an effect of psychological distance when we examine the words people employ to describe themselves and others. In their *linguistic category model* (LCM), Semin and Fiedler (1991) distinguished between four levels of abstraction in language, from concrete to abstract. A descriptive action verb provides a concrete, objective and neutral statement of a situation or event, such as 'the woman threw a ball to the child'. A statement such as 'the woman plays with the child' is less specific, with the interpretive action verb 'play' (with) more general than a verb such as to 'throw' (something to), as we have to interpret how she played with the child. Now consider 'the woman cares for the child'. This is no longer tied to a specific situation but generalizes across events, with the verb 'cares for' referring to a 'state' of the woman (she is doing the caring) so is a state verb. Finally, we can be even more general in a description by employing an adjective, such as 'the woman is caring', indicating an attribute of the person, stable across events. The important point to note here is that any behaviour can be described by any of these four descriptive categories. Furthermore, the choice of descriptive category represents the behaviour at a different level of abstraction, from a concrete description of the situation through to an abstract statement about a person's character.

The choice of linguistic categories to describe the behaviour of in-group and out-group members was examined by Maass et al. (1989; see also Maass, 1999). There was a clear tendency to describe positive in-group behaviour, and negative out-group behaviour in more abstract terms, and negative in-group behaviour and positive out-group behaviour in concrete terms. For example, two competing sporting teams are asked to describe a good play and a bad play by their team and the opposition. There is a tendency for a good play by the in-group team to be described in terms of skill but when performed by the opposition as a result of the particular situation. Alternatively, a bad play by the in-group was viewed as situational by the use of a concrete description but a bad play by the opposition in more abstract terms, such as a lack of skill. This is referred to as the *linguistic intergroup bias* (Maass et al., 1989). Maass et al. (1995) offered two explanations for this bias: first, as an in-group protection (to present the in-group positively and out-group negatively), as suggested by social identity theory (see Chapter 4), to maintain the self-esteem of the in-group members. A second explanation was based on differential expectancies: some behaviour is expected and other behaviour is not. Expected behaviour is described in more abstract terms and unexpected behaviour in more concrete terms. Mass (1999) argued that expectancies guide descriptions but are then moderated by in-group protection. Consequently, group relationships are particularly important in a competitive situation, at which times in-group protection may dominate the descriptions. However, there is a more general cognitive bias based on expectancy that can explain the differences in these descriptions. This has been termed the *linguistic expectancy bias* (LEB).

The LEB is particularly relevant to the study of stereotypes, as stereotypes, as group attributes, are abstract descriptions of expected behaviour. In an examination of the LEB, Wigboldus et al. (2000) asked participants to think of a good friend (either male or female) and then describe examples of the person's behaviour that were stereotypically female or stereotypically male. In the study, expected behaviour was defined as a person behaving in accordance with their gender stereotype and unexpected behaviour was defined as behaving according to the opposite gender stereotype. These descriptions were rated for their level of abstraction (according to the LCM categories). Participants were given descriptions from another person and asked to make dispositional inferences about the behaviour: how much was it due to the person (or the situation) and how likely was it to be repeated by that person. The results, for both male and female friends, showed that gender stereotype-consistent behaviour was described more abstractly and rated as being more dispositional (than situational). The reverse occurred when the behaviour described was stereotypically inconsistent. They concluded that the linguistic expectancy bias leads to stereotype-consistent behaviour being described more abstractly. Furthermore, the participants also showed, when reading the stories, that behaviours described abstractly led to dispositional inferences (that this behaviour was characteristic of the person). Thus, it indicates that people are communicating an expectancy bias in their use of language both in the words of the writer and the interpretation of the reader (which can be labelled as 'a stereotype').

A subsequent study by Wigboldus et al. (2005), examined the role of social context on the LEB. In a similar study to Wigboldus at el. (2000), participants from the University of Amsterdam were given behavioural descriptions to judge. The description presented a brief story about a student from either the University of Amsterdam (the in-group) or the Free University (also in Amsterdam but, in this study, the out-group). The former are viewed in Amsterdam as stereotypically independent but sloppy and the latter as serious but boring. At the end of the story were four sentences to complete the description, which differed in their level of abstraction (according to the LCM). The participants were asked to rate these sentences in terms of their relationship to the rest of the story. Finally they were asked to rate the story in terms of how typical the action was for a student of the university indicated. Again, a linguistic expectancy bias was found, in that, generally, abstract sentences were judged more likely to complete the story when stereotype consistent behaviours were being performed. However, this was shown to be essentially an intergroup phenomenon. There was a strong LEB in the intergroup context (reading a description about someone from a different university). However, there was not an LEB effect (or it was reversed) when a person was judging someone from the same university, an intragroup judgement. This implies that the behavioural expectancies ('stereotypes') are particularly relevant when group membership is activated in the context of an in-group and an out-group. It appears therefore that we pay more attention to psychologically close people and less attention to more distant people, and judge them accordingly. When people are psychologically distant we have little information about them (often only characteristics such as gender, age or nationality). Employing cultural associations about group membership – stereotypes – can allow us, in these limited circumstances to make rapid judgements about them. However, as people become closer to us then we will tend to view them less abstractly, probably because we pay more attention to them. Tincher et al. (2016) employed a typical LEB design, and asked participants to select a description that best described a person (as either a friend or an enemy) performing a positive or a negative behaviour as illustrated in a cartoon. They found the expected linguistic bias, with more abstract descriptions of the expected behaviours (friend–positive and enemy–negative). However, in an 'observing perspective' condition that encouraged mindful attention, the abstraction level, describing the expected behaviour, was reduced. While the LEB was not eliminated, it did provide support for the role of attention in the LEB effect.

Stereotypes and communication in social networks

Lyons et al. (2008) argued that stereotypes, as shared cultural beliefs, are disseminated through interpersonal and mass media communication, particularly as discussions about people, typically as group members, form much of everyday conversation (Kellerman and Palomares, 2004). Crucial to stereotype diffusion are *social networks*, where a social network is the collection of people involved in an ongoing communicative interaction (Lyons et al., 2008). These may be networks of family, friends or colleagues or a variety of online social networks. These networks form groups of people who share common understandings. For example, in one scene from the US television series, *The Big Bang Theory*,[1] about university scientists, the character Amy is with her two girlfriends, Penny and Bernadette, in Penny's apartment preparing for a date with a new boyfriend, whom they know nothing about. She tells them his name and lets slip that he is tall. The two friends, sitting on the sofa, demand more details and ask if they have kissed. Amy replies: 'Just a little peck on the lips', to which they respond gleefully. Penny continues, 'Well, we're your best friends, give us one more detail and we promise we'll leave you alone.' Amy thinks for a moment and then responds, 'Fine. Um, he's British.' Penny squeals with delight and Bernadette, smiling, bangs the sofa with her hand. Amy, smiling, says, 'All right, that is a juicy one.' Clearly they all agree that the boyfriend being British is positive. Also with no other knowledge, the friends' reaction indicates that they are relying on their shared understanding, which Amy also understands (which is why she said it). Speakers and listenes share *common ground* to communicate meaning (Clark and Brennan, 1991; Kashima, 2014), such as a shared stereotype of a British man as charming and polite. Grice (1975) argued that a speaker must assume certain information is known by the listener (the *given* information, such as 'British men are charming'), which they supplement (the *new* information, such as 'I have a British boyfriend'). Without the given information, the new information may not make any sense. However, common ground does more than allow communication; it also establishes the people within it as sharing common interests and identities (Brown and Levinson, 1987). Thus a culture or social group can be defined by their shared common ground or 'common sense' (see Moscovici, 1998; Chapter 5), which creates the social reality of the group (Kashima, 2014; Liu and Morris, 2014). In another group or social network, British men may not be viewed as charming.

As stereotypes (as learnt associations about people) are known in a culture, they form one aspect of the common ground in communication. Consequently, as noted above, stereotype-consistent information is expected (or given) but stereotype-inconsistent information is unexpected (or new). Research has shown that stereotype-consistent information is often well-remembered (Macrae et al., 1994) as it is expected – such as the librarian being quiet at the office party. However, sometimes stereotype-inconsistent information is better remembered – such as the librarian dancing on a table at the office party – as it is argued that we pay more attention to unexpected information (Hastie, 1981). Unexpected information presents a problem of why it occurred, so we attend to it. In a series of studies Kashima and his colleagues simulated a social network by a method of serial reproduction. A participant read a story that was deliberately constructed by the researchers to contain stereotype-consistent and stereotype-inconsistent information. This story was communicated from one participant to the next, who then communicated it to the next in a four- or six-person chain. Kashima

(2000) and Lyons and Kashima (2001) showed that as the information passed along the chain it became more stereotypical. Furthermore, this indicated that the stereotype was already shared by the people in the group (or network), otherwise this tendency would not have happened. The stereotype-consistent effect was shown to be related to the intention of the speaker or writer to communicate a coherent story to the listener or reader in the network (Kashima et al., 2013; Lyons and Kashima, 2006). This leads to the question of why we emphasize information that the audience already knows (stereotype-consistent information), rather than novel information (stereotype-inconsistent information)? Clark and Kashima (2007) argued that while stereotype-inconsistent information was more informative, stereotype-consistent information served a *social connectivity* function, of maintaining and enhancing social relationships and reinforcing shared group membership and social identity.

Hence, stereotypes play a role in cultural dynamics: the formation and maintenance of a cultural group (Kashima, 2014). Members of a social network (or culture) in communication with each other will, for reasons of group dynamics such as maintaining social cohesion, tend to bias their representation of another social group (in their communication) in the direction of what is contextually socially appropriate. Neutral information may be presented positively (or negatively) if the social group under discussion are viewed positively (or negatively). This positive (or negative) representation may then be disseminated through the social network by its reproduction. Bratanova and Kashima (2014) argued that cultural stereotypes can develop in this way. They cite the example of the Hans Christian Anderson story 'The Emperor's New Clothes'[2] to illustrate how a representation can be disseminated throughout a network for reasons of social cohesion and group maintenance rather than its accuracy. Indeed, everyday communication relies on a common understanding of social reality that itself can be based on stereotypical constructions. Kashima (2014, p. 82) gave the example of everyday communication between male office colleagues talking by the water cooler. One says to the other, 'Gary brought a ring for Mary'. Not only is this statement grounded in a shared knowledge of Gary and Mary (who they are), but also relies on specific social representations in order to make sense of it:

> [T]he grounded meaning implies that it is men that buy rings for women, and that men take an active role and women take a passive role in courtship. It is a gender stereotype – active men and passive women – that is reproduced in this mundane, and seemingly innocuous, interaction that can happen anywhere.
>
> *Kashima, 2014, p. 83*

Communication within a social network is not simply transferring information between its members but involves the transmission of culture, grounded in a particular formation of social reality (Kashima, 2014). Communicating stereotypes is part of that process of cultural transmission (see Chapter 5).

Opinion polarization in social networks

In the second decade of the twenty-first century, concern was raised about *filter bubbles* (Pariser, 2011). Online social media sites included algorithms that could personalize information for users based on their content preferences. The implication of these algorithms was that people then only viewed content that was consistent with their own ideological and political opinions, so their media space would metaphorically become an *echo chamber* (Flaxman et al., 2016). The concern is that people are not aware of these filters and therefore gain a distorted view of the social world, such as liberals viewing only a liberal perspective or conservatives only a conservative perspective. Political opinion therefore becomes polarized as people are not exposed to alternative views. Pariser (2011, p. 5) represented it as a threat to the overall political system: 'Democracy requires citizens to see things from one another's point of view, but instead we're more and more enclosed in our own bubbles. Democracy requires a reliance on shared facts; instead we're being offered parallel but separate universes.' This was examined in a study by Bakshy et al. (2015) of over 10 million users on the Facebook social media platform in the United States. The results confirmed that generally conservative (liberal) people tended to have conservative (liberal) friends and share conservative (liberal) content. While the News Feed algorithms did rank news items concordant with their views there still remained the potential to access some discordant content. However, individual choice was a stronger influence in limiting access to alternative viewpoints than the algorithms, as people chose not to click on it. In a study of online news consumption in the United States, Flaxman et al. (2016) found that only 4 per cent of the population were regular readers of online news opinion articles. Of the 50,000 such users, it was found that the majority of users accessed their news from traditional, mainstream news outlets, so were not dissimilar to offline users who accessed their news from mainstream providers via traditional means (such as television or newspapers). However, it was also found that people typically visited news sites and read articles that were ideologically similar.

These results indicate that opinion polarization is not entirely a function of social media algorithms, but that people actively choose to access news content that is consistent with their political views. This is not surprising from the research of Kashima and his colleagues (above): shared common ground – shared beliefs and stereotypes – makes sense of information circulating within a social network. Also, ideological polarization can be considered as identifying different cultural groups, with which individuals' self-identify. For example, there is a common belief in the United States that academics are liberals. Honeycutt and Freberg (2017) found this to be the case in a study of over 600 academics across a range of disciplines, the majority of whom were liberals, indicating an academic social network of liberal opinions. If we refine it further, social scientists, and in particular psychologists, are viewed as liberals. As Jussim (2012b, p. 504) pointed out, this is a stereotype, yet, 'as a probabilistic generalization, it is also accurate'. This was demonstrated in a study by Inbar and Lammers (2012), who surveyed over 500 psychology academics (members of a social and personality psychology society). Over 90 per cent identified as liberal on social issues, with around two-thirds being liberal on economic issues and social policy. In a second, follow up survey, with just under 300 of the original sample, they found that: 'More than one in three would discriminate against [conservatives] in hiring decisions' (Inbar and Lammers, 2012, p. 6). Jussim et al. (2015) argued that, with only 23 per cent of the wider population identifying as liberal (with up to 38 per cent as moderates and up to 40 per cent as conservatives) there is a potential for a risk of liberal bias in, for example, describing the characteristics of liberals and conservatives in psychological research.

Stereotypes, explanations and cultural stories

We are constantly telling stories about our own lives. In communication we are not simply exchanging pieces of information but creating narratives; that is, a sequence of events with a storyline. The storyline must be internally consistent to make sense. Bruner (1990) argued that narratives have no requirement to be true or accurate, although they need to be believable for an audience to accept them. However, people normally assume that the events described occurred (Labov, 2001). For example, in an autobiography, a politician might claim responsibility for a period of economic success in their country (as the hero of the story). Readers of this autobiography will usually accept that the period of economic success occurred, but they may or may not agree that it was due to the activities of this particular politician. Narratives usually have a conventional or canonical form that makes them understandable. Thus, the autobiographical story follows a well-known success-from-failure 'script' (Schank and Abelson, 1977). These scripts reflect expectations learnt within the culture, with canonical elements including social norms and moral imperatives, such as a 'strong leader' 'taking control' of the country. However, a narrative has to manage 'departures from the canonical' or else it doesn't make sense (Bruner, 1990, p. 50), For example, the politician, to maintain their hero characterization, has to explain why they made a political blunder (such as by claiming: 'It taught me a valuable lesson about whom I could trust for advice'). A key assumption in narratives is that the characters in the story have wishes and desires, goals and intentions: they have agency so their actions are for a purpose (Bruner, 1990). Stories often gain their power and interest when characters are put in a difficult position and, despite their best intentions, bring about unexpected, adverse or destressing consequences; revealing the complexities of human existence and challenging stereotypical assumptions, such as bad things are only done by bad people. Finally, stories have a *voice* (Bruner, 1990). The autobiography is the politician's story, which other people (other voices) might tell very differently.

Bruner (1991) argued that human cognition involves the narrative construction of meaning. We do have the potential for rational, logical scientific analysis but much of the time we are using stories to explain our lives. By being born into a culture, children 'are entering a story that has begun before them and one in which they will be helped in understanding through the aid of elders' (Mattingly et al.,

2008, p.11). Human psychology is therefore cultural (Bruner, 1990). Our life stories are constructed within the ongoing stories of our own culture. We construct stories of our own lives, our *personal myths* (McAdams, 1993). Just like the politician's autobiography is written in a certain way to enhance their reputation, any person's life story presents themselves within a cultural and moral framework in which they seek to portray *themselves* to the world. Personal narratives are used to construct identity, a concept referred to as the *storied self* (McAdams, 2008). Autobiographical accounts assume an audience (even when absent) and can be considered as *cultural texts* as they are created with the framework of the socio-political structure of the culture (McAdams, 2008).

National history is a cultural story. American independence is represented in the United States as pioneering colonial people throwing off the oppressive British yoke to forge a new country based on freedom and equality.[3] Paul (2014) identified the important myths in the formation of American culture, which present the idea of the discovery of a 'new world', a virgin territory or a 'promised land' where decent, honest folk could create a new social order, unencumbered by the intolerance and restrictions of the 'old world'. This was achieved by the 'Founding Fathers', in the Declaration of Independence in 1776, setting out the ideas of freedom, equality and democracy. Comprising the positive qualities of fatherhood, family and kinship, these men were heroes of the new republic (having gained independence through their military and strategic abilities) and established a collective sense of national identity. European immigrants of different religions and backgrounds could come to the new country and, in the 'melting pot', would emerge as Americans with a new identity and common values. With this spirit, pioneers spread across the West, taming and civilizing the vast territory through the 'sweat of their brows'. The United States as a land of opportunity meant that anyone could become a 'self-made man' achieving success through their own ingenuity and hard work (Paul, 2014). These cultural myths are told through the cultural products of the society, from written histories, school books, statuary and architecture, through to novels, films and television. However, within these stories, certain sociocultural groups who are not part of the dominant narrative have to be represented in specific (and negative) stereotypical ways in order to maintain these myths. Thus, the native peoples of North America were, in the early twentieth century, stereotypically represented as undifferentiated savages, as in an early film *The Pioneers* (1903). As Lutz (1990, p. 32) argued: 'the stereotype was functionalized according to the colonizer's interests', noting that native people were sometimes stereotyped as 'noble savages' and at others as 'blood-thirsty savages', depending on the context. Kilpatrick (1999) plotted the representations of the Native American in films throughout the twentieth century, noting that, in the 1980s and 1990s, movies presented a more complex and contextualized representation that she termed 'sympathetic', in films such as *Dances with Wolves* (1990) and *Geronimo: An American Legend* (1993). These films followed from challenges to the traditional telling of American history, by works such as Dee Brown's (1970) book *Bury My Heart at Wounded Knee*, which tells the story through a different 'voice': of peaceful native people, living in sophisticated societies, welcoming the Europeans, supporting and trading with them, only to be forced off their own lands by trickery, broken agreements and military might. The changing historical perspective can also be seen in the representation of African Americans. If the country is built on equality, democracy and the pursuit of happiness, then how can there have been slavery? How can this 'departure from the canonical' be narratively dealt with? To retain the foundation myth, slaves were depicted as ideologically and stereotypically different in terms of their 'nature': physical (suited to their societal role) and childlike (as unsuited for other roles), as in the notorious D. W. Griffiths film *Birth of a Nation* 1915. And for at least the first half of the twentieth century media representations of African Americans were limited to subordinate and comic roles (Allport, [1954] 1979; Holte, 1984). With social change and new civil rights legislation, in the latter decades of the twentieth century, different stories of African American history began to be told, such as Alex Haley's Pultizer Prize winning book *Roots* (1976) and Alice Walker's *The Color Purple* (1982), also a Pulitzer Prize winner, and in the twenty-first century, the film *12 Years a Slave* (2013) directed by Steve McQueen, which won the Academy Award for Best Picture. Thus, the telling of history becomes a matter of competing stories in a cultural context. The presence of other voices means that stories may be told – and retold – with different narrative storylines – for different purposes.

National stories provide a cultural framework for the life stories of the individual citizens of the nation. McAdams (2006), in examining different American autobiographical stories, focused on a particular story that he calls the *redemptive self*. Importantly, '[t]he redemptive self is an American identity' McAdams (2006, p. 271). He looked in particular at the stories of generative adults of middle age, a life period that Erikson (1982) argued involved a challenge between generativity and stagnation. A generative adult seeks to contribute to the good of society, preserving its values and actively contributing to the family and the community. Opposing this tendency is self-absorption and self-indulgence leading to a lack of interest in the wider good, and stagnation. McAdams (2006) took generative adults as his topic of study as 'they are highly attuned to society's central ideas and practices' (even if they don't agree with them). These people are located in the heart of society's powerful and influential in-group. McAdams (2006) argued that their personal stories – their narrative identities – provide an insight into American culture and its values. This is not to say that these people crudely believe in well-known cultural ideas, such as 'the American Dream', but that there is a complex relationship of culture and personal identity. For example, individualism (Triandis, 1995) is a central aspect of American culture, where independence, individual happiness, individual responsibility and personal agency are stressed.[4] Thus, an American identity will focus on the self as an independent agent, with the narrative involving details of 'my' life and what 'I' did. The cultural myths of a nation promoting individual freedom and opportunity are linked to an individual's own story. Individual narratives will acknowledge individual personality characteristics, such as 'I have always been a shy person', but also adaptation, such as 'which I learnt to overcome when I became a politician'. However, the integrated narrative about the self (a person's autobiography) will draw on a repertoire of culturally familiar stories, such as 'rags to riches', or 'overcoming initial failure to achieve success'. McAdam (2006) argued that the redemptive self is particularly American as the culture contains an anthology of such stories. However, redemptive stories are not the only stories in the culture. In a complex society, there are many competing stories, but certain ones characterize the culture and influence the stories that the members of that culture tell about themselves.

In later research, McAdams et al. (2013) examined the life stories of 128 liberal and conservative Americans. Drawing on Lakoff's strict father and nurturant parent metaphors and moral foundations theory (see Chapter 6), they examined 12 key scenes from each of the stories. In a first study, the stories were analysed in terms of rules-reinforcement and self-discipline (associated with strict father morality) and nurturant caregiving and empathy-openness (associated with nurturant parent morality). As predicted there was a significant correlation between their self-reported political attitudes and the story narratives. Conservatives tended to tell stories about learning self-discipline and gaining rewards from following rules. Liberals tended to tell stories about developing empathy and learning to be open to new perspectives but, contrary to expectation, did not feature stories involving authority in caregiving roles. It was argued that there did not seem to be a focus on the specific qualities of nurturance or caring of an authority but more on what the participant had learnt from them. Both conservatives and liberals had learnt from authority figures but different moral values: self-discipline for conservatives and openness for liberals. In a second study, based on moral foundations theory, the stories were coded according to the five moral foundations. Liberal stories were related more to the care–harm and the fairness–reciprocity foundations, with conservative stories related more to in-group–loyalty, authority–respect and purity–sanctity (with authority–respect producing the strongest correlation with conservativism). This provided strong support for the predictions of moral foundations theory. McAdams et al. (2013) argued that people construct their personal narratives within their moral framework; so there is a question about how much of an autobiographical story is 'as it was lived' or 'as it is reconstructed'. The researchers suggested that the events described (and the experiences) must in many aspects be accurate accounts of the author's lives (as would also be argued from Bruner, 1990, above), but there remains the intriguing question to how and when the specific narrative identities (within the moral frameworks) are formed.

Consequently, there are no 'correct' stories, be it of national or personal lives, otherwise historians and biographers would have nothing new to write, as the actual events are explained within a particular storyline (and a different narrative could describe the same events in a different way to present an alternative interpretation of them). However, one particular narrative may be dominant in the history of a culture or the self-story of an individual. As Bruner (1990) pointed out, these accounts present an explanation of events through a particular voice. A narrative will have a purpose and a storyline, which constructs the characters within it in particular ways. Stereotypes can serve a useful rhetorical purpose for the speaker in the story construction. For example, how does a Scotswoman explain her success in the music business (see Chapter 1)? She explains that a woman has to be tough to be successful in the music business and she is Scottish – who are tough people. It is up to the audience to decide if they believe the explanations as 'true' or not (Williams, 2002), but a stereotype can provide an explanation for the events within a coherent life story. Different stories – narratives of people's lives – make up the communication within a culture (Bruner, 1990), and are being constructed and reconstructed all the time. Indeed, novelist Lawrence Durrell (1958, p. 14) has one of his characters say: 'We live ... lives based upon selected fictions.' Stories make up our personal histories and the histories of our societies. However, novelist Chimamanda Adichie (2009) argued that the greatest danger to our understanding of the multi-voiced social world, in which we live, is the dominance of a single story that denies all other voices.

Communication as argument

From the invention of the stereotype by Lippmann (1922), it has been claimed that the world 'out there' is too complex for people to perceive it fully, so they simplify and distort it by imposing social categories upon it (Billig, 1996). The 'problem' of this simplification is that people employ stereotypes, which implies that a 'biased' view of the world is inevitable: 'an outgrowth of normal cognitive processes' (Taylor, 1981, p. 83 – a quote selected by Billig to illustrate the point). Billig (1996) analyses this approach to stereotypes in terms of the metaphor of a bureaucrat. The person, like the bureaucrat, cannot deal with the complexity of the world so must process information about people by slotting it into the correctly labelled 'folder' (or social category) from a predetermined set of 'folders' (given to them by others); so that 'thinking has been reduced to the unthinking operations of the filing clerk' (Billig, 1996, p. 159). However, this approach, which constructs the human thinker in terms of a rule-following bureaucrat, also criticizes the bureaucrat for not being very good at their job, relying on old-fashioned folders and categorization rules, which 'biases' their filing system and maintains an objectively 'inaccurate' set of stereotypical folders (social categories). The human thinker has become characterized as a *biased bureaucrat* who must be constantly alerted to their failings. Yet, as Billig (1996, p. 159) points out, 'this approach offers a very one-sided image' of the human thinker, in ignoring the flexibility and creativity of human thought. Billig (1996) noted that not even (real) bureaucrats always rigidly follow a fixed set of rules. They bend the rules, create new ones and debate the rules with the boss. Human '[f]lair, wit and sagacity seem to have been edged out by the demands of organization and stability ... The categorization approach ... ignores the capacity for transcendence' (Billig, 1996, pp. 159–160).

While people may not always be logical, they are fast and flexible thinkers, often relying on pragmatic learnt cultural associations (e.g. Gigerenzer and Gaissmaier, 2011). They can give an opinion on almost any topic quickly (Kahneman, 2011), including those concerning their moral beliefs (Haidt, 2001). However, if they are challenged on their views or asked to explain them, they may then take time to provide justifications. However, they do not typically abandon their opinions on being presented with a contradiction. They are not dispassionate bureaucrats simply following rules. Their sense of self is invested in their opinions. They argue in support of their views. They act as *lawyers* (Haidt, 2001). Consider a defence lawyer in a criminal case. They may not know whether their client really committed the crime or not; or even wish to know. The lawyer's task is to present a convincing case to the judge and jury to get a verdict of not guilty, by using their persuasive skills, drawing on selective evidence and arguments to achieve their goal. People – in this model as lawyers – express themselves in language for persuasive intent. The lawyer in the courtroom thinks of a counterargument to deal with a criticism rather than abandoning a case. Similarly, people in everyday life are not seeking, in their arguments, to be objectively 'right' but 'right', as in persuasive, to achieve a goal; and they will employ different linguistic techniques (rhetoric) to be so. Argument – the exchange and discussion of views – is central to people's lives, which indicates that, according to Billig (1996, p. 173), 'the rhetorical context is one of justification and criticism'. Billig (1996, p. 74) pointed out that the study of persuasive communication can be traced back to the ancient Greeks: 'Plato recognizes, along with Protagoras, the world of everyday experience is full of shifting opinions and impressions ... filled with contradictory arguments.' However, whereas Plato argued that there are fundamental truths to be found, Protagoras in his famous maxim denied this, as human beings are 'the measure of all things'. Billig (1996, p. 74) concluded, 'Plato may have dreamt of an end to argument, but in Protagoras' philosophy there is no escape from rhetoric.' In the modern world of instant worldwide communication, 24-hour news and social media users in their billions, it is clear that we live in a rhetorical world. Rather than seeking a hidden 'truth' about the social world behind these communications, we can examine how the social world is constructed within them. People are not biased bureaucrats but, like lawyers, they are flexible arguers.

Rhetoric is typically defined as the art of persuasive communication, but is sometimes considered a skill and, more critically, as a collection of persuasive techniques or tricks. A rhetorical approach to social psychology challenges some of the basic assumptions of traditional psychology. For example, Billig (1996) argued that *categorization* is a rhetorical strategy. While traditionally social psychologists employ social categories in their experiments, such as examining stereotypes of 'White' people and 'Black' people, as if these categorizations are incontestable or 'given', by viewing them as rhetorical strategies it emphasizes that their construction is for a political and ideological purpose in an ongoing argument about the nature of human beings within a culture (rather than identifying an underlying 'reality' about them). Furthermore, as Protagoras argued, in the construction of one argument it opens up the possibility of arguing the opposite. Consequently, Billig (1996) argued that we can employ a rhetorical strategy of *particularization* in opposition to categorization. A categorization combines a set of people (or things) according to a common characteristic, as in all Xs are Y, but a particularization states that a particular X is not Y in a particular context (Billig, 1996). Representing people as relying on categorization is only half the story according to Billig. Human categories are not fixed and people are not bureaucratically only making sense of the world through a given set of fixed categories. In argument, for every categorization there is a particularization that can deny the construction of the original category; and a particularization can then be responded to by a new categorization.

Consider this example from Flew (1975). There is a categorization of Scotsmen and Englishmen. A Scotsman learns that an Englishman has committed a particular crime, and claims: 'No Scotsman would do that'. On the following day he learns that a Scotsman has committed the same crime. Rather than giving up his stereotypical belief, he states: 'He is no true Scotsman', a particularization. Rather than rejecting the original categorization (of Englishmen who commit the crime and Scotsmen who do not), he denies the criminal Scot as a 'true' member of the Scotsman category and, in his argument, distinguishes between a category of 'true' Scotsmen, who don't commit the crime, and 'no true' Scotsmen, who do. This is the same argument that Adorno et al.'s (1950) anti-Semitic interviewees used when presented with evidence contrary to their stereotypical beliefs, such as Jewish generosity (see Chapter 2). Categorization and particularization operate as strategies in argument to maintain – or challenge – social categories and their attributes. There are cases when such a particularization strategy might be regarded as making a valid differentiation of a category in a society. For example, in a hypothetical country, a law states that any citizen who kills another citizen belongs to the category of 'committed murder' (or murderer) and should, according to law, go to prison for the rest of their lives. However, a lawyer argues that their client, who has definitely killed another citizen, did not intend to do it, it was an accident that they could not have foreseen (it was a misadventure), and for this reason their client does not belong to the category of 'committed murder'. They can do this by identifying a contradiction in the purpose of the law and its enactment: a law should be proportionate and just, and in this case it is neither. Even though the lawyer knows the law, they are arguing that in this case it is inappropriately applied. In response, the society might accept this argument and change the law such that only some killers are now placed in the category of 'committed murder' (when the killing is intentional), and other killers are put in a new categorization, 'committed manslaughter' (unintentional killing), which does not require a life sentence. Now, killing for reasons of self-defence, mental illness or accident will result in a lesser sentence or potentially no incarceration at all. In this case the lawyer has not sought to 'explain away' the contradiction but argued persuasively that it identifies an injustice that should be corrected by making a differentiation of the original category, or a recategorization.

Rhetorical categorization and particularization strategies can also be used to support opposing ideologies in argument, as we saw in the politics of 'not belonging' in Chapter 6, which excluded Black slaves from the category of equal men at the founding of the United States. Consequently, this argument was countered by abolitionists who challenged the narrow categorization of 'men'. The image of a manacled African slave kneeling with hands outstretched, with the slogan 'Am I not a man and a brother?' was employed by British abolitionist Josiah Wedgwood (1730–1795) on medallions that he produced in his pottery factory. Subsequently, the phrase was widely employed by abolitionists in Britain and the United States. Defining the category of 'men' as adult males, regardless of their origin (or 'race'), meant that it was a contradiction to treat them differently in a society based on equality. Feminists, from Olympe de Gourges (see Chapter 6) onwards, have argued that privileging men as 'citizens' excluded women unfairly from the category. Other categorization and particularization arguments have been employed to exclude certain subgroups of adults from equal rights, such as categorizing people as 'criminals' or 'mentally ill', who then may be deprived of their freedom on the basis of justification arguments, which are also open to criticism. The flexibility of supposed fixed categories is clearly illustrated in the difficult problem of US government census designers in the categorization and particularization of 'race'. On the one hand is the awareness that a social categorization of 'race' is a biologically meaningless category. Yet on the other hand there is the understanding that the historical classification still impacts on society and only by collecting demographic data associated with ethnicity can population trends and current societal discrimination be determined (and addressed to bring about a fairer society). The history of the US census classification reflects the arguments within the culture about what are the appropriate racial classifications for people in society. Indeed, the chosen classifications have changed from census to census, with the nineteenth-century groupings very different to today's categories, reflecting changing cultural ideas and patterns of immigration. A key problem for the US census in 2000 and 2010 was how to classify 'Hispanic' people. Demby (2014) pointed out that some population forecasters assumed that they were 'not-White', yet when they were allowed to self-categorize on the 2010 census a large number classified themselves as White. The census data shows that the categorical division of White–not-White is not a fixed category (Demby, 2014), with 10 million people changing their classification on the US census between 2000 and 2010 (Cohn, 2014). Thus, the census, as well as recording statistical information, is also reflecting the current state of the argument about ethnic groupings in the society.

Argument, stereotypes and positioning in discourse

Harré (2001) argued that we can understand human interaction as an ongoing conversation, within which people take up various positions that have associated rights and duties. For example, a professor talking to a student has a right to ask the student to complete a coursework assignment and a duty to advise the student on how to complete it. In any interaction these rights and duties will correspond to the social norms of the various positions people adopt. People will seek to influence the storyline being constructed in the discourse in their positioning, such as the student positioning themselves as an enthusiastic and intelligent student by their questions and comments to the professor. Consequently, 'stereotypes can only be understood when placed in their conversational context' (van Langenhove and Harré, 1994, p. 364). In an interview, a politician is told of academic research that contradicts their view and responds: 'what do these so-called experts in their ivory towers know about the life of the hard-working man or woman in the street'. By employing a known professor stereotype, as out of touch with the 'real world', the politician is able to rhetorically demean and dismiss the research without engaging with it, and also claim a moral superiority. Van Langenhove and Harré (1994) argued that there is no one 'right' representation of a social group (such as professors or politicians); but there are a variety of social representations of any group. However, a specific known representation (or cultural association) is employed for the purpose of positioning a character in a storyline. They also suggested that stereotype change is not going to occur by telling people that stereotypes are false, but by 'pointing out to people how they position themselves while 'using' stereotypes' (van Langenhove and Harré, 1994, p. 370).

Consider, for example, the category of 'migrants'. The members of this category may have very little in common with each other, so the categorization itself is a cultural and political act. By the rhetorical use of a particular stereotype of a 'migrant' as poor and alien (a cultural Other, see Chapter 6), a politician can position themselves as a determined protector of the cultural and national heritage, rather than a xenophobe, in seeking to restrict immigration. Furthermore, by employing the metaphor of migration as an inundation, statements like 'we cannot cope with waves of migrants in our communities', a politician can position migrants as a damaging flood, with the implication that flood protection (tighter immigration controls) are the only protection from disaster (widespread damage to the social order). Like metaphors, stereotypes are rhetorical tools employed within language and literature to exaggerate difference and claim moral superiority (e.g. Holliday, 2010a; Shi xu, 1995). While there are a variety of different stereotypes of social groups, different ones are employed in argument for different purposes. Furthermore, people can employ positioning strategies to rhetorically place themselves 'outside' an argument to make socially disapproved of statements about social groups, as if they are not their own personal opinion (Ladegaard, 2011). In modern Western societies, people are aware that making racist or sexist statements are unacceptable, so may choose to employ rhetorical strategies, such as justification, victim blaming or denial, before making stereotypical statements by, for example, beginning a statement with 'I am not a racist, but ...' (van Dijk, 1992). Speakers may add hedges and provisos to police their speech to avoid the opprobrium of overtly expressing cultural stereotypes that they know will be viewed negatively in the context (Condor et al., 2006). Another such rhetorical strategy is when the speaker implies that they have access to general group opinions rather than simply expressing their personal view. Rather than saying, 'I think that ...' people will say 'Everyone knows that ...' or 'The working people of this country want ...', or 'The public are fed up with ...' which are frequently employed by politicians in the news media. By using this generalization strategy, the speaker seeks to persuade the audience that their own ideological position is representative of a wider social group and that their view is – or should be – the accepted norm. Arguably, every time someone makes such a claim it is, by definition, stereotypical as the group almost certainly do not have a homogeneous view or possibly even the opinion claimed for them.

The language of binary opposition

There are certain social categories that have been traditionally employed as binary oppositions, such as men–women, White–Black and West–East in literature and the media. These are the social categories whose stereotypes have been of the greatest public concern in Western societies. It has been argued by the linguist Ferdinand de Saussure that there is a structural role of binary oppositions in language, in creating meaning: *good* is reciprocally determined in a complementary relationship with its opposite, *evil*. We only know what *blackness* means by the contrast of its opposite, *whiteness* (Hall, 1997; Jeffries, 2010). The anthropologist Claude Lévi-Strauss developed this idea, to claim that binary oppositions were related to how people think, with folk tales and cultural narratives structured in terms of such oppositional binaries. Popular culture presents stories of binary oppositions such as the hero and the villain, the young and the old, even the human and the alien (e.g. Deliège, 2004). However, this implied a universal or fixed structure of meaning that was challenged by philosopher Jacques Derrida, who argued that the 'web of language' is contextualized through time (for example, new words and new meanings are continually being introduced into a language). Even more importantly, 'In a classical philosophical opposition [i.e. within Western thought] we are not dealing with a peaceful co-existence of a vis-à-vis, but rather with a violent hierarchy. One of the two terms governs the other' (Derrida, 1981, p. 41). We can show this by simply reversing the opposition to reveal the privileged term and the implicit assumptions contained within the text employing it. These binaries have a political and social significance. They reflect societal power relationships, between men and women, White and Black people, Westerners and Orientals, with the first group listed being the dominant group in Western societies. This then relates to sexism, racism and Orientalism in the society as these terms, by definition, claim discrimination between the binary pairs, both in terms of difference and privilege (Hall, 1997). Consequently, a major theme within modern literary and media analysis has been the deconstruction of 'texts' (be they novels, plays, films or television, or even conversations and discussions) to reveal their underlying (binary) patterns of privilege (McQuillan, 2001).

Jeffries (2010) noted that English language practice has traditionally employed the man–woman dichotomy as a mutually exclusive categorization. Consequently, 'such a socially entrenched conceptual division as gender is not affected by the historical existence of hermaphrodites; transsexuals or any other challenges to the distinction between being a man or a woman' (Jeffries, 2010, p. 19). The historic binary division constructs a rigid stereotypical distinction between men and women, by which means it excludes all variation. Hence, the stereotypes of men and women are structured through the use of language in a society. The key point in the above quote from Jeffries (2010) is the phrase 'socially entrenched' as this is precisely what

Derrida wished to highlight in the deconstruction of a text, as well as seeking to destabilize the 'fixed' binary oppositions themselves. This is not simply a destructive process but reveals the underlying values creating the binary oppositions, which are contingent rather than essential divisions of dominance, opening up the opportunity for ambiguity and reconstruction using alternative values. Carter (2011) explicitly challenged this historical binary classification: 'Categorization imposes a false binary on the sexes while at the same time ignoring those who do not fit the binary.' Hekman (1997) argued that there is not an underlying truth (of gender) to be discovered, but that social constructions are not simply relative (or equivalent), but are guided by values. Hence, social binaries based on ideologies of difference can be challenged through arguments based on alternative values (such as equality and inclusion) and by undermining the idea of essential differences. For example, de Beauvoir ([1949] 2010, p. 17) claimed that '[o]ne is not born, but rather becomes, a woman'. Butler (1988, 1990), in her analysis of gender, argued that people are not essentially gendered but that gender is a *performance*.[5] A person's gender is not *what they are* but *what they do*. Butler (1990) challenged the acceptance of heterosexuality as a dominant frame for gender, which has constructed dominant gender norms. Thus, the socialization of girls and boys has produced cultural rituals of gender that are normalized. Gender has traditionally been viewed as a 'natural manifestation of sex' (Butler, 1990, p. 20), whereas it is constructed within a normative structure. She took the example of 'drag' to question the reality of gender, arguing that a statement such as 'a man dressed as a woman' reveals – and challenges – the gender norm or assumption that 'man' in this statement is 'real' whereas 'woman' is not. Thus, this argument suggests, the cultural binary division of gender into male and female (heterosexual) roles is not a 'natural' binary division but a particular historical 'theatre' upon which particular scripts about gender are performed. When people refer to gender stereotypes or make statements like 'boys don't cry' or 'girls don't do mathematics', rather than claiming anything 'natural' about gender, they are identifying the gender performance norms of a particular culture at a particular time. Morgenroth and Ryan (2018, p. 4) made the link between Butler and gender-role theory clear: 'gender stereotypes provide the "script" for the performance of gender with negative consequences of those who fail to "learn their lines" or "stick to the script"'. Just as Garfinkel (1967; see Chapter 5) noted that breaches to social norms can result in annoyance in the observers, Rudman et al. (2012) showed how deviations from normative scripts can lead to social sanction (Morgenroth and Ryan, 2018).

The debate about historic binaries, such as gender, sexuality and race, has led to some complex philosophical arguments about these issues when considered in non-binary terms. Brubaker (2016a, p. 414) has argued that there is both the opportunity for reformulation of historic binary dimensions (recategorizations) but also social anxieties about 'fraudulent identity claims' in terms of both gender and race, such as in gendered sport, or a person of exclusively European (White) heritage self-identifying as being 'a person of colour' (Brubaker, 2016b, p. 414). This is part of an ongoing cultural and political argument about both the social 'policing' of such categories and, at the same time, challenging the policing of such categories (see, for example, Brubaker, 2016a; Meadow, 2017; Phoenix, 2017). This indicates that, while these traditional binaries may be broken down, there remain arguments about what different representations of gender *should be* or *should not be*, indicating that, while old stereotypes might be rejected, new stereotypes may also be constructed based on different ideologies of gender and other traditional binary divisions in the culture.

Stereotypes and the media representation of social groups

Giddens (1990) has argued that a feature of the modern world is the proliferation of choice. In the twenty-first century, the numerous media sources contrast with the limited range of newspapers, television channels, books and films of the previous century. Despite this increase in choice there remains a power imbalance between the broadcasters and the audience (Curran, 2002). Broadcasters have power in terms of their ability to construct media messages in specific ways by two key processes: what stories they tell (*agenda setting*) and how they tell those stories (*framing*). They tell us what is going on in the world and what it means. This is particularly relevant to news reporting, as the media has the power to influence the news agenda (McCombs and Shaw, 1993). The power of the media is that it tells people what are the (media-selected) important news stories of the day (Cohen, 1963). For example, Hall et al. (1978) discussed how 'mugging' (street crime) became a major media story in Britain in the early 1970s. Incidents of street crime were combined together in the media reports along with the storyline that 'something had to be done about it', creating a moral panic (see Chapter 5). By claiming an increase in street violence, governmental force could be justified in targeting certain groups as the focus of police action (particularly, working-class men of African Caribbean origin in London). As with many moral panics, the response had a self-fulfilling effect, as media stories drew their material from the police and the courts, which justified their actions in making more arrests (rather than questioning such actions). While Hall et al. (1978) accepted that the moral panic was not a government and media conspiracy, they argued that the widespread media coverage presented cultural and economic issues in terms of criminal violence associated with specific social groups rather than offering alternative explanations for such social issues. Not only had the coverage set 'mugging' at the top of the media agenda, but it also contextualized current social issues in terms of social control that required harsh policing and was likely to have reinforced stereotypical associations between a social group and crime in the perceptions of the audience. As well, as influencing the selection of news stories, the media also influence the way these stories are told. Communicating the same information in different ways can result in it being understood differently. For example, Kahneman and Tversky (1986) found that people were much more likely to agree to a medical procedure when expressed in a form such as '90 per cent of the people who have the procedure survive' compared to '10 per cent of the people who have the procedure die'; yet the information is the same. Goffman (1974) argued that people understand events through (media) framing, which often relies on learnt schemas from culture, such as the association of a social group with criminality. Happer and Philo (2013) demonstrated this with the reporting of disability in Britain during the first decade of the twenty-first century. While there was an increase in reports about disability, there was actually a reduction in sympathetic reporting of the topic and a rise in stories framed in terms of welfare benefit and fraudulent claims. Happer and Philo (2013) argued that this had an influence on the audience who estimated the percentage of fraudulent claimants as between 10 and 70 per cent whereas the actual figure was merely a half of 1 per cent. These high estimations were also accompanied by resentment at the 'large numbers of people believed to be fraudulently claiming benefit' (Happer and Philo, 2013, p. 327). Thus, agenda setting and news framing can construct cultural associations between social groups and stereotypical attributes.

Media reporting is undertaken within a context, of what is defined as 'news' and how it should be presented, which is a political decision. However, news, in a democratic society, does not reflect the actual state of the world but highlights social problems (Shoemaker, 2006), so there is likely to be a degree of consistency across the media sources as to what are the important news topics of the day. Broadcasters are also competing for 'audience share', which often relates to their income. Thus, media producers must construct stories that will attract audiences. Due to the need to maintain audience interest, complex stories are often simplified in various ways. Robinson (2017), a BBC journalist, suggested that there is a risk of modern news reporting being reduced to attention-grabbing stories exaggerating their extraordinariness, either in a good way (amusing or LOL) or in a bad way (shocking or OMG or WTF[6]). The ordinary, or the expected, therefore is not newsworthy – as it is not 'news'. Consequently, bad news stories predominate, as 'people naturally pay attention to things that are dangerous or threatening' (Shoemaker, 2006, p. 107). Various rhetorical devices may be employed to make stories more attention grabbing and maintain audience interest. For example rhetorical exaggeration produces headlines such as 'cure for cancer' or 'risk of world war', which are more attention grabbing than 'new medical advance may improve cancer survival rates in the future' or 'current diplomatic efforts fail to resolve a territorial dispute'. Such rhetorical devices can be employed to reduce complex issues to media binaries: as a simple two-choice argument. Rather than dealing with the complexities of issues such as illegal drug use, the political use of violence or health and illness, the metaphor of war (a rhetorical device) is often employed. This reduces the issue to 'good guys' (whom it is assumed the audience supports) 'fighting' the 'enemy' or the bad guys. Representations such as the 'war on drugs', the 'war on terror' or the 'war on cancer' simplify complex issues in this way. Stories gain drama by characters being represented as heroes and villains (Shoemaker, 2006). By using the metaphor of war, the police, the army and the medical profession become the 'heroes' and the drug dealers, terrorists and disease become the 'villains' to be vanquished. This generalizes to other stories, such as firefighters becoming 'heroes' for rescuing people from burning buildings and landlords becoming 'villains' for increasing rents. However, the media representation of stories as a battleground (if only a 'war of words') makes issues where there is a common consensus appear more ambiguous, despite the vast weight of scientific evidence favouring one 'side' or the other. In news reports, and particularly in interviews, the 'two sides' of an argument are given equal air time, in an illusion of impartiality. Happer and Philo (2013) demonstrated how, in the discussion on climate change, organizations funded by businesses with a vested interest in presenting a sceptical view of climate change were given equivalent status alongside the scientists and engineers in a 'battle' of opinion. Rather than the media reports acknowledging the weight of scientific evidence, it overemphasized the time allocated to the minority sceptical opinion, leading to audience confusion and distrust in such communications. Thus, each media argument can be 'won' by rhetorical means (such as undermining evidence with statements such as 'what do experts know?') rather than a detailed analysis of the issues. By always presenting an opposing argument in the cause of 'impartiality' the media promotes scepticism and cynicism in the minds of the audience, and ignores the balance of opinion or weight of evidence (Happer and Philo, 2013; Mills, 2016).

This media emphasis, in news coverage, on the unusual and the extreme has also resulted in the construction of a number of stereotypical associations; for example, the stereotype of the criminal as the stranger, the Other, the lone predator, who might strike an innocent victim at any moment (Surette, 1994). The image of this predatory criminal character has been present in numerous fiction stories, television and film dramas throughout the nineteenth and twentieth centuries, employed for its dramatic effect. Whereas stranger murder is rare (only 2 to 3 per cent in 1990), and serial killing even rarer, the public estimated the figure for the predatory stranger at 25 per cent (Surette, 1994). The threat is exacerbated by the implication that the predator can strike anyone at any time, so the risk is the same for everyone. Yet this is not the case. The media distortion of the prevalence of the predator in society has influenced public policy addressing this perception of crime, rather than the social reality of crime, which represents policing as a dangerous battle against the criminal 'stranger'. Surette (1994) explained this fascination with the predatory criminal in terms of American culture constructing the criminal – the bad guy – as fundamentally different to ordinary people – the good guys. This is particularly the case with sex crimes. Despite sex crimes decreasing over a 20-year period, the media has paid them increasing attention (Klein, 2016). As Klein (2016) argued, sex offenders are frequently referred to as 'predators', with the fear of 'stranger danger' perpetuating a myth of the stalking 'predator', contrary to the evidence of who actually perpetrates such crimes: 'The image of the reviled "monster" offender is much easier to comprehend than having to imagine that an uncle, a cousin, or even a mother could be the real monster' (Klein, 2016, p. 488). Crucially, the media mediate the actual events, influencing the audience interpretation to the extent that: 'Mediated events blot out actual ones, so that media renditions often supplant and conflict with what actually happened' (Surette, 2018), creating a mythological world with the criminal as a dangerous stranger or stereotypical Other.

The media construction of stereotypical associations is also illustrated in the portrayal of mental illness. Nairn (2007) compared 21 articles examining media reports of mental illness from the United States, the United Kingdom, Australia and New Zealand. A consistent theme was that news reports depicted mentally ill people as being 'mad' or suffering from 'madness', constructing the stereotypical view that such people are unpredictable, dangerous and prone to violence, which specifically represents them as a threatening Other, despite the evidence of such patients' ordinariness (Nairn, 2007). A similar conclusion was formed by Happer and Philo (2013) in a study of the British media's coverage of mental illness, which tended to focus on violent incidents. The evidence is that mental illness is not associated with violence, with only a very small minority of mentally ill people potentially violent (Scheff, 1999). However, the media focus can result in people (the audience) believing that the mentally ill are a threat to them. Furthermore, the media-constructed association between mental illness and violence is much more likely to be learnt and believed when there are no alternative messages contradicting this relationship (Happer and Philo, 2013). The media-constructed stereotype of the mentally ill is once again the image of a dangerous, unpredictable Other.

Stereotypes, active audiences and interpretive communities

There is a temptation from the research on media stereotypes to view the audience as passively absorbing media representations and replicating them in their social perception. But this idea has been challenged in studies of *audience reception*. Audience interpretation does not only depend on the broadcaster's construction of events, but also the way the audience *actively* interpret that message (Livingstone, 2000). Hall (1999) referred to the process as one of encoding and decoding. The media do not simply 'transmit' a message but *encodes* it (Hall, 1999), as discussed above. However, the audience is not simply a passive receiver of 'information' but actively *decodes* the message (Hall, 1999; Livingstone, 2000). For example, consider a local news report about teenagers representing them as causing problems in the local town, about which 'something must be done'. Most of the audience may interpret the news report in terms of juvenile delinquency, the *dominant reading* of the story constructed by the broadcaster (Hall, 1999). However, this is not the only reading. A teenager, viewing the report, might strongly object to the representation and argue that the report is biased and unfair. This is referred to as an *oppositional reading* (Hall, 1999), as the audience is rejecting the dominant reading. For this particular audience, this news report might be interpreted as perpetuating an offensive stereotype of young people. Finally, a viewer might accept aspects of the message but not accept the dominant reading, such as acknowledging that there is a problem but arguing that it requires additional community facilities and not law enforcement. Hall (1999) referred to this as a *negotiated reading*. These differences of media interpretation – different readings – have been shown to be related to cultural group membership, such as social class (Morley, 1980), which are related to different group-based ideologies. This means that an ideologically conservative (liberal) media producer will encode news stories in such a way that an ideologically conservative (liberal) audience will accept the dominant reading. The representation is one that both producer and audience are likely to view as a 'correct' interpretation of social reality. However, if a liberal (conservative) audience access the same media source, then they are likely to view the news story in terms of an oppositional reading, even to the extent of viewing it as a complete distortion of social reality, replete with false stereotypes and biased representations.

This idea can be linked to the concept of *interpretive communities* (Fish, 1980). Fish argued that the meaning of a 'text' (such as a media story) is not contained in the text or the individual audience member but in the interpretive community to which the audience belongs.

> An interpretive community is not objective because, as a bundle of interests, of particular purposes and goals, its perspective is interested rather than neutral; but by the very same reasoning, the meanings and texts produced by an interpretive community are not subjective because they do not proceed from an isolated individual but from a public and conventional point of view.
>
> *Fish, 1980, p. 14*

For the purposes of this book, this idea is associated with a cultural group, by arguing that the active audience, as an interpretive community, is guided by their common understandings (see Chapters 5 and 7). This occurs through their shared knowledge of *cultural codes* (Hall, 1997). Communication occurs through a shared language of signs. It is not just that people in a cultural group employ the same spoken language (such as English) but they have learnt the specific associations of signs and signification (such as a 'red' traffic light meaning 'stop') in their culture. Cultural codes exist in language (such as the arbitrary word 'dog' for a particular group of animals) but more broadly in visual media (such as gestures, clothing, music, photographs, video and even traffic lights). To understand other people we must have both a common conceptual system and a common language system. These are learnt within a culture and so are referred to as 'cultural codes' (Hall, 1997). Thus, meaning does not lie inherently in things (a green-light traffic light does not inherently mean 'go') but is constructed within the practice of signification in a culture. People from different cultures will interpret media stories through their own cultural codes, which can lead to a different understanding of a media output when it comes from a different culture. This explains why some drama serials may be successful in their home culture but not in other cultures. For example, in a focus group study, Katz et al. (1991) showed Japanese viewers the 1980s American soap opera *Dallas*, about the lives of a family of oil millionaires in Texas. The hugely popular program, in its own country, was not successful in Japan. The results suggested why this might have been. First, the program violated the conventions of Japanese home-produced drama series, so did not follow their cultural expectations. Second, inconsistencies in the storyline that might have been considered exciting in its home country, such as two characters hating each other one week and working together the next, were considered confusing (and not believable). This combination of the unexpected and the inconsistent led the Japanese audience to be critically distant from the story (they simply could not 'get into it'). While there is evidence that people from one culture can enjoy a program from another culture, there is no guarantee that they are interpreting it in the same way, and may be enjoying it for its exoticism or melodrama rather than picking up the same cultural codes of the broadcaster (Hinton, 2007).

Therefore, a key aspect of cultural sophistication (i.e. being able to make sense of the social world in one's own culture) is that members of the culture are able to interpret cultural signs and symbols in terms of their *denotation* and *connotation*, which refer to levels of meaning (Barthes, 1977) that members of a culture readily understand. Denotation is a more basic common-sense level of signification, such as a Stetson 'denoting' a type of American headgear, familiar in films of the old West. However, in a 1950s cowboy story (as in *The Lone Ranger*) a black Stetson 'connotes' a bad guy and a white Stetson connotes the hero. Connotations are related to myths, such as the triumph of the white-hat-wearing good guy over the black-hat-wearing bad guy, and the combination of denotation and connotation draws on an ideology that is embedded within the culture. By performing a *semiotic analysis*[7] we can reveal the patterns of denotation and connotation in a text, a film or a book, which support certain values and ideas and are understood by the characters within the text, and the audience as an interpretive community who are able to 'read' (understand) the signs and their cultural signification, as knowledgeable members of the culture. These ideas can be brought together in examining the popular 1995 teen comedy movie *Clueless*, directed by Amy Heckerling, which was loosely based on the 1815 Jane Austin novel *Emma*, about the misperceptions and misunderstandings of a young woman seeking to manage the romantic lives of the people around her. In the film the story was transferred to a modern American high school. Rather than being the sophisticate she believes herself to be, the central character is clearly naive, as the (American) audience soon determines.

The film is set in a Beverly Hills high school where students are the children of very wealthy parents, so can afford the latest in cars, phones and fashion. Furthermore, it presents a catalogue of 1990s teenage argot, fashion and stereotypes; from the long-haired skateboard dude to the nerdy teachers with their lunchtime sandwiches and thermos flasks. Indeed, the film gains much of its appeal and humour from these representations (assuming cultural knowledge). Initially, Cher (the central, Emma, character) appears to have some success in making her new friend, Tai, more fashionable and bringing two of the teachers together through her machinations. Yet all along she is making comments, particularly to her former step-brother Josh, which both he and the audience pick up, which demonstrate her misunderstanding of the world around her. Then a new boy arrives in her class, and she decides that the handsome, well-dressed Christian will make the perfect boyfriend for her. However, from the very moment that Christian appears, as Sinatra (2011, p. 125) put it, 'Heckerling [the director] then bombards the audience with one gay stereotype after another to exaggerate Cher's self-absorption and naiveté.' Christian likes listening to Billie Holliday music and is interested in art. Cher and Christian hang out together watching Christian's old movies (*Some Like It Hot* and *Spartacus*) and going shopping for clothes. Confusingly (to her), he seems unresponsive to her moves towards intimacy. In a sequence where she is sitting in the back of her friend Dionne's car, with Dionne and her boyfriend Murray sitting in the front, she decides to confess her confusion to them. Murray bursts out laughing in surprise and asks her if she is 'blind or something'. Seeing the confused blank look on Cher's face, he exclaims: 'He's gay'. At first Cher cannot believe it, but Dionne says: 'He does like to shop, Cher, and the boy can dress.' Finally, Cher is convinced: 'Oh, my God. I am totally buggin'. I feel like such a bonehead.'

Cher's naivety was because she did not recognize the stereotypes of her own culture.

Notes

1 Series 8, episode 9 'The Mysterious Date Observation' (2014).
2 An emperor is duped by tailors into believing that they have made him a wonderful new suit of clothes that is invisible to the foolish. This is communicated to the townsfolk who, not wanting to appear foolish, marvel at his new attire until a small child cries out that the emperor is not wearing any clothes.
3 In the British historical story, American independence is viewed as a setback in the ongoing global battle against the French (whose military involvement was seen as a significant factor in the colonial victory), which was ultimately successful in the defeat of French emperor Napoleon in 1815, cementing the rise of the British Empire (Jasanoff, 2011).
4 Compared to other cultures where interdependency, obligation to others and group cohesion are emphasized (called *collectivism*), such as in East Asian societies and religions (Hofstede, 1984).
5 This can be considered alongside the dramaturgical model of Erving Goffman (1959) arguing that social life can be analysed in terms of people as actors in the performance of their own lives, taking on roles and following normative scripts.
6 LOL (Laugh Out Loud) for amusing stories, and OMG (Oh My God) or WTF (What the F★★K) for stories that are shocking.
7 An analysis of the signs and associated cultural codes in a text to reveal their meaning.

8

'STEREOTYPES' AND THE CONSTRUCTION OF THE SOCIAL WORLD

What are stereotypes?

The vast majority of the research into stereotypes, since Lippmann's proposal in 1922, has concerned the relationship between certain stereotypes and discrimination in the United States. For example, in his book, Allport ([1954] 1979) has a chapter entitled 'stereotypes in our culture'. Yet this chapter focused almost entirely on two stereotypes, the Jewish and the Black stereotypes. If we move forward 65 years, and look at the social categories examined on the Project Implicit website (see Chapter 3), we find 14 different comparisons that, apart from presidential popularity, all concern issues of discrimination in that culture: race (Black–White), gender and science, gender and careers, weapons, presidential popularity, disability (disabled–abled), skin tone (dark skin–light skin), native (Native–White American), weight (fat–thin), sexuality (gay–straight), Asian (Asian–European American), religions, age (old–young) and Arab-Muslim (Arab-Muslim–other people). Stereotypes have had a significant position in the battle against prejudice in American society, in particular in the fight against anti-Semitism, racism and sexism. The stereotypes of the discriminated-against groups associate them with negative attributes or in the case of the Black stereotype and the stereotype of women, as lacking in capability compared to Whites and men. These are a problem for two reasons. When the group members are given equal opportunities – and a level playing field – to demonstrate their abilities, they clearly are not lacking in capability, despite the added pressure of stereotype threat. For example, successful African American and women professors and politicians (and other leaders) demonstrate the association to be false. In addition, the stereotypes are ideologically offensive in supporting societal discrimination that should not be (in the society). While, in the classical model of stereotypes it was argued that people who expressed such stereotypes were demonstrating simplistic, faulty, rigid thinking, the more recent work on implicit bias has argued that stereotypes may have an insidious influence even on people in the society seeking to act in non-discriminatory ways, resulting in implicit prejudice. Why is this? The answer is given by Devine and Sharp (2009, p. 62): 'during socialization, a culture's beliefs about various social groups are frequently activated and become well learned'. Thus, stereotypes are in the culture and acquired by its member during socialization. Yet, from Allport ([1954] 1979) to Hardin and Banaji (2013), these particular stereotypes have been viewed as a pernicious influence in society as they support societal discrimination and violate a fundamental egalitarian ideology. As Hardin and Banaji (2013, p. 21) point out: 'Implicit prejudice not only reflects stable social and organizational hierarchies, but research shows that changes in social organization also predict corresponding changes in implicit prejudice, a finding that has promising implications for public policy.' Thus, to solve the problem of these discriminatory stereotypes, as social group-attribute associations that are present in the culture, is to change the society.

This focus on stereotypes – seeking to find ways of reducing discrimination in American society – has led to a tendency to see *all* stereotypes as 'bad'; that is, all stereotypes are 'wrong' (as in not an accurate representation of the social world) and 'wrong' (as in ideologically objectionable). However, Perkins (1979) argued that rather than the stereotypes associated with societal discrimination being 'typical' stereotypes, they might actually be a special type of stereotype: the ones that are objectionable in terms of an egalitarian ideology. Most other stereotypes – as cultural associations – might be accepted by the people doing the stereotyping and the people being stereotyped and accord with their ideological beliefs. To take one example important in British culture: the British 'stiff upper lip'. If you look up the word 'phlegmatic' in the *Oxford Dictionary*,[1] the first example it gives is 'the phlegmatic British character'. The British 'stiff upper lip' is a stoical ability to keep calm in stressful situations and not react emotionally. It is a widely known stereotype in American culture to describe the British, with all the top circulation newspapers[2] in the United States having employed it at some point in the twenty-first century, on the assumption that their readers are familiar with it. Yet it is not a stereotype of a discriminated-against group in society. More significantly, the phlegmatic British stereotype has been of particular importance to the British as a way of viewing themselves. In the Second World War British cities were regularly bombed by enemy aircraft creating widespread destruction (referred to as the Blitz). It has been argued that, in this situation, 'the British people behaved as they had been taught to behave – courageously, stoically and good-humouredly' (Richards, 1997, p. 17). Wartime patriotic films, such as *In Which We Serve* (1942) emphasized this phlegmatic aspect of the British character. It was important to the British that this was an attribute they 'truly' had. In a 2006 interview, a British woman recalled: 'When the war began I was 8 years old ... You mustn't forget that we were entreated to *endure*, be courageous, grin and bear it' (Wilkins, 2016, p. 133).

Yet British culture changed and the British engagement with this cultural association changed. In the second half of the twentieth century, Britain was dealing with the loss of both its empire and its status as a world power. The British stiff upper lip began to be affectionately mocked in British culture for comedic effect in books, such as P. G. Woodhouse's *Stiff Upper Lip, Jeeves* (1963), or films, such as the deliberately ridiculous comedy *Carry On Up the Khyber* (1968). In the film, set in nineteenth-century India, a British governor, his officers and families are eating a formal meal as the governor's residence is shelled by local insurgents. They continue stoically eating and making small talk as if nothing is happening, as the building (or rather the harmless film set) gradually disintegrates around them, covering them in dust and 'debris'. Thus, in the latter part of the twentieth century, the stiff upper lip was viewed (in Britain) as an archaic concept that was often the subject of self-deprecating humour. A twist in the story of British stoicism occurred near the end of the twentieth century, when it was argued that having a stiff upper lip was not a good way to deal with stress and disguised unreported mental problems. In 2001 a liberal-oriented national newspaper reported on a government campaign to encourage emotional literacy under the heading of 'Antidote to the stiff upper lip' (Browne, 2001). The approach of stress counselling was later criticized in a more conservative-oriented newspaper under the heading 'Stiff upper lip beats stress counselling' (Baxter and Rogers, 2003), which was then criticized by medical researchers as a misunderstanding of stress counselling (Kimble and Kaufman, 2004). More recently, in a damning criticism of the British upper-class boarding school system, which he experienced, Renton (2017) presents a catalogue of abuses hidden by a culture of not speaking out, under the title of *Stiff Upper Lip*.

This stereotype of the phlegmatic British appears to have none of the qualities of the American stereotypes above. Yet they have one crucial aspect in common. They are products of their culture. They exist as associations between social groups and attributes that the people in the culture have learnt. While anti-racists in the United States object to the negative stereotype of Black people in their culture, and fight to change their culture, they do not deny the history and existence of racism within that culture. The key feature of all stereotypes is that they are formed within a particular culture for a particular purpose at a particular time. Thus, their 'reality' is a cultural reality, not an objective accuracy (or inaccuracy). These associations between social groups and attributes are not 'irrational' generalizations but gain their meaning – their rationality – from the structure of the culture in which they are formed. Generalizations about social groups, present in the historical structure of the culture, may be viewed as morally right or morally wrong, depending on the ideological viewpoint of the person or group making the judgement. Stereotypes are learnt cultural associations. Recall that modern definitions are simply that 'stereotypes are qualities perceived to be associated with particular groups or categories of people', Schneider (2004, p. 24). Hence, stereotypes as a general category, are not indicative of simplistic, rigid, irrational 'wrong-headedness'. Of course, stereotypes may endure over a period of time as they reflect the culture that constructed them. But cultures are dynamic and stereotypes are not 'fixed'. A person of 100 years ago, brought miraculously forward to the modern state of their culture, would find it radically different, with different associations between groups and attributes. Similarly, children of today sent back 100 years would find it equally surprising, if not shocking, due to the different generalizations and expectations about people. Cultures change and the cultural associations change with it.

This explains why there are stereotypes of accountant and librarians, and of *every* meaningful social category in a culture, be it Californians or check-out clerks or truck drivers or trailer-park inhabitants. Indeed, these associations reveal the culture itself. To learn about a culture is to learn its cultural associations about the meaningful social groups within it – its stereotypes. Stereotypes are not providing accounts of the 'real' or 'true' psychology of social groups but a cultural psychology of them – a folk psychology:

> All cultures have as one of their most powerful constitutive instruments a folk psychology, a set of more or less connected, more or less normative descriptions about how human beings 'tick', what our own and other minds are like, and what one can expect situated action to be like, what are the possible modes of life, how one commits oneself to them, and so on. We learn our culture's folk psychology early, learn it as we learn to use the very language we acquire and to conduct the interpersonal transactions required in communal life.
>
> *Bruner, 1990, p. 35*

These 'more or less connected, more or less normative descriptions' are the cultural associations relating people (as group members) to attributes – its stereotypes. This folk psychology represents both the cultural fabric and the construction of the people within it. This means, as Lippmann (1922, p, 81) insightfully put it, 'we pick out what our culture has already defined for us, and we tend to perceive that which we have picked out in the form stereotyped for us by our culture'. Implicit mental 'biases' are not indicative of some sort of 'faulty' individual cognition but of learnt associations as 'culture in mind' (Hinton, 2017). To understand how the people of a culture 'tick' we must learn its cultural associations, which is the task of every young child during socialization. The meaningful social categories in a society and their associated attributes – what the group members are like and what they do – construct a model of the social world, a framework of power and control that enables the prediction of the conduct of people in that culture, who otherwise would be inexplicable. Therefore, to understand stereotypes, we need to shift the focus from cognition to culture. And to understand how they are constructed in, and form the fabric of, a culture we must ask three questions.

1. What are the meaningful social categories in this culture?

The social world is made up of different social categories and the task of understanding a culture is to work out what those categories are and what they mean. Social categories are units of culture. Social categories are constructed within a culture as a result of a history of power and ideological dominance. The ideological construction of social groups also constructs the members of them:

who they are, what they do and what they should and should not do. This defines their position in the culture, their status and their access to resources; such as in the division of society into nobles and peasants, bourgeoisie and workers, men and women or White people and Black people. Members of social institutions, such as the government, police, priests, teachers, doctors (and others) regulate the social categories to control deviance. The child will soon learn who has power and authority and who does not in the culture and the meaning of the different social groups (based on the dominant ideology). They will also learn which categories they inhabit by the treatment they receive from others in this culture, and the consequent social control over their own behaviour.

2. Who are the members of the social groups in terms of other social categories in this culture?

Children learn that, in their culture, certain social categories go together. For example, at one period in the history of a culture, children may learn that, in the commercial sphere, all the company managers tend to be men and all the secretaries are predominantly women. In another cultural period, they may learn that, although the students in state-run elementary schools are ethnically mixed, the majority of teachers are White women. Social groups are not independent of each other, but are interdependent. These relationships – the constitution of the social categories in terms of other categories – provide important information about the culture. These interrelationships reveal the structure of the culture (the 'web of culture'), as social categories are related to each other in a complex framework – often hierarchical – of the relationships between them. There will be significant correlations (associations) between social groups. For example, at one time the senior executives of major corporations and the low-paid manual workers in those same corporations may tend to come from specific but different ethnic groups in this culture.

3. What do the members of a social group (normally) do in this culture?

Children will learn that there are consistencies of conduct related to social group membership. While people have the capacity for idiosyncratic behaviour, much of human conduct is socially defined by, or normatively related to, social group membership. Role requirements associated with a social category – with its associated rights and duties – identify different 'types' of people related to their role in the culture, be it an occupational role such as accountant or a social role such as mother, or the expectations concerning the conduct of any other culturally meaningful group, such as those related to old age. These roles and their associated norms are cultural. Different societies may employ similar category labels (such as priest, teacher, mother) but the normative activities of people in those categories will differ according to the cultural formation. Once the child is fully socialized into the culture then they too can interact with other people in their culture in terms of shared meanings of social categories and associated conduct, as the 'common-sense' or the social reality of society.

A model of stereotypes as a culture's folk psychology

The answers to the three questions above do not simply reveal the structure and organization of the culture but provide a framework for understanding stereotypes as a cultural folk psychology. In particular, it helps us to answer some of the complex issues about stereotypes debated over the last 100 years. Crucially, it argues that none of the social categories, the interrelationships between categories or the conduct of category members are 'fixed' or permanent but are part of a dynamic process of cultural change that can be fast and radical (as in the French and Russian Revolutions) or slow and incremental. To illustrate how the whole range of stereotypical associations, from those of ethnic groups to accountants, are constructed within a culture, I have (somewhat artificially) separated them into three types of generalization in this model. However, it is important to note that these generalizations are not independent of each other.

Category construction: stereotypes as prescriptive generalizations (ideological prescriptions)

At any moment in history we can observe the social organization of a culture and its patterns of dominance created to support a particular ideology. The meaning of the constructed social categories derives from the relationships of power in the culture, with dominant groups imposing ideological prescriptions and proscriptions on how these category members behave. The members and supporters of a dominant ideology will seek to maintain and justify their dominance in support of the social structure, others will seek to challenge it based on alternative ideological beliefs and values, working to reconstruct the social categories and the patterns of dominance. Therefore different social groups make generalizations about people based on their ideological beliefs and not on their scientific 'accuracy'. These can be considered as *prescriptive generalizations* as they are generalizations about how people are (and *should be*) based on an ideology of difference in terms of specific characteristics (see Chapter 6). For example, someone with strong religious beliefs will learn their views of social groups from that religion's teachings. The religion may employ a theological argument distinguishing between, say, men and women in terms of their God-given place in the 'natural order', about the nature of men and women, which, it is argued, *should* influence their societal roles. This may or may not be concordant with the actual structure of the society dependent on the power of that religious group in that society (such as whether it is the state religion or not). However, someone else, as a member of a secular political organization (for example) holding strong egalitarian values, will argue on the basis of their beliefs that in general (i.e. culturally relevant terms) men and women do not differ on the important aspects of their membership of the social category of citizen and so

Stereotypes and the social world

should have equal status and equal opportunities. Again, these ideological beliefs may or may not correspond to the actual structure of the society. While it is theoretically possible to argue for an 'objective' or 'outside' stance, such as in a scientific analysis of 'real' gender differences (or lack therefore), this type of analysis is fraught with philosophical and methodological difficulties, and a person with strong religious beliefs or a fundamental belief in egalitarianism is unlikely to change their views on evidence that will almost certainly be open to debate, given their investment in their beliefs and the importance of their ideology to their identity (see Chapter 4). For this reason, prescriptive generalizations based on an ideology (particularly those that the speaker disagrees with) are often represented as 'fixed' or 'rigid' stereotypes (see Chapter 2). Thus, stereotypes such as 'the rich are greedy' or 'the poor are lazy' are prescriptive generalizations based on ideological beliefs and values. A decision about their validity (as 'true' or 'false') does not necessarily relate to the state of the social world but to an ideological position (such as a Marxist viewing the bourgeoisie as having a 'false consciousness' or an egalitarian regarding an ideology of difference as morally wrong).

Category constitution: stereotypes as predictive generalizations (category associations)

People learn the correlations between social categories in a culture by their frequency of co-occurrence in the media and personal experience. For example, nurses care for people and typically work in hospitals alongside doctors, and engineers design, build and maintain systems and typically employ complex mathematics: neither role requirement is associated with gender by definition. Yet in a particular culture, at a particular time, most nurses are women (say, 90 per cent) and most engineers are men (say, 80 per cent). This is not true of other cultures, and, indeed, it is possible to imagine a society where the reverse is the case. However, these percentages provide reliable statistical probabilities present in the society: there is a 9 out of 10 chance that an (unknown) nurse will be a woman and an 8 out of 10 chance that an (unknown) engineer will be a man. Statistically, the associations are present in the culture. A member of that culture will learn a huge variety of such between-category associations present within their culture, including these two specific associations. This forms their cultural knowledge and helps them negotiate their social world. A *predicative generalization* is not an ideological belief about what should or should not be the case – it is not a value judgement about, for example, whether it is a good or bad thing that, in this culture, nurses are typically women and engineers typically men. A person (or their unconscious mind) is simply acquiring predictive generalizations (probabilities of association). (This may be occurring in a similar way to a Bayesian artificial intelligence (AI) system; see Chapter 3. Hence, artificial intelligence systems and the human implicit knowledge system can be viewed as performing similar activities.) These predictive generalizations may be labelled as 'stereotypes', but these stereotypes (or predicative generalizations) can be probabilistically accurate in the culture (Jussim, 2012a; Lee et al., 2013). It is important to note that predictive generalizations are learnt associations about how the culture is actually structured (and acquired through personal experience, cultural resources and media occurrences). These predictions are only inaccurate if they are probabilistically incorrect: for example, a person predicts that most doctors in the culture are men when statistically most doctors in the culture are actually women. As the culture changes, then so will the probabilities of category association change and members of the culture will gradually unlearn the old associations and the next generation will learn the new social structure. However, for a cultural group member, despite societal change, it will take time to learn the new cultural association (like changing a well-learnt habit). It is important to note what is meant by 'the culture' here. Large societies – or the global community – comprise many cultures and, if people only communicate within restricted social networks or segregated communities, which form cultures within a wider society, then the predictive generalizations may reflect the former rather than the latter culture. Therefore, the accuracy of predictive generalizations depends on which particular culture is being considered (see Chapter 7).

Category conduct: stereotypes as normative generalizations (normative descriptions)

Social group members typically behave in normative ways as defined in their culture. Normative behaviours are socially expected behaviours. They relate to the formation, structure and organization of the culture, which determine the roles of the members of different social groups in the society and their conduct. Hence, normative behaviour is regulated (see Chapters 4 and 7): behaving non-normatively (often labelled as deviance) can result in social disapproval, to formal sanction and ultimately punishment, such as imprisonment. Therefore the behaviour of people is generally normative as they will follow the prescriptions of the roles they inhabit as group members. Stereotypes, particularly occupational stereotypes, can be considered as *normative generalizations* that are associations between the normative in-role conduct and the people performing them. For example, the stereotype of the boring accountant (undertaking numerical activities generally considered as dull in the culture) or the introverted librarian (required to work in a quiet environment surrounded by books), relate the in-role activities with the character or type of person carrying out the role. In-role behaviour can also be considered as in-character behaviour. This is supported by research showing that stereotypes are related to social roles, particularly those related to men and women (Eagly and Wood, 2012). Normative generalizations can be made about any social group and its role in society. Indeed, normative generalizations can be considered as attributions of character from normative behaviour associated with a social category (see Chapter 5). Assuming a relationship between characteristic behaviour and an underlying character ('a type') allows for generalization. While this may be considered an 'error' in terms of personality attribution – the people do not actually have the characteristic – in terms of seeking to maximize the predictability of other people it has rationality. While a social group member may not ('really') have the inferred characteristic associated with their normative group behaviour, they may act as if they do (due to the role requirements) and so the generalization may still be pragmatic if it results in a successful expectation (prediction) of their actual behaviour, which is likely to be the case if group members continue to behave normatively for their social group.

Stereotypes and the cycle of cultural association and generalization

What has been referred to as 'stereotypes' in the research literature has been demonstrated here to be integral in the dynamic cultural process of social category construction and reconstruction. Stereotypes are generalization about the characteristics of social group members. Three types of generalization have been identified: prescriptive generalization, predicative generalization and normative generalization. Each one serves a particular purpose in understanding the social organization of a culture and navigating through it in terms of being able to predict the behaviour of others. However, they are all interrelated in terms of the structure (and ideology) of the culture. Consider a culture based on an ideology of difference that discriminates against a particular social group in a range of activities from housing, education, employment and health. Ideological discriminatory *prescriptive generalizations* about them (they are lazy and low in intelligence) support the discriminatory social structure and the dominant ideology of difference (but are offensive and inaccurate stereotypes from an egalitarian point of view). Members of the culture will learn that other certain social categories (domestic service, the unemployed or the criminal, for example) disproportionately feature in this group, so members of the culture learn these associations as *predictive generalizations* about the group. Finally, the restricted roles the group members are required to carry out in the society (such as menial activities and physical work) lead to normative generalizations about the characteristic behaviour of those roles in the society, which may lead to an attribution of characteristics of the group members: that is, they are lazy and unintelligent – which supports the dominant ideological beliefs in the culture. The cycle has now returned to the beginning again (see Figure 8.1).

While there are pressures for maintaining the social structure, none of these generalizations are fixed or determined, despite the cycle leading to the system being self-justifying (see Chapter 4). Natural disasters (floods, droughts) or plagues can upset the social order. External threats from invaders or internal threats from within, such as the effect of Martin Luther's criticisms of the Catholic Church in 1517 or the French and Russian Revolutions, can all bring about a structural reorganization. However, social change can be less dramatic but just as transformative, through argumentation and political activity (see Chapter 7). In the communication of a culture there will be dissenting views and alternative ideologies that, despite attempts to suppress them, can ultimately bring about a paradigm shift in the organization of the culture. Throughout history people have learnt about the structure of their society and where this organization conflicts with their own ideological beliefs

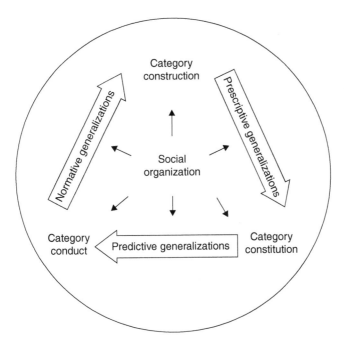

FIGURE 8.1 Stereotypes in the dynamic cycle of social category construction and reconstruction in culture

they have sought to change it. Human beings have the capabilities to construct their own cultures and they have the capabilities to reconstruct them. This can be done by challenging the ideological beliefs on which the structure of dominance is constructed. The meaningful social groups in a society can be reconstructed and reformulated by challenging traditional ideas of, for example, race and gender. The structure of the society in terms of its interrelated social categories can be reorganized, breaking down traditional relationships between social categories and constructing new ones. Finally, roles can be challenged and normative conduct can be extended and changed, which may change the meaningful categories in the society. And the cycle can return to the beginning again with a new set of associations and a reorganized culture.

Conclusion

There have been almost 100 years of research into stereotypes in the United States and other Western countries, which have focused on issues of societal discrimination. Research on this specific set of stereotypes led to the common belief that all stereotypes were indicative of an individual's psychological and mental 'irrationality' (a 'fallacy', 'fault', 'error' or 'bias'). Yet, as this book has demonstrated, rather than being fixed and faulty cognitions about people 'etched' in the minds of individuals, generalizations about people (or 'stereotypes') are constructed by people in communication in a culture for an ideological purpose. Generalizations about people are learnt from the culture that the person inhabits. Socialization, in terms of formal and informal education, means that people acquire these associations to become cultural beings, able to interact with fellow cultural group members in communication. As Leslie (2014, p. 227) pointed out:

> [A]dults have certain ways of carving up the social world, and these ways are very salient to us. To the extent that our ways of thinking and speaking are shaped by this, children will find a way to glean the relevant information from our utterances, so as to 'sync up' with the adults in their community as quickly as possible.

However, as Billig (1996) has pointed out, the current set of social categories (and their related generalizations), present in a culture at any one time, are only half the story. These social categories and their associated attributes are not fixed, even though it is in some people's ideological interest to claim that they are. The second half of the story is one of dissent, of argument and cultural change. Cultures are dynamic and not fixed. We may not like the way our society is organized. We may consider its structure ideologically and morally wrong. We may challenge it and argue for a different social structure, seeking to undermine apparently rigid categorizations through political actions. While it is within culture that the formation and perpetuation of generalizations about social groups (called 'stereotypes') occurs, which are then passed on to its members, it should not be forgotten that those same members might reject them and decide to change things. Therefore the real question of which stereotypes emerge and persist in a culture fundamentally depends on how each generation of adults choose to carve up their social world.

Notes

1 See https://en.oxforddictionaries.com/definition/phlegmatic.
2 I looked at the top ten highest circulation US newspapers.

REFERENCES

Acevedo, G. A. (2005). Turning anomie on its head: Fatalism as Durkheim's concealed and multidimensional alienation theory. *Sociological Theory*, 23(1), 75–85.

Adichie, C. (2009). The danger of a single story. Retrieved from www.ted.com/talks/chimamanda_adichie_the_danger_of_a_single_story.

Adorno, T. W., Frenkel-Brunswik, E., Levinson, D. J. and Sanford, R. N. (1950). *The authoritarian personality*. New York: Harper & Row.

Ajzen, I. (1991). The theory of planned behavior. *Organizational Behavior and Human Decision Processes*, 50(2), 179–211.

Ajzen, I. (1985). From intentions to actions: A theory of planned behavior. In J. Kuhl and J. Beckmann (Eds.) *Action-control: From cognition to behavior* (pp. 11–39). Heidelberg: Springer.

Ajzen, I. and Fishbein, M. (1980) *Understanding attitudes and predicting social behavior*. Englewood Cliffs, NJ: Prentice-Hall.

Albu, N., Albu, C. N., Gîrbină, M. M. and Sandu, M. I. (2011). A framework for the analysis of the stereotypes in accounting. *World Academy of Science, Engineering and Technology*, 5, 732–736.

Alesina, A., Glaeser, E. and Sacerdote, B. (2001). Why doesn't the US have a European-style welfare system?. National Bureau of Economic Research Working Paper no. w8524. Retrieved from www.nber.org/papers/w8524.

Allport, F. H. (1924). The group fallacy in relation to social science. *American Journal of Sociology*, 29(6), 688–706.

Alport, G. W. [1954] (1979). *The nature of prejudice*. Reading, MA: Addison-Wesley.

Andersen, H. and Hepburn, B. (2015). Scientific method. *Stanford Encyclopedia of Philosophy*. Retrieved from https://plato.stanford.edu/entries/scientific-method.

Andrews, P. (2016). Understanding the cultural construction of school mathematics. In B. Lavor (Ed.) *Mathematical cultures* (pp. 9–23). Cham, Switzerland: Springer.

Angwin, J., Larson, J., Mattu, S. and Kirchner, L. (2016). Machine bias: There is software that is used across the county to predict future criminals. And it is biased against blacks. Retrieved from www.propublica.org/article/machine-bias-risk-assessments-in-criminal-sentencing.

Ariès, P. (1962). *Centuries of childhood*: New York: Cape.

Arkes, H. R. and Tetlock, P. E. (2004). Attributions of implicit prejudice, or 'would Jesse Jackson "fail" the Implicit Association Test?'. *Psychological Inquiry*, 15(4), 257–278.

Armstrong, A. C. (2015) 'Princeton University does not discriminate …': African American exclusion at Princeton. Retrieved from https://blogs.princeton.edu/mudd/2015/02/princeton-university-does-not-discriminate-african-american-exclusion-at-princeton.

Armstrong, K. (2004). *A short history of myth*. Edinburgh: Canongate Books.

Arnett, J. J. (2000). Emerging adulthood: A theory of development from the late teens through the twenties. *American Psychologist*, 55(5), 469–480.

Aronson, E. (1976). *The social animal*. San Francisco, CA: W. H. Freeman.

Aronson, J., Fried, C. and Good, C. (2002). Reducing the effects of stereotype threat on African American college students by shaping theories of intelligence. *Journal of Experimental Social Psychology*, 38, 113–125.

Asch, S. E. (1952). *Social psychology*. New York: Prentice-Hall.

Augoustinos, M. and Walker, I. (1998). The construction of stereotypes within social psychology: From social cognition to ideology. *Theory & Psychology*, 8(5), 629–652.

Axt, J. R., Ebersole, C. R. and Nosek, B. A. (2014). The rules of implicit evaluation by race, religion, and age. *Psychological Science*, 25(9), 1804–1815.

Bailey, S. R. and Telles, E. E. (2006). Multiracial versus collective black categories: Examining census classification debates in Brazil. *Ethnicities*, 6(1), 74–101.

Bakshy, E., Messing, S. and Adamic, L. A. (2015). Exposure to ideologically diverse news and opinion on Facebook. *Science*, 348(6239), 1130–1132.

Banaji, M. R., Bhaskar, R. and Brownstein, M. (2015). When bias is implicit, how might we think about repairing harm? *Current Opinion in Psychology*, 6, 183–188.

Banaji, M. R. and Greenwald, A. G. (2013). *Blindspot: Hidden biases of good people*. New York: Delacorte Press.

Bandura, A. (1977). *Social learning theory*. Englewood Cliffs, NJ: Prentice-Hall.

Bandura, A. (1969). Social-learning theory of identificatory processes. In D. A. Goslin (Ed.) *Handbook of socialization theory and research* (pp. 213–262). Chicago, IL: Rand McNally.

Banks, J. A. and McGee Banks, C. A. (Eds.) (2016). *Multicultural education: Issues and perspectives*. 9th edition. Hoboken, NJ: Wiley.

Barden, J., Maddux, W. W., Petty, R. E. and Brewer, M. B. (2004). Contextual moderation of racial bias: The impact of social roles on controlled and automatically activated attitudes. *Journal of Personality and Social Psychology*, 87, 5–22.

Bargh, J. A. (1999). The cognitive monster: The case against controllability of automatic stereotype effects. In S. Chaiken and Y. Trope (Eds.) *Dual process theories in social psychology* (pp. 361–382). New York: Guilford Press.

Bargh, J. A. (1994). The four horsemen of automaticity: Awareness, efficiency, intention, and control in social cognition. In R. S. Wyer Jr and T. K. Srull (Eds.) *Handbook of social cognition*. 2nd edition (pp. 1–40). Hillsdale, NJ: Lawrence Erlbaum Associates.

Bargh, J. A. and Morsella, E. (2008). The unconscious mind. *Perspectives on Psychological Science*, 3(1), 73–79.

Barker, C. (2004). *The Sage dictionary of cultural studies*. London: Sage.

Barker, C. and Jane. E. A. (2016). *Cultural studies: Theory and practice*. London: Sage.

Barthes, R. (1977). *Image–music–text*. London: Fontana.

Barthes, R. (1972). *Mythologies* (Annette Lavers, trans.). New York: Hill & Wang.

Bartlett, F. C. (1932). *Remembering: A study in experimental and social psychology*. Cambridge, UK: Cambridge University Press.

Baxter, S. and Rogers, L. (2003). Stiff upper lip beats stress counselling. *Sunday Times*, 2 March, p. 12.

Becker, H. S. (1963). *Outsiders: Studies in the sociology of deviance*. Glencoe, IL: Free Press.

Bell, K. (Ed.) (2013). Open education sociology dictionary. Retrieved from http://sociology dictionary.org.

Bem, D. J. (1972). Self-perception theory. In L. Berkowitz (Ed.) *Advances in Experimental Social Psychology* (Vol. 6, pp. 1–62). New York: Academic Press.

Bengtson, V. L., Copen, C. E., Putney, N. M. and Silverstein, M. (2009). A longitudinal study of the intergenerational transmission of religion. *International Sociology*, 24(3), 325–345.

Bennett, J. M. (2006). *History matters: Patriarchy and the challenge of feminism.* Philadelphia: University of Pennsylvania Press.

Benson, L., Harkavy, I. R. and Puckett, J. L. (2007). *Dewey's dream: Universities and democracies in an age of education reform – civil society, public schools, and democratic citizenship.* Philadelphia, PA: Temple University Press.

Berger, P. L. (1967). *The sacred canopy: Elements of a sociological theory of religion.* New York: Anchor.

Bernstein, R. (2011). *Racial innocence: Performing American childhood and race from slavery to civil rights.* New York: NYU Press.

Bertman, M. A. (1973). The function of the rational principle in Aristotle. *The Thomist: A Speculative Quarterly Review*, 37(4), 686–701.

Bicchieri, C. (2006). *The grammar of society: The nature and dynamics of social norms.* Cambridge, UK: Cambridge University Press.

Bigler, R. S., Jones, L. C. and Lobliner, D. B. (1997). Social categorization and the formation of intergroup attitudes in children. *Child Development*, 68, 530–543.

Bigler, R. S. and Liben, L. S. (2007). Developmental intergroup theory: Explaining and reducing children's social stereotyping and prejudice. *Current Directions in Psychological Science*, 16(3), 162–166.

Bigler, R. S. and Liben, L. S. (2006). A developmental intergroup theory of social stereotypes and prejudice. In R. V. Kail (Ed.) *Advances in child development and behavior* (Vol. 34, pp. 39–89). San Diego, CA: Elsevier.

Big State Plumbing (2018). Top 5 plumbing stereotypes. Retrieved from www.bigstateplumbing.com/top-5-plumbing-stereotypes.

Billig, M. (2008) *The hidden roots of critical psychology.* London: Sage.

Billig, M. (1996). *Arguing and thinking: A rhetorical approach to social psychology.* 2nd edition. Cambridge, UK: Cambridge University Press.

Billig, M. (1985). Prejudice, categorization and particularization: From a perceptual to a rhetorical approach. *European Journal of Social Psychology*, 15, 79–103.

Billig, M. (1978). *Fascists: A social psychological view of the National Front.* London: Academic Press.

Black, J. (2015). The middling sort of people in the eighteenth-century English-speaking world. XVII–XVIII. *Revue de la Société d'études Anglo-Américaines des XVIIe et XVIIIe siècles*, 72, 41–56.

Blakey, M. L. (1999). Scientific racism and the biological concept of race. *Literature and Psychology*, 45(1/2), 29–43.

Bodenhausen, G.V., Kang, S. K. and Peery, D. (2012). Social categorization and the perception of social groups. In S. T. Fiske and C. N. Macrae (Eds.) *SAGE handbook of social cognition* (pp. 311–329). Los Angeles, CA: Sage.

Bodenhausen, G. V., Todd, A. R. and Becker, A. P. (2007). Categorizing the social world: Affect, motivation and self-regulation. In B. H. Ross and A. B. Markman (Eds.) *Psychology of learning and motivation* (Vol. 47, pp. 123–155). Amsterdam: Elsevier.

Borowczyk-Martins, D., Bradley, J. and Tarasonis, L. (2017). Racial discrimination in the U.S. labor market: Employment and wage differentials by skill. *Labor Economics*, 49, 106–127.

Bosak, J., Eagly, A., Diekman, A. and Sczesny, S. (2018). Women and men of the past, present, and future: Evidence of dynamic gender stereotypes in Ghana. *Journal of Cross-Cultural Psychology*, 49(1), 115–129.

Bourne, J. (2008). Slavery in the United States. Retrieved from http://eh.net/encyclopedia/slavery-in-the-united-states.

Bousfield, C. and Hutchison, P. (2010). Contact, anxiety, and young people's attitudes and behavioral intentions towards the elderly. *Educational Gerontology*, 36(6), 451–466.

Bramel, D. (2004). The strange career of the contact hypothesis. In L. Yueh-Ting, C. McCauley, F. Moghaddam and S. Worchel (Eds.) *The psychology of ethnic and cultural conflict* (pp. 49–68). New York: Praeger.

Branscombe, N. R. and Baron, R. A. (2017). *Social psychology*. 14th edition. London: Pearson.

Branscombe, N. R., Ellemers, N., Spears, R. and Doosje, B. (1999). The context and content of social identity threat. In N. Ellemers and R. Spears (Eds.) *Social identity: Contexts, commitment, content* (pp. 35–59). Oxford: Blackwell Science.

Bratanova, B. and Kashima, Y. (2014). The 'saying is repeating' effect: Dyadic communication can generate cultural stereotypes. *Journal of Social Psychology*, 154(2), 155–174.

Brigham, J. C. (1971). Ethnic stereotypes. *Psychological Bulletin*, 76, 15–38.

Broadbent, D. E. (1958). *Perception and communication*. Oxford: Pergamon Press.

Brons, L. L. (2015). Othering, an analysis. *Transcience: A Journal of Global Studies*, 6(1), 69–90.

Brown, P. and Levinson, S. C. (1987). *Politeness: Some universals in language usage*. Cambridge, UK: Cambridge University Press.

Brown, R. (2010). *Prejudice: Its social psychology*. Oxford: Wiley-Blackwell.

Brown, R. (1965). *Social psychology*. New York: The Free Press.

Brown, R. (1958). *Words and things*. Glencoe, IL: The Free Press.

Brown, W. (2014). A map of China, by stereotype. Retrieved from http://foreignpolicy.com/2014/03/04/a-map-of-china-by-stereotype.

Browne, A. (2001). Antidote to the stiff upper lip. *Observer*, 21 January. Retrieved from www.theguardian.com/uk/2001/jan/21/theobserver.uknews.

Brubaker, R. (2016a). *Gender and race in an age of unsettled identities*. Princeton, NJ: Princeton University Press.

Brubaker, R. (2016b). The Dolezal affair: Race, gender, and the micropolitics of identity. *Ethnic and Racial Studies*, 39(3), 414–448.

Bruner, J. S. (1991). The narrative construction of reality. *Critical Inquiry*, 18(1), 1–21.

Bruner, J. S. (1990). *Acts of meaning*. Cambridge, MA: Harvard University Press.

Bruner, J. S. (1959). Myth and identity. *Daedalus*, 88(2), 349–358.

Bruner, J. S. (1957). On perceptual readiness. *Psychological Review*, 64(2), 123–152.

Bruner, J. S., Goodnow, J. J. and Austin, J. G. (1956). *A study of thinking*, New York: Wiley.

Bryant, I. J. and Oliver, M. B. (2009). *Media effects: Advances in theory and research*. 3rd edition. New York: Routledge.

Bubic, A., von Cramon, D. Y. and Schubotz, R. I. (2010). Prediction, cognition and the brain. *Frontiers in Human Neuroscience*, 4(25), 1–15.

Bullough, V. L. (2005). Age of consent: A historical overview. *Journal of Psychology & Human Sexuality*, 16(2–3), 25–42.

Bureau of Labor Statistics (2016). *Occupational outlook handbook*. Washington, DC: Bureau of Labor Statistics.

Burke, E. (2015). *Reflections on the revolution in France and other writings*. New York: Everyman's Library.

Burr, V. (2015). *Social constructionism*. Abingdon, UK: Routledge.

Burris, C. T., Branscombe, N. R. and Jackson, L. M. (2000). 'For God and country': Religion and the endorsement of national self-stereotypes. *Journal of Cross-Cultural Psychology*, 31(4), 517–527.

Butler, J. (1990). *Gender trouble*. London: Routledge.

Butler, J. (1988). Performative acts and gender constitution: An essay in phenomenology and feminist theory. *Theatre Journal*, 40(4), 519–531.

Cameron, C. D., Payne, B. K. and Knobe, J. (2010). Do theories of implicit race bias change moral judgements? *Social Justice Research*, 23(4), 272–289.

Campbell, D. T. (1967). Stereotypes and the perception of group differences. *American Psychologist*, 22(10), 817.

Cantor, N. and Mischel, W. (1979). Prototypes in person perception. In L. Berkowitz (Ed.) *Advances in experimental social psychology* (Vol. 12). New York: Academic Press.

Carlson, D. L. and Knoester, C. (2011). Family structure and the intergenerational transmission of gender ideology. *Journal of Family Issues*, 32(6), 709–734.

Carmichael, D. J. C. (1990). Hobbes on natural right in society: The Leviathan account. *Canadian Journal of Political Science/Revue Canadienne de Science Politique*, 23(1), 3–21.

Carpenter, J. (1995). Doctors and nurses: Stereotypes and stereotype change in inter-professional education. *Journal of Interprofessional Care*, 9(2), 151–161.

Carr, D. (2003). *Making sense of education: An introduction to the philosophy and theory of education and teaching*. London: Routledge.

Carter, C. (2011). Sex/gender and the media: From sex roles to social construction and beyond. In K. Ross (Ed.) *The handbook of gender, sex and media* (pp. 365–382). Oxford: Wiley-Blackwell.

Cauthen, N. R., Robinson, I. E. and Krauss, H. H. (1971). Stereotypes: A review of the literature 1926–1968. *Journal of Social Psychology*, 84(1), 103–125.

Cerami, C. A. (2002). *Benjamin Banneker: Surveyor, astronomer, publisher, patriot*. New York: John Wiley.

Chaiken, S. and Trope, Y. (Eds.) (1999). *Dual-process theories in social psychology*. New York: Guilford Press.

Chaiklin, H. (2011). Attitudes, behavior, and social practice. *Journal of Sociology & Social Welfare*, 38(1), 31–54.

Chambers, J. R., Schlenker, B. R. and Collisson, B. (2013). Ideology and prejudice: The role of value conflicts. *Psychological Science*, 24(2), 140–149.

Chua, P. (2008). Orientalism as cultural practices and the production of sociological knowledge. *Sociology Compass*, 2(4), 1179–1191.

Cialdini, R. B. (2011). The focus theory of normative conduct. In P. A. M. van Lange, A. W. Kruglanski and E. T. Higgins (Eds.) *Handbook of theories of social psychology* (pp. 295–312). Thousand Oaks, CA: Sage.

Cialdini, R. B. (2007). Descriptive social norms as underappreciated sources of social control. *Psychometrika*, 72(2), 263–268.

Cialdini, R. B. (2003). Crafting normative messages to protect the environment. *Current Directions in Psychological Science*, 12, 105–109.

Cialdini, R. B., Reno, R. R. and Kallgren, C. A. (1990). A focus theory of normative conduct: Recycling the concept of norms to reduce littering in public places. *Journal of Personality and Social Psychology*, 58, 1015–1026.

Cikara, M. and Fiske, S. T. (2012). Stereotypes and schadenfreude: Affective and physiological markers of pleasure at outgroup misfortunes. *Social Psychological and Personality Science*, 3(1), 63–71.

Clark, A. (2016). *Surfing uncertainty: Prediction, action, and the embodied mind*. Oxford: Oxford University Press

Clark, A. (2013). Whatever next? Predictive brains, situated agents, and the future of cognitive science. *Behavioral and Brain Sciences*, 36, 181–253.

Clark, A. E. and Kashima, Y. (2007). Stereotypes help people connect with others in the community: A situated functional analysis of the stereotype consistency bias in communication. *Journal of Personality and Social Psychology*, 93(6), 1028–1039.

Clark, H. H. and Brennan, S. E. (1991). Grounding in communication. In L. B. Resnick, J. M. Levine and S. D. Teasley (Eds.) *Perspectives on socially shared cognition* (pp. 127–149). Washington, DC: American Psychological Association.

Clemente, D. (2008). Caps, canes, and coonskins: Princeton and the evolution of collegiate clothing, 1900–1930. *Journal of American Culture*, 31(1), 20–33.

Clulow, A. (2014). *The company and the Shogun: The Dutch encounter with Tokugawa Japan*. New York: Columbia University Press.

Coben, L. A. (2015). The events that led to the Treaty of Tordesillas. *Terrae Incognitae*, 47(2), 142–162.

Cohen, B. (1963). *The press and foreign policy*. New York: Harcourt.

Cohen, R. D. (1997). The delinquents: Censorship and youth culture in recent US history. *History of Education Quarterly*, 37(3), 251–270.

Cohen, S. (2002). *Folk devils and moral panics*. 3rd edition. Abingdon, UK: Routledge.

Cohn, D'V. (2014). Millions of Americans changed their racial or ethnic identity from one census to the next. Retrieved from www.pewresearch.org/fact-tank/2014/05/05/millions-of-americans-changed-their-racial-or-ethnic-identity-from-one-census-to-the-next.

Collins, A. M. and Loftus, E. F. (1975). A spreading activation theory of semantic processing. *Psychological Review*, 82, 407–428.

Colman, A. and Lambley, P. (1970). Authoritarianism and race attitudes in South Africa. *Journal of Social Psychology*, 82, 161–164.

Condor, S. (1988). 'Race stereotypes' and racist discourse. *Text*, 8, 69–91.

Condor, S., Figgou, L., Abell, J., Gibson, S. and Stevenson, C. (2006). 'They're not racist ...': Prejudice denial, mitigation and suppression in dialogue. *British Journal of Social Psychology*, 45, 441–462.

Correll, J., Hudson, S. M., Guillermo, S. and Ma, D. S. (2014). The police officer's dilemma: A decade of research on racial bias in the decision to shoot. *Social and Personality Psychology Compass*, 8(5), 201–213.

Correll, J., Park, B., Judd, C. M. and Wittenbrink, B. (2002). The police officer's dilemma: Using ethnicity to disambiguate potentially threatening individuals. *Journal of Personality and Social Psychology*, 83(6), 1314–1329.

Correll, J., Park, B., Judd, C. M., Wittenbrink, B., Sadler, M. S. and Keesee, T. (2007). Across the thin blue line: Police officers and racial bias in the decision to shoot. *Journal of Personality and Social Psychology*, 92(6), 1006–1023.

Creutz-Kämppi, K. (2008). The Othering of Islam in a European context. *Nordicom Review*, 29(2), 295–308.

Crisp, R. J. (2006). Commitment and categorization in common ingroup contexts. In R. J. Crisp and M. Hewstone (Eds.) *Multiple social categorization: Processes, models and applications* (pp. 90–111). Hove, UK: Psychology Press.

Crisp, R. J. and Hewstone, M. (2006). Multiple social categorization: Context, process, and social consequences. In R. J. Crisp and M. Hewstone (Eds.) *Multiple social categorization* (pp. 3–22). Hove, UK: Psychology Press.

Crosnoe, R., Riegle-Crumb, C., Field, S., Frank, K. and Muller, C. (2008). Peer group contexts of girls' and boys' academic experiences. *Child Development*, 79(1), 139–155.

Cuddy, A. J., Fiske, S. T. and Glick, P. (2008). Warmth and competence as universal dimensions of social perception: The stereotype content model and the BIAS map. *Advances in Experimental Social Psychology*, 40, 61–149.

Cuddy, A. J., Fiske, S. T. and Glick, P. (2007). The BIAS map: behaviors from intergroup affect and stereotypes. *Journal of Personality and Social Psychology*, 92(4), 631–648.

Cunningham, H. (2006). *The invention of childhood*. London: BBC Books.

Cunningham, H. (2000). The decline of child labour: Labour markets and family economies in Europe and North America since 1830. *Economic History Review*, 53(3), 409–428.

Cunningham, M. (2001). The influence of parental attitudes and behaviors on children's attitudes toward gender and household labor in early adulthood. *Journal of Marriage and Family*, 63(1), 111–122.

Curran, J. (2002). *Media and power*. Abingdon, UK: Routledge.

Cvencek, D, Greenwald, A. G. and Meltzoff, A. N. (2012). Balanced identity theory: Review of evidence for implicit cognitive consistency in social cognition. In B. Gawronski and F. Strack (Eds.) *Cognitive consistency: A fundamental principle in social cognition* (pp. 157–17). New York: Guilford Press.

Danesi, M. (2009). *Dictionary of media and communications*. London: M. E. Sharpe.

Dastin, J. (2018). Amazon scraps secret AI recruiting tool that showed bias against women. Retrieved from www.reuters.com/article/us-amazon-com-jobs-automation-insight/amazon-scraps-secret-ai-recruiting-tool-that-showed-bias-against-women-idUSKCN1MK08G.

Davies, S. and Tanner, J. (2003). The long arm of the law: Effects of labeling on employment. *Sociological Quarterly*, 44(3), 385–404.

Davis, S. S. (2015) What role does an accountant play in business operations? Retrieved from http://smallbusiness.chron.com/role-accountant-play-business-operations-411.html.

de Beauvoir, S. [1949] (2010). *The second sex*. New York: Vintage books.

Deliège, R. (2004). *Lévi-Strauss today: An introduction to structural anthropology*. New York: Bloomsbury Academic.

Demby, G. (2014) What is your race? For millions of Americans, a shifting answer. Retrieved from www.npr.org/sections/codeswitch/2014/06/09/319584793/what-is-your-race-for-millions-of-americans-a-shifting-answer.

Derrida, J. (1981). *Positions* (Alan Bass, trans. and Ed.). 1st edition. Chicago, IL: University of Chicago Press.

Deschamps, J.-C. and Doise, W. (1978). Crossed category memberships in intergroup relations. In H. Tajfel (Ed.) *Differentiation between social groups* (pp. 141–158). London: Academic Press.

Devine, P. G. (2003). A modern perspective on the classic American dilemma. *Psychological Inquiry*, 14(3–4), 244–250.

Devine, P. G. (1989). Stereotypes and prejudice: Their automatic and controlled components. *Journal of Personality and Social Psychology*, 56(1), 5.

Devine, P. G. and Elliot, A. J. (1995). Are racial stereotypes really fading? The Princeton trilogy revisited. *Personality and Social Psychology Bulletin*, 21(11), 1139–1150.

Devine, P. G., Forscher, P. S., Austin, A. J. and Cox, W. T. (2012). Long-term reduction in implicit race bias: A prejudice habit-breaking intervention. *Journal of Experimental Social Psychology*, 48(6), 1267–1278.

Devine, P. G. and Monteith, M. J. (1999). Automaticity and control in stereotyping. In S. Chaiken and Y. Trope (Eds.) *Dual process theories in social psychology* (pp. 339–360). New York: Guilford Press.

Devine, P. G. and Sharp, L. B. (2009). Automaticity and control in stereotyping and prejudice. In T. D. Nelson (Ed.) *Handbook of prejudice, stereotyping, and discrimination* (pp. 61–88). New York: Psychology Press.

Dewey, J. (1916). *Democracy and education: An introduction to the philosophy of education.* New York: Macmillan.

Dickinson, T. E. (2003) Looking at the male librarian stereotype. *Reference Librarian,* 37(78), 97–110.

Diekman, A. B. and Eagly, A. H. (2000). Stereotypes as dynamic constructs: Women and men of the past, present, and future. *Personality and Social Psychology Bulletin,* 26(10), 1171–1188.

Dijksterhuis, A. and Nordgren, L. F. (2006). A theory of unconscious thought. *Perspectives on Psychological Science,* 1(2), 95–109.

DiMaggio, P. (1997). Culture and cognition. *Annual Review of Sociology,* 23(1), 263–287.

Dinnerstein, L. (1994). *Anti-Semitism in America.* New York: Oxford University Press.

Disney, A. R. (2009). *A history of Portugal and the Portuguese empire: Volume 1, Portugal: From beginnings to 1807.* Cambridge, UK: Cambridge University Press.

Dixon, J. (2001). Contact and boundaries: Locating the social psychology of intergroup relations. *Theory & Psychology,* 11(5), 587–608.

Dobbin, F. and Kalev, A. (2018). Why doesn't diversity training work? The challenge for industry and academia. *Anthropology Now,* 10(2), 48–55.

Dobbin, F. and Kalev, A. (2016). Why diversity programs fail. *Harvard Business Review,* 94(7). Retrieved from https://hbr.org/2016/07/why-diversity-programs-fail.

Dodge, N. T. (1966). *Women in the Soviet economy.* Baltimore, MD: Johns Hopkins University Press.

Doise, W. (1993). Debating social representations. In G. M. Breakwell and D. V. Canter (Eds.) *Empirical approaches to social representations* (pp. 157–170), Oxford: Oxford University Press.

Domhoff, G. W. (2006). Mills's 'the power elite' 50 years later. *Contemporary Sociology,* 35(6), 547–550.

Donaldson, M. (1978). *Children's minds.* Glasgow: Fontana/Collins.

Dorn, S. (1996). *Creating the dropout: An institutional and social history of school failure.* Westport, CT: Praeger.

Downes, D., Rock, P. E. and McLaughlin, E. (2016). *Understanding deviance: A guide to the sociology of crime and rule-breaking.* Oxford: Oxford University Press.

Dressel, J. and Farid, H. (2018). The accuracy, fairness, and limits of predicting recidivism. *Science Advances,* 4(1), eaao5580.

Duehr, E. E. and Bono, J. E. (2006). Men, women, and managers: Are stereotypes finally changing? *Personnel Psychology,* 59(4), 815–846.

Dunham, Y. (2013). Balanced identity in the minimal groups paradigm. *PloS one,* 8(12), e84205.

Durkheim, E. (1956). *Education and sociology.* New York: Free Press.

Durrell, L. (1958). *Balthazar.* New York: Dutton.

Dweck, C. S. and Sorich, L. (1999). Mastery-oriented thinking. *Coping,* 11, 232–251.

Eagly, A. H. and Chaiken, S. (1993). *The psychology of attitudes.* Fort Worth, TX: Harcourt Brace Jovanovich College.

Eagly, A. H. and Karau, S. J. (2002). Role congruity theory of prejudice toward female leaders. *Psychological Review,* 109(3), 573.

Eagly, A. H., Nater, C., Miller, D., Kaufmann, M. and Sczesny, S. (2019). Gender stereotypes have changed: A cross-temporal meta-analysis of US public opinion polls from 1946 to 2018. *American Psychologist.* dx.doi.org/10.1037/amp0000494.

Eagly, A. H. and Steffen, V. J. (1984). Gender stereotypes stem from the distribution of women and men into social roles. *Journal of Personality and Social Psychology,* 46(4), 735–754.

Eagly, A. H. and Wood, W. (2012). Social role theory. In P. A. van Lange, A. W. Kruglanski and E. T. Higgins, *Handbook of theories of social psychology* (Vol. 2, pp. 458–476). London: Sage.

Eagly, A. H., Wood, W. and Diekman, A. B. (2000). Social role theory of sex differences and similarities: A current appraisal. In T. Eckes and H. M. Trautner (Eds.) *The developmental social psychology of gender* (pp. 123–174). Mahwah, NJ: Lawrence Erlbaum Associates.

Eakin, M. C. (2017). *Becoming Brazilians: Race and national identity in twentieth century Brazil.* Cambridge, UK: Cambridge University Press.

Echabe, A. E. (2013). Relationship between implicit and explicit measures of attitudes: The impact of application conditions. *Europe's Journal of Psychology*, 9(2), 231–245.

Eckhardt, W. (1991). Authoritarianism. *Political Psychology*, 12(1), 97–124.

Ellemers, N., van Knippenberg, A., De Vries, N. and Wilke, H. (1988). Social identification and permeability of group boundaries. *European Journal of Social Psychology*, 18(6), 497–513.

Ehrlich, H. J. and Rinehart, J. W. (1965). A brief report on the methodology of stereotype research. *Social Forces*, 43(4), 564–575.

Elcheroth, G., Doise, W. and Reicher, S. (2011). On the knowledge of politics and the politics of knowledge: How a social representations approach helps us rethink the subject of political psychology. *Political Psychology*, 32(5), 729–758.

Epstein, R. (2007). *The case against adolescence: Rediscovering the adult in every teen.* Sanger, CA: Quill Driver.

Erikson, E. H. (1982). *The life cycle completed.* New York: Norton.

Erikson, E. H. (1968). *Youth: Identity and crisis.* New York: Norton.

Erikson, E. H. (1963). *Childhood and society.* 2nd edition. New York: Norton.

Evans, J. St B. T. (2008). Dual-processing accounts of reasoning, judgment and social cognition. *Annual Review of Psychology*, 59, 255–278.

Eveleth, R. (2013). Soviet Russia had a better record of training Women in STEM than America does today. Retrieved from www.smithsonianmag.com/smart-news/soviet-russia-had-a-better-record-of-training-women-in-stem-than-america-does-today-180948141.

Ewoldsen, D. R., Rhodes, N. and Fazio, R. H. (2015). The MODE model and its implications for studying the media. *Media Psychology*, 18(3), 312–337.

Eyerman, R. (1981). False consciousness and ideology in Marxist theory. *Acta Sociologica*, 24(1–2), 43–56.

Eysenck, H. J. (1961). Personality and social attitudes. *Journal of Social Psychology*, 53(2), 243–248.

Eysenck, H. J. and Crown, S. (1948). National stereotypes: An experimental and methodological study. *International Journal of Opinion and Attitude Research*, 2, 26–39.

Fara, P. (2004). *Sex, botany and empire: The story of Carl Linnaeus and Joseph Banks.* New York: Columbia University Press.

Farr, R. M. (1998). From collective to social representations: Aller et Retour. *Culture & Psychology*, 4(3), 275–296.

Farr, R. M. (1993). Common sense, science and social representations. *Public Understanding of Science*, 2(3), 189–204.

Fazio, R. H. (1990) Multiple processes by which attitudes guide behavior: The MODE model as an integrative framework. In M. Zanna (Ed.) *Advances in experimental social psychology* (pp. 75–109). San Diego, CA: Academic Press.

Fazio, R. H. and Olson, M. A. (2014). The MODE model: Attitude-behavior processes as a function of motivation and opportunity. In J. W. Sherman, B. Gawronski and Y. Trope (Eds.) *Dual-process theories of the social mind* (pp. 155–171). New York: Guilford Press.

Fazio, R. H. and Olson, M. A. (2003). Implicit measures in social cognition research: Their meaning and use. *Annual Review of Psychology*, 54(1), 297–327.

Fazio, R. H., Sanbonmatsu, D. M., Powell, M. C. and Kardes, F. R. (1986). On the automatic activation of attitudes. *Journal of Personality and Social Psychology*, 50(2), 229–238.

Ferguson, M. J. and Bargh, J. A. (2004). How social perception can automatically influence behavior. *Trends in Cognitive Sciences*, 8(1), 33–39.

Festinger, L. (1957). *A theory of cognitive dissonance*. Stanford, CA: Stanford University Press.

Fish, S. (1980). *Is there a text in this class? The authority of the interpretive community*. Cambridge, MA: Harvard University Press.

Fishbein, M. and Ajzen, I. (1975). *Belief, attitude, and behavior: An introduction to theory and research*. Reading, MA: Addison Wessley.

Fishbein, M. and Ajzen, I. (1974). Attitudes towards objects as predictors of single and multiple behavioral criteria. *Psychological Review*, 81(1), 59.

Fiske, S.T. (2004). Intent and ordinary bias: Unintended thought and social motivation create casual prejudice. *Social Justice Research*, 17(2), 117–127.

Fiske, S. T. (2003). Five core social motives, plus or minus five. In S. J. Spencer, S. Fein, M. P. Zanna and J. Olson (Eds.) *Motivated social perception: The Ontario Symposium*, 9, 233–246. Mahwah, NJ: Lawrence Erlbaum Associates.

Fiske, S. T., Bersoff, D. N., Borgida, E., Deaux, K. and Heilman, M. E. (1991). Social science research on trial: Use of sex stereotyping research in *Price Waterhouse v. Hopkins*. *American Psychologist*, 46(10), 1049.

Fiske, S. T., Cuddy, A. J., Glick, P. and Xu, J. (2002). A model of (often mixed) stereotype content: Competence and warmth respectively follow from perceived status and competition. *Journal of Personality and Social Psychology*, 82(6), 878–902.

Fiske, S. T. and Stevens, L. E. (1993). What's so special about sex? Gender stereotyping and discrimination. In S. Oskamp and M. Costanzo (Eds.) *Gender issues in contemporary society* (pp. 173–196). Newbury Park, CA: Sage.

Fiske, S. T. and Taylor, S. E. (2017). *Social cognition: From brains to culture*. 3rd edition. London: Sage.

Fiske, S. T. and Taylor, S. E. (2013). *Social cognition: From brains to culture*. 2nd edition. London: Sage.

Fiske, S.T. and Taylor, S. E. (1991). *Social cognition*. 2nd edition. New York: McGraw-Hill.

Flaxman, S., Goel, S. and Rao, J. M. (2016). Filter bubbles, echo chambers, and online news consumption. *Public Opinion Quarterly*, 80(S1), 298–320.

Flew, A. (1975). *Thinking about thinking: Or, do I sincerely want to be right?* Glasgow: Fontana/Collins.

Fong, C., Bowles, S. and Gintis, H. (2006). Strong reciprocity and the welfare state. In S. C. Kolm and J. M. Ythier (Eds.) *Handbook of giving, reciprocity, and altrusim* (pp. 1439–1464). Amsterdam: Elsevier.

Forbes, H. D. (2004). Ethnic conflict and the contact hypothesis. In Y.-T. Lee, C. McCauley, F. Moghaddam and S. Worchel (Eds.) *The psychology of ethnic and cultural conflict* (pp. 69–88). Westport, CT: Praeger/Greenwood.

Forscher, P. S., Lai, C. K., Axt, J. R., Ebersole, C. R., Herman, M., Devine, P. G. and Nosek, B. A. (2019). A meta-analysis of procedures to change implicit measures. *Journal of Personality and Social Psychology*. Retrieved from https://psyarxiv.com/dv8tu.

Foucault, M. [1975] (1995). *Discipline and punish: The birth of the prison* (Alan Sheridan, trans.). New York: Vintage.

Foucault, M. [1961] (2001). *Madness and civilization: A history of insanity in the age of reason*. London: Routledge.

Fox, R. (1992). Prejudice and the unfinished mind: A new look at an old failing, *Psychological Inquiry*, 3, 137–152.

Franklin, J. H. and Gates, H. L. (2001). Race in America: Looking back, looking forward. *Bulletin of the American Academy of Arts and Sciences*, 55(1), 42–49.

Freeden, M. (2003). *Ideology: A very short introduction*. Oxford: Oxford University Press.

Frenkel-Brunswik, E. and Sanford, R. N. (1945). Some personality factors in anti-Semitism. *Journal of Psychology*, 20(2), 271–291.

Friedan, B. (1963). *The feminine mystique*. New York: W. W. Norton & Company.

Friedrich, J. (2014). Vygotsky's idea of psychological tools. In A. Yasnitsky, R. van der Veer and M. Ferrari (Eds.) *The Cambridge handbook of cultural historical psychology* (pp. 47–61). Cambridge, UK: Cambridge University Press.

Fromm, E. [1932] (1982). The method and function of an analytic social psychology. Notes on psychoanalysis and historical materialism. In A. Arato and E. Gebhardt (Eds.) *The essential Frankfurt School reader* (pp. 477–496). New York: Continuum.

Fuchs, R. G. (2005). *Gender and poverty in 19th-century Europe*. Cambridge, UK: Cambridge University Press.

Fulcher, J. and Scott, J. (2011). *Sociology*. 4th edition. Oxford: Oxford University Press

Fuller, G., Stecker, R. and Wright, J. P. (2000). *John Locke: An essay concerning human understanding in focus*. London: Routledge.

Gaertner, S. L. and Dovidio, J. F. (2000). *Reducing intergroup bias: The common ingroup identity model*. Philadelphia, PA: Psychology Press.

Garfinkel, H. (1967). *Studies in ethnomethodology*. Englewood Cliffs, NJ: Prentice-Hall

Garland, D. (2008). On the concept of moral panic. *Crime, Media, Culture*, 4(1), 9–30.

Gates, S., Hegre, H., Jones, M. P. and Strand, H. (2006). Institutional inconsistency and political instability: Polity duration, 1800–2000. *American Journal of Political Science*, 50(4), 893–908.

Gawronski, B. and Bodenhausen, G. V. (2007). What do we know about implicit attitude measures and what do we have to learn? In B. Wittenbrink and N. Schwarz (Eds.) *Implicit measures of attitudes* (pp. 265–286). New York: Guilford Press.

Gawronski, B. and Bodenhausen, G. V. (2006). Associative and propositional processes in evaluation: An integrative review of implicit and explicit attitude change. *Psychological Bulletin*, 132(5), 692–731.

Geddes, L. (2016). Is being reserved a bad thing? Retrieved from www.bbc.com/future/story/20160517-is-being-reserved-such-a-bad-thing.

Geertz, C. (1974). 'From the native's point of view': On the nature of anthropological understanding. *Bulletin of the American Academy of Arts and Sciences*, 28(1), 26–45.

Geertz, C. (1973). *The interpretation of cultures*. New York: Basic Books.

Gelman, S. A. (2003). *The essential child: Origins of essentialism in everyday thought*. Oxford: Oxford University Press.

Genner, S. and Süss, D. (2017). Socialization as media effect. In P. Rössler (Ed.) *The international encyclopedia of media effects* (pp. 1–15). Oxford: Wiley-Blackwell.

Gerbner, G. (1998). Cultivation analysis: An overview. *Mass Communication and Society*, 1(3–4), 175–194.

Gergen, K. J. (2015). *An invitation to social construction*. 3rd edition. London: Sage.

Gergen, K. J. (1973). Social psychology as history. *Journal of Personality and Social Psychology*, 26(2), 309–320.

Gerhardt, U. (2016). *The social thought of Talcott Parsons: Methodology and American ethos*. Abingdon, UK: Routledge.

Gerrig, R. J. (2013). *Psychology And life*. 20th edition. Boston, MA: Pearson.

Gibson, J. J. (1979). *The ecological approach to visual perception*. Boston, MA: Houghton-Mifflin.

Giddens, A. (1990). *The consequences of modernity*. Cambridge, UK: Polity Press.

Giddens, A. and Sutton, P. W. (2017). *Sociology*. 8th edition. Cambridge, UK: Polity Press.

Gigerenzer, G. and Gaissmaier, W. (2011). Heuristic decision-making. *Annual Review of Psychology*, 62, 451–482.

Gigerenzer, G., Todd, P. M. and the ABC Research Group (1999). *Simple heuristics that make us smart*. Oxford: Oxford University Press.

Gilbert, D. T. and Malone, P. S. (1995). The correspondence bias. *Psychological Bulletin*, 117(1), 21–38.

Gilbert, G. M. (1951). Stereotype persistence and change among college students. *Journal of Abnormal and Social Psychology*, 46, 245–254.

Gillespie, A. (2008). Social representations: Alternative representations and semantic barriers. *Journal for the Theory of Social Behaviour*, 38(4), 375–391.

Glick, P. and Fiske, S. T. (1997). Hostile and benevolent sexism: Measuring ambivalent sexist attitudes toward women. *Psychology of Women Quarterly*, 21(1), 119–135.

Glick, P. and Fiske, S. T. (2001). An ambivalent alliance: Hostile and benevolent sexism as complementary justifications for gender inequality. *American Psychologist*, 56(2), 109–118.

Goffman, E. (1974). *Frame analysis: An essay on the organization of experience*. New York: Harper & Row.

Goffman, E. (1963). *Stigma*. Englewood Cliffs, NJ: Spectrum.

Goffman, E. (1959). *The presentation of self in everyday life*. New York: Anchor Books.

Goldstein, D. G. and Gigerenzer, G. (2002). Models of ecological rationality: The recognition heuristic. *Psychological Review*, 109(1), 75–90.

Goode, E. (2016). *Deviant behaviour*. 11th edition. Abingdon, UK: Routledge.

Goode, E. (2004). Is the sociology of deviance still relevant? *American Sociologist*, 35(4), 46–57.

Goode, E. and Ben-Yehuda, N. (2010). *Moral panics: The social construction of deviance*. New York: John Wiley & Sons.

Gorman, K. A. and Fritzsche, B. A. (2002). The good-mother stereotype: Stay at home (or wish that you did!). *Journal of Applied Social Psychology*, 32(10), 2190–2201.

Graham, J., Haidt, J., Koleva, S., Motyl, M., Iyer, R., Wojcik, S. P. and Ditto, P. H. (2013). Moral foundations theory: The pragmatic validity of moral pluralism. In P. Devine and A. Plant (Eds.) *Advances in experimental social psychology* (Vol. 47, pp. 55–130). San Diego, CA: Academic Press.

Graham, J., Haidt, J. and Nosek, B. A. (2009). Liberals and conservatives rely on different sets of moral foundations. *Journal of Personality and Social Psychology*, 96(5), 1029–1046.

Graham, J., Nosek, B. A. and Haidt, J. (2012). The moral stereotypes of liberals and conservatives: Exaggeration of differences across the political spectrum. *PloS one*, 7(12), e50092.

Graham, J., Nosek, B. A., Haidt, J., Iyer, R., Koleva, S. and Ditto, P. H. (2011). Mapping the moral domain. *Journal of Personality and Social Psychology*, 101(2), 366–385.

Grant, C. A. (Ed.) (1992). *Research in multicultural education: From the margins to the mainstream*. Washington, DC: Falmer Press.

Grattet, R. (2011). Societal reactions to deviance. *Annual Review of Sociology*, 37, 185–204.

Graupner, H. (2005). The 17-year-old child: An absurdity of the late 20th century. *Journal of Psychology & Human Sexuality*, 16(2–3), 7–24.

Greenberg, J., Schimel, J. and Martens, A. (2002). Ageism: Denying the face of the future. In T. Nelson (Ed.) *Ageism: Stereotyping and prejudice against older persons* (pp. 27–48). Cambridge, UK: MIT Press.

Greenwald, A. G. and Banaji, M. R. (1995). Implicit social cognition: attitudes, self-esteem, and stereotypes. *Psychological Review*, 102(1), 4–27.

Greenwald, A. G., Banaji, M. R. and Nosek, B. A. (2015). Statistically small effects of the Implicit Association Test can have societally large effects. *Journal of Personality and Social Psychology*, 108(4), 553–561.

Greenwald, A. G., Banaji, M. R., Rudman, L. A., Farnham, S. D., Nosek, B. A. and Mellott, D. S. (2002). A unified theory of implicit attitudes, stereotypes, self-esteem, and self-concept. *Psychological Review*, 109(1), 3–25.

Greenwald, A. G., McGhee, D. E. and Schwartz, J. L. K. (1998). Measuring individual differences in implicit cognition: The implicit association test. *Journal of Personality and Social Psychology*, 74(6), 1464–1480.

Greenwald, A. G. and Nosek, B. A. (2001). Health of the Implicit Association Test at age 3. *Zeitschrift für Experimentelle Psychologie*, 48(2), 85–93.

Greenwald, A. G., Poehlman, T. A., Uhlmann, E. L. and Banaji, M. R. (2009). Understanding and using the Implicit Association Test: III. Meta-analysis of predictive validity. *Journal of Personality and Social Psychology*, 97(1), 17–41.

Grice, H. P. (1975). Logic and conversation. In P. Cole and J. Morgan (Eds.) *Syntax and semantics: Vol. 3 speech acts* (pp. 43–58). New York: Academic Press.

Grusec, J. E. (2011). Socialization processes in the family: Social and emotional development. *Annual Review of Psychology*, 62, 243–269.

Grusec, J. E. and Hastings, P. D. (Eds.). (2015). *Handbook of socialization: Theory and research.* 2nd edition. New York: Guilford Press.

Haidt, J. (2012). *The righteous mind: Why good people are divided by politics and religion.* New York: Vintage Books.

Haidt, J. (2006). *The happiness hypothesis: Finding modern truth in ancient wisdom.* New York: Basic Books.

Haidt, J. (2001). The emotional dog and its rational tail: A social intuitionist approach to moral judgment. *Psychological Review*, 108(4), 814–834.

Haidt, J. and Graham, J. (2007). When morality opposes justice: Conservatives have moral intuitions that liberals may not recognize. *Social Justice Research*, 20(1), 98–116.

Haines, E. L., Deaux, K. and Lofaro, N. (2016). The times they are a-changing … or are they not? A comparison of gender stereotypes, 1983–2014. *Psychology of Women Quarterly*, 40(3), 353–363.

Hall, E. V., Phillips, K. W. and Townsend, S. S. (2015). A rose by any other name? The consequences of subtyping 'African-Americans' from 'Blacks'. *Journal of Experimental Social Psychology*, 56, 183–190.

Hall, S. (1999). Encoding, decoding. In S. During (Ed.) *The cultural studies reader.* 2nd edition (pp. 477–481). London: Routledge.

Hall, S. (1997). The work of representation. In S. Hall (Ed.) *Representation: Cultural representations and signifying practices* (pp. 13–74). London: Sage.

Hall, S. (1992). The West and the rest. In S. Hall and B. Gieben (Eds.) *Formations of modernity* (pp. 275–332). Cambridge, UK: Polity Press.

Hall, S., Critcher, C., Jefferson, T., Clarke, J. and Roberts, B. (1978). *Policing the crisis.* London: Macmillan

Hamilton, D. L., Sherman, S. J. and Ruvolo, C. M. (1990). Stereotype-based expectancies: Effects on information processing and social behavior. *Journal of Social Issues*, 46(2), 35–60.

Hanchard, M. (1999). *Racial politics in contemporary Brazil.* Durham, NC: Duke University Press.

Happer, C. and Philo, G. (2013). The role of the media in the construction of public belief and social change. *Journal of Social and Political Psychology*, 1(1), 321–336.

Haralambos, M., Holborn, M., Chapman, S. and Moore, S. (2013). *Sociology: Themes and perspectives.* London: Collins.

Hardin, C. D. and Banaji, M. R. (2013). The nature of implicit prejudice: Implications for personal and public policy. In E. Sahfir (Ed.) *The behavioral foundations of public policy* (pp. 13–31). Princeton, NJ: Princeton University Press.

Harré, R. (2001). The discursive turn in social psychology. In D. Schiffrin, D. Tannen and H. E. Hamilton (Eds.) *The handbook of discourse analysis* (pp. 688–706). Oxford: Blackwell.

Harris, M. (1968). *The rise of anthropological theory: A history of theories of culture*. New York: Crowell.

Harris, P. L. (2012). *Trusting what you're told: How children learn from others*. Cambridge, MA: Harvard University Press.

Hastie, R. (1981). Schematic principles in human memory. In E. T. Higgins, P. Herman and M. Zanna (Eds.) *Social cognition*. Hillsdale, NJ: Lawrence Erlbaum Associates.

Hekman, S. (1997). Truth and method: Feminist standpoint theory revisited. *Signs: Journal of Women in Culture and Society*, 22(2), 341–365.

Heider, F. (1958). *The psychology of interpersonal relations*. New York: Wiley.

Hewstone, M. and Swart, H. (2011). Fifty-odd years of inter-group contact: From hypothesis to integrated theory. *British Journal of Social Psychology*, 50(3), 374–386.

Hewstone, M., Stroebe, W. and Jonas, K. (2015). *An introduction to social psychology*. 6th edition. New York: Wiley.

Hewstone, M., Turner, R. N., Kenworthy, J. B. and Crisp, R. J. (2006). Multiple social categorization: Integrative themes and future research priorities. In R. J. Crisp and M. Hewstone (Eds.) *Multiple social categorization: Advances in experimental social psychology* (pp. 271–310). Hove, UK: Psychology Press.

Higonnet, A. (1998). *Pictures of innocence: The history and crisis of ideal childhood*. London: Thames & Hudson.

Hinton, P. R. (2017). Implicit stereotypes and the predictive brain: Cognition and culture in 'biased' person perception. *Palgrave Communications*, 3(17086).

Hinton, P. R. (2016a). *The perception of people: Integrating cognition and culture*. Abingdon, UK: Routledge.

Hinton, P. R. (2016b). The cultural construction of the girl 'teen': A cross-cultural analysis of feminine adolescence portrayed in popular culture. *Journal of Intercultural Communication Research*, 45(3), 233–247.

Hinton, P. R. (2007). The cultural context of media interpretation. In H. Kotthoff and H. Spencer-Oatey (Eds.) *The handbook of applied linguistics: Volume 7, intercultural communication* (pp. 323–339). Berlin: Mouton de Gruyter.

Hofstede, G. (1984). *Culture's consequences: International differences in work-related values*. Beverly Hills, CA: Sage.

Hogg, M. A. and Sunderland, J. (1991). Self-esteem and intergroup discrimination in the minimal group paradigm. *British Journal of Social Psychology*, 30(1), 51–62.

Höijer, B. (2011). Social representations theory: A new theory for media research. *Nordicom Review*, 32(2), 3–16.

Holliday, A. (2010a). Interrogating the concept of stereotypes in intercultural communication. In S. Hunston and D. Oakey (Eds.) *Introducing applied linguistics: Concepts and skills* (pp. 134–140). London: Routledge.

Holliday, A. (2010b). *Intercultural communication & ideology*. London: Sage.

Holte, J. C. (1984). Unmelting images: Film, television, and ethnic stereotyping. *Melus*, 11(3), 101–108.

Honeycutt, N. and Freberg, L. (2017). The liberal and conservative experience across academic disciplines: An extension of Inbar and Lammers. *Social Psychological and Personality Science*, 8(2), 115–123.

Hornsey, M. J. (2008). Social identity theory and self-categorization theory: A historical review. *Social and Personality Psychology Compass*, 2(1), 204–222.

Housman [1896] (2017). *A Shropshire lad*. London: Penguin Classics.

Houtman, D. (2003). Lipset and 'working-class' authoritarianism. *The American Sociologist*, 34(1–2), 85–103.

Hung, K. S. (2014). Perceptions of accounting and accountants in the eyes of the people from Mainland China and Macau. In *2014 International Conference on Global Economy, Commerce and Service Science (GECSS-14)*. Paris: Atlantis Press.

Hunt, L. (2016). *The French Revolution and human rights: A brief documentary history*. 2nd edition. New York: Bedford Books.

Hyde, J. S. and Kling, K. C. (2001). Women, motivation, and achievement. *Psychology of Women Quarterly*, 25, 364–378.

Inbar, Y. and Lammers, J. (2012). Political diversity in social and personality psychology. *Perspectives on Psychological Science*, 7(5), 496–503.

Ingraham, C. (2017). Somebody just put a price tag on the 2016 election. It's a doozy. Retrieved from www.washingtonpost.com/news/wonk/wp/2017/04/14/somebody-just-put-a-price-tag-on-the-2016-election-its-a-doozy/?utm_term=.64ede14d21f7.

Inness, S. (Ed.). (2007). *Geek chic: Smart women in popular culture*. New York: Palgrave Macmillan.

Israel, J. I. (2001). *Radical enlightenment: Philosophy and the making of modernity, 1650–1750*. Oxford: Oxford University Press.

Jackson, J. (2014). *Introducing language and communication*. London: Routledge.

Jacob, M. C. (1981). *The radical enlightenment: Pantheists, freemasons, and republicans*. London: George Allen & Unwin.

Jacobson, R. P., Mortensen, C. R. and Cialdini, R. B. (2011). Bodies obliged and unbound: Differentiated response tendencies for injunctive and descriptive social norms. *Journal of Personality and Social Psychology*, 100(3), 433–448.

James, W. [1890] (1950). *The principles of psychology*. Vols. I and II. New York: Dover.

Janowitz, M. (1975). Sociological theory and social control. *American Journal of Sociology*, 81(1), 82–108.

Jarvis, P. (2006). *Towards a comprehensive theory of human learning*. Abingdon, UK: Routledge.

Jasanoff, M. (2011). *Liberty's exiles: The loss of America and the remaking of the British empire*. London: Harper Press.

Jeacle, I. (2008). Beyond the boring grey: The construction of the colourful accountant. *Critical Perspectives on Accounting*, 19(8), 1296–1320.

Jeffries, L. (2010). *Opposition in discourse: The construction of oppositional meaning*. London: Bloomsbury.

Jennings, M. K., Stoker, L. and Bowers, J. (2009). Politics across generations: Family transmission reexamined. *Journal of Politics*, 71(3), 782–799.

Jones, E. E. and Colman, A. M. (1996). Stereotypes. In A. Kuper and J. Kuper (Eds.) *The social science encyclopedia* (pp. 843–844). London: Routledge.

Jones, E. E. and Harris, V. A. (1967). The attribution of attitudes. *Journal of Experimental Social Psychology*, 3(1), 1–24.

Jones, E. E. and McGillis, D. (1976). Correspondent inferences and the attribution cube: a comparative reappraisal. In J. H. Harvey, W. J. Ickes and R. F. Kidd (Eds.) *New directions in attribution research* (Vol. 1, pp. 389–420). Hillsdale, NJ: Lawrence Erlbaum Associates.

Jones, M. N., Willits, J., Dennis, S. and Jones, M. (2015). Models of semantic memory. In J. R. Busemeyer, Z. Wang, J. T. Townsend and A. Eidels (Eds.) *The Oxford handbook of mathematical and computational psychology* (pp. 232–254). Oxford: Oxford University Press.

Joshel, S. R. (2010). *Slavery in the Roman world*. Cambridge, UK: Cambridge University Press.

Jost, J. T. and Banaji, M. (1994). The role of stereotyping in system justification and the production of false consciousness. *British Journal of Social Psychology*, 22, 1–27.

Jost, J. T., Banaji, M. R. and Nosek, B. A. (2004). A decade of system justification theory: Accumulated evidence of conscious and unconscious bolstering of the status quo. *Political Psychology*, 25(6), 881–919.

Jost, J. T., Chaikalis-Petritsis, V., Abrams, D., Sidanius, J., van Der Toorn, J. and Bratt, C. (2012). Why men (and women) do and don't rebel: Effects of system justification on willingness to protest. *Personality and Social Psychology Bulletin*, 38, 197–208.

Jost, J. T. and Hamilton, D. L. (2005). Stereotypes in our culture. In J. F. Dovidio, P. Glick and L. A. Rudman (Eds.) *On the nature of prejudice: Fifty years after Allport* (pp. 208–224). Oxford: Blackwell.

Jost, J. T. and Kay, A. C. (2005). Exposure to benevolent sexism and complementary gender stereotypes: Consequences for specific and diffuse forms of system justification. *Journal of Personality and Social Psychology*, 88(3), 498–509.

Jost, J. T., Kivetz, Y., Rubini, M., Guermandi, G. and Mosso, C. (2005). System-justifying functions of complementary regional and ethnic stereotypes: Cross-national evidence. *Social Justice Research*, 18(3), 305–333.

Jost, J. T., Rudman, L. A., Blair, I. V., Carney, D. R., Dasgupta, N., Glaser, J. and Hardin, C. D. (2009). The existence of implicit bias is beyond reasonable doubt: A refutation of ideological and methodological objections and executive summary of ten studies that no manager should ignore. *Research in Organizational Behavior*, 29, 39–69.

Jovchelovitch, S. (2019). Discourse and representation: A comment on Batel and Castro 're-opening the dialogue between the theory of social representations and discursive psychology'. *British Journal of Social Psychology*, 58, 415–422.

Jovchelovitch, S. (2008). Rehabilitation of common sense: Social representations, science and cognitive polyphasia. *Journal for the Theory of Social Behaviour*, 38(4), 431–449.

Jussim, L. (2012a). *Social perception and social reality: Why accuracy dominates bias and self-fulfilling prophecy*. Oxford: Oxford University Press.

Jussim, L. (2012b). Liberal privilege in academic psychology and the social sciences: Commentary on Inbar & Lammers (2012). *Perspectives on Psychological Science*, 7, 504–507.

Jussim, L., Crawford, J. T., Anglin, S. M. and Stevens, S. T. (2015). Ideological bias in social psychological research. In J. P. Forgas, K. Fiedler and W. D. Crano (Eds.) *Social psychology and politics* (pp. 91–109). New York: Routledge.

Kahneman, D. (2011). *Thinking, fast and slow*. London: Penguin Books.

Kahneman, D. (1973). *Attention and effort*. Englewood Cliffs, NJ: Prentice-Hall.

Kahneman, D., Slovic, P. and Tversky, A. (Eds.) (1982) *Judgement under uncertainty: Heuristics and biases*. Cambridge, UK: Cambridge University Press.

Kahneman, D. and Tversky, A. (1986). Rational choice and the framing of decisions. *Journal of Business*, 59(4), 251–278.

Kahneman, D. and Tversky, A. (1973). On the psychology of prediction. *Psychological Review*, 80, 237–251.

Karlins, M., Coffman, T. L. and Walters, G. (1969). On the fading of social stereotypes: Studies in three generations of college students. *Journal of Personality and Social Psychology*, 13, 1–16.

Kashif, M., Sarifuddin, S. and Hassan, A. (2015). Charity donation: Intentions and behaviour. *Marketing Intelligence & Planning*, 33(1), 90–102.

Kashima, Y. (2014). Meaning, grounding, and the construction of social reality. *Asian Journal of Social Psychology*, 17(2), 81–95.

Kashima, Y. (2000). Maintaining cultural stereotypes in the serial reproduction of narratives. *Personality and Social Psychology Bulletin*, 26(5), 594–604.

Kashima, Y., Lyons, A. and Clark, A. (2013). The maintenance of cultural stereotypes in the conversational retelling of narratives. *Asian Journal of Social Psychology*, 16(1), 60–70.

Kassin, S., Fein, S. and Markus, H. R. (2017). *Social psychology*. 10th edition. London: Cengage.

Katz, D. and Braly, K. W. (1933). Racial prejudice and racial stereotypes. *Journal of Abnormal and Social Psychology*, 30, 175–193.

Katz, E., Liebes, T. and Iwao, S. (1991). Neither here nor there: Why 'Dallas' failed in Japan. *Communication*, 12, 99–110.

Kaufmann, M. (2017). *Black Tudors: The untold story*. London: Oneworld Publications.

Kay, A. C. and Jost, J. T. (2003). Complementary justice: Effects of 'poor but happy' and 'poor but honest' stereotype exemplars on system justification and implicit activation of the justice motive. *Journal of Personality and Social Psychology*, 85, 823–837.

Keevak, M. (2011). *Becoming yellow: A short history of racial thinking*. Princeton, NJ: Princeton University Press.

Keller, C. (2001). Effect of teachers' stereotyping on students' stereotyping of mathematics as a male domain. *Journal of Social Psychology*, 141(2), 165–173.

Kellerman, K. and Palomares, N. A. (2004). Topical profiling: Emergent, co-occurring, and relationally defining topics in talk. *Journal of Language and Social Psychology*, 23, 308–337.

Kelley, H. H. (1973). The processes of causal attribution. *American Psychologist*, 28(2), 107–128.

Khamelyanin, G. (2018). Kremlin expects US to distance itself from Russophobia gripping numerous countries. Retrieved from http://tass.com/politics/1001370.

Killewald, A. (2016). Money, work, and marital stability: Assessing change in the gendered determinants of divorce. *American Sociological Review*, 81(4), 696–719.

Kilpatrick, J. (1999). *Celluloid Indians: Native Americans and film*. Lincoln: University of Nebraska Press.

Kimble, M. and Kaufman, M. (2004). Clinical correlates of neurological change in posttraumatic stress disorder: An overview of critical systems. *Psychiatric Clinics of North America*, 27(1), 49–65.

King, M. L. Jr (1963). I have a dream. Retrieved from www.archives.gov/files/press/exhibits/dream-speech.pdf.

Kitsuse, J. I. (1980). Coming out all over: Deviants and the politics of social problems. *Social Problems*, 28(1), 1–13.

Klein, J. L. (2016). The media responses to sex crimes. In T. Sanders (Ed.) *The Oxford handbook of sex offences and sex offenders* (pp. 482–497). Oxford: Oxford University Press.

Klineberg, O. (1951). The scientific study of national stereotypes. *International Social Science Bulletin*, 3, 505–515.

Koenig, A. M. and Eagly, A. H. (2014). Evidence for the social role theory of stereotype content: Observations of groups' roles shape stereotypes. *Journal of Personality and Social Psychology*, 107(3), 371–392.

Korsgaard, C. M. (2018). Rationality. In L. Gruen (Ed.). *Critical terms for animal studies* (pp. 294–306). Chicago, IL: University of Chicago Press.

Korman, S. (1996). *The right of conquest: The acquisition of territory by force in international law and practice*. Oxford: Clarendon Press.

Kowner, R. (2014). *From White to Yellow: The Japanese in European thought, 1300–1735*. Montreal: McGill-Queen's University Press.

Krieger, L. H. (1995). The content of our categories: A cognitive bias approach to discrimination and equal employment opportunity. *Stanford Law Review*, 47(6), 1161–1248.

Krieger, L. H. and Fiske, S. T. (2006). Behavioral realism in employment discrimination law: Implicit bias and disparate treatment. *California Law Review*, 94, 997–1062.

Kruglanski, A. W. and Orehek, E. (2007). Partitioning the domain of social inference: Dual mode and systems models and their alternatives. *Annual Review of Psychology*, 58, 291–316.

Kukla, J. (2008). *Mister Jefferson's women*. New York: Vintage.

Kumaravadivelu, B. (2007). *Cultural globalization and language education*. New Haven, CT: Yale University Press.

Labov, W. (2001). Uncovering the event structure of narrative. In D. Tannen and J. E. Alatis (Eds.) *Georgetown University Round Table 2001: Linguistics, language and the real world – discourse and beyond* (pp. 63–83). Washington, DC: Georgetown University Press.

Ladegaard H. J. (2011). Stereotypes and the discursive accomplishment of intergroup differentiation: Talking about 'the other' in a global business organization. *Pragmatics*, 21(1), 85–109.

Lai, C. K., Skinner, A. L., Cooley, E., Murrar, S., Brauer, M., Devos, T., … Nosek, B. A. (2016). Reducing implicit racial preferences: II. Intervention effectiveness across time. *Journal of Experimental Psychology: General*, 145, 1001–1016.

Lakoff, G. (2016). *Moral politics. How conservatives and liberals think*. 3rd edition. Chicago, IL: Chicago University Press.

Lakoff, G. and Johnson, M. (1980). *Metaphors we live by*. Chicago, IL: University of Chicago Press.

Lapidus, G. W. (1978). *Women in Soviet society: Equality, development, and social change*. Berkeley: University of California Press.

Lapidus, M. and King, S. (2019). Leisure activities and personality traits of medical librarians. *Reference Librarian*, 60(1), 1–13.

LaPiere, R. T. (1934). Attitudes vs. actions. *Social Forces*, 13(2), 230–237.

Larrivée, P. and Longhi, J. (2012). The foundations of discourse: The case of British stereotypes of the French. *Corela*, 10(1). Retrieved from http://journals.openedition.org/corela/2676.

Leaper, C., Farkas, T. and Brown, C. S. (2012). Adolescent girls' experiences and gender-related beliefs in relation to their motivation in math/science and English. *Journal of Youth and Adolescence*, 41(3), 268–282.

Lee, Y. T., McCauley, C. and Jussim, L. (2013). Stereotypes as valid categories of knowledge and human perceptions of group differences. *Social and Personality Psychology Compass*, 7(7), 470–486.

Lemert, E. M. (1942). The folkways and social control. *American Sociological Review*, 7(3), 394–399.

Lenard, P. T. (2018). Wither the Canadian model? Evaluating the new Canadian nationalism (2006–2015). In J. E. Fossum, R. Kastoryano and B. Siim (Eds.) *Diversity and contestation over nationalism in Europe and Canada* (pp. 211–236). London: Palgrave Macmillan.

Leslie, S. J. (2017). The original sin of cognition: Fear, prejudice, and generalization. *Journal of Philosophy*, 114(8), 393–421.

Leslie, S. J. (2014). Carving up the social world with generics. *Oxford Studies in Experimental Philosophy*, 1, 208–232.

Leslie, S. J. (2008). Generics: Cognition and acquisition. *Philosophical Review*, 117(1), 1–47.

Leslie, S. J. (2007). Generics and the structure of the mind. *Philosophical Perspectives*, 21(1), 375–403.

Liben, L. S. (2017). Gender development: A constructivist-ecological perspective. New perspectives on human development. In N. Budwig, E. Turiel and P. D. Zelazo (Eds.) *New perspectives on human development* (pp. 145–164). Cambridge, UK: Cambridge University Press.

Lippert-Rasmussen, K. (2015). Luck egalitarians versus relational egalitarians: On the prospects of a pluralist account of egalitarian justice. *Canadian Journal of Philosophy*, 45(2), 220–241.

Lippmann, W. (1922). *Public opinion*. New York: Harcourt Brace.

Lipset, S. M. (1960). *Political man: The social bases of politics*. New York: Doubleday & Company.

Liu, Z. and Morris, M.W. (2014). Intercultural interactions and cultural transformation. *Asian Journal of Social Psychology*, 17(2), 100–103.

Livingstone, S. (2000). Television and the active audience. In D. Fleming (Ed.) *Formations: 21st-century media studies* (pp. 175–195) Manchester, UK: Manchester University Press.

Lloyd, G. (2002). *The man of reason: 'Male' and 'female' in Western philosophy*. London: Routledge.

Lopez, G. (2017). For years, this popular test measured anyone's racial bias. But it might not work after all. Retrieved from www.vox.com/identities/2017/3/7/14637626/implicit-association-test-racism.

Lutz, H. (1990). 'Indians' and Native Americans in the movies: A history of stereotypes, distortions, and displacements. *Visual Anthropology*, 3(1), 31–48.

Lyons, A., Clark, A., Kashima, Y. and Kurz, T. (2008). Cultural dynamics of stereotypes: Social network processes and the perpetuation of stereotypes. In Y. Kashima, K. Fiedler and P. Freytag (Eds.). *Stereotype dynamics: Language-based approaches to the formation, maintenance, and transformation of stereotypes* (pp. 59–92). New York: Lawrence Erlbaum Associates.

Lyons, A. and Kashima, Y. (2006). Maintaining stereotypes in communication: Investigating memory biases and coherence-seeking in storytelling. *Asian Journal of Social Psychology*, 9(1), 59–71.

Lyons, A. and Kashima, Y. (2001). The reproduction of culture: Communication processes tend to maintain cultural stereotypes. *Social Cognition*, 19(3), 372–394.

Maass, A. (1999). Linguistic intergroup bias: Stereotype perpetuation through language. In M. P. Zanna (Ed.) *Advances in experimental social psychology* (Vol. 31, pp. 79–121). San Diego, CA: Academic Press.

Maass, A., Milesi, A., Zabbini, S. and Stahlberg, D. (1995). Linguistic intergroup bias: Differential expectancies or in-group protection? *Journal of Personality and Social Psychology*, 68(1), 116–126.

Maass, A., Salvi, D., Arcuri, L. and Semin, G. R. (1989). Language use in intergroup contexts: The linguistic intergroup bias. *Journal of Personality and Social Psychology*, 57(6), 981.

Macionis, J. J. and Plummer, K. (2011). *Sociology: A global introduction*. 5th edition. Harlow, UK: Pearson Prentice-Hall.

Macrae, C. N., Hood, B. M., Milne, A. B., Rowe, A. and Mason, M. (2002). Are you looking at me? Eye gaze and person perception. *Psychological Science*, 13, 460–464.

Macrae, C. N., Milne, A. B. and Bodenhausen, G. V. (1994). Stereotypes as energy-saving devices: A peek inside the cognitive toolbox, *Journal of Personality and Social Psychology*, 66, 37–47.

MacPherson, W. (1999). *The Stephen Lawrence Inquiry*. Retrieved from https://assets.publishing.service.gov.uk/government/uploads/system/uploads/attachment_data/file/277111/4262.pdf.

Madon, S., Guyll, M., Aboufadel, K., Montiel, E., Smith, A., Palumbo, P. and Jussim, L. (2001). Ethnic and national stereotypes: The Princeton trilogy revisited and revised. *Personality and Social Psychology Bulletin*, 27(8), 996–1010.

Mandel, W. M. (1971). Soviet women in the work force and professions. *American Behavioral Scientist*, 15(2), 255–280.

Manning, P. D. (Ed.). (2017). *On folkways and mores: William Graham Sumner then and now*. New York: Routledge.

Marín, G. and Salazar, J. M. (1985). Determinants of hetero-and autostereotypes: Distance, level of contact, and socioeconomic development in seven nations. *Journal of Cross-Cultural Psychology*, 16(4), 403–422.

Martin, C. L. and Ruble, D. (2004). Children's search for gender cues: Cognitive perspectives on gender development. *Current Directions in Psychological Science*, 13(2), 67–70.

Martin, J. L. (2015). What is ideology? *Sociologia, Problemas e Práticas*, 77, 9–31.

Mastro, D. (2009). Effects of racial and ethnic stereotyping. In J. Bryant and M. B. Oliver (Eds.) *Media effects: Advances in theory and research*. 3rd edition (pp. 325–341). New York: Routledge.

Mattingly, C., Lutkehaus, N. C. and Throop, C. J. (2008). Bruner's search for meaning: A conversation between psychology and anthropology. *Ethos*, 36, 1–28.

McAdams, D. P. (2008). Personal narratives and the life story in O. John, R. Robins and L. A. Pervin (Eds.) *Handbook of personality: Theory and research* (pp. 241–261). New York: Guilford Press.

McAdams, D. P. (2006). *The redemptive self: Stories Americans live by*. Oxford: Oxford University Press.

McAdams, D. P. (1993). *The stories we live by: Personal myths and the making of the self*. New York: Guilford Press.

McAdams, D. P., Hanek, K. J. and Dadabo, J. G. (2013). Themes of self-regulation and self-exploration in the life stories of religious American conservatives and liberals. *Political Psychology*, 34(2), 201–219.

McArthur, J. A. (2009). Digital subculture: A geek meaning of style. *Journal of Communication Inquiry*, 33(1), 58–70.

McCombs, M. E. and Shaw, D. L. (1993). The evolution of agenda-setting research: Twenty-five years in the marketplace of ideas. *Journal of Communication*, 43(2), 58–67.

McCrae, R. R. and Costa, P. T. (1982). Self-concept and the stability of personality: Cross-sectional comparisons of self-reports and ratings. *Journal of Personality and Social Psychology*, 43, 1282–1292.

McKinnon, A. M. (2005). Reading 'Opium of the People': Expression, protest and the dialectics of religion. *Critical Sociology*, 31(1–2), 15–38.

McLaughlin, E. (2005). From reel to ideal: The Blue Lamp and the popular cultural construction of the English 'bobby'. *Crime, Media, Culture*, 1(1), 11–30.

McLeod, J. (2010) *Beginning postcolonialism*. 2nd edition. Manchester: Manchester University Press.

McQuillan, M. (2001). *Deconstruction: A reader*. New York: Routledge.

Meadow, T. (2017). Whose chosenness counts? The always-already racialized discourse of trans–response to Rogers Brubaker. *Ethnic and Racial Studies*, 40(8), 1306–1311.

Mendham, M. D. (2011). Gentle savages and fierce citizens against civilization: Unraveling Rousseau's paradoxes. *American Journal of Political Science*, 55(1), 170–187

Miles, E. and Crisp, R. J. (2014). A meta-analytic test of the imagined contact hypothesis. *Group Processes & Intergroup Relations*, 17(1), 3–26.

Mills, C. W. (1956). *The power elite*. Oxford: Oxford University Press.

Mills, T. (2016). *The BBC: Myth of a public service*. London: Verso Books.

Minard, R. D. (1952). Race relationships in the Pocahontas coal field. *Journal of Social Issues*, 8(1), 29–44.

Minda, J. P. and Smith, J. D. (2011). Prototype models of categorization: Basic formulation, predictions, and limitations. In E. M. Pothos and A. J. Wills (Eds.) *Formal approaches in categorization* (pp. 40–64). Cambridge, UK: Cambridge University Press.

Moghaddam, F. M. and Stringer, P. (1986). Trivial and important criteria for social categorization in the minimal group paradigm. *Journal of Social Psychology*, 126(3), 345–354.

Morewedge, C. K. and Kahneman, D. (2010). Associative processes in intuitive judgment. *Trends in Cognitive Sciences*, 14(10), 435–440.

Morgenroth, T. and Ryan, M. K. (2018). Gender trouble in social psychology: How can Butler's work inform experimental social psychologists' conceptualization of gender? *Frontiers in Psychology*, 9(1320).

Morley, D. (1980). *The Nationwide audience*. London: British Film Institute.

Moscovici, S. (2000). *Social representations: Explorations in social psychology*. Cambridge, UK: Polity.

Moscovici, S. (1998). The history and actuality of social representations. In U. Flick (Ed.) *The psychology of the social* (pp. 209–247). Cambridge, UK: Cambridge University Press.

Moscovici, S. (1993). Introductory address, *Papers on Social Representations*, 2(3), 1–11.

Moscovici, S. (1988). Notes towards a description of social representations. *European Journal of Social Psychology*, 18, 211–250.

Moscovici, S. (1984). The phenomenon of social representations. In R. M. Farr and S. Moscovici (Eds.) *Social representations* (pp. 3–69). Cambridge, UK: Cambridge University.

Moscovici, S. [1961] (2008) *Psychoanalysis: Its image and its public* (D. Macey, trans.). Cambridge, UK: Polity.

Moses, P. (2017). *An unlikely union: The love-hate story of New York's Irish and Italians*. New York: NYU Press.

Mosley, P. A. (2003). Shedding the stereotypes: Librarians in the 21st century. *Reference Librarian*, 37(78), 167–176.

Mumby, D. K. (1989). Ideology and the social construction of meaning: A communication perspective. *Communication Quarterly*, 37(4), 291–304.

Mummendey, A. and Schreiber, H. J. (1984). 'Different' just means 'better': Some obvious and some hidden pathways to in-group favouritism. *British Journal of Social Psychology*, 23(4), 363–367.

Myrdal, G. (1944). *An American dilemma: The Negro problem and modern democracy*. New York: Harper & Brothers.

Nairn, R. G. (2007). Media portrayals of mental illness, or is it madness? A review. *Australian Psychologist*, 42(2), 138–146.

Napier, J. L. and Jost, J. T. (2008). The 'antidemocratic personality' revisited: A cross-national investigation of working-class authoritarianism. *Journal of Social Issues*, 64(3), 595–617.

Newmyer, J. (1976). The image problem of the librarian: Femininity and social control. *Journal of Library History*, 11(1), 44–67.

Nieuwenhuis, A. J. (2012). State and religion, a multidimensional relationship: Some comparative law remarks. *International Journal of Constitutional Law*, 10(1), 153–174.

North, M. S. and Fiske, S. T. (2012). A history of social cognition. In A. W. Kruglanski and W. Stroebe (Eds.) *Handbook of the history of social psychology* (pp. 81–99). New York: Psychology Press.

Nosek, B. A., Banaji, M. R. and Greenwald, A. G. (2002). Harvesting implicit group attitudes and beliefs from a demonstration web site. *Group Dynamics: Theory, Research, and Practice*, 6(1), 101–115.

Nosek, B. A., Smyth, F. L., Hansen, J. J., Devos, T., Lindner, N. M., Ranganath, K. A., … Banaji, M. R. (2007). Pervasiveness and correlates of implicit attitudes and stereotypes. *European Review of Social Psychology*, 18(1), 36–88.

Nosofsky, R. M. (2011). The generalized context model: an exemplar model of classification. In E. M. Pothos and A. J. Wills (Eds.) *Formal approaches in categorization* (pp. 18–39). Cambridge, UK: Cambridge University Press.

Nosofsky, R. M. (1986). Attention, similarity and the identification-categorization relationship. *Journal of Experimental Psychology: General*, 115(1), 39–57.

NWLC (2013). Sex stereotypes: How they hurt women in the workplace – and in the wallet. Retrieved from https://nwlc.org/resources/sex-stereotypes-how-they-hurt-women-workplace-and-wallet.

Nyland, C. (1993). John Locke and the social position of women. *History of Political Economy*, 25(1), 39–63.

O'Brien, R. D. (2018). Martin Shkreli's former lawyer sentenced to 18 months in prison. *Wall Street Journal*. Retrieved from www.wsj.com/articles/martin-shkrelis-former-lawyer-sentenced-to-18-months-in-prison-1534541458.

O'Bryan, M., Fishbein, H. D. and Ritchey, P. N. (2004). Intergenerational transmission of prejudice, sex role stereotyping, and intolerance. *Adolescence*, 39(155), 407–426.

Olneck, M. R. (1990). The recurring dream: Symbolism and ideology in intercultural and multicultural education. *American Journal of Education*, 98(2), 147–174.

O'Neill, D. (2016). *Edmund Burke and the conservative logic of empire*. Oakland: University of California Press.

Osborne, D., Sengupta, N. K. and Sibley, C. G. (2018). System justification theory at 25: Evaluating a paradigm shift in psychology and looking towards the future. *British Journal of Social Psychology*, bjso.12302.

Osborne, D. and Sibley, C. G. (2013). Through rose-colored glasses: System-justifying beliefs dampen the effects of relative deprivation on well-being and political mobilization. *Personality and Social Psychology Bulletin*, 39(8), 991–1004.

Oswald, F. L., Mitchell, G., Blanton, H., Jaccard, J. and Tetlock, P. E. (2015). Using the IAT to predict ethnic and racial discrimination: Small effect sizes of unknown societal significance. *Journal of Personality and Social Psychology*, 108(4), 562–571.

Oswald, F. L., Mitchell, G., Blanton, H., Jaccard, J. and Tetlock, P. E. (2013). Predicting ethnic and racial discrimination: A meta-analysis of IAT criterion studies. *Journal of Personality and Social Psychology*, 105(2), 171–192.

Palladino, G. (1996). *Teenagers: An American history*. New York: Basic Books.

Pangle, T. L. (1988) *The spirit of modern republicanism: The moral vision of the American founders and the philosophy of Locke*. Chicago, IL: University of Chicago Press.

Pagden, A. (2013). *The Enlightenment: And why it still matters*. Oxford: Oxford University Press.

Pariser, E. (2011). *The filter bubble: How the new personalized web is changing what we read and how we think*. London: Penguin.

Parker, B. and Hart, J. (1971). *The wizard of Id: Remember the golden rule!* New York: Fawcett.

Parsons, T. [1951] (1991). *The social system*. London: Routledge.

Paul, H. (2014). *The myths that made America: An introduction to American studies*. Bielefeld: Transcript Verlag.

Payne, B. K. and Cameron, C. D. (2013). Implicit social cognition and mental representation. In D. Carlston (Ed.) *Oxford handbook of social cognition* (pp. 220–238). Oxford: Oxford University Press.

Payne, M. A. (2012) 'All gas and no brakes!': Helpful metaphor or harmful stereotype? *Journal of Adolescent Research*, 27(1), 3–17.

Pearse, R. and Connell, R. (2016). Gender norms and the economy: Insights from social research. *Feminist Economics*, 22(1), 30–53.

Pechar, E. and Kranton R. (2017) Moderators of intergroup discrimination in the minimal group paradigm: A meta-analysis. Retrieved from https://sites.duke.edu/rachelkranton/files/2016/09/Moderators-of-Intergroup-Discrimination.pdf.

Perkins, T. E. (1979). Rethinking stereotypes. In M. Barrett, P. Corrigan, A. Kuhn and J. Wolff (Eds.) *Ideology and cultural production* (pp. 135–159). London: Croom Helm.

Pettigrew, T. F. (1971). *Racially separate or together?* New York: McGraw-Hill.

Pettigrew, T. F. (1960). Social distance attitudes of South African students. *Social Forces*, 38(3), 246–253.

Pettigrew, T. F. and Tropp, L. R. (2006). A meta-analytic test of intergroup contact theory. *Journal of Personality and Social Psychology*, 90(5), 751–783.

Pettigrew, T. F., Tropp, L. R., Wagner, U. and Christ, O. (2011). Recent advances in intergroup contact theory. *International Journal of Intercultural Relations*, 35(3), 271–280.

Philogène, G. (2001). Stereotype fissure: Katz and Braly revisited. *Social Science Information*, 40(3), 411–432.

Phinney, J. S., Ong, A. and Madden, T. (2000). Cultural values and intergenerational value discrepancies in immigrant and non-immigrant families. *Child Development*, 71(2), 528–539.

Phoenix, A. (2017). Unsettling intersectional identities: historicizing embodied boundaries and border crossings. *Ethnic and Racial Studies*, 40(8), 1312–1319.

Piaget, J. (1954). *The construction of reality in the child* (M. Cook, trans.). New York: Basic Books.

Piaget, J. and Cook, M. (1952). *The origins of intelligence in children*. New York: International Universities Press.

Piaget, J. and Inhelder, B. (1969). *The psychology of the child*. New York: Basic Books.

Pickering, M. (2001). *Stereotyping: The politics of representation*. New York: Palgrave.

Posner, M. I. (1978). *Chronometric analysis of mind*. Hillsdale, NJ: Lawrence Erlbaum Associates.

Pratto, F., Sidanius, J. and Levin, S. (2006). Social dominance theory and the dynamics of intergroup relations: Taking stock and looking forward. *European Review of Social Psychology*, 17(1), 271–320.

Pratto, F., Sidanius, J., Stallworth, L. M. and Malle, B. F. (1994). Social dominance orientation: A personality variable predicting social and political attitudes. *Journal of Personality and Social Psychology*, 67(4), 741–763.

Prentice, D. A. and Carranza, E. (2002). What women should be, shouldn't be, are allowed to be, and don't have to be: The contents of prescriptive gender stereotypes. *Psychology of Women Quarterly*, 26(4), 269–281.

Prot, S., Anderson, C. A., Gentile, D. A., Warburton, W., Saleem, M., Groves, C. L. and Brown, S. C. (2015). Media as agents of socialization. In J. E. Grusec and P. D. Hastings (Eds.) *Handbook of socialization*. 2nd edition (pp. 276–300). New York: Guilford Press.

Puddifoot, J. E. and Cooke, C. A. (2002). Representations of handguns by young adults in the US and UK. *Journal of Community and Applied Social Psychology*, 12, 256–270.

Punch, S., Marsh, I., Keating, M. and Harden, J. (Eds.) (2013). *Sociology: Making sense of society*. 5th edition. London: Pearson.

Ramakrishnan, A., Sambuco, D. and Jagsi, R. (2014). Women's participation in the medical profession: Insights from experiences in Japan, Scandinavia, Russia, and Eastern Europe. *Journal of Women's Health*, 23(11), 927–934.

Ramasubramanian, S. (2011). The impact of stereotypical versus counterstereotypical media exemplars on racial attitudes, causal attributions, and support for affirmative action. *Communication Research*, 38(4), 497–516.

Rawls, J. (2007). *Lectures on the history of political philosophy*. Cambridge, MA: Harvard University Press.

Ray, A. G. (1998). 'In my own hand writing': Benjamin Banneker addresses the slaveholder of Monticello. *Rhetoric & Public Affairs*, 1(3), 387–405.

Ray, J. J. and Bozek, R. S. (1981). Authoritarianism and Eysenck's P scale. *Journal of Social Psychology*, 113(2), 231–234.

Reeder, G. D. (2009). Mindreading: Judgments about intentionality and motives in dispositional inference. *Psychological Inquiry*, 20(1), 1–18.

Reeder, G. D. and Spores, J. M. (1983). The attribution of morality. *Journal of Personality and Social Psychology*, 44(4), 736–745.

Reeder, G. D., Vonk, R., Ronk, M. J., Ham, J. and Lawrence, M. (2004). Dispositional attribution: Multiple inferences about motive-related traits. *Journal of Personality and Social Psychology*, 86(4), 530–544.

Renton, A. (2017). *Stiff upper lip: Secrets, crimes and the schooling of a ruling class*. London: Hachette UK.

Reppy, A. (1950). The Grotian doctrine of the freedom of the seas reappraised. *Fordham Law Review*, 19(3), 243–285.

Reskin, B. (2012). The race discrimination system. *Annual Review of Sociology*, 38, 17–35.

Rhodes, M. and Gelman, S. A. (2009). A developmental examination of the conceptual structure of animal, artifact, and human social categories across two cultural contexts. *Cognitive Psychology*, 59, 244–274.

Richards, J. (1997). *Films and British national identity: From Dickens to Dad's Army*. Manchester, UK: Manchester University Press.

Roberts, B. W., Kuncel, N. R., Shiner, R., Caspi, A. and Goldberg, L. R. (2007). The power of personality: The comparative validity of personality traits, socioeconomic status, and cognitive ability for predicting important life outcomes. *Perspectives on Psychological Science*, 2(4), 313–345.

Robertson, S. I. (2017). *Problem solving: Perspectives from cognition and neuroscience*. New York: Routledge.

Robinson, N. (2017). Steve Hewlett memorial lecture. Retrieved from www.bbc.co.uk/news/uk-politics-41439172.

Roets, A. and van Hiel, A. (2011). Allport's prejudiced personality today: Need for closure as the motivated cognitive basis of prejudice. *Current Directions in Psychological Science*, 20(6), 349–354.

Rogers, C. A. and Frantz, C. (1962). *Racial themes in Southern Rhodesia: The attitudes and behavior of the white population*. New Haven, CT: Yale University Press.

Romano, S. (2017). *Moralising poverty: The 'undeserving' poor in the public gaze*. Abingdon, UK: Routledge.

Rosch, E. (1978). Principles of categorization. In E. Rosch and B. B. Lloyd (Eds.) *Cognition and categorization* (pp. 27–48). Hillsdale, NJ: Lawrence Erlbaum Associates, Inc.

Rosch, E. and Mervis, C. B. (1975). Family resemblances: Studies in the internal structure of categories. *Cognitive Psychology*, 7, 573–605.

Rosenberg, M. J. and Hovland, C. I. (1960) Cognitive, affective and behavioral components of attitudes. In M. J. Rosenberg and C. I. Hovland (Eds.) *Attitude organization and change: An analysis of consistency among attitude components* (pp. 1–14). New Haven, CT: Yale University Press.

Rosenthal, A. S. (1999). The gender-coded stereotype: An American perception of France and the French. *French Review*, 72(5), 897–908.

Ross, E. A. (1901). *Social control: A survey of the foundations of order*. New York: Macmillan.

Ross, L. D. (1977). The intuitive psychologist and his shortcomings: Distortions in the attribution process. In L. Berkowitz (Ed.) *Advances in experimental social psychology* (Vol. 10, pp. 173–220). San Diego, CA: Academic Press.

Rudman, L. A., Moss-Racusin, C. A., Glick, P. and Phelan, J. E. (2012). Reactions to vanguards: Advances in backlash theory. In P. G. Devine and E. A. Plant (Eds.) *Advances in experimental social psychology* (Vol. 45, pp. 167–227). San Diego, CA: Academic Press.

Said, E. W. (1978). *Orientalism*. New York: Pantheon.

Saito, A. (2000). *Bartlett, culture & cognition*. London: Psychology Press.

Saito, A. (1996). 'Bartlett's way' and social representations: The case of Zen transmitted across cultures. *Japanese Journal of Experimental Social Psychology*, 35, 263–277.

Sakala, L. (2014). Breaking down mass incarceration in the 2010 census: State-by-state incarceration rates by race/ethnicity. Retrieved from www.prisonpolicy.org/reports/rates.html.

Sakamoto, A. and Yamazaki, K. (2004). Blood-typical personality stereotypes and self-fulfilling prophecy: A natural experiment with time-series data of 1978–1988. *Progress in Asian Social Psychology*, 4, 239–262.

Saunders, P. (1990). *Social class and stratification*. London: Routledge.

Schank, R. C. and Abelson, R. P. (1977). *Scripts, plans, goals and understanding: An inquiry into human knowledge structures*. Hillsdale, NJ: Lawrence Erlbaum Associates.

Scharrer, E. and Ramasubramanian, S. (2015). Intervening in the media's influence on stereotypes of race and ethnicity: The role of media literacy education. *Journal of Social Issues*, 71(1), 171–185.

Scheff, T. J. (2010). Updating labelling theory: Normalizing but not enabling. *Nordic Journal of Social Research*, 1. Retrieved from https://doi.org/10.7577/njsr.2044.

Scheff, T. J. (1999). *Being mentally ill*. 3rd edition. New York: Aldline de Gruyter.

Schneider, D. J. (2004). *The psychology of stereotyping*. New York: Guilford Press.

Scribner, S. (1977). Modes of thinking and ways of speaking: culture and logic reconsidered. In P. N. Johnson-Laird and P. C. Wason (Eds.) *Thinking: Readings in cognitive science* (pp. 483–500). Cambridge, UK: Cambridge University Press.

Semin, G. R. (1980). A gloss on attribution theory. *British Journal of Social and Clinical Psychology*, 19, 291–300.

Semin, G. R. and Fiedler, K. (1991). The linguistic category model, its bases, applications and range. *European Review of Social Psychology*, 2(1), 1–30.

Seneca, S. (2016). *Letters from a Stoic*. Irving, CA: Xist Publishing.

Sercombe, H. (2014). Risk, adaptation and the functional teenage brain. *Brain and Cognition*, 89, 61–69.

Seyfarth, R. M., Cheney, D. L. and Marler, P. (1980). Monkey responses to three different alarm calls: Evidence of predator classification and semantic communication. *Science*, 210(4471), 801–803.

Shapiro, I. and Calvert, J. E. (2014). *The selected writings of Thomas Paine*. New Haven, CT: Yale University Press.

Shattell, M. (2004). Nurse–patient interaction: A review of the literature. *Journal of Clinical Nursing*, 13(6), 714–722.

Shaver, K. G. (1983). *An introduction to attribution processes*. Hillsdale, NJ: Lawrence Erlbaum Associates.

Sherman, S. J., Sherman, J. W., Percy, E. J. and Soderberg, C. K. (2013). Stereotype development and formation. In D. E. Carlston (Ed.) *Oxford library of psychology: The Oxford handbook of social cognition* (pp. 548–574). New York: Oxford University Press.

Sherif, M. (1936). *The psychology of social norms*. Oxford: Harper.

Sherif, M., Harvey, O. J., White, B. J., Hood, W. R. and Sherif, C. W. (1961). *Intergroup conflict and cooperation: The Robbers Cave experiment*. Norman, OK: University Book Exchange.

Shiffrin, R. M. and Schneider, W. (1977). Controlled and automatic human information processing: II. Perceptual learning, automatic attending and a general theory. *Psychological Review*, 84(2), 127–190.

Shi xu (1995). Cultural perceptions: Exploiting the unexpected of the Other. *Culture & Psychology*, 1(3), 315–342.

Shoemaker, P. J. (2006). News and newsworthiness: A commentary. *Communications*, 31(1), 105–111.

Shone, S. J. (2004). Cultural relativism and the savage: The alleged inconsistency of William Graham Sumner. *American Journal of Economics and Sociology*, 63(3), 697–715.

Shore, B. (1996). *Cognition in mind: Cognition, culture, and the problem of meaning*. New York: Oxford University Press.

Sidanius, J. and Pratto, F. (2012). Social dominance theory. In P. A. M. van Lange, A. W. Kruglanski and E. T. Higgins (Eds.) *Handbook of theories of social psychology* (Vol. 2, pp. 418–438). London: Sage.

Sidanius, J. and Pratto, F. (1999). *Social dominance: An intergroup theory of social hierarchy and oppression.* Cambridge, UK: Cambridge University Press.

Siegel, A. E. and Siegel, S. (1957). Reference groups, membership groups, and attitude change. *Journal of Abnormal and Social Psychology*, 55(3), 360–364.

Silva, D. M. (2017). The othering of Muslims: Discourses of radicalization in the New York Times, 1969–2014. *Sociological Forum*, 32(1), 138–161.

Sim, J. J., Correll, J. and Sadler, M. S. (2013). Understanding police and expert performance: When training attenuates (vs. exacerbates) stereotypic bias in the decision to shoot. *Personality and Social Psychology Bulletin*, 39(3), 291–304.

Simmons, J. L. and Chambers, H. (1965). Public stereotypes of deviants. *Social Problems*, 12(2), 223–232.

Sinatra, M. E. (2011). Totally clueless: Heckerling and queer sexuality in Austen's *Emma*. In A. B. Bloom and M. S. Pollack (Eds.) *Victorian literature and film adaptation* (pp. 123–133). New York: Cambria Press.

Sindic, D. and Condor, S. (2014). Social identity theory and self categorization theory. In P. Nesbitt-Larking, C. Kinnvall, T. Capelos and H. Dekker (Eds.) *The Palgrave Handbook of Global Political Psychology* (pp. 39–54). Basingstoke: Palgrave Macmillan.

Skinner, B. F. (1948). *Walden two.* New York: Macmillan

Smith, C. (Ed.) (1996). *Disruptive religion: The force of faith in social movement activism.* London: Routledge.

Smith, E. E. and Medin, D. L. (1981). *Categories and concepts.* Cambridge, MA: Harvard University Press.

Smith, J. R. and McSweeney, A. (2007). Charitable giving: The effectiveness of a revised theory of planned behaviour model in predicting donating intentions and behaviour. *Journal of Community & Applied Social Psychology*, 17(5), 363–386.

Smith, J. R. and Terry, D. J. (2003). Attitude-behaviour consistency: The role of group norms, attitude accessibility, and mode of behavioural decision-making. *European Journal of Social Psychology*, 33(5), 591–608.

SmithBattle, L. I. (2013). Reducing the stigmatization of teen mothers. *MCN: The American Journal of Maternal/Child Nursing*, 38(4), 235–241.

Snyder, M., Tanke, E. D. and Berscheid, E. (1977). Social perception and interpersonal behavior: On the self-fulfilling nature of social stereotypes. *Journal of Personality and Social Psychology*, 35(9), 656–666.

Spears, R. (2011). Group identities: The social identity perspective. In S. J. Schwartz, K. Luyckx and V. L. Vignoles (Eds.) *Handbook of identity theory and research* (pp. 201–224). New York: Springer.

Spencer-Oatey, H. (Ed.). (2008). *Culturally speaking: Culture, communication and politeness theory.* 2nd edition. London: Bloomsbury.

Srivastava, S., John, O. P., Gosling, S. D. and Potter, J. (2003). Development of personality in early and middle adulthood: Set like plaster or persistent change? *Journal of Personality and Social Psychology*, 84(5), 1041.

Staerklé, C., Clémence, A. and Spini, D. (2011). Social representations: A normative and dynamic intergroup approach. *Political Psychology*, 32(5), 759–768.

Stangor, C. (2009). The study of stereotyping, prejudice, and discrimination within social psychology: A quick history of theory and research. In T. D. Nelson (Ed.) *Handbook of prejudice, stereotyping, and discrimination* (pp. 1–22). New York: Psychology Press.

Steele, C. M. (2010). *Whistling Vivaldi: And other clues to how stereotypes affect us*. New York: W. W. Norton & Co.

Steele, C. M. (1997). A threat in the air: How stereotypes shape intellectual identity and performance. *American Psychologist*, 52(6), 613–629.

Steinberg, L. and Monahan, K. C. (2007). Age differences in resistance to peer influence. *Developmental Psychology*, 43(6), 1531–1543.

Stewart, C. O., Pitts, M. J. and Osborne, H. (2011). Mediated intergroup conflict: The discursive construction of 'illegal immigrants' in a regional US newspaper. *Journal of Language and Social Psychology*, 30(1), 8–27.

Stigler, J. W., Shweder, R. A. and Herdt, G. E. (1990). *Cultural psychology: Essays on comparative human development*. Cambridge, UK: Cambridge University Press.

Stephan, E., Liberman, N. and Trope, Y. (2010). Politeness and psychological distance: A construal level perspective. *Journal of Personality and Social Psychology*, 98(2), 268–280.

Stoet, G. and Geary, D. C. (2018). The gender-equality paradox in science, technology, engineering, and mathematics education. *Psychological Science*, 29(4), 581–593.

Stråth, B. (2006). Ideology and history. *Journal of Political Ideologies*, 11(1), 23–42.

Stuurman, S. (2010). Global equality and inequality in enlightenment thought. *Reeks Burgerhartlezingen Werkgroep 18e eeuw* [Bergerhart Lecture Series Working Group 18th century], number 3. Amsterdam: Felix Meritis.

Sumner, W. G. [1919] (2007). *The forgotten man and other essays*. New York: Cosimo Classics.

Sumner, W. G. [1913] (1980). *Earth-hunger and other essays*. London: Transaction Books.

Sumner, W. G. (1906). *Folkways: A study of the sociological importance of usages. Manners, customs, mores, and morals*. Boston, MA: Gin & Company.

Surette, R. (2018). Media, criminology and criminal justice. *Oxford Research Encyclopedia of Criminology*. Retrieved from http://oxfordre.com/criminology/view/10.1093/acrefore/9780190264079.001.0001/acrefore-9780190264079-e-473.

Surette, R. (1994). Predator criminals as media icons. In G. Barak (Ed.) *Media, process, and the social construction of crime* (pp. 131–158). New York: Garland.

Tajfel, H. (1981). *Human groups and social categories: Studies in social psychology*. Cambridge, UK: Cambridge University Press.

Tajfel, H. (1970). Experiments in intergroup discrimination. *Scientific American*, 223(5), 96–103.

Tajfel, H. (1969). Cognitive aspects of prejudice. *Journal of Social Issues*, 25(4), 79–93.

Tajfel, H., Sheikh, A. A. and Gardner, R. C. (1964). Content of stereotypes and the inference of similarity between members of stereotyped groups. *Acta Psychologica*, 22, 191–201.

Tajfel, H. and Turner, J. (1986). The social identity theory of intergroup behaviour. In S. Worchel and W. G. Austin (Eds.) *Psychology of intergroup relations*. 2nd edition (pp. 7–24). Chicago, IL: Nelson Hall

Tattersall, I. (2009). Human origins: Out of Africa. *Proceedings of the National Academy of Sciences*, 106(38), 16018–16021.

Taylor, D. M. (1981). Stereotypes and intergroup relations. In R. C. Gardner and R. Kalin (Eds.) *A Canadian social psychology of ethnic relations* (pp. 151–171). Toronto: Methuen.

Taylor, D. M. and Porter, L. E. (1994). A multicultural view of stereotyping. In W. J. Lonner and R. Malpass (Eds.) *Psychology and culture* (pp. 85–90). Boston, MA: Allyn & Bacon.

Taylor, M. C. (2000). Social contextual strategies for reducing racial discrimination. In S. Oskamp (Ed.). *Reducing prejudice and discrimination* (pp. 81–100). London: Psychology Press.

Taylor, M. G., Rhodes, M. and Gelman, S. A. (2009). Boys will be boys; cows will be cows: Children's essentialist reasoning about gender categories and animal species. *Child Development*, 80(2), 461–481.

Taylor, S. E. (1981). A categorization approach to stereotyping. In D. L. Hamilton (Ed.) *Cognitive processes in stereotyping and intergroup behavior* (pp. 83–114). Hillsdale, NJ: Lawrence Erlbaum Associates.

Tetlock, P. E. and Mitchell, G. (2009). Implicit bias and accountability systems: What must organizations do to prevent discrimination? *Research in Organizational Behavior*, 29, 3–38.

Thomas, D., Newcomb, P. and Fusco, P. (2018). Perception of caring among patients and nurses. *Journal of Patient Experience*, 1–7. doi.org/10.1177/2374373518795713

Thompson, M. J. (2015). False consciousness reconsidered: A theory of defective social cognition. *Critical Sociology*, 41(3), 449–461.

Thompson, M. P. (1976). The reception of Locke's two treatises of government 1690–1705. *Political Studies*, 24(2), 184–191.

Thornton, H. (2004). Hugo Grotius and the freedom of the seas. *International Journal of Maritime History*, 16(2), 17–38.

Tincher, M. M., Lebois, L. A. and Barsalou, L. W. (2016). Mindful attention reduces linguistic intergroup bias. *Mindfulness*, 7(2), 349–360.

Tiosano, D., Audi, L., Climer, S., Zhang, W., Templeton, A. R., Fernández-Cancio, M., … Hochberg, Z. (2016). Latitudinal clines of the human vitamin D receptor and skin color genes. *G3: Genes, Genomes, Genetics*, 6(5), 1251–1266.

Todd, P. M. and Gigerenzer, G. (Eds.) (2012). *Ecological rationality: Intelligence in the world*. New York: Oxford University Press.

Tonry, M. (2010). The social, psychological, and political causes of racial disparities in the American criminal justice system. *Crime and Justice*, 39(1), 273–312.

Toyama, E. (2006). The stereotype and the nationality. *Visio*, 35, 17–23.

Triandis, H. C. (1995). *Individualism and collectivism*. London: Routledge.

Treisman, A. (1960). Contextual cues in selective listening. *Quarterly Journal of Experimental Psychology*, 12, 242–248.

Trope, Y. and Liberman, N. (2010). Construal-level theory of psychological distance. *Psychological Review*, 117(2), 440–463.

Trope, Y., Liberman, N. and Wakslak, C. (2007). Construal levels and psychological distance: Effects on representation, prediction, evaluation, and behavior. *Journal of Consumer Psychology*, 17, 83–95.

Tsri, K. (2016). *Africans are not black: The case for conceptual liberation*. New York: Routledge.

Turner, B. S. (1991). Preface to new edition. In T. Parsons *The social system* (pp. xiii–xxx). London: Routledge.

Turner, J. C. (1991). *Social influence*. Milton Keynes, UK: Open University Press.

Turner, J. C., Hogg, M. A., Oakes, P. J., Reicher, S. D. and Wetherell, M. S. (1987). *Rediscovering the social group: A self-categorization theory*. Oxford: Basil Blackwell.

Turner, R. N. and Crisp, R. J. (2010). Explaining the relationship between ingroup identification and intergroup bias following recategorization: A self-regulation theory analysis. *Group Processes & Intergroup Relations*, 13(2), 251–261.

Tversky, A. and Kahneman, D. (1982). Judgments of and by representativeness. In D. Kahneman, P. Slovic and A. Tversky (Eds.) *Judgement under uncertainty: Heuristics and biases* (pp. 84–98). Cambridge, UK: Cambridge University Press.

Twenge, J. M., Martin, G. N. and Spitzberg, B. H. (2018). Trends in US adolescents' media use, 1976–2016: The rise of digital media, the decline of TV, and the (near) demise of print. *Psychology of Popular Media Culture*. dx.doi.org/10.1037/ppm0000203

US National Archives. (n.d.) *The Declaration of Independence.* The National Archives and Records Administration. Retrieved from www.archives.gov/founding-docs/declaration.

van Ausdale, D. and Feagin, J. R. (2001). *The first R: How children learn race and racism.* Lanham, MD: Rowman & Littlefield.

van den Berghe, P. L. (1966). Checklists versus open-ended questions: A comment on 'A brief report on the methodology of stereotype research'. *Social Forces,* 44(3), 418–419.

van Dijk, T. (1992) Discourse and the denial of racism. *Discourse & Society,* 3(1), 87–118.

van Langenhove, L. and Harré, R. (1999). Introducing positioning theory. In R. Harré and L. van Lagenhove (Eds.) *Positioning theory: Moral contexts of intentional action* (pp. 14–31). Oxford: Blackwell.

van Langenhove, L. and Harré, R. (1994). Cultural stereotypes and positioning theory. *Journal for the Theory of Social Behaviour,* 24(4), 359–372.

van Ravenzwaaij, D., van der Maas, H. L. and Wagenmakers, E. J. (2011). Does the name-race Implicit Association Test measure racial prejudice? *Experimental Psychology,* 58(4), 271–277.

van Rossum, H. (2010). Black alumni looking back, 1996. Retrieved from https://blogs.princeton.edu/reelmudd/2010/10/black-alumni-looking-back-1996.

Vinacke, W. E. (1957). Stereotypes as social concepts. *Journal of Social Psychology,* 46(2), 229–243.

Vygotsky, L. S. (1997). *The collected works of L.S. Vygotsky: Problems of the theory and history of psychology* (Vol. 3). New York: Plenum Press.

Vygotsky, L. S. (1978). *Mind in society: The development of higher psychological processes.* Cambridge, MA: Harvard University Press.

Wacquant, L. (2009). *Punishing the poor: The neoliberal government of social insecurity.* Durham, NC: Duke University Press.

Wason, P. C. (1966). Reasoning. In B. M. Foss (Ed.) *New horizons in psychology* (pp. 135–151). Harmondsworth, UK: Penguin.

Watson, J. and Hill, A. (2015). *Dictionary of media and communication studies.* 9th edition. London: Bloomsbury.

Weber, R. and Crocker, J. (1983). Cognitive processes in the revision of stereotypic beliefs. *Journal of Personality and Social Psychology,* 45, 961–977.

Wells, W. D., Goi, F. J. and Seader, S. (1958). A change in a product image. *Journal of Applied Psychology,* 42, 120–121.

Whitney, G. (2006). Slaveholding Presidents. *Ask Gleaves,* paper 30. Retrieved from http://scholarworks.gvsu.edu/ask_gleaves/30.

Wicker, A. W. (1969). Attitudes versus actions: The relationship of verbal and overt behavioral responses to attitude objects. *Journal of Social Issues,* 25(4), 41–78.

Wiedemann, T. E. (1985). The regularity of manumission at Rome. *Classical Quarterly,* 35(1), 162–175.

Wigboldus, D. H., Semin, G. R. and Spears, R. (2000). How do we communicate stereotypes? Linguistic bases and inferential consequences. *Journal of Personality and Social Psychology,* 78(1), 5–18.

Wigboldus, D. H., Spears, R. and Semin, G. R. (2005). When do we communicate stereotypes? Influence of the social context on the linguistic expectancy bias. *Group Processes & Intergroup Relations,* 8(3), 215–230.

Wilkins, R. (2016). The optimal form and its use in cross-cultural analysis: A British 'stiff upper lip' and a Finnish matter-of-fact style. In D. Carbaugh (Ed.) *The handbook of communication in cross-cultural perspective* (pp. 129–141). New York: Routledge.

Williams, B. A. O. (2002). *Truth & truthfulness: An essay in genealogy.* Princeton, NJ: Princeton University Press.

Williams, R. (1977). *Marxism and literature*. Oxford: Oxford University Press.

Williams, R. M. (1964). *Strangers next door: Ethnic relations in American communities*. Englewood Cliffs, NJ: Prentice-Hall.

Willyard, C. (2011). Men: A growing minority. *GradPSYCH Magazine*, 40. Retrieved from www.apa.org/gradpsych/2011/01/cover-men.aspx.

Wittenbrink, B., Judd, C. M. and Park, B. (2001). Spontaneous prejudice in context: Variability in automatically activated attitudes. *Journal of Personality and Social Psychology*, 81, 815–827.

Woodcock, A., Hernandez, P. R., Estrada, M. and Schultz, P. (2012). The consequences of chronic stereotype threat: Domain disidentification and abandonment. *Journal of Personality and Social Psychology*, 103(4), 635–646.

Worchel, S. and Rothgerber, H. (1997). Changing the stereotype of the stereotype. In R. Spears, P. J. Oakes, N. Ellemers and S. A. Haslam (Eds.) *The social psychology of stereotyping and group life* (pp. 72–93). Malden, MA: Blackwell.

World Economic Forum (2018). *The global gender gap report 2018*. Retrieved from www.weforum.org/reports/the-global-gender-gap-report-2018.

Wundt, W. M. (1916). *Elements of folk-psychology* (E. L. Schaub, trans.). London: Allen & Unwin.

Wundt, W. M. (1874). *Grundzüge der physiologischen Psychologie*. Leipzig: Engelmann.

Yoder, B. L. (2017). *Engineering by the numbers*. Washington, DC: American Society for Engineering Education. Retrieved from www.asee.org/documents/papers-and-publications/publications/college-profiles/2017-Engineering-by-Numbers-Engineering-Statistics.pdf.

Young, L. C. (1988). Regional stereotypes in China. *Chinese Studies in History*, 21(4), 32–57.

Zaeske, S. (1995). The 'promiscuous audience' controversy and the emergence of the early woman's rights movement. *Quarterly Journal of Speech*, 81(2), 191–207.

Zhu, G. and van der Aa, S. (2017). Trends of age of consent legislation in Europe: A comparative study of 59 jurisdictions on the European continent. *New Journal of European Criminal Law*, 8(1), 14–42.

Zosuls, K. M., Miller, C. F., Ruble, D. N., Martin, C. L. and Fabes, R. A. (2011). Gender development research in sex roles: Historical trends and future directions. *Sex Roles*, 64(11–12), 826–842.

AUTHOR INDEX

SUBJECT INDEX

activated actor 76
active audience 188–189
American dilemma 75–76, 78
American Revolution 156; Declaration of Independence 8, 150, 155, 175
anchoring *see* social representations theory
anti-miscegenation laws *see* segregation
Apartheid South Africa 50, 110, 142
argument 52–53, 55, 146, 148, 165, 168, 178–188, 200; *see also* rhetoric
Aristotle 62
artificial intelligence systems 72, 80–81, 198
associative learning 63–67, 81
associative network 64–66
attention 62–64, 67, 69, 97, 170–171, 186
attitudes 35, 41–42, 47, 87–94, 103–104; and behaviour 89–91; explicit attitudes 91–94; implicit attitudes 91–94; and norms 127–129; social attitudes 42, 94, 99–101, 122–123; *see also* prejudiced person
attribution 78, 99, 105, 130; dispositional attribution 130, 199–200
authoritarianism 40–44, 50–52, 87, 97, 99–100, 144
automaticity 63–66, 69, 72–76, 91–92, 96; automatic activation of stereotypes 73–76, 97

'bad apples' 96, 97; *see also* prejudiced person
balance-congruity principle 104
balanced identity theory 103–104

Bayes' theorem 72–73, 81, 198; and artificial intelligence systems 81, 198; and the predictive brain 72
bias 6–7, 27, 47, 49, 69–73, 77–83, 88, 94–96, 99–100, 108–109, 111, 117–118, 130, 136, 139, 165–167, 169; cognitive bias 6–7, 27; intergroup bias 6, 108–109, 169; linguistic expectancy bias 169–170; unconscious bias (implicit bias) 77–83, 88, 94–96, 99–100, 111
biased bureaucrat model 178–179
binary opposition 159, 183–185

capitalism 138
categorization (social categories) 10, 24, 42–43, 47, 50, 59–61, 85, 101–103, 108–109, 115–118, 121, 129, 132, 147, 158, 158, 178–184, 202
categorization and particularization (rhetorical techniques) 179–181
characteristic property 116
checklist method 34, 48–49, 167; *see also* Princeton trilogy
children (childhood) 21, 41–43, 63, 72, 86, 108, 114–126, 128–129, 135, 155, 157–159, 174, 194–196, 202
citizen (social category) 9, 12, 78, 80, 87, 95–96, 118, 141–142, 145, 149–150, 156, 162, 173, 176, 180–181, 197; as child of the government metaphor 162–164
civil rights 8–11, 18, 75, 83, 87, 105, 132, 153–156, 176
class consciousness 143

CPSIA information can be obtained
at www.ICGtesting.com
Printed in the USA
LVHW051602080221
678722LV00004B/274

9 781138 637559